OXFORD CLASSICAL MONOGRAPHS

*Published under the supervision of a Committee of the
Faculty of Literae Humaniores in the University of Oxford*

OXFORD CLASSICAL MONOGRAPHS

The aim of the Oxford Classical Monographs series (which
replaces the Oxford Classical and Philosophical
Monographs) is to publish outstanding revised theses on Greek and
Latin literature, ancient history, and ancient philosophy
examined by the faculty board of Literae Humaniores.

Xenophon's *Cyropaedia*

STYLE, GENRE,
AND LITERARY TECHNIQUE

DEBORAH LEVINE GERA

CLARENDON PRESS · OXFORD
1993

Oxford University Press, Walton Street, Oxford OX2 6DP
Oxford New York Toronto
Delhi Bombay Calcutta Madras Karachi
Kuala Lumpur Singapore Hong Kong Tokyo
Nairobi Dar es Salaam Cape Town
Melbourne Auckland Madrid
and associated companies in
Berlin Ibadan

Oxford is a trade mark of Oxford University Press

Published in the United States
by Oxford University Press Inc. New York

British Library Cataloguing in Publication Data
Data available
ISBN 0–19–814477–6

Library of Congress Cataloging in Publication Data
Gera, Deborah Levine.
Xenophon's Cyropaedia: style, genre, and literary technique /
Deborah Levine Gera.
—(Oxford classical monographs)
Includes bibliographical references and index.
1. Xenophon. Cyropaedia. 2. Cyrus, King of Persia, d. 529 BC,
in fiction, drama, poetry, etc. 3. Political fiction, Greek—
History and criticism. 4. Kings and rulers in literature.
5. Rhetoric, Ancient. 6. Literary form. I. Title. II. Series.
PA4494.C9G4 1993
883′.01—dc20
ISBN 0–19–814477–6

3 5 7 9 10 8 6 4 2

Set by Joshua Associates Limited, Oxford
Printed in Great Britain
on acid-free paper by
Bookcraft (Bath) Ltd., Midsomer Norton, Avon

IN MEMORY OF MY FATHER

לזכר אבי מורי

Preface

CONSIDERED by all too many to be one of the most tedious books to have survived classical antiquity, Xenophon's *Cyropaedia* is a complex, varied work. It has generally been approached by scholars with a specific interest or angle in mind: be it the political, biographical, military, novelistic, or Persian features of the work. It seems at times that too little attention is paid to the text as a literary composition in its own right. This book is first and foremost a study of the *Cyropaedia*: not of the long, multifarious composition in its entirety, but of three particular literary strands which feature prominently in the work. Chapter 1 is a general introduction, touching upon questions of genre, date, and possible Persian sources. Chapters 2, 3, and 4 deal respectively with three literary influences which have left their mark on the work: Socratic dialogue, literary symposia, and dramatic stories or novellas. In these three chapters the characteristic features of each literary genre are first described and discussed in relation to Xenophon's predecessors and contemporaries. A detailed commentary on specific sections of the *Cyropaedia*, exhibiting this literary influence, then follows. These commentaries are best read with Xenophon's text close at hand; all quotations are from the 1910 OCT edition of E. C. Marchant. In the concluding chapter an attempt is made to examine Xenophon's attitude towards his hero, Cyrus the Great.

This book is a much-revised version of my Oxford D.Phil. thesis, 'The Dialogues of the *Cyropaedia*'. Professor D. A. Russell supervised my research, and it is a pleasure to thank a man who is as kindly as he is learned for his sage advice and warm encouragement over the years. My examiners, Dr C. Pelling and Mr S. Usher, had many perceptive comments and criticisms to offer, and I have made free use of their suggestions here. Professor S. Shaked was kind enough to look at an earlier draft of the section on Persian sources. Professor D. M. Lewis was my adviser in the difficult process of turning an unwieldy dissertation into a more readable book. His enviable scholarship and exacting reading of the manuscript have led to many improvements, large and small.

I owe a great deal to members of the Classics Department of

the Hebrew University of Jerusalem, particularly Joseph Geiger, Ra'anana Meridor, Lisa Ullmann, Abraham Wasserstein, and the late Alexander Fuks. Teachers, colleagues, and friends, they have been a source of inspiration over many years.

Various institutions have afforded me financial support during stays at Oxford. I am very grateful to the British Council, the Rothschild Foundation (Yad Avi Hayishuv), the Humanitarian Trust, the Frederick Rau Memorial Trust, the Overseas Research Students Awards Scheme, and the British Friends of the Hebrew University for their financial aid. My college in Oxford, Wolfson, was—and remains—an exceptionally congenial place to pursue research.

Finally, I should like to thank my husband, Dov, who claims to believe, along with Samuel Johnson, that 'a man is . . . better pleased when he has a good dinner upon his table than when his wife talks Greek', but whose support, encouragement, and genuine partnership in raising our children consistently demonstrate just how dubious that claim is.

D.L.G.

Hebrew University of Jerusalem
September 1991

Contents

x   *Contents*

Abbreviations

AC	*L'Antiquité classique*
AJP	*American Journal of Philology*
BICS	*Bulletin of the Institute of Classical Studies*
BSOAS	*Bulletin of the School of Oriental and African Studies*
C&M	*Classica et Mediaevalia*
CA	*Classical Antiquity*
CJ	*Classical Journal*
CP	*Classical Philology*
CQ	*Classical Quarterly*
DK	H. Diels and W. Kranz, *Die Fragmente der Vorsokratiker*[6] (Berlin, 1951)
EMC	*Échos du monde classique*
FGrH	F. Jacoby, *Die Fragmente der griechischen Historiker* (Leiden, 1923–57)
G&R	*Greece and Rome*
GRBS	*Greek, Roman and Byzantine Studies*
IG	*Inscriptiones Graecae*
JAOS	*Journal of the American Oriental Society*
JHI	*Journal of the History of Ideas*
JHS	*Journal of Hellenic Studies*
JRAS	*Journal of the Royal Asiatic Society*
K.	T. Kock, *Comicorum Atticorum Fragmenta* (Leipzig, 1880–8)
K.–A.	R. Kassell and C. Austin, *Poetae Comici Graeci* (Berlin and New York, 1983–)
Kai.	G. Kaibel, *Comicorum Graecorum Fragmenta* i/1 (Berlin, 1899)
MH	*Museum Helveticum*
OSAP	*Oxford Studies in Ancient Philosophy*
Pack[2]	R. A. Pack, *The Greek and Latin Literary Texts from Greco-Roman Egypt*[2] (Ann Arbor, 1965)
PSI	*Pubblicazioni della Società Italiana per la Ricerca dei Papiri Greci e Latini in Egitto*
QUCC	*Quaderni urbinati di cultura classica*
RE	*Real-Encyclopädie der classischen Altertumswissenschaft*, ed. A. Fr. von Pauly, rev. G. Wissowa *et al.* (Stuttgart, 1894–1980)

RM	*Rheinisches Museum für Philologie*
SEG	*Supplementum Epigraphicum Graecum*
Sturz	F. W. Sturz, *Lexicon Xenophonteum* (Leipzig, 1801; repr. Hildesheim, 1964)
TAPA	*Transactions of the American Philological Association*
YCS	*Yale Classical Studies*
ZPE	*Zeitschrift für Papyrologie und Epigraphik*

DB, XPh, etc. are the standard abbreviations for Persian royal inscriptions. The first letter indicates the name of the king (e.g. Darius, Xerxes), the second the site of the inscription (e.g. Behistun, Persepolis), while the third, lower-case letter indicates position in a sequence.

1

An Introduction to
the *Cyropaedia*

I. GENRE, PURPOSE, AND PREDECESSORS

What is the *Cyropaedia*? It can be described as a biography of Cyrus the Great, a history of the beginnings of the Persian empire, a romance, an encomium, a military handbook, a guide to the political administration of an empire, a didactic work on ethics, morals, and education, etc.; it is, in fact, all of these things. Cicero's famous statement—'Cyrus ille a Xenophonte non ad historiae fidem scriptus sed ad effigiem iusti imperi'[1]—is perhaps the best starting-point when attempting to define or narrow down the genre of this work: the *Cyropaedia* was not written as history and is a portrait of a model, just ruler. Cicero may have needed to point this out to his brother Quintus because Xenophon himself nowhere indicates—either in his preface to the work or in the course of narrating the deeds of Cyrus the Great—that he is not presenting a purely historical account. He begins the *Cyropaedia* with a discussion of the instability of political regimes and observes that man is the most difficult of creatures to rule. None the less, states Xenophon, the example of Cyrus serves as proof that governing men is not an impossible task, since the Persian king successfully ruled a great empire and commanded the willing obedience of his many subjects. Hence Xenophon turned to an investigation of Cyrus the Great, concentrating on the Persian's family background, character, and education. The *Cyropaedia* is, according to Xenophon's preface, the result of these researches (*Cyr.* 1. 1. 1–6).[2]

In reality the *Cyropaedia* contains a great deal more than Xenophon has promised at the outset. There is a description in Book 1 of Cyrus' family, appearance, and personality, and of the education he

---

[1] *Q. fr.* 1. 1. 23; cf. Dion. Hal. *Ep. ad Pomp.* 4.

[2] Cf. 1. 1. 6 ὅσα οὖν καὶ ἐπυθόμεθα καὶ ᾐσθῆσθαι δοκοῦμεν περὶ αὐτοῦ, ταῦτα πειρασόμεθα διηγήσασθαι.

received; so too part of Book 8, the final book, is devoted to a detailed exposition of the way the Persian ruler administered his vast empire and the means he used to school his many subjects to obedience. In the intervening books Xenophon tells of Cyrus' rise to power: how he acquired useful allies, won important victories, and established an empire. This is, however, only a small portion of the work, which includes much that is less directly related to Cyrus' actions and achievements. The story of Panthea and Abradatas, Tigranes' sophistic debate with Cyrus, Cambyses' exposition of the various branches of tactics, Xenophon's own thoughts on the principle of division of labour[3]—to name just a few examples—all reflect Xenophon's interests and enthusiasms, but are not directly related to his Persian hero's success as a ruler. The *Cyropaedia* is above all a didactic work, its author's vehicle for developing and discussing his own cherished ideas and interests. In this work Xenophon touches upon many areas covered in his other writings, and he uses a variety of literary forms which he has used elsewhere—philosophical dialogue, encomium, history, military memoirs, technical handbook—to present these favourite themes and topics. The narration of the life and deeds of Cyrus the Great is, in essence, a convenient framework, a peg upon which Xenophon hangs reflections and ideas of his own. Cyrus is not the real impetus for the *Cyropaedia* but is more akin to a tailor's dummy, a useful figure to be clothed as his author likes. Thus Xenophon improvises freely with the facts of Cyrus' life, altering historical circumstances to suit his literary and didactic purposes, even while making use of the narrative framework which the historical Persian's well-known deeds provide.

If this view of the *Cyropaedia* is correct—that is, it is first and foremost the author's vehicle for presenting favourite themes and concerns to his readers—it remains to be seen how Xenophon came to choose this particular format. Why a biography? Why is Cyrus, a Persian ruler of long ago, the hero of the work? Why does Xenophon begin the work with reflections on the instability of governments and the near impossibility of ruling contented subjects? Let us deal with each of these questions in turn, looking at the writings of Xenophon's predecessors and contemporaries, in an attempt to find possible influences on his choice of framework for the *Cyropaedia*.

We begin with biography. The text opens with an account of

---

[3] Panthea and Abradatas: 5. 1. 2 ff., 6. 1. 31 ff., 6. 4. 2 ff., 7. 3. 2 ff.; Tigranes: 3. 1. 14–30; Cambyses: 1. 6. 43; Xenophon: 8. 2. 5–6.

Cyrus' boyhood and closes with his death, presenting in between a chronological narrative of many of the Persian's deeds, and hence can be considered a biography. Xenophon deals selectively with Cyrus' career, concentrating on certain periods (e.g. his visit to Media as a teenager, the conquest of Lydia and Babylon) and ignoring others (such as Cyrus' early childhood or most of the years after he captured Babylon), but the work is none the less recognizably a biography. In fact, one scholar terms the *Cyropaedia* 'the most accomplished biography we have in classical Greek literature'.[4] Who were Xenophon's predecessors in the writing of biographies, and which writings, if any, could have prompted or influenced the biographical form of the work?

Two early names associated with the writing of biographies are Scylax of Caryanda and Xanthus of Lydia. We know nothing of the work that Scylax, the explorer employed by Darius (Hdt. 4. 44), may have written about a contemporary ruler, Heraclides of Mylasa, other than its name, τὰ κατὰ Ἡρακλείδην τὸν Μυλασσῶν βασιλέα.[5] So too the account of Empedocles by Xanthus mentioned by Diogenes Laertius may have been a monograph on—or life of—the Sicilian philosopher by Herodotus' contemporary, Xanthus of Lydia, but the matter is uncertain.[6]

A more interesting figure for our purposes is Herodorus of Heraclea Pontica, father of the sophist Bryson. Herodorus wrote the story of Heracles (ὁ καθ' Ἡρακλέα λόγος or τὰ καθ' Ἡρακλέα) in seventeen books, at the very end of the fifth century.[7] He used a rationalizing approach when narrating the deeds of Heracles and was a pioneer of allegorical interpretation of the Heracles myths.[8] In Herodorus Heracles became, apparently, an ethical figure, a model of some kind, as in the works of Prodicus and Antisthenes.[9] The extant fragments describe Heracles' famous labours and touch upon

[4] Momigliano 1971: 55.

[5] The name is found in the *Suda*—see *FGrH* 709 T 1. For very different evaluations of the evidence on Scylax cf. Momigliano 1971: 29–30 with Meister 1978: 292.

[6] D.L. 8. 63 = *FGrH* 765 F 33; cf. Pearson 1939: 119; Momigliano 1971: 30–2; Meister 1978: 291–2.

[7] For the little that is known of Herodorus' life see Jacoby 1912: 980–1 (= 1956b: 241–2).

[8] Cf. e.g. *FGrH* 31 F 14, where the three apples of the Hesperides are said to represent three virtues.

[9] On this aspect of Herodorus' composition see Galinsky 1972: 56 and 78 n. 37; Höistad 1948: 29–31. Jacoby on *FGrH* 31 (ia. 502) is more sceptical about Herodorus' Heracles serving as a model of ethical behaviour.

the education he received, but often deal with geographical, zoologi-
cal, and cosmological matters, i.e. Herodorus' own 'interests.[10] It
seems that Herodorus used the story of Heracles' life and deeds as a
convenient backdrop or framework for presenting discussions of
topics that were close to his heart.[11] The similarity with Xenophon's
own approach in the Cyropaedia is evident: both writers present the
life and deeds of a well-known figure of old not so much for its own
sake but as a means to bring to their readers their views on a variety of
subjects.

Our next writer of biographies, Stesimbrotus of Thasos, was perhaps closest of all to Xenophon in his approach to biographical
accounts of famous men of action. This fifth-century author[12] wrote a
series of biographical portraits of contemporary (or near contemporary) Athenian politicians in his περὶ Θεμιστοκλέους καὶ Θουκυδίδου
καὶ Περικλέους. While the exact scope and intention of the work are
not known—scholars debate whether Stesimbrotus' main concern
was political, ethical, or biographical[13]—the extant fragments (FGrH
107 F 1–11) indicate that Stesimbrotus discussed both the public and
private faces of the men he portrayed. The surviving fragments—all
but one derive from Plutarch—tell of Themistocles, Cimon, and
Pericles, but nothing remains on Thucydides son of Melesias.
Stesimbrotus describes the political policies of these men (F 2, F 8)
and quotes some of their public pronouncements (F 7, F 9), but he
was also interested in the character of these politicians, their childhood, and the education they received (F 1, F 4, F 6).[14] In addition,

[10] See FGrH 31 F 1–4, 13–37; cf. 41, 60, 62, 63. F 17 is the fragment on education.

[11] Cf. Jacoby 1912: 984–5 (= 1956b: 243–4).

[12] Stesimbrotus is called a contemporary of Cimon and Pericles (FGrH 107 T 1, T 2),
and it is clear from the reference in F 11 to the death of Pericles' son in the plague that
his work on Themistocles, Thucydides, and Pericles was written after 429. Schachermeyr 1965: 9–10 argues persuasively that his composition appeared in about 420; other
scholars date the work earlier.

[13] Schachermeyr 1965 contends that Stesimbrotus was interested in the character
and behaviour of demagogues and that his composition was a forerunner of later works
περὶ δημαγωγῶν, περὶ τυράννων, etc. He finds no evidence in the fragments of any
malice towards the Athenians and their policies. Other scholars—cf. e.g. Jacoby on
FGrH 107 (iiB. 343) and the further references there—consider the work 'eine politische
Tendenzschrift', although there is no real agreement as to which political policies are
being attacked; cf. Frost 1980: 16–17. Meister 1978 emphasizes Stesimbrotus' pioneer-
ing role as a writer of biographies.

[14] The fragment dealing with the education of Themistocles (F 1) is particularly
interesting in view of the later debate by the Socratics as to whether Themistocles owed
his success to his natural abilities or to the teachers he had. See—in addition to Thucydides' famous description of Themistocles' intellect (Thuc. 1. 138. 3)—Mem. 2. 6. 13,

Stesimbrotus included details of the private lives and families of his subjects (F 3, F 5, F 10, F 11), some of them rather spicy. His presentation seems to have been lively, for he quotes the politicians' words directly (F 7, F 9) and reproduces conversations they held (F 5).

Plutarch makes it clear that Stesimbrotus was not a careful historian or painstaking biographer: he was careless about chronology (F 1) and did not always tell a consistent tale (F 3). Stesimbrotus was known chiefly as a rhapsode, an interpreter of Homer,[15] and he wrote a book on Homer which included elucidations of difficult passages (F 23–5), besides a discussion of the date and birthplace of the poet (F 21, F 22). In addition, Stesimbrotus wrote a work on religious rites, περὶ τελετῶν (F 12–20), which contained mythological material. It seems likely, then, that Stesimbrotus, whose interests were pedagogical as well as political, was as concerned with the characters of the statesmen he portrayed as their actual deeds. If he did indeed recount the lives and actions of these Athenian leaders, examining their characters and the education they received, without being too scrupulous about the actual historical facts, the affinities with Xenophon's approach in the *Cyropaedia* are obvious. Stesimbrotus' inclusion of rather scandalous stories about these statesmen (e.g. F 5, F 10, F 11) would seem to indicate, however, that his subjects, unlike Xenophon's Cyrus, were not meant to be model figures.

Another fifth-century figure associated with the writing of biographies is Ion of Chios, a slightly older contemporary of Stesimbrotus.[16] In his Ἐπιδημίαι Ion described famous men of his time whom he had encountered either when they came to visit his native Chios or on his visits to Athens (and elsewhere).[17] In these memoirs, which, to judge by the extant fragments, were written in a vivid and graceful fashion,[18] Ion mentions not only important political personages such as Cimon (*FGrH* 392 F 12–15), Pericles (F 15–16), and Themistocles (F 11, F 13), but also the leading cultural figures of his

4. 2. 2; *Symp.* 8. 39; Aeschines, *Alcibiades*, frr. 7–9 Dittmar and *P. Oxy.* 13. 1608; cf. Gigon 1956: 137–9. Pelling 1990: 215 notes Stesimbrotus' prominent interest in the childhood of these political figures.

[15] Cf. *FGrH* 107 T 3 = Pl. *Ion* 530c–d; T 4 = Xen. *Symp.* 3. 6.

[16] Jacoby 1947: 1–2 (= 1956a: 144–5) dates Ion from *c.* 480 to 422 BC; cf. Dover 1986: 27 (= 1988: 1); West 1985: 71–3. The Ἐπιδημίαι was written after 440 BC (cf. *FGrH* 392 F 6) and Jacoby thinks it may have appeared as late as the first years of the Peloponnesian war—cf. his commentary on *FGrH* 392 (iiiʙ (text), 193–4).

[17] West 1985: 75–6 and Dover 1986: 32–5 (= 1988: 7–9) have useful discussions of the content, form, and genre of the Ἐπιδημίαι.

[18] Cf. in particular *FGrH* 392 F 6, F 13.

time, including Aeschylus (F 7; cf. F 22), Sophocles (F 6; cf. F 23), and Socrates (F 9). His portraits were wide-ranging and included descriptions of his subjects' physical appearance (F 12), character and manner (F 6, F 15), travels (F 9), memorable deeds (F 7, F 13), and notable sayings, both in the public and private spheres (F 6, F 14). In these memoirs Ion provides lively, charming portraits of his contemporaries, as seen from his own particular vantage-point (cf. F 15), while in the *Cyropaedia* Xenophon presents a full-scale, seemingly objective account of a famous figure who lived well before his own time. None the less, Ion's character sketches in the Ἐπιδημίαι and his lighthearted, skilful use of anecdotes and conversations to illuminate the personalities he describes may have influenced Xenophon. We shall see that Ion's effect on the *Cyropaedia* is probably most prominent in the work's more playful scenes.

Herodotus presented a full account of Cyrus the Great, including details of his birth, youth, major conquests, final campaign, and death, thus including many biographical elements in his narrative.[19] We can also assume that Ctesias included biographical material on Cyrus in the five books of the *Persica* devoted to the Persian king.[20] However, both Herodotus and Ctesias wrote history rather than biography, and included an account of Cyrus as only a part of their work; he is not their central axis.

Xenophon himself makes use of biographical materials in several of his other works.[21] The *Memorabilia*, Xenophon's recollections, so to speak, of Socrates and his conversations, is a form of biography; as with Cyrus of the *Cyropaedia*, the portrait of Socrates is often more idealized fiction than actual fact.[22] The *Anabasis* is, of course, an autobiographical work, memoirs of a campaign (written, however, in the third person), and it includes several character sketches or

---

[19] Hdt. 1. 107–30, 177–91, 201–14. See Homeyer 1962: 76–8 on the formal biographical elements found in Herodotus' account of Cyrus. She considers Herodotus a forerunner of later Greek biography and thinks that the nature of Herodotus' Persian sources, dealing mainly with tales of kings, led him to arrange his material this way. Momigliano 1971: 33–8 notes the interest in biographical details found in the east.

[20] For Ctesias' account of Cyrus see below chs. 3. 2, 4. 3.

[21] See the survey in Momigliano 1971: 46–57.

[22] Dihle 1956: 13 ff. sees such portraits of Socrates, particularly Plato's *Apology*, as the first true biography. For the more general problem of the relation between the historical Socrates and his portrayal in the writings of the Socratics, see Breitenbach 1966: 1771–6 and the further references there; Morrison 1988: 12–18 has a detailed bibliography of works on Xenophon and the Socratic problem.

portraits—of Cyrus the Younger and the dead Greek generals.[23] The encomium *Agesilaus* is in part a biography and contains a brief chronological survey of the Spartan king's deeds (*Ages.* 1–2), followed by a longer list of his various virtues (3–9). The Spartan king is meant to serve as a model to others who wish to cultivate virtue,[24] and in this laudatory work Xenophon glosses over those unpleasant facts which do not suit his portrait of an ideal leader;[25] the parallels with the *Cyropaedia* are plain.

The *Agesilaus* is often thought to have been influenced by Isocrates' *Evagoras*,[26] which may have been the earliest Greek prose encomium of a contemporary figure.[27] Isocrates includes a selective, chronological survey of his hero's deeds, even mentioning Evagoras' childhood (*Evag.* 21–2), and he describes the many outstanding qualities of the ruler of Salamis. He too is careful to omit any unsavoury events—such as the fact that Evagoras was assassinated —perhaps because one of his aims in writing is to encourage young men to emulate the ruler (76–7). It is interesting to note that in the *Evagoras* Isocrates mentions Cyrus the Great as one hero of the past who might be thought an equally worthy subject for such an encomium; but, adds Isocrates, the Persian ruler is inferior to his own subject (37–8).

This brings us to the question of Xenophon's choice of hero. Why did he select the Persian king to serve as an idealized, didactic model? As the last-mentioned passage from Isocrates indicates, Cyrus and his achievements were well known to the Greeks of Xenophon's time. Cyrus enjoyed, on the whole, a good reputation in Greek literature from Aeschylus onwards.[28] We have already seen that the Persian king featured prominently in the popular works of Herodotus and Ctesias; more generally, Greeks of the fourth century appear to have

[23] *Anab.* 1. 9, 2. 6. On the difference in style and content between the sketches of Cyrus and Clearchus on the one hand, and Meno and Proxenus on the other, see Bruns 1896: 137–44; Breitenbach 1966: 1642–3; Momigliano 1971: 51–2.

[24] *Ages.* 10. 2 καλὸν ἄν μοι δοκεῖ ἡ Ἀγησιλάου ἀρετὴ παράδειγμα γενέσθαι τοῖς ἀνδραγαθίαν ἀσκεῖν βουλομένοις.

[25] For a comparison between the *Ages.* and the *Hell.* (where many of the less admirable facts concerning Agesilaus *are* reported), see Breitenbach 1966: 1702–5; Hirsch 1985: 46–9, 56–7.

[26] The *Evag.* is generally given a date shortly after the death of Evagoras, *c.* 370 BC; see Hirsch 1985: 57–60 for an interesting comparison between the *Evag.* and the *Ages.*

[27] Compare Isocrates' claim (*Evag.* 5) with Arist. *Rhet.* 1368ᵃ17.

[28] Cf. Aes. *Pers.* 767–72 εὐδαίμων . . . ἀνὴρ . . . ἔθηκε . . . εἰρήνην . . . εὔφρων ἔφυ; cf. also Hdt. 3. 89 πατήρ; [Pl.] *Epist.* 4, 320D ἔδοξεν ἤθει καὶ πολιτείᾳ διενεγκεῖν; and see Pl. *Laws* 694A–B, *Menex.* 239D–E; Isoc. *Philip* 5. 66.

been fascinated by all things Persian.[29] Xenophon had, of course, first-hand knowledge of the Persians and their ways. The author of the *Cyropaedia* could rely, then, upon his readers' interest in, and perhaps sympathy for, Cyrus. The fact that Cyrus was a Persian king of long ago, rather than a present-day Greek, may have made it easier for Xenophon to fashion his life, character, and deeds as freely as he chose,[30] although elsewhere he does not hesitate to present contemporary Greeks such as Agesilaus and Socrates in an idealized way as well.

Antisthenes' *Cyrus* may have been the most influential factor when Xenophon chose the Persian ruler as the central axis of his didactic work. Antisthenes is an elusive figure, and it is particularly difficult to reconstruct his lost writings on Cyrus. There is also no firm chronological evidence that his *Cyrus* was earlier than the *Cyropaedia*, although it is generally considered to be so.[31] Despite the dearth of concrete evidence, it is worth examining the patchy and troublesome *Cyrus* fragments in some detail, since Antisthenes is often mentioned as Xenophon's chief predecessor or source of inspiration for the *Cyropaedia*.

To begin with, Antisthenes apparently wrote more than one work entitled Κῦρος. Diogenes Laertius, in his list of Antisthenes' works (D.L. 6. 15–18 = fr. 1)[32] knows of one Κῦρος which appeared (together with a work entitled Ἡρακλῆς ὁ μείζων) in book 4 of Antisthenes' writings, and of another composition, in book 5, with the double title Κῦρος ἢ περὶ βασιλείας. In addition, according to one manuscript tradition of Diogenes Laertius, there were two other compositions entitled *Cyrus* in the tenth and final book of Antisthenes' collected writings: Κῦρος ἢ ἐρώμενος and Κῦρος ἢ κατάσκοποι. Most scholars do not think that the last two titles refer to actual works by Antisthenes on Cyrus; they either reject or emend the manuscript reading, or else

---

[29] See e.g. [Pl.] *Alc. I* 120E–123E, and cf. Lévy 1976: 203–5 for further references; he describes the Greek attitude towards Persians as 'un mélange de fascination et de répulsion' (203). Cf. also Starr 1975: 48–61; Hirsch 1985: 1–5 and *passim*.

[30] Cf. Breitenbach 1966: 1708 for this point.

[31] Antisthenes' fragments and testimonia are collected by Caizzi 1966 and Giannantoni 1983; for his life and writings in general see e.g. Gigon 1947: 289–99 and Guthrie 1969: 304–11. Giannantoni 1985: 269–81 has a detailed survey of modern scholarship on Antisthenes' *Cyrus*, including opinions on the relation (chronological and otherwise) between the *Cyr.* and the *Cyrus*; cf. Höistad 1948: 73–94. Joël 1901 believes in the all-pervasive influence of Antisthenes on Xenophon and the *Cyr.*; see esp. 381–90, 1053–64.

[32] The numbering of the fragments here is that of Caizzi 1966.

consider the works inauthentic.[33] We are left, then, with the two compositions of books 4 and 5, and one of the difficulties raised by the *Cyrus* fragments is deciding to which of the two works each fragment should be assigned. A further complication is that in one of the two works entitled *Cyrus* reference is made to Alcibiades,[34] but there may have been another, separate *Alcibiades* as well (in book 10 of Antisthenes' collected writings—cf. fr. 1)—and it is not clear how the various fragments mentioning Alcibiades are related to the *Cyrus* ones.

The next problem concerns the identity of Cyrus: did Antisthenes write about Cyrus the Great or Cyrus the Younger or both—with, for example, each Persian the main character of one of the two works? Again, scholars are divided, but here a look at the actual fragments seems to establish what is important for our purposes, namely, that at least one of the two compositions dealt with Cyrus the Great. One fragment begins Κῦρος ὁ βασιλεὺς ἐρωτηθείς . . . (fr. 21a), and this can only mean Cyrus the Great, for his younger namesake was never king. Another fragment (fr. 20a) touches upon the duties of a king— βασιλικόν, ὦ Κῦρε, πράττειν μὲν εὖ, κακῶς δ' ἀκούειν—and again makes more sense if it is meant for the ears of an actual king, i.e. our Cyrus. This latter fragment is interesting for another reason as well: the vocative ὦ Κῦρε shows that Cyrus is addressed by another, so that this composition may have been a dialogue. We know that Antisthenes wrote Socratic dialogues, and several individual works of his are specifically given this name: not all of Antisthenes' dialogues need have been Socratic ones.[35]

A third *Cyrus* fragment (fr. 19) tells us καὶ ὅτι ὁ πόνος ἀγαθὸν συνέστησε [sc. Antisthenes] διὰ τοῦ μεγάλου Ἡρακλέους καὶ τοῦ Κύρου, i.e. Antisthenes, in his works about Heracles and Cyrus, used these two figures to demonstrate the rewards of hard labour. Once again Cyrus the Great suits the context of this fragment better than Cyrus the Younger, for his rise to power and conquest of an empire provide a most convincing illustration of the principle ὁ πόνος ἀγαθόν. It seems likely, then, that in one of his *Cyrus* compositions Antisthenes told of Cyrus the Great's ascent to the throne and used

[33] See Giannantoni 1985: 269–73 and Höistad 1948: 74–5 for a survey of the various solutions proposed. Susemihl 1887: 210 argues that the two works entitled *Cyrus* found in bks. 4 and 5 respectively are, in fact, two halves of the same work and that Antisthenes wrote only one Κῦρος.

[34] Fr. 29a Ἀντισθένης δ' ἐν θατέρῳ τῶν Κύρων κακολογῶν Ἀλκιβιάδην . . .

[35] Cf. frr. 5, 7, 36, 37, 43, and see Hirzel 1895: 118–29; Patzer 1970: 94–5.

the life of the Persian as an ethical model meant to demonstrate ideas
of his own: the similarities with (and hence possible influence upon)
the *Cyropaedia* are apparent. Fragment 20, in which Cyrus is advised
on the duties of a king, would fit the context of such a work well. The
sentence was probably spoken by someone who taught or advised
Cyrus at an early stage of his career; in the parallel *Heracles* Antisthenes tells of Heracles being educated by Chiron (fr. 24). It would
seem, then, that Antisthenes' work on Cyrus included a certain
amount of Κύρου παιδεία, and perhaps there was even a conversation akin to the Cambyses–Cyrus teaching dialogue of the *Cyropaedia*
(1. 6. 1 ff.). In fr. 21, where Cyrus is termed a king, he is no longer
being educated but teaches others instead. When asked what is the
most necessary thing to learn, Cyrus replies 'to unlearn evil'. If this
fragment belongs to the same *Cyrus* as the other two, the Persian has
changed or developed in the course of the work from pupil to teacher;
a similar process takes place in the *Heracles*.[36] If this interpretation of
frr. 19–21 is correct,[37] we can conclude that Antisthenes, in a work
called *Cyrus*—which may have been a dialogue—described the
Persian king's rise to power and showed how Cyrus learnt, laboured,
and developed into a wise king. It is possible that Antisthenes
discussed political matters in this *Cyrus* as well; elsewhere he
investigates questions of νόμος and πολιτεία.[38] If the *Cyropaedia* is
later than this *Cyrus* by Antisthenes, it would seem that Xenophon
adopted a great deal from his fellow Socratic when fashioning the
framework of his book. One answer to the question 'Why did
Xenophon choose Cyrus as a didactic model?' would be, then, that
Antisthenes had already paved the way.

Another likely influence upon Xenophon's choice of Cyrus the
Great as his hero was his own personal acquaintance with Cyrus the

[36] Cf. fr. 26 vs. fr. 24.

[37] It will be obvious that the discussion here owes much to Dittmar 1912: 68–76,
even if not all of his hypotheses are accepted. Caizzi 1966: 93–4 seems to be correct in
seeing frr. 19–21 as the sole remnants of one *Cyrus* composition, for the simplest hypothesis is that this *Cyrus*, a companion piece to Antisthenes' *Heracles*, was found together
with the *Heracles* in bk. 4. Fragment 29a, the remaining fragment specifically assigned
to a work entitled *Cyrus* by Antisthenes, tells us that Alcibiades was reprimanded for his
incestuous behaviour, similar to that of the Persians. This Alcibiades-related fragment
should, if only for simplicity's sake, be separated from the *Heracles*-linked fragments we
have seen so far and assigned to the second *Cyrus* Κύρος ἢ περὶ βασιλείας of bk. 5.
Perhaps, as Dittmar 1912: 82 suggests, Antisthenes contrasted the decadent Persians of
his time with the noble contemporaries of Cyrus the Great, just as Xenophon does in
the final chapter of the *Cyr.*

[38] Cf. frr. 1, 100–5.

Younger. It has long been recognized that the leading character of the *Cyropaedia* has much in common with Cyrus the Younger in the *Anabasis*. The two are similar in character and personality, both go through the same educational curriculum, and they even have friends and followers of the same name.[39] Xenophon's portrait of Cyrus the Younger makes it clear that he admired the Persian prince, and he seems to have seen the younger Cyrus as taking after his famous ancestor in more than name alone, for he claims that of all the Persians who lived after Cyrus the Great, Cyrus the Younger was the most kinglike and the most deserving of an empire (*Anab.* 1. 9. 1). It seems that at first Xenophon compared Cyrus the Younger to his illustrious namesake and then later,[40] when writing the *Cyropaedia*, reversed the situation and projected qualities of the younger man backwards in time, assigning them to his ancestor of long ago. When painting the portrait of his model hero in the *Cyropaedia*, Xenophon had the figure of an authentic Persian leader (actually named Cyrus), whose qualities of leadership he particularly admired, ready at hand.

The remaining question raised by the framework of the *Cyropaedia* is Xenophon's choice of introduction. Why does he present the *Cyropaedia*—a wide-ranging, varied work—as the end-product of his reflections on the various types of constitutions and the difficulties involved in ruling men well? The answer appears to be that Xenophon wished to ensure the work a place within the tradition of political treatises or πολιτεία literature.[41] By Xenophon's time various kinds of writings on civic constitutions were in circulation. There were political pamphlets describing the constitution or way of life of an existing polis, with its advantages and drawbacks (e.g. the 'Old Oligarch' on Athens or Xenophon's own *Lacedaemonion Politeia*),[42] as well as more theoretical discussions of the best possible form of government. The debate on the three constitutions (democracy,

---

[39] For a detailed comparison of the two Cyruses in Xenophon see e.g. Hirsch 1985: 72–5, 82, 85–9, 172–5, and Holden's introduction to his commentary on the *Cyr.* (vol. i), pp. lii–liii. Breitenbach 1966: 1712–14 shows how in the *Cyr.* Xenophon uses the names of contemporary Persians who appear in the *Anab.*

[40] Cawkwell 1972: 16 argues that the *Anab.* is later than the *Cyr.*, but this seems unlikely; see Breitenbach 1966: 1639–44 for a detailed discussion of the date of the *Anab.*

[41] For a brief, useful survey of πολιτεία literature see Treu 1966: 1935–47 and cf. Connor 1989: 49–51.

[42] The opening of the *Lac. Pol.* (1. 1–2) is very like that of the *Cyr.* (1. 1. 1–3). There too Xenophon begins by wondering why a certain form of government succeeds so well, but further reflection supplies him with the answer, which he then relates to his reader; cf. Breitenbach 1966: 1747.

monarchy, and oligarchy) found in Herodotus (3. 80–2)—a discussion, it should be noted, between Persian nobles[43]—is one of the earliest extant examples of such theoretical reflections. Xenophon's own *Hiero*, a conversation between Hiero and Simonides on the uneasy life of the tyrant and ways for him to become more benevolent and improve his regime, can be seen as another work of this kind. Other contemporaries of Xenophon shared his interest in monarchy and the possibilities inherent in the rule of an enlightened monarch —Isocrates' *To Nicocles* and *Evagoras*, and Antisthenes' lost work *Archelaus or On Kingship* come to mind—and perhaps these fourth-century writers were influenced by the strong men of their time: Evagoras of Cyprus, Dionysius of Syracuse, Jason of Pherae, and Archelaus of Macedonia.[44]

Other πολιτεία compositions were more imaginative works, in which ideal constitutions were constructed and described in detail. Hippodamus of Miletus may have been the first to describe an ideal πολιτεία,[45] and Plato's *Republic* is, of course, the outstanding representative of writings of this kind. Xenophon, it seems, wants his readers to view the *Cyropaedia* as another such work. In fact, the *Republic* has been described by one modern commentator as a '*Cyropaedia* without the historical setting of Xenophon'.[46] Ancient commentators too saw a link between Plato's political writings and the *Cyropaedia*. Diogenes Laertius (3. 34) describes Plato and Xenophon as two rivals who often wrote on the same subjects. He mentions each author's ethical works, *Symposium*, and *Apology*, and then pairs the *Republic* with the *Cyropaedia*: διαφιλονεικοῦντες τὰ ὅμοια γεγράφασι . . . , ὁ μὲν Πολιτείαν, ὁ δὲ Κύρου παιδείαν. Diogenes also notes that in his *Laws* Plato objects to Xenophon's idealized portrait of Cyrus and his upbringing, calling it, according to Diogenes, a fiction. Aulus Gellius (14. 3), writing even earlier than Diogenes, notes that some commentators describe the *Cyropaedia* as Xenophon's critical reaction to a part of Plato's *Republic*.[47] According to

---

[43] Despite Herodotus' Persian setting and his words at 6. 43, it seems clear that the debate reflects contemporary sophistic ideas and concerns: see e.g. Kerferd 1981: 150 ff., but cf. Lateiner 1989: 167, 272 and Dandamaev 1989: 105–6.

[44] Cf. Morrow 1962: 133–5 and Stroheker 1953: 406 ff.

[45] Cf. Arist. *Pol.* 1267^{b}22 ff. and Sinclair 1967: 63–4.

[46] Barker 1960: 115. Barker hastens to add that Xenophon lacks Plato's deep philosophical approach.

[47] On Gellius' problematic statement concerning the 'duo fere libri' of the *Republic* which were published separately, see Diès's introduction to the Budé *Rep.*, pp. xxxix–xliii.

these ancient commentators, an angry Plato then went out of his way to criticize Xenophon's description of Cyrus and the education he received in the *Laws* (694 c).[48]

It is true that in the passage quoted by Aulus Gellius, *Laws* 694 c, Plato does seem to be criticizing or correcting Xenophon's portrait of the Persian leader, for Plato's Athenian stranger pointedly remarks that while Cyrus was a good general and a patriot, he knew nothing of education and the correct management of a household.[49] None the less, apart from this brief dig, there is little evidence to indicate that Plato and Xenophon were rivals, vying with one another to create an ideal form of government. The *Cyropaedia* is not at all like the *Republic* or the *Laws* in content and presentation; what the two authors do have in common, perhaps, is their disillusionment with the factional strife so prevalent in the Greek cities of their time and their desire to point to a better, more satisfactory form of government.[50] Xenophon, as we have noted, devotes but a small part of the *Cyropaedia* to an outline of good government, and much of the work has little to do with political reflections of any kind. So too the precise lessons to be learnt from the life and deeds of Cyrus are not always spelt out to the reader.[51] Still, in his introduction Xenophon signals to his readers that he too has been troubled by the instability and fluctuation of government in the Greek world and that the *Cyropaedia* is not merely an idealized portrait of a Persian ruler of long ago, but his contribution to the political theory of his own time.

2. PERSIAN SOURCES

So far we have looked at the Greek background to Xenophon's choice of framework and hero for the *Cyropaedia*, but there is certainly, as one commentator puts it, a Persian 'flavouring' to the

[48] Cf. Athen. 504 E–505 A for a similar report.

[49] μαντεύομαι ... περί γε Κύρου ... παιδείας δὲ ὀρθῆς οὐχ ἧφθαι τὸ παράπαν, οἰκονομίᾳ τε οὐδὲν τὸν νοῦν προσεσχηκέναι. Hirsch 1985: 97–100 is probably right in suggesting that Plato's favourable description of the relationship between Cyrus and his subjects at *Laws* 694 A–B was influenced by the *Cyr.*

[50] For a brief survey of political conditions and attitudes in the time of Plato and Xenophon, a time of 'crise spirituelle et évasion', see Reverdin 1962; Field 1967: 77–90, 107–21; Morrow 1962: 123–37.

[51] Hence modern scholars hold a variety of opinions on the political message of the *Cyr.*: see Scharr 1919: 25–45, 102–8, and Carlier 1978: 139–40 for a brief survey of scholarly views, and cf. below, ch. 5. 2.

work as well,[52] for Xenophon includes many Persian customs, concerns, and motifs. Where do these Persian spices come from? What Persian sources were available to Xenophon and what use does he make of them in the *Cyropaedia*?

The only Persian writings extant from the Achaemenian era are the royal inscriptions written from the reign of Darius (521–486) onwards;[53] the inscriptions attributed to Cyrus the Great may be much later.[54] It seems unlikely, however, that Xenophon knew of these inscriptions or made use of them in any way. There were also written royal Persian chronicles, as we know from the Books of Esther (6: 1; cf. 2: 23) and Ezra (4: 15). Ctesias, in fact, claims to have consulted the βασιλικαὶ διφθέραι or royal leather records for his *Persica*.[55] The Iranologist Christensen has suggested that these royal writings were not a dry, annalistic record of events, but rather a royal epic, 'une littérature d'amusements' containing more than a simple chronicle of Achaemenid royal activities. He bases his argument on Esther 6: 1, where the sleepless Ahasuerus has ספר הזכרונות, דברי הימים 'the Book of Memorable Deeds, the Chronicles' read to him and is reminded to reward Mordecai; presumably the insomniac king wanted to be entertained rather than listen to a dry, dull record of events. In addition, argues Christensen, the royal Persian epics of a much later era—the (largely lost) Pahlavian work *Xwaday Namag* 'Book of Rulers' and the eleventh-century Modern Persian *Shahnamah* 'Book of Kings'—may well be, in both title and content, a continuation of the tradition of Old Persian royal annals.[56] Christensen's rather speculative theory has not been generally accepted;[57] in any

---

[52] Higgins 1977: 44. Cf. Tuplin 1990, who argues that the 'Persian decor' of the *Cyr.* is minimal.

[53] See Kent 1953 for a convenient collection of the texts; Mayrhofer 1978 supplements the corpus of extant Old Persian inscriptions. For other epigraphical sources—Persepolis treasury tablets, Aramaic inscriptions, etc.—see the survey in Frye 1984: 87–8.

[54] The authenticity of the Old Persian inscriptions attributed to Cyrus is hotly debated by Iranian scholars; see Frye 1984: 95–6 for a brief discussion and further references.

[55] *FGrH* 688 F 5; see 696 F 3–11 for other evidence in Greek sources for written Persian records.

[56] Christensen 1936: 117ff. The 'Royal Memoirs' or βασιλικὰ ἀπομνημονεύματα (cf. the Hebrew ספר הזכרונות) used by Agathias in his history of the Sasanian period (*Histories*, 4. 30. 3) should also be noted in this context; cf. Klima 1968: 23.

[57] Posner 1972: 126 thinks that the Persian chronicle was 'the daily record of royal actions and activities into which every royal decree was entered . . . termed daybooks (ἐφημερίδες) by the Greeks'; cf. the Hebrew דברי הימים. Such registers, says Posner, could be found in the courts of Egypt, Babylonia, and Assyria, as well as the princely courts of Israel and Judaea. Momigliano 1977: 27 calls Christensen's theory 'incredible'; see too the objections of Boyce 1957: 33 n. 4.

event, it is again unlikely that Xenophon consulted the Persian royal chronicles, whatever their form.

A source much more likely to have been tapped by the author of the *Cyropaedia* would be oral Persian tales, in poetry or prose, telling of the marvellous deeds of Cyrus the Great—a Persian epic. Although Xenophon may not have been particularly interested in historical research (and we must bear in mind that Cyrus the Great lived almost two hundred years before the writing of the work), it surely would have been simple and convenient for him to listen to Persian tales relating to Cyrus.[58] Xenophon had ample opportunity to become acquainted with such Persian traditions, particularly oral ones, if he were so inclined. On the *Anabasis* expedition Persians and translators were, of course, present. Later too, while residing at Scillus, where in all likelihood he first turned to writing the story of Cyrus the Great, Xenophon could have met many of the Persians in contact with Agesilaus at Sparta. We do not know what stories Xenophon may have heard, for the Persian literature of his time—not to mention the time of Cyrus the Great—is a great unknown. The very existence of Persian epic during Xenophon's period is doubted by some.[59] It would seem, however, that the burden of proof lies upon those who would deny the Persians (or any other people) any kind of folk narrative dealing with men of the past. Cyrus the Great, in particular, left his mark upon Babylonian and Jewish literature; it is difficult to believe that his own people did not commemorate him in some fashion.

The actual evidence for early Persian or Iranian epic is of four kinds: (1) references in Greek sources to Persian and Median tales of gods and men; (2) stories found in Iranian epic of a much later period which can be traced back to our period; (3) gaps or obscure allusions in the tales of the *Avesta* which presuppose widespread knowledge of mythical lore; (4) stories found in Greek writers (e.g. Herodotus, Ctesias, Xenophon) which seem to stem from Persian sources. We shall examine each of the four categories in turn.

[58] For a brief survey of Xenophon's sources of information on Cyrus and Persia, see Hirsch 1985: 68–9. Briant 1982: 491–506 has a thoughtful, more general discussion of the nature of Achaemenid sources available to classical Greek writers and their use of these sources.

[59] See e.g. Momigliano 1977: 27, who recognizes Eastern stories in Herodotus, Xenophon, and Ctesias, but explains them as stemming from 'international storytelling with a Persian background'. Drews 1973: 107 refuses to grant the Persians (or Babylonians) any sort of historical spirit, claiming 'the average man had little knowledge of what was happening or what *had* happened . . . not all peoples were fascinated with, and remembered, great *erga*'; cf. Reinhardt 1960 (= Marg 1965: 320–69).

Our most general piece of information in Greek sources comes from Strabo (15. 3. 18), who, when describing Persian mores, tells us of Persian teachers who blend useful instruction with the recitation of myths (ἔργα θεῶν τε καὶ ἀνδρῶν τῶν ἀρίστων) in prose and poetry. Herodotus (1. 132) tells us of a theogony recited by the Magi, the Median priests, during sacrifices, and we learn from Athenaeus of a well-established tradition of court poetry in the first half of the sixth century in Media. Athenaeus first commends the barbarians for using song as the ancient Greeks did, to celebrate the deeds of heroes and to praise the gods, and then brings as an example of their poetry a story from Dinon's *Persica*. Dinon tells how Angares, the most celebrated of the minstrels (ᾠδοί) at Astyages' court, once sang songs from his usual repertoire and then turned to political allegory, warning the king of a beast more dangerous than a wild boar (i.e. Cyrus).[60]

Athenaeus also furnishes evidence for a folk-tale widely told among the barbarians, i.e. Persians and Medes, during the fourth century—the love story of Odatis and Zariadres.[61] Chares of Mytilene, the Alexander historian who is Athenaeus' source here, first recounts this tale of love at first sight and then describes how popular the story is among the Asians of his time (in the second half of the fourth century BC). Odatis, the heroine of this ancient Median romance,[62] is, like Panthea in the *Cyropaedia*, the fairest woman in Asia.[63] She first sees—and falls in love with—Zariadres in a dream. When Odatis is about to be wed to another against her will, Zariadres arrives opportunely on the scene and carries her off to be his wife, so that the tale has a happy end.

There is also Greek evidence for Persian (and Median) tales featuring Cyrus the Great. Xenophon himself mentions stories and poems about Cyrus current in his day[64] and Herodotus, when presenting his version of the life of Cyrus, mentions that he knows of three other (Persian) accounts as well.[65] Thus there is, if not an

[60] Athen. 633c–e = *FGrH* 690 F 9; for a discussion of this passage and the Iranian minstrel tradition in general see Boyce 1957, esp. 19–20.

[61] Athen. 575a–f = *FGrH* 125 F 5.

[62] Cf. Boyce 1955: 470.

[63] See Schwartz 1943: 75–7, who discusses the influence of Ionian or eastern stories like that of Odatis and Zariadres on the Panthea episode of the *Cyr.*; cf. below, ch. 4. 2.

[64] *Cyr.* 1. 2. 1 ὁ Κῦρος λέγεται καὶ ᾄδεται ἔτι καὶ νῦν ὑπὸ τῶν βαρβάρων; cf. 1. 4. 25 οἱ . . . πάντες τὸν Κῦρον διὰ στόματος εἶχον καὶ ἐν λόγῳ καὶ ἐν ᾠδαῖς and see 8. 5. 28.

[65] Hdt. 1. 95; cf. 1. 214. Fehling 1989: 110–12 argues that Herodotus' claim to know four accounts of the life of Cyrus is fictitious.

abundance, an ample amount of Greek evidence attesting to Persian and Median tales current in classical times, including stories of Cyrus.

Next comes the trickier question of late Persian epic reflecting, many centuries later, traditions already current in Xenophon's time. It is generally accepted that Persian literature began to evolve from an oral to a written form only during the Sasanian era (third to seventh centuries AD). Oral tradition seems, however, to have been tenacious and to have survived in transmission over hundreds of years.[66] Thus, in theory at least, a Persian story of the classical era could have been transmitted orally, generation after generation, and have first been written down sometime in the Sasanian period, many centuries later. Sometimes this first, written Middle Persian version then survived, if only indirectly, in Arab derivatives or in reshaped form in the *Shahnamah*.[67] Hence it is not altogether unreasonable to suggest that a Persian tale of Xenophon's time can be found, in altered form, in Modern Persian writings such as the eleventh-century *Shahnamah*. An outstanding example of this process at work is the survival of the romance of Odatis and Zariadres mentioned above, a tale already current in the fourth century BC. A strikingly similar, but not identical,[68] story is told by Firdausi in the *Shahnamah* over 1,300 years later.[69]

A second, more complex illustration of Persian material seemingly preserved (in altered form) in Persian epic of a much later date is the tale of the boyhood and rise to power of Ardashir I, the founder of the Sasanian dynasty. His story, which is preserved both in the *Karnamag i Ardashir i Papakan* ('Book of the Deeds of Ardashir, son of Papakan'), a short historical novel written towards the end of the Sasanian era, and in a later, fairly close redaction of the *Karnamag* in the *Shahnamah*,[70] has much in common with the tale of the rise of Cyrus the

---

[66] See Boyce 1968: 31–2; Yarshater 1988: 8–10.

[67] This was, for example, the fate of the *Xwaday Namag* ('Book of Rulers'); see Boyce 1968: 57–9.

[68] The two versions of this story are of particular interest to Iranian scholars, for they seem to furnish proof of the early diffusion of eastern Kayanian legends to western, Achaemenian Persia in the wake of Zoroastrianism. For a detailed comparison of the two versions see Boyce 1955.

[69] For a convenient, but somewhat abridged, translation of the Odatis tale in the *Shahnamah* see Levy 1967: 181–8.

[70] See Klima 1968: 44–5 and Boyce 1968: 32, 59–60. There is a very abridged translation of the *Karnamag* in Browne 1902: 137 ff.; for the *Shahnamah* version see Levy 1967: 252 ff. More details about Ardashir can be found in other Persian writers as well.

Great as found in Ctesias–Nicolaus (*FGrH* 90 F 66).[71] Although this coincidence may be merely a repetition of a 'dynasty founder' motif popular with Persian story-tellers,[72] another way to explain the correspondences between the Cyrus and Ardashir tales is to postulate a (more or less) direct link: legends surrounding the founder of Persia's first great empire have been transferred to the founder of its second. Despite the existence of accurate historical records for the reign of Ardashir I, the historical details were effaced by legends of Cyrus the Great still in circulation. These legends were then written down in the *Karnamag* and subsequently reproduced in the *Shahnamah*. This would mean that Ctesias' version of Cyrus' youth and rise to power came from Persian sources and that the *Karnamag* itself stems from Old Persian traditions (unlike most of surviving Iranian epic, which comes from eastern Iran). If these assumptions are correct, we would then have evidence of (1) a Persian source reproduced by a classical Greek author which (2) later appeared (in revised form) in a written Sasanid source and (3) subsequently was incorporated into the *Shahnamah*.

Although we are no longer on very firm ground methodologically, certain Iranian scholars carry their investigations one stage further. Relying upon the continuity of Persian tradition for over a thousand years, they look for rough parallels between classical Greek writings dealing with Persian affairs and the *Shahnamah*, in an attempt to reconstruct early Persian epic. The *Shahnamah*, which is derived indirectly from the late Sasanian chronicle *Xwaday Namag*, tells the story of Iran in a fairly continuous way, from the creation of the world down to the Arab conquest, using the successions of kings and dynasties as a framework. Ideally, then, in our attempt to find traces of early Persian epic in the *Cyropaedia* we should compare stories of Cyrus the Great found in Xenophon with those of the *Shahnamah*. Unfortunately Cyrus—along with the Medes and most of the other Achaemenian kings—does not appear in the *Shahnamah* at all.[73] In all

[71] Both Ctesias' Cyrus and Ardashir come from a poor family, have their future greatness predicted by interpreters of a dream, do menial tasks in the king's palace, flee to their homeland, rebel, etc. For a detailed comparison see Gutschmid 1892: 133–4, who was the first, apparently, to point out the similarities; cf. also Christensen 1936: 120ff. On Ctesias–Nicolaus see below, ch. 4 n. 24.

[72] So Frye 1976: 86–7, who thinks that Ardashir's story resembles the version of Cyrus' rise to power found in Herodotus.

[73] Of all the Achaemenian rulers, only two appear briefly in the 11th-cent. epic— Dara son of Darab (= Darius III), who was conquered by Sekandar (= Alexander), and the earlier Darab (= Darius I or II). Some scholars think that Artaxerxes appears in the

likelihood Cyrus is missing from the eleventh-century epic not only because ancient lists of kings were incomplete or lost when the *Xwaday Namag* was compiled but also because Cyrus is completely absent from eastern, Zoroastrian traditions and it is these that underlie the *Xwaday Namag* and thus, indirectly, the *Shahnamah*.[74] To trace Cyrus' disappearance from late Iranian epic we must turn from traditions of the west, i.e. Persia and Media, to those of eastern Iran, the homeland of Zoroaster and the *Avesta*, the scripture of the Zoroastrians.

The extant *Avesta*[75] is all that remains of a collection, three or four times the size, of religious texts in the Avestan language—some of which go back to Zoroaster himself—made in Sasanian times; our manuscripts date from 1278 onwards. The *Avesta* contains many stories of mythical heroes and eastern rulers or *Kavis*, particularly in the *Yasht*s, the hymns dedicated to divinities. These stories in the *Yasht*s are often not told in full and many people and details are alluded to in an obscure way, making them almost incomprehensible to us. Clearly, however, the stories were known and understood when the *Yasht*s were composed (i.e. some time after Zoroaster), so that a mere hint was sufficient for the original audience. This would mean that there was a well-developed cycle of stories of heroes and rulers, an epic tradition, in eastern Iran as well. Some of the missing details of the *Avesta* stories can be found in the *Shahnamah* or in Pahlavi (Middle Persian) literature, and scholars are divided as to whether these details survived through Zoroastrian texts that are now lost to us or through an unbroken secular oral tradition.[76] In any event, the fact that the patron of Zoroaster, Vishtaspa (Hystaspas), was a *Kavi* meant that Zoroaster was introduced into the Kayanian cycle. This seems to have ensured both the survival of east Iranian, Kayanian traditions and their use much later on as the basis for the early sections of all-Iranian epic, i.e. the *Shahnamah*, since the *Xwaday Namag*, the indirect source of the *Shahnamah*, was a chronicle arranged by priests in accordance with the Zoroastrian world-view. In the past many scholars thought that there was no trace of Cyrus in Zoroastrian writings simply because he (along with other early

Shahnamah as well (as Bahman, grandson of Vishtaspa)—see e.g. Boyce 1968: 58 n. 3. Shahbazi 1977: 32–4 has an explanation of why these Achaemenians were included.

[74] See Boyce 1968: 57 ff. on the Zoroastrian shaping of the *Xwaday Namag*.

[75] For an excellent, concise introduction to the *Avesta* see Gershevitch 1968: 10 ff.

[76] A discussion of the opposing views and bibliography can be found in Gershevitch 1968: 25–6.

Achaemenian kings) was not a Zoroastrian. The long-established Sasanian tradition that Zoroaster is to be dated 258 years before Alexander would make Zoroaster a contemporary of Cyrus, and it is unlikely that the prophet's teachings would have spread from eastern to western Iran during his lifetime. Now, however, there is some evidence (archaeological and otherwise) that the early Achaemenids were indeed Zoroastrians, while the date of Zoroaster has been pushed further back.[77] None the less, Cyrus and most of the Achaemenians do not appear in the east Iranian literary tradition, and scholars have had to devise a variety of theories to explain their absence.[78]

In any event, Cyrus' absence from the *Shahnamah* and, more generally, the preponderance of east (rather than west) Iranian traditions in that work make the task of reconstructing Persian (or Median) epic—with which the Greeks may have been acquainted— quite difficult. However, as the example of Cyrus–Ardashir shows, certain old, authentic Persian elements are to be found in the *Shahnamah* (and the few surviving pre-Islamic writings). Consequently, stories or bits of stories with a Persian setting which appear in Herodotus, Ctesias, Xenophon, etc. are scrutinized by Iranian scholars for any broad similarity to tales in the *Shahnamah*. The common elements are then said to be traces of, or motifs from, Old Persian epic.[79]

The *Cyropaedia* is used by Christensen and other Iranologists in

---

[77] On the Zoroastrianism of the early Achaemenids cf. Cook 1983: 156–7, and see below, ch. 2 n. 113. For an attempt to push the date of Zoroaster back on linguistic grounds, see Burrow 1973.

[78] Yarshater 1983: 388–91 argues that in the Parthian period tales of western and southern Iran, i.e. tales of the Medes and the Persians, faded from memory, so that eastern traditions became the 'national' traditions and subsequently were committed to writing in the Sasanian period. Boyce 1982: 68–9 has an ingenious theory according to which Cyrus was thought by the Zoroastrian priests to be the father of Darius the Great (and hence named Hystaspas). This Cyrus–Hystaspas was then taken to be identical with the homonymous *Kavi* Vishtaspa (or Hystaspas) of the *Avesta*, the patron of Zoroaster, and thus Cyrus was completely erased from Zoroastrian sources, name and all; cf. Shahbazi 1977: 32 ff.

[79] Christensen 1936: 107–40 has done the most comprehensive work on the subject; Pizzagalli 1942 adds very little to Christensen's arguments. Nöldeke 1930: 5 ff. discusses Persian influence on Ctesias and Herodotus, but does not think that there are many Persian elements to be found in the *Cyr.*—see 7 n. 5. Knauth 1975 is the best-sourced attempt to show the relationship between Xenophon's model hero and Iranian sources. Knauth is less interested, however, in recovering traces of early Iranian epic and concentrates upon demonstrating the link between monarchic ideals in the *Cyr.* and those found in the *Shahnamah*.

just this fashion—both as a quarry for mining traces of Old Persian epic and as proof of Xenophon's dependence upon such Persian sources. Some of the arguments and parallels adduced by these scholars are stronger than others; none is conclusive nor can be because of the nature of the material available. Two examples will suffice to illustrate the difficulties involved in trying to pinpoint Persian influences; a third instance is discussed in detail below.[80]

In the *Cyropaedia* we learn that Gobryas' only son was killed by the Assyrian crown prince, in the course of a hunting expedition. Gobryas' son had been competing freely with the prince, and proved more successful than his royal friend, shooting down two animals after the prince had missed them both. When Gobryas' son expressed delight at his own prowess, the jealous prince stabbed his companion to death (*Cyr.* 4. 6. 3–4). Christensen compares a similar tale told of Ardashir I; it is found both in the *Karnamag* and the *Shahnamah*.[81] Ardashir, who had been accepted by Ardavan, the last of the Arsacid kings, as a privileged member of his household, went hunting with the king's son. Ardashir killed a wild ass with an expert shot, but Ardavan's son claimed that *he* had hunted down the animal. Ardashir then reprimanded the prince for lying, but Ardavan took his son's side and punished Ardashir by sending him to work in the stables. The similarities between the two incidents are apparent; can we assume, as Christensen does, that there is a direct connection? We have already seen that the *Karnamag* stems from Old Persian traditions and that the story of Ardashir has probably been influenced (directly or indirectly) by tales of Cyrus. This story from the *Cyropaedia*, however, concerns not Cyrus himself, but the son of one of his allies. The custom that no one is to shoot before the king is clearly a Persian or Oriental one; Xenophon himself terms it βασιλικῶς in the *Cyropaedia* and has his idealized young hero reject this royal prerogative (1. 4. 14). So too tales of the dire consequences resulting from outdoing a royal despot at a hunt naturally belong to the Oriental world, not to the Greek one; similar stories are told both by Ctesias and Curtius Rufus.[82] Clearly, then, Xenophon is making use of a Persian motif here, but he is not necessarily adapting a story found in Persian epic. What Momigliano terms 'international storytelling with a Persian background'[83] would seem a more accurate description of Xenophon's source here.

[80] Cf. below, ch. 2. 7.
[81] See Levy 1967: 255–6; Browne 1902: 137; Christensen 1936: 125.
[82] Cf. below, ch. 4. 3.   [83] Momigliano 1977: 27; cf. above, n. 59.

A second test case from the *Cyropaedia* concerns the lovely and virtuous Panthea. Did Xenophon make use of Persian traditions when writing this famous and influential romance? Here, Christensen—or, to be just, the very limited Persian material available—disappoints. The Iranian scholar is reminded of love stories in the *Shahnamah* but he does not mention any specific parallel, other than comparing Panthea's lament for Abradatas (*Cyr.* 7. 3. 8–14) to a mother's much more violent lament for her son,[84] and it seems that in fact there is no similar heroine to be found in that long work.[85] The story of Panthea (or her Persian equivalent) may have been part of the Persian traditions of Xenophon's time—we have already seen that another romance, that of Odatis and Zariadres, was in circulation at about that time—but without even a foothold in the *Shahnamah* we can only speculate. Panthea's story, like that of Gobryas' son, is only loosely connected with Cyrus the Great, and may well have come from traditions totally unrelated to the Persian leader. This would mean in turn either that Xenophon had a fairly broad acquaintance with Persian epic and his knowledge was not restricted to a Cyrus cycle of tales, or that we are dealing with the rather nebulous 'internationally circulating stories' of his era. Again, much as we would like to know, we can only guess.

To sum up, the evidence seems to indicate that there was some sort of Persian epic, including stories of Cyrus, in circulation when the *Cyropaedia* was written. Xenophon could have been—and probably was—acquainted with parts of this epic. Unfortunately Old Persian epic has disappeared, leaving very few traces behind; those that remain are chiefly found in the eleventh-century *Shahnamah*. While these vestiges tempt us to conjecture links between the *Cyropaedia* and Old Persian epic, since they are no more than traces we are unable to go beyond conjecture. Time and again we shall encounter in the *Cyropaedia* features which seem to be Persian, but any real knowledge of the origin or sources of this Persian material is, at present, tantalizingly out of reach.

---

[84] The mother and son of the *Shahnamah* are Tahmina and Sohrab; cf. Christensen 1936: 125–6.

[85] Cf. Nöldeke 1930: 88–9, who discusses the limited role women play in the *Shahnamah*. He notes that women such as Penelope, Andromache, and Nausicaa, who are as important as men, are not found in the Persian epic. Panthea is, of course, another such strong-minded heroine.

3. THE DATE OF THE *CYROPAEDIA*

Another question which will arise several times is that of the date of the *Cyropaedia*. It is difficult to date Xenophon's writings, and this work is no exception. There are several different approaches used to assign a date to the *Cyropaedia*, and no one method leads to a certain or incontestable result. Most scholars would agree, however, that the *Cyropaedia* is a late work and was written in the 360s.

The final chapter (8. 8) seems to give us a *terminus post quem* of 362/1 BC, for mention is made there of two key figures in the satraps' revolt, Mithridates and Rheomithres, and their treacherous behaviour towards their relatives, which took place during that year.[86] This final chapter or epilogue, a scathing attack on the degenerate Persians of Xenophon's day, raises many problems. There are several discrepancies between descriptions of Persian customs found in the main body of the *Cyropaedia* and those of the final chapter, while the polemical, anti-Persian tone of the epilogue is inconsistent with Xenophon's attitude throughout the rest of the work. Hence the epilogue seems to many readers (and scholars) an abrupt, surprising, and inappropriate end to the *Cyropaedia*.[87] Several commentators consider this final chapter a late addition, tacked on by Xenophon after he wrote the rest of the text: his response, perhaps, to criticisms of the work's excessively favourable attitude towards the Persians or simply his second thoughts on the subject. Other scholars reject the epilogue outright, declaring it inauthentic.[88] Thus, the chronological information supplied by the epilogue is open to question and depends upon one's acceptance of the final chapter as authentic. It will be argued in detail below that there is no real reason to reject the authenticity of the epilogue,[89] and this would mean that the *Cyropaedia was* written after 362/1 BC. However, if those who condemn *Cyr.* 8. 8 are correct and the epilogue is indeed a later addition, either by Xenophon or by some unknown author, then the reference to events of 362/1 found there is, of course, of little use in determining when the rest of the work was written.

[86] *Cyr.* 8. 8. 4; cf. Diod. Sic. 15. 90 ff.; cf. Weiskopf 1989: 38, 82, 88–9 n. 116.

[87] Miller, in the Loeb edition of the *Cyr.* (ii. 439), is so disconcerted by this ending that he recommends his readers 'to close the book . . . and read no further'.

[88] For a survey of the problems raised by the epilogue and modern views on the question, see e.g. Holden in his commentary ad loc.; Bizos' introduction to the Budé *Cyr.*, p. xxvii; Hirsch 1985: 91–6 with nn.

[89] Cf. below, ch. 5. 3.

A second approach used to date the work is based upon the assumption that Xenophon is addressing an Athenian audience. Once, when referring, it seems, to Athenian education, Xenophon uses the phrase παρ' ἡμῖν (*Cyr.* 1. 2. 6; cf. 1. 6. 32). He also includes in the *Cyropaedia* a description of an Armenian 'Socrates', a sophist who is accused by the Armenian king of corrupting his son and executed for the crime (*Cyr.* 3. 1. 38–40).[90] When Cyrus hears of the incident, he declares that the Armenian king should be forgiven for his very human failing, and commentators interpret the forgiving attitude displayed by the hero of the *Cyropaedia* as a conciliatory overture made by Xenophon to the Athenians after his recall from exile, i.e. some time after 369 BC.[91] This pair of assumptions—that the work was written first and foremost for an Athenian reading public and that Xenophon would address the Athenians sympathetically only after the repeal of his banishment—is difficult to substantiate.

A third argument used in assigning a late date to the *Cyropaedia* is the fact that the work includes almost all the various features found in Xenophon's other works: (pseudo-)history as in the *Hellenica*, a Persian setting as in the *Anabasis*, philosophical and ethical conversations as in the *Memorabilia*, convivial dinner parties as in the *Symposium*, encomium as in the *Agesilaus*, horsemanship and hunting as in the περὶ ἱππικῆς and the Ἱππαρχικός, etc.[92] It is hazardous, of course, to date the *Cyropaedia* according to its relation to Xenophon's other works. Our author frequently repeats himself and reworks the same material several times in different compositions, and it is usually quite difficult to determine which of two or more variations came first.[93] So too scholars are agreed that Xenophon's works do not lend themselves to stylometric analysis, and his writings cannot be arranged in an approximate chronological order on the basis of a statistical investigation of linguistic features.[94] None the less it is worth noting that no other work by Xenophon encompasses so many

[90] See below, ch. 2. 4.

[91] For this approach to the dating of the *Cyr.* see Carlier 1978: 137 n. 13; Scharr 1919: 40 n. 78; Schwartz 1943: 70. On the probable date of Xenophon's recall from exile see Breitenbach 1966: 1576 and cf. Cawkwell 1972: 15 n. 3.

[92] See e.g. Nickel 1979: 56–8 and Anderson 1974: 2.

[93] Schwartz 1889: 191–2 (= 1956: 171–2) thinks that the many cross-references and repetitions in Xenophon's writings indicate that he wrote most of his works (in his old age) during a relatively short period; this view has found favour with several scholars— see Gautier 1911: 133 and Higgins 1977: 131–2. We shall encounter several instances of such repetitions and variations below (see chs. 2. 2 at nn. 130, 144, 3. 6 at n. 157).

[94] See Gautier 1911: 131–2; Nickel 1979: 131; Breitenbach 1966: 1901.

of its author's varied interests and it is difficult to resist the impression that the *Cyropaedia* is a kind of summary of Xenophon's literary activity and consequently is a late work.

Finally, some of the fictional military material included in the *Cyropaedia* serves as an indication of the work's date. The battles described in the *Cyropaedia* do not reflect the real order, location, or types of battles fought by the historical Cyrus, but constitute a fairly exhaustive military treatise on various types of battles and the ways to wage them. There is little doubt that these military engagements are the fruit of Xenophon's own expertise and interests: he invents almost all the details of these clashes, making use of the lessons he has learnt from the actual battles of his time, in order to instruct his readers. The main battle of the *Cyropaedia*, that which takes place between Cyrus and Croesus at Thymbrara (*Cyr.* 7. 1. 1 ff.), is particularly interesting in this respect, for it seems to have been written in the light of the conflict between Thebes and Sparta at Leuctra in 371.[95] In other words, Xenophon included in the *Cyropaedia* a clash which seems modelled upon the battle of Leuctra of 371, and this gives us a *terminus post quem* of 371, at the earliest, for the work.[96]

To sum up, the *Cyropaedia* should be dated in the 360s; the two strongest arguments for this date are that the epilogue, if genuine, shows that the work was written after 362/1, while the indirect allusions to the tactics used at Leuctra point to a date after 371. This approximate date will be used in what follows chiefly in order to establish that other works which may have influenced the *Cyropaedia*—Ctesias' *Persica*, Plato's *Symposium*, Isocrates' *To Nicocles*, Aeschines' *Aspasia*, etc.—were indeed written earlier.

---

[95] For a detailed, convincing demonstration of this point see Anderson 1970: 165–91, 211, 217, 218. See also Pease 1934 for an appreciation of the *Cyr.* as a military treatise.

[96] Delebecque 1957: 400–4 uses other military information in the *Cyr.* to arrive at an even later date for the work. He argues that the important military role assigned to the Egyptians in the *Cyr.* is due to the attention which the Egyptians aroused in Agesilaus' final campaigns, and concludes that the *Cyr.* was written after the winter of 361/60.

2

Socrates in Persia

I. INTRODUCTION

At first sight one would not expect Socrates—the man, his life, ideas, and techniques of argument—to exercise any real influence over the *Cyropaedia*. Cyrus and his Persian soldiers are, after all, far removed in time, geography, and way of life from the world of the Athenian philosopher. None the less Socrates, Xenophon's Socrates,[1] is a real presence in the *Cyropaedia*, and this chapter deals with Socratic echoes in the work. For a start, Cyrus the Great has several character traits in common with Socrates: both have temperate habits and moderate material needs, both are capable of enduring a great deal of physical discomfort, and both have a tendency towards preachy didacticism.[2] These characteristics are not, of course, restricted solely to these two heroes in Xenophon. Agesilaus, Jason of Thessaly, Cyrus the Younger, and, for that matter, Xenophon himself in the *Anabasis* all believe in ἐγκράτεια and καρτερία—self-control, moderation, and physical endurance[3]—and these men generally enjoy making moralizing, didactic pronouncements as well.[4] In fact many of the positive, leading figures in Xenophon are virtuous in much the

[1] It should perhaps be stressed at the outset that our chief concern here is with Socrates *as he is portrayed by Xenophon*, without entering into the question of his relation to the actual, historical figure of Socrates. We shall see that Xenophon's Socrates bears some resemblance to Plato's philosopher and has certain traits in common with the sophists as well, but only those features which are regularly associated with the philosopher in Xenophon's writings are termed here 'Socratic'.

[2] Cyrus' temperate habits and self-control: *Cyr.* 1. 3. 4, 10, 1. 5. 1, 1. 6. 8, 25, 5. 1. 8, 12, 16; cf. also Due 1989: 170–81, but cf. below, ch. 5. 2. His didacticism: *Cyr.* 2. 4. 5–6, 8. 3. 3–4, 8. 4. 32–6, etc. Socrates' physical endurance and modest needs: *Mem.* 1. 2. 1, 1. 3. 5–6, 14, 1. 5. 6, 4. 8. 11. Socrates' didacticism is evident throughout the *Mem.* —see 1. 3. 8–14, 1. 5. 1–5, 1. 6. 7–8, 2. 1. 1–7, etc.

[3] Agesilaus: *Ages.* 5. 1–5, 9. 3; Jason of Thessaly: *Hell.* 6. 1. 15–16; Cyrus the Younger: *Anab.* 1. 9. 3; *Oec.* 4. 24; Xenophon: *Anab.* 4. 4. 12; cf. also *Hipparch.* 6. 3. See Breitenbach 1950: 60–70 and Due 1989: 185–206.

[4] See e.g. *Hell.* 3. 4. 9; *Ages.* 1. 21, 28, 4. 6 (Agesilaus); *Hell.* 6. 1. 7–8 (Jason of Thessaly); *Anab.* 1. 9. 23 (Cyrus the Younger); *Anab.* 3. 4. 44–9, 7. 3. 44–5 (Xenophon).

same way, and it is an interesting (and perhaps unanswerable) question as to why this is so. One explanation is that the figure of Socrates—the Athenian philosopher as Xenophon perceived him— has left his mark upon all of his follower's writings. In other words, Xenophon portrays his positive characters as variations on his ideal model, Socrates. Another possibility is that Xenophon's own view of life, his moralistic, didactic way of thought, dominates his writing (and thinking) so thoroughly that he fashions all his heroes, including a figure as unique as Socrates, along the same lines.[5]

In any event, the resemblance between Socrates and Cyrus is not the only indication that the Athenian philosopher has influenced our work. In the *Cyropaedia* Xenophon alludes several times to the circumstances surrounding Socrates' trial and death. We shall see that he actually introduces a Socrates-like character, a sophist who is executed for corrupting his young charge, and his depiction of the death of Cyrus the Great has overtones of Socrates' end. But the strongest and most frequent indication of the philosopher's presence is the Socratic tenor of many of the conversations in the *Cyropaedia*. The philosophical or didactic tone of these dialogues—as well as their structure and means of argument—are very like Socrates' conversations as recorded by Xenophon.

Of the three kinds of Socratic influence to be found in the *Cyropaedia*—personal traits shared by Socrates and Cyrus, issues and events related to Socrates' trial and final days which are incorporated into the work, and didactic, dialectical conversations—the last is the most difficult to pin down and define. The circumstances of Socrates' trial, the charges made against the philosopher, and his manner of death are, of course, well known and easy to recognize even in the new guise they take on in the *Cyropaedia*. So too the correspondences in Xenophon between the Athenian philosopher's teachings and moderate way of life and those of the Persian ruler are, again, not difficult to identify; one can easily quote many parallels between the *Cyropaedia* and (for example) the *Memorabilia*.[6] But while Socrates'

[5] Xenophon's didactic tendencies are so pronounced that even his most historical or 'objective' work, the *Hell.*, is regarded by some as primarily didactic and his chief concern is thought to be moral rather than the recording of history. See C. H. Grayson 1975 for an extreme statement of this position and compare Gray 1989, *passim*; see also Breitenbach 1950: 87–8 n. 143. Luccioni 1953 is an attempt to trace this didactic strain in all of Xenophon's works under the guise of pointing out *Socratic* influence.

[6] For a detailed demonstration, based on a collection of parallels between the *Mem.* and the *Cyr.*, that Xenophon's Cyrus 'is not a Persian at all . . . but a Grecian of the

words can be, at times, little more than topoi often found elsewhere in Xenophon, the clothing or method of presentation of the philosopher's ideas—through his dialogues—is often more individual. More than anything else, Socrates' characteristic features as an interlocutor, the form and 'feel' of his conversations, have left their mark on the *Cyropaedia*, and it is these features of Socratic conversation that must first be characterized if we are to identify Socratic influence on the work.

A short and seemingly simple conversation, *Cyr.* 1. 4. 13–14, well illustrates the presence of these Socratic methods. Young Cyrus, on a visit to Media, is trying to persuade his grandfather, the despot Astyages, to allow him and his Mede friends to go hunting outside the παράδεισος, the royal enclosed park, and he uses an interesting technique of argument in order to do so. Cyrus, we are told, feels tongue-tied and is wary of approaching Astyages,[7] but pressed by his companions to intercede on their behalf, he summons up his courage and plans (1. 4. 13 ἐπιβουλεύσας) how best to achieve his aims. The Persian youngster does not put forth the request to his grandfather directly but opens the conversation with a hypothetical question, asking Astyages how he would treat a runaway servant who had been caught. When the despot replies that he would put the man to work in chains, Cyrus then asks how a fugitive servant who had returned of his own free will would be handled, once again requesting Astyages' verdict on a theoretical case, which seems to have little to do with the two of them. Only after Astyages answers that he would flog such a servant and then treat him as before does Cyrus reveal that the despot is, in fact, pronouncing judgement on his own grandson, for he is the runaway servant who plans to go off hunting with his friends and then return. Astyages then forbids Cyrus to carry out his plan, because he does not want his grandson harmed through carelessness. Cyrus' conversational ploy has failed; later (1. 4. 14) sulking proves a more effective means of achieving his aim.

The technique used here by Cyrus, of having a conversational partner discuss a hypothetical question—one seemingly unrelated to his own situation—and then suddenly applying the (analogous) outcome to himself, is one used time and again by Socrates in the

school of Socrates', whose every quality and action can be attributed to Socratic influence, see Dadachanjee 1904: 552–61, esp. 554.

[7] Compare the difficulties Archidamus has in facing Agesilaus with a request to save Sphodrias—*Hell.* 5. 4. 27–30.

Memorabilia.[8] Ischomachus, Socrates' 'teacher' in the *Oeconomicus*, also makes use of this questioning technique (*Oec.* 10. 3–7), and the practice may well be genuinely Socratic. Plato, for instance, has Nicias point out that no matter what the starting-point of a discussion is, Socrates' interlocutors always end up having to give an account of themselves (*Laches* 187 E–188 A). Cyrus' method here is, then, Socratic[9] and his casual opening words to his grandfather— εἰπέ μοι—actually echo Socratic usage in the *Memorabilia*, for every instance there of Socrates first inviting an interlocutor to judge a hypothetical case and then having him apply the judgement to himself begins with the philosopher's εἰπέ μοι.[10]

In our short dialogue, *Cyr.* 1. 4. 13–14, young Cyrus plays the role of Socrates, whereas his grandfather is the conversational partner who unwittingly gives a verdict affecting himself while discussing a different, but analogous, situation (runaway servant : master = Cyrus : Astyages).[11] Cyrus, Xenophon tells us, thought that such indirect questioning was the best way to achieve his aim without paining his grandfather, but the Persian lad fails to win over Astyages and has to resort to sulking instead. Why does Cyrus fail? Surely not because Xenophon wishes to impugn Socrates' method as such: one could well imagine Astyages delighting in his grandson's cleverness and granting him his request at once. The reason behind Cyrus' lack of success is to be found, perhaps, in the Mede ruler's final remark χαρίεν γάρ . . . εἰ ἕνεκα κρεαδίων τῇ θυγατρὶ τὸν παῖδα ἀποβουκολήσαιμι—Astyages does not want to lose his daughter her son, as one loses a stray sheep, for the sake of a bit of meat. With these words we have moved suddenly from the world of Socrates to that of Herodotus. According to Herodotus, Astyages set out to destroy his daughter's child and Cyrus was almost left to die of exposure at the hands of a βουκόλος (Hdt.

---

[8] *Mem.* 2. 1. 1–7, 16–17, 2. 2. 1–3, 12–13, 2. 3. 11–13, 2. 9. 1–3, 2. 10. 1–3, and 3. 7. 1–2 are all instances of Socrates employing this method; cf. 1. 4. 2–9.

[9] Socrates was not, of course, the first to employ this method of teaching by analogy. We find, for example, several instances of this technique in Herodotus: Bias/Pittacus uses this kind of reasoning (ἐπίλογος) to guide Croesus (Hdt. 1. 27), as does Cambyses' sister when reproving her brother (3. 32; cf. 1. 159).

[10] *Mem.* 1. 4. 2, 2. 1. 1, 2. 2. 1, 2. 9. 2, 2. 10. 1, 3. 7. 1; cf. *Oec.* 10. 3 and contrast *Mem.* 2. 3. 11. See too Radermacher 1967: 287. Needless to say, εἰπέ μοι is not used exclusively (either in the *Mem.* or the *Cyr.*) for this purpose and often opens conversations of an entirely different sort.

[11] See Tatum 1989: 106–10 for a different interpretation of Cyrus' conversation with his grandfather.

1. 108 ff.); bits of meat play a gruesome part in the subsequent tale
(1. 119). Xenophon by his use of the colourful ἀποβουκολήσαιμι
seems to hint here at Herodotus' tale of Cyrus' cruel grandfather,
even while presenting Astyages in an altogether more positive light.[12]
Thus this brief dialogue is an intriguing blend of Persian and Socratic
elements, and we shall see that several other conversations in the
Cyropaedia also feature such a combination of influences.

It is time to see what 'Socratic' or, more specifically, 'Socratic
dialogue' means in Xenophon. What are Socrates' teaching
methods? What kinds of arguments does the Athenian philosopher
use? Who are his partners in these conversations? How do they react
to his words? The *Memorabilia* is a good starting-point for such an
enquiry because it includes—in addition to a small number of
speeches—a large group of dialogues which are fairly uniform in
length, form, and presentation, and Socrates is, of course, the leading
figure in these conversations.[13] The philosopher is presented in
consistent fashion in the *Memorabilia*, so that we can safely generalize
about Socrates' practices, mannerisms, etc. in the work.

The most immediate thing that one notices about Socrates in the
Memorabilia is that conversations or dialogues are his preferred
medium of instruction. Xenophon's philosopher is a most didactic
figure, eager to teach, advise, and guide, and he prefers to do so in
conversation rather than by means of continuous discourses or
diatribes. While Socrates discourses and exhorts at great length in the
Memorabilia, he almost always does so within the framework of a
dialogue: there are very few pure speeches in the work.[14] The
conversations of the *Memorabilia* are all fairly short and, with one
exception (*Mem.* 1. 2. 32–8), Socrates converses with only one other
person: Xenophon's philosopher prefers to deal with one interlocutor at a time. This does not mean that others are not present at
these conversations, and Socrates, who is sensitive to a surrounding
audience, knows how to make use of these onlookers. Generally, we
hear of these spectators in the *Memorabilia* only when their presence
affects the tenor of the conversation in some way.[15] The philosopher is,

[12] Cf. below, ch. 3. 2, for another such indirect allusion to Herodotus' portrait of
Astyages.
[13] Socrates participates in all but one dialogue of the *Mem.*, a conversation between
Alcibiades and Pericles (1. 2. 40–6).   [14] See *Mem.* 1. 5, 1. 7, 2. 4, 3. 2; cf. 4. 7.
[15] We can ignore Xenophon's references to his own presence at Socrates' conversations, for they are meant to lend authority and authenticity to the *Mem.*, not to reflect
reality. See Breitenbach 1966: 1779–80 and Field 1967: 140 n. 1.

for instance, tackled by his critics Antiphon (1. 6), Aristippus (3. 8),
and Hippias (4. 4) in front of a crowd of his supporters, since one of
the objectives of these opponents is to discredit Socrates in the eyes of
his followers. (As is to be expected, these critics do not succeed in
their aim.) Elsewhere in the *Memorabilia* there are several light-
hearted conversations where a wider group of friends is invited to join
in the fun (3. 1. 4, 3. 11. 2). In another type of dialogue the presence
of a (silent) third party is significant. In these conversations Socrates
addresses didactic or admonitory remarks to one interlocutor but his
words are actually intended to serve as an indirect reproach to
another person present.[16] Perhaps the most interesting use of a
surrounding audience is to be found in Socrates' early encounters
with Euthydemus (4. 2). At first Socrates speaks to Euthydemus only
indirectly, addressing the words meant for the youngster's ears to his
followers. Later, when he feels that Euthydemus is ripe for serious
discussion and 'conversion', Socrates approaches the young man by
himself and submits him to a long and searching elenchus in private
(4. 2. 8–39).

In his conversations in the *Memorabilia* Socrates generally gets
straight to the point. Xenophon has a specific aim in mind—usually
that of showing Socrates instructing his fellow conversationalist in an
area in which the latter is deficient—and little else is allowed to
intervene. This means that very little description of the circumstances
or locale of these conversations, or of the speakers themselves, is
included in the dialogues. Xenophon's Socrates does not, on the
whole, indulge in light chit-chat before turning to his main concern,
so that both the dramatic background—narrated by the author,
Xenophon—and the actual conversational preludes of Socrates
himself are compressed and succinct. Often we are given the essential
background information—the name of Socrates' interlocutor and his
specific problem—in a short opening frame which precedes the
actual dialogue: in this way, for example, the impious Aristodemus,
undisciplined Aristippus, unfilial Lamprocles, and shy Charmides
are introduced to us.[17] Sometimes only the name and profession
of Socrates' partner are mentioned at the outset, or the specific

---

[16] See *Mem.* 1. 3. 8–15, 2. 5. 1–5, 4. 2. 1–7; cf. 1. 2. 30 and 3. 14. 2–4. Gigon 1946:
133–41 was the first to identify and discuss this indirect technique of reproach in the
Mem.; he notes that Plato's Socrates does not make use of this method. See also Gigon
1953: 56 and cf. Xen. *Symp.* 4. 23–8.

[17] See *Mem.* 1. 3. 8, 1. 4. 2, 2. 1. 1, 2. 2. 1, 2. 3. 1, 2. 5. 1, 2. 9. 1, 3. 6. 1, 3. 7. 1,
3. 12. 1, 4. 2. 1; cf. also 1. 6. 1, 3. 8. 1, 4. 8. 4.

circumstances of the conversation are sketched briefly, and the
discussion between the philosopher and his partner then follows with
no further ado.[18] The breathless opening of Plato's *Meno*, which
plunges straight into the matter at hand, is perhaps the closest
instance in Plato's Socratic dialogues to the kind of presentation often
found in the *Memorabilia*.[19] None the less, Xenophon, in his role as
narrator, does not eschew dramatic effects altogether. One outstanding instance is Socrates' encounter with the courtesan Theodote (3. 11): the elaborate opening, vivid background detail, and
large surrounding audience add considerably to the conversation.
Two elenctic conversations, Socrates' cross-examinations of Euthydemus and Glaucon, are also enhanced by the fact that we are first
told why Socrates approaches the youngsters (3. 6. 1–2, 4. 2. 1–2) and
are then shown their similar reactions to the philosopher's questions
—vanity which rapidly turns to bewilderment (3. 6. 3–4, 4. 2. 9–
10).[20] Xenophon skilfully characterizes another of Socrates' interlocutors, Nicomachides, by describing a single gesture of his (3. 4. 1).

The functional, no-nonsense approach generally adopted by
Socrates (and Xenophon) in the conversations of the *Memorabilia*
may be related to the scale or brevity of these rather short dialogues.
(We shall see that the *Symposium* and the *Oeconomicus*, Socratic
dialogues on a much greater scale, proceed at a more leisurely pace,
while another lengthy dialogue by Xenophon, the *Hiero*, does not.)
Recent scholarship postulates the existence of a literary subgenre of
Socratic dialogues, *Kurzdialoge* or 'short dialogues', which were first
composed in the first half of the fourth century; the dialogues of the
Memorabilia seem to belong to this category of short conversations
between Socrates and one other person.[21] In any event, the majority

---

[18] Name or profession of Socrates' interlocutor: *Mem.* 2. 7. 1, 2. 8. 1, 2. 10. 1, 3. 4. 1,
3. 5. 1, 3. 10. 1, 3. 10. 6, 3. 10. 9, 4. 4. 5; cf. 1. 2. 40. Circumstances: 1. 2. 32–3, 3. 1. 1,
3. 3. 1.

[19] The *Meno* is, of course, a direct, dramatic dialogue. While Plato uses a variety of
means to present his dialogues—direct dramatic form, narrated conversations, and a
combination of the two (see e.g. Tarrant 1955: 84–5)—all of Socrates' conversations in
the *Mem.* are narrated by Xenophon.

[20] Cf. also Hippias' conversation with Socrates (4. 4. 5 ff.).

[21] Müller 1975 was the first to designate this class of *Kurzdialoge* on the basis of the
short pseudo-Platonic dialogues; cf. 320–6 for a summary of the main characteristics of
the group. Slings 1981: 24–41 continues Müller's work and, making use of Gigon's
analysis of the *Mem.* as well, again analyses the chief features of the 'short dialogues'.
These short conversations between Socrates and one other (often anonymous) interlocutor are generally presented directly and dramatically, and include little scenic
background. They are usually restricted to one central theme or question—e.g. τί τὸ

of Socrates' conversations in the *Memorabilia* are much shorter than Plato's dialogues, for example, and it is only natural that this should affect the manner in which they are presented.

While long addresses by Socrates are often found in the dialogues of the *Memorabilia*, we frequently find the very opposite of lengthy exhortations, a series of brief exchanges in the form of questions and replies. In a majority of the dialogues Socrates at some point turns to his interlocutor with a string of short, leading questions which can often be answered with a simple 'yes' or 'no'.[22] Such rapid exchanges of question and reply are associated with Socrates elsewhere as well: we find examples of this kind of cross-examination in Plato,[23] the pseudo-Platonic works,[24] and the minor Socratics.[25] Hence it is tempting to conclude that this use of brief, leading questions was a genuine trait of Socrates or at least was associated with the philosopher from a very early stage. But while all the early Socratic writers seem to include these 'question and reply' interrogations, the resemblance is in their external form alone. Socrates uses this technique in quite different ways in the various writers, and this is particularly noticeable in comparing Xenophon and Plato.

In Plato the 'question and reply' form of discussion beloved of Socrates is frequently linked with the ability to speak briefly, βραχυλογία, and contrasted with μακρολογία, the delivery of lengthy speeches.[26] Socrates regularly employs this kind of interrogation in Plato's early dialogues when conducting an ἔλεγχος, a cross-examination which reduces his interlocutor to helplessness or

καλόν;—which is introduced at the very start of the conversation, and Socrates' interlocutor in the *Kurzdialoge* is little more than a 'yes man', agreeing with the philosopher's thesis and raising no arguments or objections of his own. The main difference between such short conversations and the narrated dialogues of the *Mem.* is, as we shall see, the more substantial role assigned at times to Socrates' fellow conversationalists in the *Mem.*

[22] See *Mem.* 2. 1. 1–3, 2. 2. 1–3, 7–9, 11–12, 2. 3. 11–14, 2. 6. 1–4, 2. 7. 3–5, 2. 10. 1–2, 3. 1. 10–11, 3. 3. 1–15, 3. 4. 7–10, 3. 5. 1–3, 3. 6. 3–13, 3. 8. 2–3, 3. 10. 3–5, 6–8, 3. 11. 4, 3. 13. 3, 6, 4. 2. 8–22, 31–9, 4. 3. 3–8, 4. 4. 10–14, 20–5, 4. 5. 2–9, 4. 6. 2–11, 13–14, and cf. 1. 2. 40–6.

[23] For the 'question-and-reply' form of conversation in Plato see Schaerer 1969: 25–38 and Thesleff 1967: 35–41.

[24] See e.g. *De Iusto* 374 A–E and cf. Müller 1975: 323–5.

[25] See in particular Aeschines, *Alcibiades* (*P. Oxy.* 13. 1608, fr. 1) and compare Aspasia's interrogation of Xenophon and his wife in Aeschines' *Aspasia* (fr. 31 Dittmar).

[26] On βραχυλογία and μακρολογία see Pl. *Prot.* 329 B, 334 D–335 A; *Gorg.* 449 B–C, 461 E–462 A; *Phaedr.* 267 B; cf. Δισσοὶ Λόγοι (DK 90) 8. 1, 13. For a good discussion of the two methods of discussion in relation to Socrates and the sophists see Kerferd 1981: 32–4.

bafflement.[27] In the *Memorabilia* Xenophon tells us that Socrates questions and refutes know-it-alls—favourite targets of the Platonic Socrates—and occasionally we actually see him doing so: that is, we find the philosopher posing a chain of leading questions in order to cross-examine, refute, and chastise another.[28] Socrates' examination of the young and over-confident Euthydemus (*Mem.* 4. 2) is the most outstanding instance of a Platonic-style, negative ἔλεγχος found in the *Memorabilia*, along with Alcibiades' refutation of Pericles (1. 2. 40–6). Glaucon, another proud young man, and the sophist Hippias are two others who emerge somewhat battered after an inter-rogation—in the form of leading questions which call for brief replies—by Socrates.[29] Hippias, even before undergoing a cross-examination at the hands of Socrates, accuses the philosopher of constantly ridiculing others and arguing them down without reveal-ing his own views (*Mem.* 4. 4. 9; compare 4. 8. 11), but this descrip-tion—not an inaccurate picture of Socrates at work in Plato's early dialogues—is in reality a very one-sided view of Socrates' activities in the *Memorabilia*. Only rarely do we see the philosopher tripping up or refuting others in Xenophon, and his Socrates is always more than anxious to reveal his own views. Thus while the philosopher in Xenophon often poses his interlocutors a series of brief questions, just as he does in early Plato, these interrogations are only rarely used in the *Memorabilia* for an ἔλεγχος and can be found on a wide variety of occasions.

Such brief cross-examinations sometimes occur in the *Memorabilia* when there are open differences of opinion between Socrates and his fellow conversationalist: the two discuss, debate, and argue by means of question and reply. In these conversations[30] Socrates does not

[27] The classic discussion of ἔλεγχος in early Plato is Robinson 1953: 7 ff.: 'The art of elenchus is to find premises believed by the answerer and yet entailing the contrary of his thesis' (15); compare the rather different approach of Vlastos 1983.

[28] Cf. *Mem.* 1. 4. 1 ἃ ἐκεῖνος κολαστηρίου ἕνεκα τοὺς πάντ' οἰομένους εἰδέναι ἐρωτῶν ἤλεγχεν. For a discussion of *Mem.* 1. 4. 1—the only passage in the *Mem.* where Xenophon touches upon the issues of continuous speeches vs. exchanges of questions and answers, and positive teachings vs. refutations and cross-examinations—see Gigon 1953: 118–22; Erbse 1961: 271–5; Slings 1981: 54 n. 11, 89–102.

[29] *Mem.* 3. 6. 3–16, 4. 4. 19–25; cf. 3. 8. 2–3, 3. 13. 3, 6. The harsh verdict of Chroust 1957: 6, that 'invariably the method of argumentation introduced by the Xenophon-tean Socrates amounts to nothing other than a rather crude effort of asking leading questions merely for the sake of arriving in a round-about fashion at a cut and dried moral commonplace', is simply not true. See Lacey 1971, esp. 38–40, for a more balanced approach.

[30] See *Mem.* 2. 2. 7–9, 2. 7. 3–5, 3. 4. 7–10, 3. 5. 1–3, 4. 4. 10–14, 20–5.

simply want to refute his opponent as in an elenchus: he is eager to establish a contrary thesis as well and tries to persuade his interlocutor of the truth of his own position. In the applied analogies discussed at the beginning of this chapter, Socrates again uses a series of brief questions to make his point and elicit agreement from his partner.[31] Socrates also uses a series of short leading questions in the *Memorabilia* in order to teach his interlocutor: here the interrogation is in essence a means of instruction, and in these exchanges the philosopher imparts information while asking questions.[32] This is, of course, a reversal of the usual teaching situation, in which the pupil asks the questions and the teacher supplies the answers; in these conversations Socrates' questions are almost always rhetorical, taking the form 'Isn't it true that . . .?' When asked these leading questions, Socrates' partner has little to do other than follow the philosopher's cue and produce the required response. In Plato we occasionally find certain such positive ἔλεγχοι as well, that is to say passages in which Socrates' characteristically brief 'yes or no' questions are employed to convey constructive (rather than negative) teachings. The most famous instance is the geometric problem Socrates puts to Meno's slave (*Meno* 84 D–85 B). Socrates, of course, supplies the solution to the problem himself, through the questions he asks: all the slave need do throughout is answer in the affirmative to the philosopher's questions. *Crito* 46 B–50 A is another instance of positive doctrine cast in the form of questions posed by Socrates to which Crito simply replies 'yes'.[33] Such 'positive' interrogations are only rarely found in Plato's early Socratic dialogues, but are quite frequent in Xenophon; this is another instance of the different use the two writers make of the same structural form of brief questions and replies.[34]

So far we have looked at Socrates' role in the *Memorabilia*. What of

[31] See esp. *Mem.* 2. 1. 1–3, 2. 2. 1–3, 11–12, 2. 3. 11–14, 2. 10. 1–2.

[32] Cf. *Mem.* 2. 6. 1–4, 3. 1. 10–11, 3. 3. 1–15, 3. 10. 3–5, 4. 3. 3–8, 4. 5. 2–9; 4. 6. 2–11, 13–14.

[33] *Crito* 49 E 4–5 is particularly noteworthy—CRITO: ἀλλὰ λέγε. SOCRATES: λέγω δὴ αὖ τὸ μετὰ τοῦτο. μᾶλλον δ᾽ ἐρωτῶ—i.e. Socrates is going to continue his positive argument by means of questions rather than a statement. See too *Phaedo* 73 A–77 A (esp. 73 C–75 C) and *Euthyd.* 278 E–282 D, Socrates' protreptic addressed to Cleinias in the form of brief questions and replies, where 'Cleinias contributes nothing more philosophically advanced than his consent' (Hawtrey 1981 on 280 D 7; cf. 282 C). Such 'positive' questioning in Plato is related to Socrates' maieutic approach and the theory of anamnesis. See Slings 1981: 149–58; Thesleff 1967: 37 n. 3; Wellman 1976: 307–8; cf. Stokes 1986: 1–27.

[34] In the *Mem.* the very same figure, Euthydemus, is interrogated by Socrates in this way for both constructive and destructive purposes—cf. *Mem.* 4. 2 vs. 4. 3, 4. 5, and 4. 6.

his partners in these dialogues? In the *Memorabilia* Socrates converses
with a wide range of men: Athenian friends and contemporaries
(Crito, Aristodemus, Aristarchus, Eutherus, etc.), craftsmen,[35] a
courtesan (Theodote), sophists (Antiphon, Aristippus, Hippias), and,
most frequently of all, young men in need of guidance.[36] Socrates'
conversational partners vary considerably in their dialectical abilities
and responsiveness—some are much more talkative and argumentative than others—and there is no 'typical' interlocutor in the
Memorabilia. Broadly speaking, we can divide Socrates' fellow conversationalists into three groups, according to the extent of their partici-
pation in the dialogues. The first type contributes nothing of
substance to the conversation; he does not disagree with Socrates in
any significant way and his role in the dialogue is restricted to an
acknowledgement of the philosopher's words or simple, affirmative
replies to his questions. These conversational partners—men such as
Antisthenes, Crito, Diodorus, Parrhasius, Cleiton, Epigenes, and
Euthydemus after his 'conversion'—serve as foils who are only too
willing to follow Socrates' lead and accept the philosopher's teachings.[37] A second group of interlocutors are also agreeable and non-
contentious, but they play a more active role in their dialogues and
are not without a personality of their own. Some of them ask
questions and raise problems, because they genuinely wish to be
instructed by Socrates (e.g. the two anonymous young men interested in military matters in *Mem.* 3. 1 and 3. 3), while others argue for
a while before falling in with Socrates' suggestions (Aristarchus,
Eutherus).[38] Yet other interlocutors found in this group are aware of
Socrates' ironic tone and respond in the same playful vein, even while

[35] *Mem.* 3. 10 is the account of three such conversations. We never actually see
Socrates conversing with craftsmen in Plato, although he describes himself interrogating craftsmen in the *Apol.* (22 C–E) and, of course, repeatedly uses analogies from the
crafts. Phaedo wrote a Socratic dialogue which featured Simon the Cobbler (Diog.
Laert. 2. 105), and the cobbler himself supposedly wrote up conversations held by
Socrates in his workship (Diog. Laert. 2. 122–4). (A house in the Athenian agora has
now been identified as belonging to Simon the Cobbler—see Thompson and Wycherley 1972: 173–4.)

[36] We are specifically told that Lamprocles, Glaucon, Epigenes, Euthydemus, and
two anonymous young men interested in military matters (Socrates' interlocutors in
Mem. 3. 1 and 3. 3 respectively) are young—they are termed νέος, νεανίσκος, νεανίας,
or the like. Critobulus, Charmides, Pericles (son of Pericles), and Xenophon himself,
while not actually called young, also give the impression of young men, not yet set in
their ways, in their encounters with Socrates.

[37] See *Mem.* 2. 5 (Antisthenes), 2. 9 (Crito), 2. 10 (Diodorus), 3. 10 (Parrhasius and
Cleiton), 3. 12 (Epigenes), 4. 3, 4. 5, and 4. 6 (Euthydemus).

[38] See *Mem.* 2. 7. 5–6, 2. 8. 4–5.

allowing themselves to be led down the conversational paths that the philosopher chooses (e.g. Xenophon, the younger Pericles, Pistias, and Theodote).[39]

The third group of interlocutors give Socrates a run for his money—they debate with him, counter his arguments, and raise serious objections to his propositions. Some of these opponents have genuine differences of opinion with the philosopher (Aristodemus, Critobulus, Nicomachides, Charmides, Euthydemus before his 'conversion', Hermogenes), while others object to the picture of themselves that Socrates has drawn (Aristippus at 2. 1, Lamprocles, Chaerecrates, Glaucon).[40] There are also some rather vocal, hostile opponents of the philosopher who seem interested in argument for argument's sake (Antiphon, Aristippus at 3. 8, Hippias);[41] naturally, Socrates runs rings around these adversaries.

In some of the conversations Socrates' partner barely speaks at all, contributing a mere sentence or two to the entire exchange. The number of times that the philosopher's partner speaks up in a conversation is, however, no real indication of the role he plays; for he may simply spend all his time saying 'yes', as Euthydemus does, for example, in his conversations with Socrates after his 'conversion' (cf. e.g. *Mem.* 4. 6). If a long exchange of brief questions and replies does not necessarily indicate that there is real disagreement or discussion between the two participants in a dialogue, neither is the converse true: a discussion with only a few statements by Socrates' interlocutor is not necessarily a friendly, positive one. Antiphon, for instance, in his two jousts with Socrates (1. 6) asks only one question, but the debate and conflict between the two men are real. Thus we cannot measure how 'dialectical' a conversation is by the number of exchanges between Socrates and his interlocutor. Dialogues which contain no real exchanges, no genuine give and take, differ only in form, but not in substance, from a continuous speech: Socrates' discussions with Antisthenes and Epigenes, for example, could have been cast in the form of a simple exhortation by the Athenian philosopher and the effect would have been the same.[42] The difference between Socrates' conversations and his speeches in the *Memorabilia* seems to be wholly one of form rather than content: three

---

[39] *Mem.* 1. 3. 8–15, 3. 5, 3. 10. 9–15, 3. 11.

[40] See *Mem.* 1. 4, 2. 6, 3. 4, 3. 7, 4. 2, 4. 8, 2. 1, 2. 2, 2. 3, 3. 6 respectively.

[41] See *Mem.* 1. 6, 3. 8, 4. 4.

[42] *Mem.* 2. 5, 3. 12. Cf. Dover on Pl. *Symp.* 199c 3–201c 9.

of the four 'pure' speeches have fairly close parallels (in content) in the dialogues.[43] None the less, as we have already seen, Xenophon's Socrates generally prefers conversations to straight speeches.

It is worth mentioning in this context a passage of Demetrius (*De Eloc.* 296–8) in which he demonstrates how in different Socratic authors the same point is made in various ways. Aristippus, says Demetrius, states the problem (e.g. men bequeath money to their children but not the knowledge of how to use it well) and accuses his audience, whereas Xenophon handles the same question by offering advice (ὑποθετικῶς). Plato and Aeschines, continues Demetrius, raise the same issue by asking the young heir a series of questions designed to make him recognize his ignorance. This last approach, the inter-rogative one, is considered by Demetrius particularly Socratic (297 τὸ δὲ ἰδίως καλούμενον εἶδος Σωκρατικόν). None the less, in essence all three methods mentioned by Demetrius—admonition, advice, and cross-examination—involving both speech and dialogue, have the same aim and lead, more or less, to the same result.

All of Socrates' interlocutors in the *Memorabilia* have to contend with certain restrictions that Socrates (or Xenophon) places on their freedom of speech in the dialogues. We have already seen that the philosopher's positive teachings often take the form of leading questions which leave little scope for reply. In fact, Socrates' frequent use of leading 'question and reply' interrogations—whether for constructive or destructive purposes—considerably curbs his part-ners' opportunity to express themselves. The questions Socrates poses in these cross-examinations are usually polar, 'yes or no' or 'either/or' (πότερον . . . ἤ . . .;) questions, and his respondent must choose between two mutually exclusive alternatives. Often only one of these two alternatives seems at all feasible, so that the interlocutor, while ostensibly given a choice by Socrates, to all intents and purposes has his answer dictated to him.[44] At times the philosopher's polar question is so patently rhetorical that his partner does not even bother to reply, and a series of such rhetorical questions is often found in Socrates' longer discourses.[45] The reduction of a problem

[43] Compare *Mem.* 1. 5 with 2. 1. 1–7 (and 4. 5); 1. 7 with 2. 6. 37–9; 2. 4 with 2. 3. *Mem.* 3. 2 has no close parallel.

[44] See e.g. *Mem.* 4. 6. 7 εἰπέ μοι, πότερά σοι δοκοῦσιν οἱ σοφοί, ἃ ἐπίστανται ταῦτα σοφοὶ εἶναι ἢ εἰσί τινες ἃ μὴ ἐπίστανται σοφοί; Cf. 1. 4. 4, 2. 1. 1–4, 2. 7. 4, 7, 8, 3. 10. 4–5, 4. 2. 22, etc.

[45] Interlocutor does not respond: *Mem.* 3. 9. 13; cf. 1. 6. 15. Series of rhetorical ques-tions: 1. 6. 5, 9, 2. 7. 7–9, etc.

into two mutually exclusive and exhaustive alternatives also enables the philosopher to dispose of a question altogether by eliminating both possibilities.[46] Just once, in his first conversation with Euthydemus, Socrates argues that such polar, black-and-white divisions (in this case into 'just' and 'unjust') are too simplistic and that further, more flexible distinctions must be made (4. 2. 13ff.). Once too Socrates' partner in a dialogue, Aristippus, refuses to allow the philosopher to reduce a situation to two antithetical opposites and argues for a middle way (2. 1. 11 μέση τούτων ὁδός). Generally, however, Socrates' questions offer a choice between an obviously correct answer and a patently wrong one—that is, they offer no choice at all.

The use of brief, leading questions is, then, a means to control and channel conversations, and in the *Memorabilia* it is only Socrates who employs interrogations of this kind. The philosopher's partners often raise queries of their own, but their questions are not of the leading 'yes or no' kind. On those rare occasions when Socrates' interlocutors do attempt to interrogate him in this fashion, he quickly squashes them, reversing the situation and taking over the role of questioner: Socrates does not allow himself to be manœuvred into the role of a passive respondent or 'yes' man.[47]

Another virtually exclusive prerogative of Socrates in the *Memorabilia* is the use of analogies: the philosopher employs them very frequently, but only once does an interlocutor of his make use of an argument by analogy.[48] The Platonic[49] Socrates was, of course, famous, even notorious, for his use of analogies, particularly those taken from the crafts,[50] and in Xenophon too Socrates' opponents have had their fill of cobblers, carpenters, and smiths, as well as the ethical discussions that follow upon the mention of these craftsmen (*Mem.* 1. 2. 37).[51] About two-thirds of the dialogues contain at least one analogy and many contain a whole cluster of such comparisons, relating to slaves and animals as well as the crafts.

[46] See e.g. *Mem.* 1. 2. 34 and 4. 8. 8.

[47] See, for instance, the futile attempts of Aristippus (3. 8. 4–5) and Hippias (4. 4. 10–13) to interrogate Socrates; cf. 2. 6. 4 and 3. 11. 10, 14, 15.

[48] Aristippus at *Mem.* 2. 1. 9. Xenophon, as narrator, employs an analogy at *Mem.* 1. 2. 27.

[49] This is true of Aristotle's Socrates as well; cf. e.g. Arist. *Metaph.* 1078^{b}27–9 and Rose ad loc. For the use of analogic argument prior to Plato, see Lloyd 1966: 384 ff.

[50] Cf. *Gorg.* 490E–491A; *Symp.* 221E.

[51] A closely related complaint directed against Socrates by his opponents is that he is always talking about the same things—see *Mem.* 4. 4. 5–6; Pl. *Gorg.* 490E; and *Symp.* 221E with Gigon 1953: 62.

There are a few technical references in the *Memorabilia* to the actual process of inference from an analogy, e.g. ὥστε κατά γε τοῦτο ἔξεστί σοι λέγειν (1. 4. 9; cf. 3. 5. 6), or to the aptness of a comparison—ἀλλὰ πάνυ ... ὅμοιον ... εἴρηκας (3. 1. 8)—but Socrates generally uses analogies in an informal, non-rigorous manner. He simply compares or contrasts two objects, introducing them with the words ὥσπερ ... οὕτω ... or the like. Sometimes the analogy is cast in the form of a hypothetical situation, 'supposing it were a question of ..',[52] We have already seen at the beginning of this chapter the technique of 'applied analogies' favoured by Socrates, where an interlocutor is made to pass judgement on a hypothetical situation which can then be applied *mutatis mutandis* to the man himself. This technique is, in a sense, maieutic, for Socrates demonstrates to his interlocutors—using their judgements of everyday, analogous situations—that they do in fact possess the knowledge of how to behave etc. Socrates is at his most midwife-like[53] at *Mem.* 2. 3. 11–14, where Chaerecrates learns, through his answers to the philosopher's questions about parallel situations, that he does indeed know of a magic formula to win over his estranged brother.[54]

Socrates' interlocutors in the *Memorabilia* do not always accept the aptness of his comparisons. In the applied analogies, for example, when Socrates discusses a hypothetical situation and asks what appear to be innocuous questions,[55] all his respondents do pronounce indirect judgement against themselves, but several refuse to apply the resulting direct verdict to their own situation.[56] Nicomachides is another argumentative interlocutor, who twice rejects analogies used by Socrates (3. 4. 3 ἀλλ' οὐδὲν ὅμοιόν ἐστι ...; cf. 3. 4. 7): the philosopher then suggests that they investigate the

[52] See e.g. *Mem.* 2. 3. 7, 2. 10. 1–2, 3. 1. 2, 9–10, 3. 5. 8, 3. 6. 14, 3. 7. 1–2.

[53] There is considerable controversy as to whether the midwife image is to be attributed to Plato or the historical Socrates—see Tomin 1987 vs. Burnyeat 1977—but fewer scholars would deny the constructive, positive side to the historical Socrates' questioning, i.e. his actual use of maieutic technique.

[54] Cf. *Mem.* 3. 10. 9–15, where it is Socrates who discovers that he knows more about something—armour-making—than he realized.

[55] Generally, the further ramifications of Socrates' questions are more obvious to a reader of the *Mem.* than they would be to Socrates' actual respondent, because Xenophon tells us at the outset why the interlocutor has been approached by the philosopher: we know at once what Socrates has in mind. Charmides is the only one of the philosopher's interlocutors to suspect something when he undergoes this kind of questioning, asking ἀτὰρ πρὸς τί με ταῦτα ἐρωτᾷς; (*Mem.* 3. 7. 2).

[56] Cf. *Mem.* 2. 1. 1–8 and 3. 7. 1–2 vs. 2. 2. 1–3, 2. 9. 1–3, 2. 10. 1–5, and compare the behaviour of the Armenian king at *Cyr.* 3. 1. 13 (below, sect. 4).

appropriateness of a comparison together (3. 4. 7). Generally, how-ever, Socrates' conversational partners accept his analogies with little ado, and they do not counter his arguments with comparisons of their own.

From a more formal point of view, Socrates uses analogies in the *Memorabilia* in two rather different ways: (1) to explain or illustrate and (2) to infer or demonstrate a point from the preceding case(s), i.e. *epagōgē*.[57] When basing an argument on a series of cases or instances, the philosopher uses a variety of logical methods. Sometimes the new proposition adduced is a co-ordinate one, i.e. another single, parallel case, and at other times it is a universal proposition, a generalization based on the preceding examples. A third use Socrates makes of these analogies, besides adducing a similar, co-ordinate case or a general proposition, is to infer a single, more powerful case. It is illuminating to compare four passages of the *Memorabilia* (1. 7. 2–3, 2. 6. 38–9, 3. 3. 9, 3. 9. 11) in which the identical point is made—namely, that the best way to seem knowledgeable in a certain field, and to persuade others that one is so, is in fact to *be* knowledgeable. In all four of these passages Socrates uses a series of analogies from the crafts in order to establish his claim, but in each instance the formal use of analogies is different.[58]

While it is not an exclusive prerogative of his, Socrates is generally the one to initiate discussions in the *Memorabilia*. He almost always has a distinctive purpose in mind when conversing with another, and so approaches his interlocutor in order to advise, exhort, or reprove (or, very rarely, in order to request information).[59] Only once does a friend in need of advice open the conversation, turning to the philosopher with his problem (2. 9. 1). Those in the *Memorabilia* who do begin a discussion with Socrates are, on the whole, antagonistic towards him and wish to attack or belittle him;[60] once, however, Socrates is approached by a friend who wishes to give him advice

[57] See Robinson 1953: 33 ff. for a useful discussion of analogy and *epagōgē* in Plato; much of his terminology and classification of arguments is used here.

[58] *Mem.* 1. 7. 2–3 begins with a generalization, which is then demonstrated (or illus-trated) through a series of examples. In 2. 6. 38–9 Socrates first mentions several specific instances and then states his general conclusion. At 3. 3. 9 a general statement is followed by a series of examples only to lead to the conclusion that the rule holds true for another particular instance as well. At 3. 9. 11 Socrates' purpose is again to establish the truth of his claim in relation to a specific occupation, and he uses a series of parallel examples without any reference to a more general rule.

[59] *Mem.* 1. 2. 32–8, 40–6, 3. 8, 3. 10, 4. 5, 4. 6 are *not* conversations of this sort.

[60] Cf. Antiphon, Aristippus, and Hippias in *Mem.* 1. 6, 3. 8, and 4. 4 respectively.

(Hermogenes in 4. 8). The philosopher almost always closes these discussions as well. When Socrates does not have the last word in the *Memorabilia*, it is usually only in order to allow his interlocutor to express agreement with his statements; very rarely, a particularly tenacious opponent is unwilling to yield and is the last to be heard.[61] Socrates often ends a conversation with a fairly long speech, and if there is no lengthy address by him at the close of a dialogue, there is usually one elsewhere in the conversation: over half of the conversations in the *Memorabilia* include a fairly long, continuous speech by Socrates. In general, only the philosopher has the prerogative of making such a long address; his interlocutors are men of fewer words[62] and none ever ends a conversation with a speech.

How persuasive is Socrates? The fact that the dialogues generally end with some sort of statement (whether lengthy or brief) by Socrates means that often there is no final indication as to how effective his arguments or exhortations have been. In a few dialogues we are actually shown that Socrates' interlocutor has been won over: such information generally comes at the end of a conversation, in the form of compliant words from the philosopher's partner.[63] There are also several two-part advice dialogues, where we first find Socrates advising another and are then shown the successful application of his advice.[64] In a third group of conversations, those in which Socrates' partner contributes virtually nothing of his own and simply goes along with the philosopher's words, the question of persuasion does not really arise. Most of the more 'dialectical' dialogues in the *Memorabilia* in which Socrates encounters a certain amount of resistance and argument—conversations with the third, more contentious type of interlocutor described above—end in a long, somewhat rhetorical speech by Socrates,[65] and it is here that the situation

[61] Critobulus (2. 6. 39), a young hipparch (3. 3. 15), Parrhasius the painter (3. 10. 5), and the flummoxed Euthydemus (4. 2. 39) all end their conversations with Socrates by accepting his words. Charicles, a member of the Thirty who is tyrannically laying down a law, appropriately enough has the last word in his conversation with Socrates (1. 2. 37), while Pistias the armour-maker teasingly sees through the philosopher's didactic methods (3. 10. 15).

[62] *Mem.* 2. 1, 2. 6, and 3. 5 are the only dialogues in which Socrates' interlocutor makes a fairly long speech.

[63] See the first four references in n. 61 and compare 1. 4. 10 and 4. 4. 18, 23, where Socrates' interlocutors are partially convinced in the course of an argument.

[64] See *Mem.* 2. 7. 11, 2. 9. 4, 2. 10. 5–6, and cf. 3. 1. 3–4.

[65] See *Mem.* 1. 4. 15–19, 1. 6. 4–10, 13–14, 2. 1. 18–34, 2. 2. 13–14, 2. 3. 17–19, 2. 8. 5–6, 3. 4. 11–12, 3. 6. 15–18, 3. 7. 8–9, 3. 12. 1–8, 4. 8. 6–10. Those dialectical conversations which do not end with a lengthy address by Socrates generally present

is most puzzling. How should we understand this final address by Socrates? Since the *Memorabilia* is an apologetic work, meant to demonstrate the value of Socrates' teachings,[66] it would seem at first sight that the philosopher's closing words have not been countered by his fellow conversationalist simply because the latter has no reply to make: Socrates has silenced (and presumably convinced) his opponent.

One piece of evidence to support this view of Socrates' closing addresses is his presentation of the tale of Heracles at the crossroads (2. 1. 21–34). In Socrates' (or Xenophon's) adaptation of the fable told by Prodicus, the story ends with a lengthy address by Arete calling upon Heracles to choose her way of life, and we are not actually told how Heracles reacts to this appeal. We know from another source[67] that in Prodicus' original account Heracles replied to Arete and indicated his preference for Virtue over her rival, but Socrates makes no mention of this final (perhaps all too obvious) outcome. The philosopher expects his listener, Aristippus, to understand that Arete's final exhortation has persuaded the youth; similarly, one might argue, Xenophon expects his readers to understand that Aristippus in this dialogue (along with the rest of Socrates' interlocutors in other such dialogues) has been won over by Socrates' culminating speech. There is no need, it seems, to labour the obvious and mention the interlocutor's final capitulation or agreement.

But Socrates does not, in fact, consistently win over his opponent with his closing address. We know specifically in the case of Aristippus that he has not been convinced by Socrates; he is only temporarily defeated and later stages a return match: Ἀριστίππου δὲ ἐπιχειροῦντος ἐλέγχειν τὸν Σωκράτην ὥσπερ αὐτὸς ὑπ᾽ ἐκείνου τὸ πρότερον ἠλέγχετο . . . (*Mem.* 3. 8. 1). Similarly, the sophist Antiphon does not seem to have been convinced by Socrates' concluding speech in their first encounter (1. 6. 1–10), for he attacks the Athenian philosopher on similar grounds on two later occasions (1. 6. 11–14, 15). Silence on the part of Socrates' interlocutors cannot, then, be taken for tacit consent—often it is more of a tactical retreat— and not all of the philosopher's opponents are convinced by his

---

his opponent as defeated, if not persuaded (2. 6, 3. 8, 4. 2, and 4. 4; cf. 1. 2. 40–6). At 1. 2. 32–8 Socrates seems to be the loser; 3. 5 does not fit this pattern.

[66] See e.g. *Mem.* 1. 4. 1–2, 19, 2. 1. 1, 3. 1. 1, 4. 7. 1–2 for outright statements to that effect.

[67] Σ ad Aristoph. *Clouds* 361 = DK 84 B 1; cf. below, sect. 2.

words, even if they have no immediate reply. In this way some of Xenophon's Socratic dialogues end in *aporia*: not in the *aporia* felt by the participants in Plato's early Socratic dialogues because of their inability to solve a specific problem (i.e. defining a certain concept), but in a more general feeling of inconclusiveness. Has Socrates said all that he might on the subject? How do his fellow conversationalists feel? What are we, the readers, meant to think?[68]

It is time to sum up what we have learnt about the Socrates of the *Memorabilia*. The philosopher—who is above all a ·didactic figure— prefers to teach by means of dialogue. These dialogues are brief conversations between Socrates and only one other person, but a wider audience may be present. The dialogues are generally narrated by Xenophon, with little dramatic background, and the conversation is restricted to one specific topic. Socrates frequently initiates the conversation and usually ends it as well, often by means of a speech. In these dialogues the philosopher does most of the talking and he often submits his partner to an interrogation consisting of short, polar questions. Socrates also regularly uses analogies taken from everyday experiences and makes one fairly long speech. His partners—who vary considerably in their dialectical abilities and willingness to participate—do virtually none of these things: only very rarely, if at all, do they conduct pointed cross-examinations, speak at great length, or use analogies. Finally, the end result of these conversations—the measure of success that Socrates has achieved with his injunctions and exhortations—is not always clear.

Before tackling the *Cyropaedia*, let us take a look at Xenophon's longer dialogues, the *Hiero*, *Oeconomicus*, and *Symposium*. How does the Socrates of the *Oeconomicus* and *Symposium* compare with Socrates in the *Memorabilia*? What of the leading figure of the *Hiero*?

The *Hiero* is not, properly speaking, a Socratic dialogue at all, but the record of a lengthy conversation between the tyrant Hiero and the poet Simonides. Xenophon makes little literary use of his role as narrator: he simply introduces the two speakers at the very beginning of the work and provides next to no additional dramatic background.[69] The dialogue falls into two uneven parts. In the first (1–7)

---

[68] Gigon 1956: 83 suggests that the point of Socrates' closing speeches is to convince the wider circle of his listeners—the συνόντες—as well as Xenophon's readers, if not his actual interlocutors.

[69] *Hiero* 1. 1 Σιμωνίδης ὁ ποιητὴς ἀφίκετό ποτε πρὸς Ἱέρωνα τὸν τύραννον. σχολῆς δὲ γενομένης ἀμφοῖν εἶπεν ὁ Σιμωνίδης . . .; (cf. 1. 31, 8. 8). Andrieu 1954: 319–20 thinks that Xenophon is not inventive enough to make better use of the *Hiero*'s narrative

Hiero describes the difficult life of a tyrant, while in the second (8–11) Simonides suggests how a tyrannical regime might be improved. The tyrant does most of the talking and leads the conversation in the longer, earlier part, but Simonides takes over the role of chief interlocutor in the second section. The dialogue ends somewhat inconclusively since we do not know for certain whether Hiero accepts Simonides' closing suggestions. The tyrant and the poet do not disagree strongly with one another and there are not many exchanges between the two (only twenty in twenty-five OCT pages). Most of these exchanges are limited to the opening chapter, which contains the only instance of a series of brief questions and replies (1. 21–5).[70] In this 'elenctic' passage Hiero asks the leading questions and refutes Simonides' contention that tyrants enjoy their food more than private individuals do. Simonides, on the other hand, opens the *Hiero* and is given a long closing exhortation (10. 2–11. 15); he also does the lion's share of the talking in the second part. There are only a few analogies used in the work (1. 36, 6. 15–16, 9. 3–6, 10. 2–3), and these are evenly divided between Hiero and Simonides. Thus, if we make use of the pattern we have found in the *Memorabilia*, there is no dominant figure, no 'Socrates', in the *Hiero*. The work is not truly Socratic and it is not by chance that the Athenian philosopher does not appear in the conversation.[71]

The *Oeconomicus*, on the other hand, must be considered a Socratic dialogue, if only because it is the record of a conversation Socrates has had. Like the *Hiero*, the *Oeconomicus* is quite long and falls into two uneven parts. The first section, the outer frame of the dialogue, is a conversation between Critobulus and Socrates on household

framework, while Strauss 1948: 11 argues that Xenophon is noticeably absent because he wishes to dissociate himself from a defence of tyranny; neither of these claims is convincing.

[70] This passage also contains one of the outstanding idioms of Socratic dialogue, πάνυ μὲν οὖν as 'yes' or 'certainly' (*Hiero* 1. 21, 22). While this expression is not restricted to philosophical dialogue (cf. e.g. Aristoph. *Pl.* 97; Xen. *Anab.* 7. 6. 4; Men. *Dysc.* 774), it was particularly favoured by the Socratic writers—see Aeschines, *Alcibiades*, fr. 8 Dittmar; Xen. *Mem.* 1. 3. 9, 2. 1. 2, 4. 6. 10, etc.; *Oec.* 1. 7, 17. 8; and esp. *Symp.* 4. 56–60, besides, of course, Plato, *passim*. Denniston 1954: 475 ff. seems to ignore these non-Platonic philosophical usages.

[71] Gray 1986 sees the *Hiero* as a new literary form, a combination—or marriage—of a Socratic dialogue with a story belonging to the tradition of meetings between wise men and tyrants. It is sometimes argued that the *Hiero* is un-Socratic in its ideas and aims as well as form; see Aalders 1953; Strauss 1948: 58–62; Strauss 1970: 208–9. Luccioni 1953: 158–61 finds a great deal of Socratic influence in the *Hiero*, but that is because the work contains several of Xenophon's favourite didactic topoi; see above, n. 5.

management, οἰκονομία. The conversation is introduced by Xenophon rather abruptly and proceeds directly to the main theme of the
dialogue in the fashion of the *Memorabilia*.[72] Socrates leads and
channels the conversation in this early part, but Critobulus plays an
active role and contributes questions and objections of his own, just
as he does during his conversation with Socrates in the *Memorabilia*.[73]

In the second and longer section of the *Oeconomicus* (7–21) Socrates
repeats to Critobulus a conversation he has earlier held with Ischomachus. Here Socrates, rather than Xenophon, is the narrator, and
he continues in that role until the very end of the dialogue: there is no
return to the opening framework of the work.[74] This second section
has a longer introduction (7. 1), which is reminiscent of the more
detailed settings found at times in Plato's dialogues (e.g. the openings
of the *Lysis*, *Charmides*, and *Republic*).[75] Another feature of the
Oeconomicus which is unusual in Xenophon's Socratic works—but is
often found, for example, in Plato's dialogues—is the short, joking
interlude at 12. 1–2, which serves as a smooth and natural transition
to the next topic to be discussed. (There are, of course, fewer transitions to be made in the shorter dialogues of the *Memorabilia*, with less
scope for elaborate preludes.)

In this second, longer section of the *Oeconomicus* Ischomachus is
the chief interlocutor. Socrates is an active partner who asks difficult
questions and raises new points,[76] but the conversational reins are in
Ischomachus' hands. He, in his role as Socrates' instructor in the art
of farming, talks most of the time—answering the philosopher's
queries, posing in turn questions of his own, and demonstrating, for
example, how he trained his wife to be a good mistress of the household. The dialogue also ends with a long discourse by Ischomachus
(21. 2–12). Thus Ischomachus seems to be the 'Socrates', the talkative teaching figure, of this section of the dialogue. He uses some of

---

[72] *Oec.* 1. 1 ἤκουσα δέ ποτε αὐτοῦ καὶ περὶ οἰκονομίας τοιάδε διαλεγομένου· Εἰπέ μοι,
ἔφη, ὦ Κριτόβουλε; cf. *Mem.* 1. 4. 2, 2. 4. 1, 4. 4. 5, 4. 5. 2 for similar opening frames.
The abrupt opening of the *Oec.* may indicate that the dialogue was originally intended
to be part of the *Mem.*—see Breitenbach 1966: 1837–8 and the references there.

[73] See *Oec.* 1. 15–2. 5, 3. 6–11, 5. 18, 6. 1, 11, and cf. *Mem.* 2. 6. 7, 12, 14–16, 18–20,
36–7.

[74] See, however, *Oec.* 10. 1.

[75] Cf. *Oec.* 7. 1 ἰδὼν οὖν ποτε αὐτὸν ἐν τῇ τοῦ Διὸς τοῦ ἐλευθερίου στοᾷ καθήμενον,
ἐπεί μοι ἔδοξε σχολάζειν, προσῆλθον αὐτῷ καὶ παρακαθιζόμενος εἶπον ... Aeschines
also seems to have described the physical settings of his Socratic dialogues—cf.
Alcibiades, fr. 2 Dittmar and *Miltiades* (*P. Oxy.* 39. 2889).

[76] See e.g. *Oec.* 11. 1, 12. 8, 15. 1–2, 9.

Socrates' favourite techniques: the discussion of a hypothetical situation which is then applied suddenly to his fellow conversationalist (10. 2–5), repeated use of analogies to demonstrate his point, and a maieutic teaching method.

The two latter techniques call for a closer look. In the first part of the *Oeconomicus*, where Socrates directs the conversation, Socrates employs some nine analogies to Critobulus' one, but in the second section it is Ischomachus who makes more frequent use of them.[77] One specific comparison made by Ischomachus leads Socrates to reflect on the value of an apt simile: *Oec.* 17. 15 ἀτὰρ ἐνθυμοῦμαι . . . ὦ Ἰσχόμαχε, οἷόν ἐστι τὸ εὖ τὰς εἰκόνας ἐπάγεσθαι. Thus Xenophon playfully has Socrates congratulate Ischomachus for using a favourite Socratic device. The philosopher also appreciates and comments upon another method of his own used by Ischomachus—the awakening of latent knowledge, unwittingly possessed by an interlocutor, through questioning. Ischomachus 'reminds' Socrates (cf. 16. 8), by means of his questions, of all that the latter unconsciously knows of farming techniques.[78] Ischomachus' interrogations in this section are often of the brief, 'question and reply' kind,[79] and Socrates gradually realizes that he is being taught through these questions. The philosopher then 'innocently' asks, 'Can it be, Ischomachus, that asking questions is teaching?'[80] Here too, then, Socrates is made to underline and applaud Ischomachus' appropriation of his own techniques; Xenophon appears to be playing with the teacher–pupil, Socrates–conversational partner relationship in the *Oeconomicus*. If in the *Hiero* neither of the two interlocutors can be considered a 'Socrates', in the *Oeconomicus* we seem, at times, to have two of them.[81]

[77] Cf. *Oec.* 1. 1–3, 7–11, 22–3, 2. 12–13, 15, 3. 9, 11, 5. 5–8, 13–16, 19–20, 11. 4–6, 12. 3, 15. 7–8, 9, 17. 7, 9, 20. 27–9 (Socrates' analogies), 6. 3 (Critobulus), 7. 17, 30, 32–8, 8. 3–10, 9. 14–15, 10. 2–5, 7, 12. 17–18, 13. 2, 6–8, 17. 14, 19. 16, 20. 6–11, 18–19, 21. 3–9 (Ischomachus).

[78] See *Oec.* 17. 6, 11, 18. 1, 3, 5, 9–10, and esp. 19. 14–16. This section of the *Oec.* (15–19) is almost a περὶ γεωργίας, a manual or handbook of farming techniques. Cf. Breitenbach 1966: 1865–71 for an excellent survey of parallels between the *Oec.* and later agricultural treatises, and a discussion of the possible sources.

[79] See *Oec.* 16. 8–12, 17. 7–8, 18. 6–8, 19. 3–7. Ischomachus, of course, imparts information while asking these questions, and in this way technical instruction is fitted neatly into the framework of a didactic *dialogue*; cf. below, sect. 2.

[80] *Oec.* 19. 15 ἆρα . . . ὦ Ἰσχόμαχε, ἡ ἐρώτησις διδασκαλία ἐστίν; The translation is that of Guthrie 1969: 337, who is very good on Socratic elements in the *Oec.* For a different view of anamnesis in the *Oec.* and its relation to Socrates' teaching see Wellman 1976: 315.

[81] Traditionally Ischomachus (who was almost certainly a historical figure—see the evidence assembled by Davies 1971: 265–8) is seen simply as Xenophon's mouthpiece,

Before leaving the *Oeconomicus* we should note that its ending is an inconclusive one, of a kind already familiar to us. Ischomachus, the chief speaker in this dialogue within a dialogue, addresses Socrates in a long concluding speech. We do not hear of Socrates' reaction to this discourse, nor do we return to the original, outer dialogue in order to learn of the effect that the entire Socrates–Ischomachus exchange has had upon Critobulus. In sum, the *Oeconomicus*, despite its greater length and more complex structure, is quite similar to the Socratic dialogues of the *Memorabilia*.

The *Symposium*, a long, lively dialogue with many participants, will be discussed in detail in the following chapter, but a few of its more Socratic features may be noted here. Socrates is, of course, one of the guests at Callias' party and participates in this (narrated) dialogue. Another guest present, Antisthenes, seems even more Socratic than Socrates—'plus royaliste que le roi', as one commentator puts it[82]—in his attempts to cross-examine and refute his fellow symposiasts. Antisthenes interrogates Niceratus and Callias, asking them sharp, pointed questions in elenctic fashion (*Symp.* 4. 2 μάλα ἐλεγκτικῶς)[83] in order to reprove them. In both instances Socrates intervenes, restraining his over-zealous follower and restoring the friendly party atmosphere.[84] Thus Antisthenes seems to represent destructive cross-examination at its worst—Callias terms him a sophist (4. 4 ὦ σοφιστά)—while Socrates behaves in a more urbane fashion. The philosopher himself conducts several discussions in question-and-reply form, admonishing or instructing other party-goers, such as the Syracusan impresario (4. 52–4), Critobulus (5. 1–8), Hermogenes (6. 1–4), and Philippus (6. 9–10), but his touch is lighter and didactic methods more skilful, as Hermogenes notes (8. 12). In these discussions Socrates' interlocutors often make contributions of their own, replying to him in kind, so that several exchanges have a lively, dialectical turn.[85]

When the guests at Callias' party take turns describing their

a figure used to express the author's own ideas on estate management, *tout court*. Thus e.g. Breitenbach 1966: 1848, 'Daß X. . . . sich schließlich selbst hineinprojiziert, ist jedem Leser klar.' Ischomachus probably does put forward a great many of his author's ideas, but it is perhaps over-simple to identify the two. Socrates, in any event, appears to have reservations about some of Ischomachus' attitudes—cf. *Oec.* 11. 11, 20. 26–9.

[82] Woldinga 1938–9: 74.

[83] See *Symp.* 3. 4, 6, 4. 2–5, 6, and cf. 6. 5.

[84] *Symp.* 3. 6 and 4. 5; cf. 2. 10 and 4. 62.

[85] See in particular Socrates' exchanges with Critobulus (5. 5–7) and Hermogenes (6. 2–3).

proudest possession or asset (3. 2 ff.), Socrates is the only one to proceed by means of question and answer,[86] eliciting his listeners' agreement to each stage of his argument (4. 56 ff.). This is a method attributed to Socrates by Xenophon in the *Memorabilia* (4. 6. 15; cf. 4. 5. 12), but we rarely see him using it there.[87] Socrates also uses analogies in the *Symposium* when propounding his ideas, but these are not found very frequently.[88] The philosopher delivers a long speech at the party, as he often does in the *Memorabilia*, and his oration is by far the longest of those found in the *Symposium*, with Antisthenes in second place. Socrates' discourse, an ἐρωτικὸς λόγος, comes towards the end of the work, but the *Symposium* closes with a dance, not with Socrates' words.

In sum, the Socrates of the *Symposium* converses as he does in the *Memorabilia*: asking questions, using analogies in his arguments, and speaking at length as well; but his manner is more playful than in the *Memorabilia*, as befits the light-hearted occasion. Antisthenes, Socrates' follower, tries to appropriate his master's elenctic technique, but is too rigid and rude in his approach. Xenophon seems to contrast the two figures deliberately, underlining the difference between the philosopher's constructive and Antisthenes' destructive approach,[89] but Socrates is undoubtedly the didactic, teaching figure, the 'Socrates' of this dialogue.

We are finally ready to investigate Socratic influence on the *Cyropaedia*, better equipped to recognize those elements and features which are particularly associated with Socrates in Xenophon's writings. We begin with *Cyr.* 1. 6, the longest and most widely quoted[90] dialogue of the work, a conversation between Cambyses and Cyrus.

---

[86] See for this point Higgins 1977: 149 n. 98, who has an interesting discussion of the *Symp.*, 15–20.

[87] *Pace* Wellman 1976: 309–10, who finds in the *Mem.* many instances of what he calls anamnesis, i.e. an enquiry in which Socrates' respondent agrees step by step with the philosopher's argument; cf. below, sect. 5.

[88] Cf. e.g. *Symp.* 2. 10, 25–6, 8. 15.

[89] For an excellent analysis of the roles of Socrates and Antisthenes in the *Symp.* and the relationship between the two see von Fritz 1935, esp. 21–5, 27–31, 40–4.

[90] Of the dozen or so papyri of the *Cyr.* now extant, no fewer than five (*P. Oxy.* 697, 698, 1018, 2101, *P. Varsov.* 1 = Pack² 1545–9) contain bits of this dialogue. This would seem to suggest that the dialogue was copied out separately at times, although three of the five papyri appear to be part of copies of the entire *Cyr.*; see Paap 1970: 16–41, 43–7.

2. A FATHER GUIDES HIS SON: *CYR*. I. 6

Cyr. 1. 6. 1–2. 1. 1 is the most explicit example of Κύρου παιδεία—
the education of Cyrus—to be found in Xenophon's lengthy work.
Cyrus has been summoned by his uncle, the Median king Cyaxares,
to head a Persian force in a joint venture against the Assyrians. The
Persian prince is setting out on his first major campaign and his
father accompanies him to the Persian–Median border, discussing
military matters and offering general advice along the way. In the
course of their conversation, Cambyses instructs, corrects, and
guides Cyrus: his didactic methods are, as we shall see, very similar
to the methods used by Socrates in the *Memorabilia*. There are also
several close parallels between *Cyr.* 1. 6 and various passages of the
Memorabilia, so the Socratic colouring of this conversation is immediately apparent. This long exchange between the Persian king and
his son should, however, also be viewed from a somewhat wider
perspective, that of the tradition of works of moral instruction and
guidance, ὑποθῆκαι.[91]

Early ὑποθῆκαι were written in verse. They were strings of
maxims, exhortations, and advice addressed to an individual
(although a wider public, of course, was meant to benefit from them).
No work actually entitled ὑποθῆκαι survives, but such collections of
precepts on the proper way to live are associated with the names of
Hesiod, Theognis, and Phocylides (cf. Isoc. *Ad Nic.* 43). The lost
composition Χείρωνος ὑποθῆκαι attributed to Hesiod (frr. 283–5
Merkelbach–West), in which the wise centaur Chiron teaches and
advises young Achilles, was, it seems, a fair representative of works of
this kind.[92] In these didactic compositions the precepts and instructions are usually addressed by an older man to a younger relative,
friend, or pupil—e.g. Hesiod and Perses, Theognis and Cyrnus,

[91] See Friedländer 1913, esp. 602–3, and Bernays 1885: 265–6 for two useful discussions of ὑποθῆκαι. Stobaeus quotes large chunks of our dialogue (*Cyr.* 1. 6. 3–6, 8, 10,
14, 17–19, 20–1, 23–8) under the heading ὑποθῆκαι περὶ βασιλείας (4. 7. 68–75).

[92] Other lost ὑποθῆκαι: (1) the semi-mythical Musaeus wrote Ὑποθήκας Εὐμόλπῳ
τῷ υἱῷ ἔπη according to the *Suda* (DK 2 A 1); (2) Aristotle (*Rhet.* 1389[b]23) knows of τὴν
Βίαντος ὑποθήκην (cf. DK i. 65, line 11 with n.); (3) in his Κένταυρος the 4th-cent. tra-
gedian Chaeremon may have included a passage in which Chiron propounded moral
precepts—see *P. Hibeh* 224 with Turner's commentary ad loc. and Arist. *Poet.* 1447[b]21;
(4) Clearchus (fr. 75 Wehrli) quotes an anonymous verse in which Amphiaraus advises
his son Amphilochus—this may have come from a ὑποθῆκαι with a mythological setting. See Kurke 1990: 104–7 for other possible allusions to mythological ὑποθῆκαι.

Chiron and Achilles—and this resembles the situation in our dialogue.[93]

By the time of the *Cyropaedia*'s composition verse ὑποθῆκαι were, it seems, a thing of the past;[94] there were prose works of moral instruction and advice instead. Democritus may have written one such prose ὑποθῆκαι (DK 68 B 119). Isocrates' *Ad Nicoclem*, a series of precepts addressed to a young man on the duties of a king, and its companion piece, *Nicocles*, on the proper conduct of his subjects, are two surviving examples of this new prose form. Isocrates' *Ad Demonicum*, a treatise on the proper way of life, again addressed to a young man, is a more general work of the same kind, which also went by the name of παραίνεσις.[95] Of the three compositions by Isocrates, *Ad Nicoclem* is closest in theme to our dialogue. The work appeared, in all likelihood, shortly before the *Cyropaedia*,[96] and some specific resemblances between the two will be noted below.

Two lost sophistic works, Hippias' Τρωϊκὸς λόγος and Prodicus' tale of Heracles at the crossroads, are also related to this genre of advice and instruction. Both sophistic compositions have a mythical setting, reminding us of the early verse ὑποθῆκαι, but unlike any of the verse or prose compositions mentioned so far, both these works seem to have been written in dialogue form, the form which Xenophon chose for Cambyses' instructions and advice to Cyrus in the *Cyropaedia*. Xenophon need not, of course, have been directly influenced by these two compositions when writing *Cyr.* 1. 6. He may well have chosen to have the Persian king converse with his son—rather than address him in one long, continuous speech—because of the Socratic influence. Dialogue, as we have seen, is the means

[93] West 1978: 3–25, in a wide-ranging survey of ancient Near Eastern didactic literature, notes that the usual pattern in Sumerian, Akkadian, Egyptian, etc. works of instruction is for a father to instruct a son, or a sage instruct a king. Cambyses, a wise father advising a future king, combines both roles here.

[94] Cf. Isoc. *Ad Nic.* 3 τῶν ποιητῶν τινες τῶν προγεγενημένων ὑποθήκας . . . καταλελοίπασιν.

[95] See Stephens 1985: 7–8 for αἱ παραινέσεις as a title for all three Isocratean works and cf. Kurke 1990: 91; αἱ πρὸς Νικοκλέα ὑποθῆκαι appears as a title for the *Ad Nic.* in some manuscripts. Gray 1985: 159–62 has a discussion of the παραίνεσις genre. She argues, chiefly on the basis of *Ad Demonicum* 5, that these works gave young men advice on 'what activities to pursue, what to avoid, what company to keep, how to live' (159) and notes that moral παραίνεσις was linked at times with technical instruction, as in Hesiod's *Works and Days* and Xenophon's own *Cynegeticus*. This combination of moral and practical, technical advice is also found in *Cyr.* 1. 6.

[96] *Ad Nicoclem* is generally dated soon after Nicocles' accession to the Cyprian throne in 374 BC; see e.g. Forster 1912: 21.

Socrates normally uses in the *Memorabilia* (and elsewhere) for his advice and exhortations. It would also be very much out of character for Xenophon's hero Cyrus simply to listen passively to another, no matter how wise. But even if there is no immediate link between the two sophistic ὑποθῆκαι and *Cyr.* 1. 6, these works may have exercised an indirect influence on our conversation, for some scholars consider them forerunners of Socratic dialogue.[97] This makes the question of the form of the compositions by Hippias and Prodicus particularly interesting and worthy of closer scrutiny.

The words attributed to Hippias in the Platonic[98] *Hippias Major* (286A 3–B 4) are our main source of evidence for that sophist's work. Hippias tells Socrates that he has an exhibition piece, an ἐπίδειξις, which he uses on his various lecture tours in Greece (286B 4–5 τοῦτον ... ἐπεδειξάμην καὶ ... μέλλω ἐπιδεικνύναι). The piece, termed a λόγος, has a mythological setting (286A 7 πρόσχημα).[99] After the capture of Troy, Neoptolemus asked Nestor what sort of activities would help a young man win a name for himself; Nestor then advised him at length. The Τρωϊκὸς λόγος described here by Hippias has all the characteristics of earlier ὑποθῆκαι: an old and wise man advises (286B 3–4 ὑποτιθέμενος) a young one on proper conduct (286A 4–5 ἃ χρὴ τὸν νέον ἐπιτηδεύειν). His advice is noble, but general (286B 4–5 πάμπολλα νόμιμα καὶ πάγκαλα)—general enough to be appreciated both in Athens and in Sparta[100]—and the characters involved are well-known mythological figures.[101]

None the less, Hippias seems to have introduced one new feature in his prose adaptation of the ὑποθῆκαι genre. Normally it is the sage and experienced adviser who approaches the young man in need of guidance, purveying his words of wisdom unsolicited, so that only he

---

[97] See esp. Gaiser 1959: 61–4 and compare the reservations of de Strycker 1962: 17. For the dialogue form of the two sophistic works see Hirzel 1895: 59–63 and compare the more sceptical views of Gigon 1956: 60–1 and Gomperz 1912: 74 n. 158.

[98] The question of the authenticity of the *Hipp. Mai.* does not really concern us here, since it is generally thought to have been written during Plato's lifetime; see Woodruff 1982: 93–105 for a recent airing of the question.

[99] See Tarrant ad loc. on the meaning of πρόσχημα here and cf. Gaiser 1959: 12–13 n. 10.

[100] See Gray 1985: 162 on the conventional moral attitudes normally found in the παραίνεσις genre.

[101] The only further bit of evidence concerning Hippias' Trojan work is Philostratus, *VS* 1. 11 (= DK 86 A 2. 4). Philostratus' comments seem to be based entirely on the Platonic passage, and hence his only original contribution—the statement that the Τρωϊκὸς λόγος is a dialogue—is generally discounted as independent evidence.

is heard in these works of instruction.[102] Here Hippias gives voice to the second figure, the young man in need of advice, having him approach the older man and seek his counsel. Neoptolemus, at the very least, opens the discussion with Nestor (286 A 8–B 1 Νεοπτόλεμος Νέστορα ἔροιτο), and he may have spoken again once Nestor had replied, asking further questions or interposing suggestions of his own.[103] Alternatively, Nestor may have simply answered the youth in one long, continuous exhortation. The versatile Hippias is supposed to have written epic verses, tragedies, and dithyrambs, as well as varied writings in prose,[104] so that such a dialogue of advice would be well within his powers.

Another mythological young man in need of guidance is found in the second lost sophistic work, Prodicus' story of Heracles' meeting with Virtue and Vice at the crossroads. Our main source for this story is Xenophon himself, for in the *Memorabilia* (2. 1. 21–34 = DK 84 B 2) Socrates paraphrases Prodicus' edifying tale in the course of a discussion with Aristippus. A scholiast on Aristoph. *Clouds* 361 (= DK 84 B 1) gives us another, independent description of the work.[105] From the scholiast's account it seems that Prodicus' composition included at least three speeches: Kakia and Arete each address Heracles, and he then announces his decision to choose the labours of Arete over the pleasures of Kakia.[106] In Xenophon's version the

---

[102] The late, anonymous introduction to *Ad Demonicum* points out that the three Isocratean παραινέσεις—which, as the anonymous author notes, are only seemingly addressed to an individual but are actually intended for a wider audience—include no discussion because there is no respondent, no second figure in the work: στάσιν δὲ οὐκ ἐπιδέχονται· οὐ γὰρ ἔχουσι τὸν ἀντιλέγοντα (liii Benseler–Blass).

[103] Since Neoptolemus has approached Nestor on his own initiative, turning to him for advice, it is unlikely that he argued with the older man or opposed him in any real way; cf. Hirzel 1895: 60. It is perhaps worth noting that in Near Eastern didactic literature the *dialogues* of instruction are contentious conversations in which a son rejects his father's advice; cf. the Sumerian dialogue *The Father and his Misguided Son* and the Egyptian *Educational Instruction of Ani*, discussed by West 1978: 5 and 10. (The parallels that West adduces to the amicable Nestor–Neoptolemus exchange are from much further afield, 9th-cent. Ireland and 13th-cent. Norway; cf. 25 n. 2.)

[104] Cf. *Hipp. Min.* 368 D = DK 86 A 12 καὶ καταλογάδην πολλοὺς λόγους καὶ παντοδαποὺς συγκειμένους.

[105] The scholiast includes two bits of information not mentioned in the *Mem.*—that the story is found in Prodicus' ὧραι and that Heracles' final decision was to follow Virtue—and hence may be treated as an independent source; cf. Guthrie 1969: 278–9 n. 2. There is also a passing reference in Pl. *Symp.* (177 B) to the fact that Prodicus wrote Ἡρακλέους . . . ἐπαίνους in prose (καταλογάδην συγγράφειν).

[106] DK 84 B 1 πεποίηκε τὸν Ἡρακλέα τῇ Ἀρετῇ καὶ τῇ Κακίᾳ συντυγχάνοντα καὶ καλούσης ἑκατέρας ἐπὶ τὰ ἤθη τὰ αὑτῆς, προσκλῖναι τῇ Ἀρετῇ τὸν Ἡρακλέα καὶ τοὺς ἐκείνης ἱδρῶτας προκρῖναι τῶν προσκαίρων τῆς κακίας ἡδονῶν.

work is plainly a dialogue, with several exchanges between the three participants, Arete, Kakia, and Heracles.[107] Nevertheless, since Socrates freely admits—both at the beginning and at the end of the fable (*Mem.* 2. 1. 21, 34)—to having reworked Prodicus' composition, we cannot be sure that the original work had the same structure as that found in the *Memorabilia*. Socrates' second disclaimer of accuracy refers only to the phrasing of the tale,[108] but his first statement is a more general one, which could apply to both form and content—καὶ Πρόδικος ... ὧδέ πως λέγων, ὅσα ἐγὼ μέμνημαι. φησὶ γὰρ ... (*Mem.* 2. 1. 21). But while Socrates (or Xenophon) may have refashioned the work in more dramatic form, there *is* one clear indication that Prodicus' fable included more than the simple speech and counter-speech of Vice and Virtue mentioned by the scholiast, for we are specifically told that Kakia takes up Arete's challenge and addresses Heracles once again in Prodicus' original version: *Mem.* 2. 1. 29 καὶ ἡ Κακία ὑπολαβοῦσα[109] εἶπεν, ὥς φησι Πρόδικος. It seems, then, that Prodicus did present his moralistic tale as a dialogue, which included not only speeches but also the reactions or replies of one speaker to another.

In sum, of the two sophistic works, Hippias' Trojan tale is more obviously related to the ὑποθῆκαι genre, while Prodicus' work is more clearly a dialogue. Neither can be said, on the available evidence, to be a direct forerunner of Socratic dialogue, but both seem to have been written as (at least rudimentary) conversations. While these sophistic dialogues of advice and exhortation cannot be shown to have influenced Xenophon here, they are in a certain sense the literary forebears of the Cambyses–Cyrus conversation.

Returning to our dialogue of advice and exhortation in the *Cyropaedia*, we find that the conversation between Cambyses and Cyrus begins—and ends—with a discussion of religious matters (*Cyr.*

---

[107] The structure of Prodicus' tale as it is found in Xenophon is as follows: (1) Kakia addresses Heracles, (2) Heracles asks her a question, and (3) she replies; (4) Arete addresses Heracles, leading (5) Kakia to speak to the youth again; (6) Arete first replies to Kakia and (7) then addresses Heracles again.

[108] *Mem.* 2. 1. 34 ἐκόσμησε [sc. Prodicus] μέντοι τὰς γνώμας ἔτι μεγαλειοτέροις ῥήμασιν ἢ ἐγὼ [i.e. Socrates] νῦν. Scholars are divided as to whether traces of Prodicus' careful distinctions between near-synonymous words can be found in the *Mem.* passage. See Guthrie 1969: 278–9; Gomperz 1912: 101 n. 225a; Gigon 1956: 60.

[109] If we understand ὑπολαβοῦσα as 'interrupt' rather than simply 'reply', this would be even stronger evidence for the conversational form of Prodicus' original composition.

1. 6. 2–6, 44–6).[110] This emphasis on religion is heightened by the fact that the talk between father and son is framed at both ends with prayers offered by Cyrus and with auspicious omens sent by the gods: thunder and lightning when the two set out (1. 6. 1) and an eagle flying overhead to the right when they cross the Persian border and arrive at Media (2. 1. 1). Cambyses begins their talk by reminding his son that he has taught him to interpret divine signs, so that Cyrus will not be dependent upon soothsayers (1. 6. 2 μὴ ἐπὶ μάντεσιν εἴης), who may trick him or simply not be available when needed. Xenophon (*Anab.* 5. 6. 29) and his Socrates (*Mem.* 4. 7. 10) also think it important to be acquainted with μαντική, and the reference here to dishonest soothsayers is seen by the commentators as an allusion to Xenophon's own experience at the hands of the treacherous seer Silanus. Cambyses may have instructed his son in the art of reading divine signs for another, particular reason: performing sacrifices was, it seems, one of the main functions of a Persian king.[111] Indeed, many years after this conversation, when Cambyses arranges a compact between his son and the Persian people, one of his chief concerns is who will fulfil this particular royal function and perform sacrifices on behalf of the Persians after he is gone (*Cyr.* 8. 5. 22 ff.). As a future king, then, Cyrus must be well acquainted with rituals, sacrifices, and omens, besides needing to understand the signs that will be sent by the gods in the course of his forthcoming campaign. If Cambyses does in fact instruct his son in the matter of sacrifices because of his role as a *Persian* crown prince, this is one of the few places in the *Cyropaedia* where there is some acknowledgement of Persian religious practices.[112] On the whole, the *Cyropaedia* is disappointing as a source for the religious beliefs and practices of the historical Cyrus the Great, and throws little light on the interesting and controversial question of the relation between the religion of the early Achaemenids and Zoroastrianism.[113] Cyrus

[110] Beginning with a discussion of religious matters may have been a regular feature of ὑποθῆκαι: see the very opening of Hesiod's Χείρωνος ὑποθῆκαι (fr. 283 Merkelbach–West); Isoc. *Ad Demonicum* 13 (the real beginning of the work, as the anonymous hypothesis notes—ἄρχεται δὲ ἀπὸ θείων); and possibly *P. Hibeh* 224, col. 2, line 2.

[111] See Widengren 1959: 251.

[112] There may be a trace of Spartan influence here as well. In Sparta too the king was in charge of all sacrifices during military campaigns—cf. *Lac. Pol.* 13. 11.

[113] Frye 1984: 120–4 is particularly sensible on the Achaemenids and Zoroastrianism; Boyce 1988: 15–31 argues strongly for the Zoroastrianism of the historical Cyrus the Great; Young 1988: 99–103 states that the evidence is too sparse to allow any conclusions about Cyrus.

generally behaves and sounds like a perfectly pious Greek, and his father Cambyses, when speaking here of religious matters, reminds us of one particular Greek, Xenophon's Socrates. The gods Cyrus sacrifices to are all Greek ones, although Xenophon may have had their Persian counterparts in mind: Zeus is actually meant to be Ahura Mazda, Hestia is the god of the hearth-fire, Helios is Mithra, etc.[114] The Magi are first mentioned about half-way through the *Cyropaedia*, and thenceforth appear fairly regularly: their role is to decide which gods should receive sacrifices and what portion of the war booty should be set aside for various divinities.[115] While the Persians, as Xenophon tells us, think it particularly important to consult experts (τεχνίταις) when dealing with the gods (*Cyr.* 8. 3. 11) and Cyrus is credited with regularizing the order of the Magi in some way,[116] the Persian leader can—and often does—perform sacrifices without their assistance.

Cyrus now tells his father that he does his utmost to propitiate the gods at all times, since he has learnt from Cambyses that the gods, like men, appreciate being remembered in good times, rather than bad. This statement has parallels in the words of Xenophon (*Hipparch.* 9. 9) and his Socrates (*Mem.* 1. 4. 18; cf. 2. 1. 28). Young Cyrus feels that the gods are his friends (*Cyr.* 1. 6. 4), reminding us of Hermogenes in the *Symposium* (3. 14, 4. 46–9), who prides himself on his good and powerful friends, the gods.

The Persian prince 'remembers' hearing about the gods from Cambyses (1. 6. 3 μέμνημαι γὰρ . . . ἀκούσας ποτέ σοῦ), and in this dialogue both father and son refer back repeatedly to earlier conversations they have had (cf. 1. 6. 3, 5, 6, 7, 8, 12). By having young Cyrus recall these previous discussions, Xenophon not only demonstrates how thoroughly and carefully Cambyses has educated his son, but also allows his hero to play a more active role in the dialogue. Cyrus presents some of his father's teachings under the guise of

[114] Cf. *Cyr.* 1. 6. 1, 3. 3. 21, 6. 4. 1, etc. and see Schwartz 1985: 684; Tuplin 1990: 26–8. The only mention of a Persian deity in the *Cyr.* is in the oath μὰ τὸν Μίθρην used by Artabazus the Mede in a semi-serious speech (*Cyr.* 7. 5. 53; cf. *Oec.* 4. 24). Boyce 1982: 211–16 gives an analysis of the Zoroastrian elements to be found in the *Cyr.*, particularly in the description of Cyrus' sacrificial procession at Babylon (*Cyr.* 8. 3). She finds only one serious mistake in Xenophon's account, the mention of whole burnt offerings (cf. *Cyr.* 8. 3. 24 ὡλοκαύτησαν).

[115] Magi in the *Cyr.*: 4. 5. 14 (first appearance), 51, 4. 6. 11, 5. 3. 4, 7. 3. 1, 7. 5. 35, 57, 8. 1. 23, 8. 3. 11, 8. 3. 24.

[116] Cf. 8. 1. 23 καὶ τότε πρῶτον κατεστάθησαν οἱ μάγοι; the text is difficult and Hug is probably right to postulate a lacuna.

recalling or reviewing what he has already learnt, and thus contributes something to the talk while still remaining an eager pupil.[117]

Continuing their discussion of religious matters, Cambyses notes that there are certain areas where men should not trouble the gods, namely those in which they can help themselves (1. 6. 5–6). Cyrus, again recalling earlier talks with his father, knows that it is wrong for men—be they horsemen, archers, navigators, farmers, or warriors—to ask the gods for success in their endeavours without mastering the basics of their profession. Such requests are contrary to the ordinances of the gods. This series of examples, taken from the crafts, already hints at the close similarity between the Persian king's words and statements made by Socrates in the *Memorabilia*. Socrates too considers it unlawful[118] for men to consult the gods about matters which they can ascertain through the use of their own intelligence (*Mem.* 1. 1. 6–9).[119]

At the close of *Cyr.* 1. 6, when Cambyses returns to the most important subject of all (1. 6. 44 τὰ μέγιστα)—man's proper attitude towards the gods—we can again detect echoes of Xenophon and his Socrates. Cyrus, warns Cambyses, should never make any moves contrary to the signs he receives from the gods, for choices made by men are no more than the random selections of a lottery and can go badly wrong. The gods, who are omniscient, are best qualified to counsel men about what should and should not be done, if they so choose. Not everyone is granted such counsel, Cambyses states: only those whom the gods favour are sent these signs (*Cyr.* 1. 6. 44–6). Cyrus, as we see by the very omens in this dialogue, is one person so favoured by the gods, and at the end of his life he thanks the gods for having indicated to him throughout what he should and should not do (*Cyr.* 8. 7. 3). Socrates, with his δαιμόνιον, is, of course, another figure in Xenophon who is fortunate enough to receive both positive and negative instructions from the gods, urging him towards—and dissuading him from—various courses of action.[120] The philosopher,

---

[117] Cf. Tatum 1989: 87–8.

[118] *Mem.* 1. 1. 9 ἀθέμιτα ποιεῖν; cf. *Cyr.* 1. 6. 6 παρὰ . . . τοὺς τῶν θεῶν θεσμούς . . . ἀθέμιτα.

[119] Cf. Ischomachus' words at *Oec.* 11. 8. For a careful comparison and analysis of *Mem.* 1. 1. 6–9 and *Cyr.* 1. 6. 2–6, 44–6, see Gigon 1953: 11–13.

[120] *Mem.* 1. 1. 2–4, 4. 3. 12, 4. 8. 1; *Apol.* 12–13. This dual function of Socrates' δαιμόνιον, both positive and negative, is an interesting difference between Xenophon's portrayal of the philosopher and that of Plato. In Plato the δαιμόνιον only prevents Socrates from acting and never urges him to undertake any action (Pl. *Apol.* 31 D ἀεὶ ἀποτρέπει με τοῦτο ὃ ἂν μέλλω πράττειν, προτρέπει δὲ οὔποτε); cf. Guthrie 1969:

whose theological outlook is shared by Cambyses, is well aware of the
fact that the gods send omens only selectively to those whom they
favour (*Mem.* 1. 1. 9, 19, 1. 4. 18, 4. 3. 12; *Apol.* 13), and he too is
careful never to act against their directions, for ignoring signs from
the gods is like preferring a blind and ignorant guide over a seeing
and knowledgeable one (*Mem.* 1. 3. 4; cf. 1. 1. 8).[121]

Cyrus follows Cambyses' advice on religious affairs, and is consistently pious throughout the *Cyropaedia*: he regularly sacrifices to
the gods before important expeditions and battles, and is always
careful to apportion to them their due share of the spoils of victory.[122]
The gods, for their part, continue to send him omens until the very
end of his life (cf. e.g. *Cyr.* 2. 4. 18–19, 7. 1. 3, 8. 7. 2). None the less,
despite Cyrus' outstanding piety—his regular sacrifices and grateful
offerings, his constant use of the expression σὺν τοῖς θεοῖς—religion
in the *Cyropaedia* is not the living, motive factor that it is, for example,
in the *Anabasis*.[123] In the *Anabasis* there are perhaps fewer theoretical
reflections on divine matters, but omens, dreams, and signs from the
gods play an important role. Xenophon himself is twice stirred to
decisive action as a result of dreams sent to him by the gods (*Anab.*
3. 1. 11–13, 4. 3. 8), and even a sneeze is taken to be a sign from
heaven (3. 2. 9). Time and again we find that an important question—such as the choice of a leader for the Ten Thousand or a
decision about despatching forces to forage for badly needed provisions—is determined solely by the outcome of sacrifices, and the gods
are consulted about a variety of matters.[124] In the *Cyropaedia* there is
not even one instance of the Persian leader having to postpone or
change his plans because of an unfavourable indication from
heaven.[125] The omens Cyrus receives are always propitious and his
sacrifices all turn out favourably: ἐπεὶ δὲ καλὰ τὰ ἱερὰ ἦν recurs

402–4. The role assigned to Socrates' δαιμόνιον in the two writers is analogous to the
philosopher's own behaviour in their writings—negative and destructive in Plato's
early dialogues, positive and protreptic in Xenophon.

[121] Hermogenes is a third pious figure in Xenophon's writings who is careful to obey
the omens sent him by his friends, the gods (*Symp.* 4. 47–8).

[122] Sacrifices: *Cyr.* 1. 6. 1, 3. 2. 3, 3. 3. 21, 34, 6. 2. 40, etc. Spoils: 4. 1. 2, 6, 4. 5. 14,
51, 5. 3. 2, 4, etc.

[123] Cf. Due 1989: 127 n. 42.

[124] See e.g. *Anab.* 3. 1. 5–7, 4. 3. 9, 5. 6. 16, 6. 1. 20–5 and 6. 6. 35–6; 6. 4. 9 ff.,
6. 5. 21.

[125] Contrast the experiences of Agesilaus (*Hell.* 3. 4. 15) and Agis (*Hell.* 3. 2. 24; cf.
4. 7. 2–7). For a detailed survey of the role played by seers, sacrifices, and various
portents during military campaigns see Pritchett 1979: 47–153.

almost as a formula at the depiction of each sacrifice Cyrus offers.[126] This makes the Persian leader's consultation of the gods seem mechanical and their approval automatic. Xenophon may have arranged matters this way because all must run smoothly for the ideal hero of the *Cyropaedia*; it is also conceivable that Xenophon's own attitude towards religion has become more routine and unthinking over the years.

The next topic raised by Cambyses is another subject that he and Cyrus have talked about in the past: the exceedingly difficult task (1. 6. 8 ὑπερμέγεθες . . . ἔργον) of ruling other men well. This is, of course, a subject raised by Xenophon himself in his introduction to the *Cyropaedia* (1. 1. 1 ff.). Xenophon tells us that he presents the story of Cyrus the Great precisely because the Persian king was able to rule over that most difficult creature of all, man: even the most distant subjects obeyed Cyrus willingly. In his introduction to the work Xenophon mentions only one task of the ruler, rendering his subjects obedient, but in our dialogue the Persian king includes a second duty: tending to the physical needs of those ruled. In the *Memorabilia* Socrates also discusses these two tasks of a leader—attending to the welfare of his 'flock' and seeing that they fulfil their function—in a similar context, when talking to a man who has just been chosen to command an army (*Mem.* 3. 2. 1 ff.).[127]

Cyrus is aware of the difficulties involved in leading others, but he thinks that he has little to fear as far as the enemy's rulers are concerned. Other leaders, including Cyrus' ally Cyaxares— ἀρξάμενος ἀπὸ τῶν ἡμετέρων φίλων is how Cyrus politely puts it— suppose that the task of a ruler is to lead an easier, richer, and more luxurious life than his subjects. Cyrus, on the other hand, thinks that a leader should differ from his subjects in his foresight and willingness to exert himself (1. 6. 8). The Persian prince looks down upon

---

[126] See *Cyr.* 2. 4. 18, 3. 2. 3, 6. 3. 1, and cf. 3. 3. 22 and 6. 4. 13. Christensen 1936: 124–5 notes that when Cyrus sacrifices to Zeus and the other gods (cf. *Cyr.* 1. 6. 1, 3. 3. 21, 7. 5. 57, 8. 7. 3) and the Magi apportion war booty to the gods (cf. 4. 6. 11, 5. 3. 4, 7. 3. 1) these actions are repeatedly described by Xenophon in similar, near-formulaic phrases.

[127] Cf. *Mem.* 3. 4. 8. This discussion is one of five chapters at the beginning of bk. 3 of the *Mem.* in which Socrates discusses military matters, and there are, as we shall see, several close parallels between these chapters of the *Mem.* and *Cyr.* 1. 6. Interestingly, the attitude of two of Socrates' partners in these discussions—the anonymous young military men of *Mem.* 3. 1 and 3. 3—is very like that of young Cyrus in our dialogue. All three aspiring military leaders play an active role in their conversations and are genuinely eager to learn.

his pampered enemies, but the Assyrians are, in fact, rather formidable opponents. We often hear of the young Assyrian king's cruelty and insolence, but never of his soft, luxurious lifestyle; Cyaxares and (to a lesser extent) Croesus are the spoiled, weak rulers of the *Cyropaedia*. This view of true leadership, Cyrus' first original contribution to the discussion, is hardly a novel one. Herodotus' Croesus, for example, is well aware of the connection between a luxurious lifestyle and military weakness (Hdt. 1. 155), and Isocrates tells Nicocles that he must be more self-restrained than his subjects (*Ad Nic.* 29; cf. 31). The need for a ruler (or for that matter any individual) to exercise self-control is a favourite theme in the *Memorabilia*, most fully elaborated in a discussion between Socrates and Aristippus, where Socrates demonstrates, point by point, how a young man trained to self-control would make a far better ruler than a self-indulgent one (*Mem.* 2. 1. 1–7).[128]

Cambyses does not take issue with his son's words, but he seems to find Cyrus' approach over-theoretical. Sometimes, observes the Persian king, leaders have to grapple with the facts themselves (1. 6. 9 αὐτὰ τὰ πράγματα), rather than personalities, and circumstances are not always easy to control. Cyrus' authority, for example, will come to nought if he does not feed his army, Cambyses warns. Cyrus replies that Cyaxares has promised to supply the Persians' needs, and the king now discovers—by means of a brief and pointed cross-examination (*Cyr.* 1. 6. 9)—that his son has made no provisions of his own for feeding the men under his command. This will not do, as Cyrus himself admits, for father and son have just agreed that providing one's subjects with an ample supply of the necessities of life is one of the chief tasks of a ruler. In effect, Cambyses conducts a Socrates-like ἔλεγχος here, asking Cyrus awkward questions and leading him to realize that he himself has not shown forethought and the ability to plan ahead—the very qualities he has just associated with genuine leadership. The Persian prince, reduced to ἀπορία, immediately turns to his father for guidance, which Cambyses is now happy to provide. Cambyses' teaching methods here are, then, both destructive and constructive: after pointing out to Cyrus the error of his ways, he gives his son practical advice on the acquisition of supplies. Once again the parallel with the Socrates of the *Memorabilia* is plain: the philosopher too, as we have seen, conducts negative or destructive

---

[128] Cf. *Mem.* 1. 5. 1, 3. 1. 6, 3. 2. 3, 3. 4. 9. We have already seen that ἐγκράτεια is a recurring characteristic of Xenophon's heroes—cf. above, sect. 1, with n. 3.

cross-examinations, but is even fonder of offering constructive advice. The chastened Cyrus, in any event, promises not to neglect the problem of supplies (*Cyr.* 1. 6. 10–11).[129]

The Persian prince now reminds his father of an incident involving a teacher he once had, a man who claimed to teach the art of military command. When Cyrus finished his course of instruction and approached his father for money to pay the man, Cambyses discovered that the instructor had simply taught tactics and had omitted all the other branches of knowledge that a good general must acquire. There is a close parallel to our passage in the *Memorabilia*: Socrates similarly unmasks the pretensions of a so-called expert who claimed to teach generalship (*Mem.* 3. 1). The similarities between this passage and *Cyr.* 1. 6. 12–15 have tantalized commentators, who try to use the two texts as a key to answering some of the weightier questions of Xenophontic scholarship—such as the relative chronology of the *Memorabilia* and *Cyropaedia*, and the authenticity of Socrates' conversations in the former[130]—so that it is worth taking a closer look at the two texts.

The situations in the *Memorabilia* and *Cyropaedia* are very similar. Cyrus and one of Socrates' followers have both gone to a teacher who professes to teach generalship (*Mem.* 3. 1. 1 ἐπαγγελλόμενον στρατη-γεῖν διδάξειν; *Cyr.* 1. 6. 12 τῷ φάσκοντι στρατηγεῖν με πεπαιδευκέ-ναι, cf. 1. 6. 14) for a fee (*Cyr.* 1. 6. 12 ἀργύριον/μισθόν; *Mem.* 3. 1. 11 ἀργύριον). Cyrus has, apparently, approached the teacher on his own initiative, while Socrates has sent his disciple to study with Dionysodorus, a military expert visiting Athens. Through Camby-ses'/Socrates' questioning it becomes clear that all that Cyrus/ Socrates' anonymous pupil has been taught is tactics. Cambyses uncovers this fact gradually, while Socrates is told so at once; both point out that the study of tactics is only a part of generalship. The Persian king then suggests that Cyrus learn more about the subject by

---

[129] The last sentence of *Cyr.* 1. 6. 11, beginning ὥς γ' ἐμοῦ (an emendation by Din-dorf; the manuscripts read ὥστε μου or ὡς ἐμοῦ), is printed by many editors (e.g. Din-dorf, Gemoll, Holden) with a capital letter, to signify that the speakers have now changed and that these are the words of Cambyses. This would mean that Cambyses is bragging, saying that he has never neglected the problem of supplies, but the words are better suited to Cyrus, who is promising to take his father's advice and tend to supplies at all times. Later in the *Cyr.* we often find Cyrus raising funds and acquiring rations for his army—see esp. 6. 2. 26–30 and cf. 2. 1. 21, 2. 4. 9–13, 32, 3. 1. 34, 3. 2. 28–30, etc.

[130] See Delatte 1933: 7–25 (who includes a detailed survey of earlier scholarly opinion on the relationship between the two works); Richter 1893: 112–18; von Arnim 1923: 186 ff.; and Marchant's introduction to the Loeb *Mem.*, p. xv.

conversing with men who are knowledgeable in military affairs, while
Socrates sends his companion back to the teacher, Dionysodorus, to
receive full value for his money.

The setting of these two stories seems far more Athenian than
Persian. Dionysodorus, the teacher in the *Memorabilia*, is probably to
be identified with the sophist of the same name who appears in
Plato's *Euthydemus*. According to Plato, Dionysodorus and his
brother Euthydemus began their careers by instructing young men
in (hoplite) warfare and then turned to teaching forensic eristic and
rhetoric (Pl. *Euthyd.* 271 D, 273 C), for pay, of course (272 A, 304 A, C).
When Socrates sends his follower back for further lessons, he is, in
essence, demonstrating that a sophist has not lived up to his claims
and does not deserve the fee he has charged (*Mem.* 3. 1. 11 ἀργύριον
εἰληφὼς ἐνδεᾶ σε ἀποπέμψασθαι) and it is here that the difficulties
arise on the Persian front. While young men who turn to specialists to
be taught for a fee are a regular part of Socrates' Athens, an outside
expert on warcraft, paid for his services, seems out of place in the
Cyropaedia. It is true that Cyrus' enemies, the Assyrians, have a Greek
(6. 3. 11 Ἕλλην τις ἀνήρ) as one of the three men in charge of drilling
their army, and in Xenophon's own time the Persians make use of
Phalinus, the Greek military expert whom Tissaphernes admires for
his supposed knowledge of tactics and hoplite warfare (*Anab.* 2. 1. 7).
None the less, in the *Cyropaedia* Xenophon has attributed to his
Persians a carefully structured educational system in which learning
and money matters are totally separate. The Persian ruling class
spend most of their time in the ἐλευθέρα ἀγορά, so named because
the sounds of the market have been banished elsewhere in order to
avoid disturbing the well-ordered life of men of culture (*Cyr.* 1. 2. 3;
cf. Hdt. 1. 155). The teachers in Persia are older members of the
ruling class, who volunteer their services (1. 2. 13) and are not paid:
teaching for a fee is simply not a part of the Persian system. Thus the
situation in which Cyrus finds himself—approaching his father for
money to pay a special teacher—seems contrived.

When discussing the expert's teachings, the Persian Cambyses
seems, paradoxically, more 'Socratic' than does Socrates in the
Memorabilia. In our dialogue Cambyses cross-examines Cyrus
sharply on the tuition he has received. His interrogation (although
reported only indirectly) is pointed and dramatic: we can sense the
Persian king's increasing incredulity as his son is forced to acknowledge over and over again that his teacher has neglected yet another

important concern of generals. In the *Memorabilia* it is not Socrates who establishes how little the military expert has taught, but the philosopher's follower, who announces at once τὰ γὰρ τακτικὰ ἐμέ γε καὶ ἄλλ᾽ οὐδὲν ἐδίδαξεν (*Mem.* 3. 1. 5), so that there is no pointed cross-examination on the subject by the philosopher. (Later in the conversation Socrates does interrogate his disciple on the subject of tactics—*Mem.* 3. 1. 9–11). Cambyses' discussion of good generalship is detailed and continues for most of our dialogue, while Socrates simply lists in a single sentence the qualities that he thinks a good military commander must possess. The actual qualities which Socrates assigns to a good general correspond only in part to those mentioned by Cambyses, but in the next four chapters of the *Memorabilia* (3. 2–5) the philosopher continues to discuss military matters, and there he covers many of the points raised by the Persian king in our passage.[131]

What can we learn from the two parallel texts? The situation described in the two passages—a young man approaches an expert and is taught by him, only to discover that the teacher is unsatisfactory and has not earned his fee—is undoubtedly one we would associate with Socrates. Plato's *Euthydemus*, *Laches*, and *Protagoras*, for example, all have settings rather similar to this. Thus it seems that Xenophon has included in the *Cyropaedia* a story associated with, or perhaps inspired by, Socrates' doings; but this does not mean that he first wrote up the scene in his book about Socrates, the *Memorabilia*. The version in the *Cyropaedia* is fuller, more readily intelligible, and in a sense more 'Socratic', but again this tells us little about the relationship between and relative chronology of the two passages—a more elaborate exposition is not necessarily an earlier one.[132]

Next comes the subject-matter of these two passages, military affairs. Could Socrates actually have held forth on the art of generalship in the way that Xenophon shows him doing? The seasoned soldier Xenophon, scholars contend, must be the source of this discussion of the art of command: he was well-versed in strategy and tactics, while the real-life Socrates had little interest in these matters and was unlikely to discuss them. Xenophon, the argument goes, first included this tale in the *Cyropaedia*, and then later put the same words into the mouth of his Socrates. But the historical Socrates, who fought at Potidaea, Delium, and Amphipolis, was not unacquainted

---

[131] For a detailed comparison of *Cyr.* 1. 6 and *Mem.* 3. 1–7 see Richter 1893: 114 ff.
[132] *Pace* Delatte 1933: 17 ff.

with soldiering and was certainly qualified to discuss what makes a good general, just as he investigated experts in other fields and crafts. In Plato's *Laches* we find Socrates in this very role: he is asked by Laches and his friends to pass judgement on the pedagogic merit of Stesilaus, an expert in hoplite warfare. Laches mentions both Socrates' interest in educating young men and his brave behaviour at the retreat from Delium as evidence of his qualifications to judge these military matters (*Laches* 180C, 181B). Hence a discussion of military affairs by Socrates need not be rejected out of hand as inauthentic or intrinsically unlikely, and Xenophon could be reporting an actual conversation, held by Socrates, in the *Memorabilia*.

In sum, a comparison of the two parallel passages *Cyr.* 1. 6 and *Mem.* 3. 1 raises interesting questions but does not lead to any definitive answers concerning the relationship between the two works. We cannot tell which version was written first or inspired the other, nor can we establish on the basis of the two passages whether or not the historical Socrates ever discussed the art of being a good general.

After Cyrus was shown by his father how little he had been taught by his teacher of generalship, he asked Cambyses to instruct him instead. The Persian king did not, in fact, teach his son himself but sent him to men considered knowledgeable in military affairs. We are once again reminded of Xenophon's Socrates, who sends his friends and followers to be instructed by men more knowledgeable than himself (*Oec.* 2. 16 πολὺ ἄλλους ἐμοῦ δεινοτέρους).[133] In Plato too we find the philosopher recommending teachers to his followers (*Laches* 180C–D; cf. 200D).[134] Thus the Persian king seems to share Socrates' modesty, his unwillingness to claim any real knowledge of his own. The reverse side of Socrates' ignorance is his recognition of how little supposed specialists in various fields actually know. We have just seen this happen with the teacher of generalship; the classic description of Socrates' unmasking of supposed experts is found in Plato's *Apology* (21C–22E). Now, on the journey to Media Cambyses too demonstrates to his son the failings of the specialists who have taught him. It soon becomes apparent in a point-by-point review of the areas that Cambyses considers essential for a general to know—supplies, health, the martial arts, inspiring soldiers and rendering them

---

[133] Cf. *Mem.* 1. 6. 14, 2. 2. 6, 4. 7. 1.

[134] See Tomin 1987: 100–1 on 'academic matchmaking' by Socrates in Plato and Xenophon: he thinks that this practice can be attributed to the historical Socrates.

obedient—that these knowledgeable Persians are not as well versed in military command as their king. They have omitted many important points, and Cambyses now proceeds to fill in the missing gaps.

Father and son begin with the question of the health and welfare of the army. Cyrus tells Cambyses that he is taking professional doctors along with him for his soldiers, but the Persian king replies that doctors, like menders of torn clothes, merely repair damage that has already been done. Cyrus should take preventive measures to ensure his men's health, such as camping in a healthy site: the salubrity of a location can be judged by the physique and complexion of its inhabitants, explains Cambyses. The Persian king, with his mention of the many discussions περὶ τῶν νοσηρῶν χωρίων καὶ περὶ τῶν ὑγιεινῶν (which sounds like the title of a Hippocratic treatise), seems to attest to widespread interest in medicine in Xenophon's time.[135] The other dietary measures mentioned here—eating moderately, 'working off' one's meals, and taking exercise—appear frequently in the pages of Xenophon.[136] Cyrus earns his father's praise for the first and only time in this conversation when he suggests warlike contests with prizes for his men, in order to keep them fit and occupied. This too is a favourite practice, often found in Xenophon.[137]

Cyrus plans to imbue his soldiers with enthusiasm (1. 6. 19 προθυμίαν ἐμβαλεῖν στρατιώταις) by inspiring them with hopes, but once again Cambyses finds it necessary to correct him. Repeatedly arousing false expectations among the troops, the Persian king warns, is like constantly crying 'wolf': in the end, when Cyrus really needs to encourage his men, he will no longer be believed. We shall see below (sect. 6) that Cyrus does not heed his father's advice on this particular point: he encourages and exhorts his men throughout the *Cyropaedia*.

The Persian prince does not consider the next task of a good general—that of keeping his soldiers obedient—difficult, for he has been taught, even compelled, to obey others from earliest youth. Cyrus considers a system of reward and punishment the best way to ensure his men's obedience, but his father again improves upon his

---

[135] On the Hippocratic echoes of our passage see Breitenbach 1950: 73 with n. 110. Cambyses uses a technical medical term here, μάρτυρες (*Cyr.* 1. 6. 16); cf. Lloyd 1979: 129 n. 15, 149 n. 124, 252–3.

[136] See e.g. *Mem.* 1. 2. 4; *Oec.* 11. 11–12; and cf. Breitenbach 1966: 1724–5, 1856–7; Due 1989: 175–9.

[137] See *Cyr.* 1. 2. 12, 2. 1. 22–3, 8. 2. 26, 8. 3. 25 ff., and Breitenbach 1950: 82–4.

plan. Cyrus, says Cambyses, will win his soldiers' willing submission if he seems to be wiser than they are. Cambyses explains that men are eager to obey those who seem more knowledgeable: those who are ill, for example, readily follow their doctor's orders and men at sea willingly obey the ship's captain (1. 6. 21). This analogy from the crafts already gives a hint that the Persian king is yet again echoing an idea expressed by Xenophon's Socrates. Socrates, in a very similar situation—he is conversing with a newly elected cavalry commander —also states that men are most anxious to obey those whom they consider best informed, and he uses almost identical examples (doctors, navigators, farmers) to illustrate his point (*Mem.* 3. 3. 8 ff.).[138]

Not surprisingly, Cyrus' next question concerns the best way to acquire such a reputation for sagacity, and Cambyses' answer is a simple one: the best way to seem wise is to *be* so. The Persian king again illustrates the truth of his words by a series of examples. A man who claims to be a good farmer, horseman, doctor, or flute-player without actually being so can acquire a fine reputation and all the external appurtenances of his craft, but will none the less be exposed as an impostor within a short time (1. 6. 22). Here too we are obviously in Socratic territory: in the *Memorabilia* Socrates argues on four separate occasions that the shortest path to seeming knowledgeable is to be so, and in each instance he uses a series of examples from various professions to support this claim.[139]

Cambyses' next piece of advice concerns a general's superiority in physical exertions. A commander must be hardier (καρτερώτερον) than his men, readily enduring heat, cold, and hardships; the respect and admiration that Cyrus will win, Cambyses adds reassuringly, will make this task seem lighter. Here perhaps we can sense the presence of Xenophon himself, the veteran leader of the Ten Thousand. In the *Anabasis* we find Xenophon naked, splitting wood in the snow, and thus rousing the other men to action in the cold (*Anab.* 4. 4. 12; cf. 7. 3. 44–5). The ability to withstand cold, heat, and hardship (*Anab.* 3. 1. 23 καὶ ψύχη καὶ θάλπη καὶ πόνους φέρειν) is one

---

[138] Cf. *Hippar.* 6. 1 ff., where Xenophon, speaking in his own person, uses this argument a third time. This piece of wisdom may not be peculiarly Socratic: Isocrates too advises Nicocles that he should demonstrate his authority, not by means of harsh punishments but by proving superior to his subjects (*Ad Nic.* 24; cf. 10), but he does not use analogies from the crafts to establish this point.

[139] *Mem.* 1. 7. 2–3, 2. 6. 38–9, 3. 3. 9, 3. 9. 11 (and cf. 3. 6. 16–17). See above, sect. 1 with n. 58.

feature of the ἐγκράτεια and καρτερία complex of qualities often associated with Xenophon's heroes: besides the soldiers of the Ten Thousand, Socrates (*Mem.* 1. 2. 1) and Agesilaus (*Ages.* 5. 2–3) are also able to endure these discomforts.[140]

Cambyses has now reviewed with his son all five areas which it is essential for a good general to know, and Cyrus feels ready to take on the enemy: he asks his father if a commander who has attended to all these matters should attack the enemy as soon as possible. The Persian king checks his son's youthful impetuousness, advising him to initiate military action against an enemy only if Cyrus has the advantage (1. 6. 26 πλέον ἔχειν). The way to gain such advantage, Cambyses warns, is not simple: one must plot and dissemble, be wily and deceitful, a thief and a robber, taking advantage of the enemy in every area: δεῖ . . . καὶ ἐπίβουλον εἶναι καὶ κρυψίνουν καὶ δολερὸν καὶ ἀπατεῶνα καὶ κλέπτην καὶ ἅρπαγα καὶ ἐν παντὶ πλεονέκτην τῶν πολεμίων (1. 6. 27).[141] Cyrus is amused and surprised by this state-ment—he laughs and uses the rare oath ὦ Ἡράκλεις—and Cam-byses compounds the surprise by adding that if Cyrus will turn out to be such a man he will be most just and law-abiding. When Cyrus points out that Persian youths are taught the very opposite of these deceitful qualities, his father explains that this sort of tricky behaviour is to be used only against enemies, but not in relation to friends and fellow citizens. The Persian prince has been trained to use deception and duplicity when hunting animals, just as he has been taught to use weapons on animals, but he has not been allowed to practise these skills on human beings for fear of harming his friends. Perhaps, retorts Cyrus, he should have been taught to harm men as well as help them, if both kinds of knowledge are useful. Cambyses now tells his son that he has heard that once, in the days of their forefathers, the Persians did indeed have such an instructor. This teacher taught Persian boys justice by instructing them in both spheres—lying and not lying, cheating and not cheating—and distinguishing between behaviour which was to be directed towards friends and that meant for enemies; even friends were to be tricked or cheated if it were for their own good. The Persian youths were made to practise these

---

[140] See Breitenbach 1966: 1784–5 and cf. above, sect. 1 with n. 3. Plato, of course, provides us with a description of Socrates in the snow (*Symp.* 219ε ff.).

[141] Socrates, in a paradoxical list of contradictory qualities that a good general must possess, mentions most of these negative features—cf. *Mem.* 3. 1. 6 . . . καὶ φιλόφρονά τε καὶ ὠμόν, καὶ ἁπλοῦν τε καὶ ἐπίβουλον καὶ φυλακτικόν τε καὶ κλέπτην, καὶ προετικὸν καὶ ἅρπαγα, καὶ φιλόδωρον καὶ πλεονέκτην . . .

negative arts just as the Greeks have their children practise deception when wrestling—the Persian king rather unexpectedly adds—but some lads became too proficient in cheating and took advantage of their own friends. Hence the Persians passed a law that children, like servants, should only be taught to tell the truth, with no lessons in deception or taking advantage. This law is still in force, Cambyses adds, but he thinks Cyrus now old enough to be taught tricks to be used against the enemy with no fear of his using these same weapons of deceit against his fellow citizens (1. 6. 21–34).

Even without Cambyses' reference to the Greeks training their children to use trickery when wrestling,[142] it is immediately apparent that the Persian teacher of old described here is a very Greek figure. Scholars raise the question of Xenophon's sources for this section of the *Cyropaedia* and try to determine which Greek thinker—Socrates, Gorgias, Protagoras, etc.—appears here in the guise of an ancient Persian teacher of justice. It is perhaps misguided to frame the question in such precise terms: when Cambyses points out that justice is a complex concept and that an individual can be righteous and law-abiding even when indulging in deception or trickery, he raises a paradox popular in classical Athens. This point is discussed by Socrates in the *Memorabilia* (4. 2. 12 ff.) and is also mentioned in the early fourth-century sophistic work Διϲϲοὶ Λόγοι (chapter 3).[143] There are also traces of such discussions in Pl. *Rep.* 331 c and [Pl.] *De Iusto* 374 B–E. Since the ideas expressed here surfaced in several places—in sophistic and Socratic circles alike—at roughly the same time, we need not assume that Xenophon has a specific Greek figure in mind when describing the Persian teacher of long ago.[144]

---

[142] Cambyses associates here the practice of forensic oratory—which is how Persian youngsters learn justice (cf. *Cyr.* 1. 2. 6–7)—with the art of wrestling. This link between physical contests and battles of words is frequently found—see e.g. Pl. *Gorg.* 456 D–E; Καταβάλλοντεϲ, the alternative title of Protagoras' Ἀλήθεια; Gorgias fr. 8 (= DK 82 B 8) (with Diels's emendation πλίγμα) and the further references in Dodds on Eur. *Ba.* 201–3 and Hawtrey on Pl. *Euthyd.* 277 D 1 f. Dionysodorus, the military expert of *Mem.* 3. 1, and his brother Euthydemus are living illustrations of this link between physical and verbal conflict: the pair of brothers went from teaching armed combat to offering instruction in forensic oratory and eristic (Pl. *Euthyd.* 271 C–272 A). Wrestling metaphors are also particularly associated with Thucydides, son of Melesias (Aristoph. *Acharn.* 703–10; Plut. *Per.* 8. 5, 11. 1), perhaps because his father was an actual wrestling master—cf. Wade-Gery 1932: 209–10 = 1958: 244–6.

[143] Robinson 1979: 34–41 dates the work to the very beginning of the 4th cent.; see also O'Brien 1967: 75–6 n. 47.

[144] Von Arnim 1923: 188–9 plumps for Socrates because of the very similar remarks attributed to him at *Mem.* 4. 2. 14–19, while Gigon 1956: 87–8, who brings even further parallels to our passage, thinks that Protagoras may be the source. Nestle 1940–1: 35–

In the parallel passage in the *Memorabilia* (4. 2. 12 ff.) Socrates questions Euthydemus about the nature of justice. Using a series of concrete illustrations—enslaving an enemy, tricking one's son into taking a beneficial drug, stealing a weapon from a suicidal friend— Socrates compels the young man to change his original position that lying, cheating, and doing wrong are always unjust. Euthydemus first admits that such actions can rightfully be taken against one's enemies, and is then led to agree that the same negative measures can, at times, be employed justly against one's friends. Eventually Euthydemus does not know how to answer Socrates' questions at all, and the self-satisfied youngster is reduced to ἀπορία (*Mem.* 4. 2. 19; cf. 23, 39). In our passage Cambyses does not question Cyrus and simply sums up the teachings of the Persian instructor: διώριζε δὲ τούτων (i.e. lying and not lying, cheating and not cheating) ἅ τε πρὸς τοὺς φίλους ποιητέον καὶ ἃ πρὸς ἐχθρούς. καὶ ἔτι γε ταῦτα ἐδίδασκεν ὡς καὶ τοὺς φίλους δίκαιον εἴη ἐξαπατᾶν ἐπί γε ἀγαθῷ καὶ κλέπτειν τὰ τῶν φίλων ἐπὶ ἀγαθῷ (*Cyr.* 1. 6. 31); but this summary is an exact description of the stages of Socrates' discussion with Euthydemus. The word διώριζε used by Cambyses reminds us of Socrates literally separating and listing various qualities under two separate headings (α for ἀδικία and δ for δικαιοσύνη) while questioning Euthydemus. Socrates' real aim seems to be to demonstrate to his over-confident young interlocutor that defining justice is a complex matter beyond his capabilities: Euthydemus still has much to learn.

Cambyses too reveals the paradoxical, 'immoral' side of justice as part of the instruction and guidance he gives in this dialogue to young Cyrus, but his ultimate aim is more pragmatic. The Persian king encourages his son actually to use such deceitful, unprincipled measures against the enemy in his forthcoming campaign, and Cyrus must first be made to understand that all is fair—or just—in war. (This is not, of course, Socrates' message in the *Memorabilia*.) Cambyses also warns of the dangers of introducing young boys to this twilight world of right and wrong, apparently agreeing with his Persian forefathers that it is better to train young men in accordance with simplistic, straightforward concepts of virtue and justice and to leave acquaintance with greyer, more complex notions for their

42 argues that both our passage and the third chapter of the Δισσοὶ Λόγοι are based upon a lost work of Gorgias, περὶ τοῦ δικαίου, which was included in his Τέχνη; he ignores *Mem.* 4. 2 entirely. Many scholars approach the question from the Δισσοὶ Λόγοι and overlook the *Cyr.* parallel; see Robinson 1979: 179–80.

maturity. Cambyses' use of the Spartan term ῥήτρα for the law for-
bidding Persian youths to engage in lying, stealing, etc. (*Cyr.* 1. 6. 33)
brings to mind Xenophon's own reports on the Spartan practice of
having their young men supplement their meagre diet by stealing
(*Lac. Pol.* 2. 5–9; cf. *Anab.* 4. 6. 14–15). The Persian king seems to
disapprove of such thefts, for he compares an early introduction to
cheating to initiation in sexual matters at too young an age, but elsewhere Xenophon notes that such dishonest activities help train boys
in the martial arts (cf. *Lac. Pol.* 2. 7 μηχανικωτέρους . . . ποιεῖν καὶ
πολεμικωτέρους).[145] Cambyses' straightforward approach to justice
—simple virtues for the young, deception and wrongdoing to be
practised by older men against the enemy—ignores one of the problems he himself raises, for he makes no provision for the Persians to
learn to deceive friends for their own good.

The next parallel to our passage, the section entitled περὶ δικαίου
καὶ ἀδίκου found in the Δισσοὶ Λόγοι (DK 90 3. 1–8), includes,
among other illustrations, all three of the examples of 'just injustice'
used by Socrates in the *Memorabilia*—enslaving enemies, stealing
weapons from a suicidal friend, and using duplicity to administer
medicine to relatives. The author of the Δισσοὶ Λόγοι is, of course,
deliberately paradoxical, and his sole intention is to bring arguments
for and against identifying the just with the unjust. One of these three
illustrations, keeping a weapon from a friend intent upon killing himself, is also used by Plato's Socrates in the *Republic* (331 C; cf. 334 A,
382 C), when pointing out to Cephalus that his definition of justice is
over-simple. In sum, Cambyses, Socrates (in Plato and Xenophon),
and the author of the Δισσοὶ Λόγοι may ultimately have different
aims in mind when discussing justice, but their initial intention is the
same in each case, to awaken their audience to an awareness of the
complex, many-sided character of justice—to tease rather than to
enlighten. This discussion of the justice of lying, cheating, and
deceiving, with its use of examples such as the suicidal friend, whatever its origin,[146] would have quickly become popular both in

---

[145] This condemnation of thefts by young boys is one of the few differences between
the Persian system of education in the *Cyr.* and its obvious source of inspiration, the
Spartan *agōgē*. Cf. Tigerstedt 1965: 178 and 459 n. 498; Rawson 1969: 50–1.

[146] It is perhaps worth noting that the discussion in the Δισσοὶ Λόγοι (3. 2–8) takes
the form of a series of leading questions, similar to those Socrates asks Euthydemus in
the *Mem.* (4. 2. 13 ff.; cf. Cambyses' string of questions at *Cyr.* 1. 6. 28). This near-
dialogue presentation may hint that Socrates is the source; cf. Ramage 1961: 420 n. 7
and 424 with n. 24.

Socratic and in sophistic circles, for despite the differences between them, both Socrates and the sophists would have found these provocative paradoxes useful teaching tools.

Next Cambyses gives his son some tips on ways to gain the upper hand over the enemy, and advises him not only to make use of military techniques that he has already learnt, but to devise new stratagems of his own. The Persian king also urges Cyrus once again to tend to his soldiers' welfare—their physical condition, good spirits, and military training—day and night. Cambyses then reviews the whole subject of tactics in one very long sentence. He mentions the various tactical problems facing the general of an army—how to lead his forces by day and night, how to travel through different kinds of terrain, how to confront the enemy or withdraw, etc.—in a series of short clauses which sound like the chapter-headings of a treatise on military tactics (e.g. 1. 6. 43 ὅπως ἱππικὸν φυλάττεσθαι).[147] It is likely that there were military manuals available when the *Cyropaedia* was written, and Xenophon's own guides to horsemanship and the command of cavalry provide evidence for other such specialist handbooks being current at the time.[148] The Πολιορκητική of Aeneas Tacticus probably appeared a little after the *Cyropaedia*;[149] it deals with siege operations rather than tactics, but Aeneas seems to have written several treatises on military matters, for he mentions ἡ παρασκευαστικὴ βίβλος (Aen. Tact. 7. 4) and ἡ ποριστικὴ βίβλος (14. 2).[150] Cambyses, in any event, does not review tactics with his son in any detail, relying on the knowledge that Cyrus has acquired from their previous discussions and on the instruction he has received from others. Thus far none of the supposed experts whom the Persian prince has consulted—including the incompetent teacher of tactics—has proved very helpful, but Xenophon may have avoided having Cambyses give detailed military advice on tactics here because he considered such information too technical to be included in this didactic dialogue. It is difficult to combine a Socratic dialogue with a

---

[147] See Breitenbach 1966: 1722, 1732–7 for a more detailed commentary on *Cyr.* 1. 6. 43 and a comparison of the *Cyr.* material with other writers on tactics.

[148] Cf. O'Brien 1967: 66 with n. 24; Whitehead 1990: 34–7.

[149] This work of Aeneas Tacticus (who may be identical with the Aeneas of Stymphalus mentioned at *Hell.* 7. 3. 1) is usually dated between 360 and 355 on the basis of internal references. See Whitehead 1990: 4–13; Oldfather in the Loeb Aeneas Tacticus, 5–7; and Bon in the Budé edition, pp. viii–ix.

[150] See too Aen. Tact. 26. 6, 12 for possible allusions to earlier military works by other writers; cf. Whitehead 1990: 13–16, 34–7.

specialist handbook: the section of the *Oeconomicus* in which Ischomachus instructs Socrates in the art of farming by means of a series of
questions (15. 6–19. 19) is perhaps the most successful marriage of
the two.[151]

Cambyses concludes this long talk with his son by returning to
religious matters, as we have seen above. Cyrus is not heard at all in
the final section of the dialogue (*Cyr.* 1. 6. 37–46), just as many
conversations in the *Memorabilia* end with a long speech by Socrates.
In this dialogue Xenophon imparts to his readers much useful
military advice in readable form[152] and also allows us a glimpse of the
easy and untroubled relationship between father and son: Cambyses
is a wise and conscientious father, while Cyrus is young and eager,
but inexperienced. The Persian king is as Socratic as can be, not only
in his didactic methods and style of argument—his use of analogies,
cross-examinations, positive exhortations, and a final, long speech—
but also in his ideas on the gods, on good generalship, on the
relativity of justice, etc. Cyrus speaks up rather more often than
Socrates' interlocutors in the *Memorabilia* usually do, but there is little
doubt that he is a willing and enthusiastic student. Indeed, Xenophon devotes much of the following book of the *Cyropaedia* to illustrating how Cyrus goes about putting his father's advice into practice,
point by point.[153] Young Cyrus has already demonstrated his ability
to hold his own with adult members of his family, and has even acted
as a kind of didactic conscience, a 'Socrates',[154] so that we might have
expected him to be on more of an equal footing with his father here.
None the less, Cyrus is the pupil, pure and simple, in our dialogue
and this is the only time that we shall find the hero of the *Cyropaedia*
cast in this role.[155]

---

[151] See Gray 1985: 159–62 and above, n. 95.

[152] It is interesting to compare our dialogue with *Cyr.* 6. 2. 24–41, a speech delivered
by Cyrus to his forces before undertaking the long march to Thymbrara. The Persian
leader touches upon many of the topics discussed by Cambyses in *Cyr.* 1. 6: provisions
for the army's health and welfare, and the food, drink, clothing, and equipment to be
taken along. Both these passages contain useful information for those embarking on a
military campaign, but Cyrus' address, unlike our dialogue, is unrelievedly dry and
dull.

[153] Supplies and finance: *Cyr.* 2. 4. 9–14, 2. 4. 32; health and exercise: 2. 1. 29;
military techniques: 2. 1. 21–4, 2. 3. 17–24; enthusiasm: 2. 1. 11–19, 25–8; obedience:
2. 1. 22, 2. 2. 10, 23–7, 30, 2. 3. 8; tactics: 2. 2. 6, 2. 4. 2–5; deception: 2. 4. 15–17;
religion: 2. 3. 1, 2. 4. 18–19; cf. Due 1989: 92–6.

[154] Cf. *Cyr.* 1. 3. 4–11, 15–18, and cf. below, sect. 3 and ch. 3. 2.

[155] See, however, *Cyr.* 8. 5. 22–7, where Cambyses again asserts his authority, and cf.
Tatum 1989: 76–82.

3. A COMPARISON OF CONSTITUTIONS: *CYR.* I. 3. 15–18

Cyr. 1. 3. 15–18 is a conversation between the young Cyrus and his mother, Mandane, which takes place during their stay in Media. Cyrus has just accepted his grandfather's persuasive invitation to remain in Media after his mother's departure, and Mandane wishes to discuss with her son the consequences of an extended stay in her native land. When she asks Cyrus why he would like to remain in Media, he replies that he is interested in improving his horsemanship. At home in Persia he is the best bowman and spearman of his age, but in Media he is inferior to his contemporaries in riding, for in Persia there are few horses (1. 3. 3). The Persian prince, ever bent on self-improvement, is anxious to remedy this failing, and his acquired skill as a horseman will in fact later stand him in good stead, when he introduces a cavalry into the Persian army (4. 3. 4–23).[156] Mandane is not, however, interested in horses: she is concerned that the 12-year-old Cyrus[157] will not be able to make progress in learning justice, for there are no teachers of justice in Media. Justice, Xenophon has told us (1. 2. 6–8), is the foremost element in the Persian curriculum for boys of Cyrus' age.

The juxtaposition of horses, bows, spears, and justice (or truth) found here seems to be particularly Persian: it is in these four areas that Persians were encouraged to excel, according to both Persian and Greek sources. Besides Herodotus' famous statement παιδεύουσι δὲ τοὺς παῖδας . . . τρία μοῦνα ἱππεύειν καὶ τοξεύειν καὶ ἀληθίζεσθαι (1. 136. 2), we have Xenophon's description of the upbringing of Cyrus the Younger (*Anab.* 1. 9. 5; cf. 1. 9. 6) and the formulaic statements found in the Old Persian autobiographical inscriptions of Darius and Xerxes. Both Achaemenid kings, using almost identical words, pride themselves upon being good horsemen, bowmen, spearmen, as well as 'friends to right, upholders of justice'.[158]

---

[156] Xenophon's statement that Cyrus first turned the Persians into horsemen (*Cyr.* 1. 3. 3 and 4. 3. 4ff.; contrast Hdt. 1. 136) is now accepted by many scholars. See How and Wells on Hdt. 1. 136 and Cook 1983: 40–1.

[157] Cf. 1. 3. 1.

[158] DNb lines 5–11, 40–5 in Kent 1953: 138–40; XPl lines 5–14, 44–50 in Gharib 1968: 54ff.; cf. Hinz 1976: 231–4. See too the tomb inscription of Arbinas, a dynast of Xanthos of the early 4th cent. BC: πάντα ἐμ πᾶσι πρέπων ὅσαπερ σοφοὶ ἄνδρες ἴ[σασιν] | τοξοσύνηι τε ἀρετῆι τε, ἵππων τε διώγματα εἰδ[ώς] in *SEG* 28 (1978), No. 1245, B, lines 14–15, and cf. Asheri 1983: 102–3 for a discussion of this variation on 'una formula iranica originale di chiara marca achemenide', with further references.

Cyrus assures his mother that he is well versed in justice, so much so that he has in the past been appointed by his teacher to judge others. This is unusual, for while Persian youngsters are encouraged to bring wrong-doing peers to trial, the judging and punishment of such children are normally left to their adult teachers (*Cyr.* 1. 2. 5–7). Cyrus tells Mandane that he was quite successful as a judge, but was once punished for producing an ill-judged verdict.[159] The Persian prince's case here is a provocative one, and Xenophon adroitly makes use of it to turn from the Persian interest in justice to very Greek controversies on the topic.

When a tall boy forcibly exchanged his too small coat for a smaller boy's too large one, Cyrus decided that each boy should keep the better-fitting coat. His teacher then flogged him for the verdict, explaining that it was his task to judge, not the fit of the garment, but its rightful owner. The coat had been taken by force, and since what is lawful is just and what is unlawful is violent or unjust (1. 3. 17 τὸ μὲν νόμιμον δίκαιον εἶναι, τὸ δὲ ἄνομον βίαιον),[160] Cyrus must decide a case according to the law. This question of the relation between τὸ νόμιμον and τὸ δίκαιον, the legal and the just, positive law and morality, was, of course, a topic avidly discussed by the Greeks, from the early sophists onwards, as part of the more general *nomos–physis* controversy.[161] The solution to the problem offered here by Cyrus' Persian teacher is identical to the one given by Socrates in a discussion with Hippias in the *Memorabilia* (4. 4. 12 ff.).[162] Socrates, when challenged by Hippias to define justice in positive terms, states categorically φημὶ γὰρ ἐγὼ τὸ νόμιμον δίκαιον εἶναι (4. 4. 12; cf. 13, 18, 25) and gradually wins the sophist over to acceptance of the equation.

This definition of justice has been termed 'a view held by the man in the street',[163] and Xenophon has been censured for attributing to Socrates such a simplistic and unthinking attitude, which overlooks the possibility that the laws and customs of a city may be

---

[159] It is interesting to note that in Herodotus too Cyrus, as a youth, is taken to task for a verdict he has delivered: the young 'king' punishes a recalcitrant 'subject' quite harshly and thus is brought to Astyages' notice—Hdt. 1. 114–15.

[160] For βίαιον and ἄνομον used as synonyms see *Mem.* 1. 2. 44; Pl. *Laws* 856c and the further references cited by Breitenbach 1966: 1786.

[161] See e.g. Guthrie 1969: 88 ff., 111 ff., 137 ff., 173 ff., and Kerferd 1981: 115 ff.

[162] See too the exchange between Euthydemus and Socrates at *Mem.* 4. 6. 5–6.

[163] Cf. Kerferd 1981: 115–16, who refers to Saunders's commentary on Antiphon's paraphrase of the νόμιμον–δίκαιον equation (DK 87 B 44, lines 6–11): δικαιοσύνη οὖν τὰ τῆς πόλεως νόμιμα ἐν ᾗ ἂν πολιτεύηταί τις, μὴ παραβαίνειν.

unjust.[164] But surely the point of the coat anecdote in the *Cyropaedia* is that it is not always easy to reconcile τὸ νόμιμον and τὸ δίκαιον, justice and the laws of the land. It is significant that young Cyrus— who is already a paragon of wisdom and deportment—does not simply state the νόμιμον–δίκαιον equation as proof of his expertise in matters of justice, but is shown to have erred when there was a conflict between 'natural' possession (τὸν ἁρμόττοντα . . . ἔχειν) and technical ownership (1. 3. 17 ποτέρου ὁ χιτὼν εἴη), i.e. between *physis* and *nomos*. Cyrus needs to be taught especially that the law may seem unfair or unreasonable at times, but must none the less be obeyed if justice is to prevail. This is a lesson that Xenophon himself may well have had impressed upon him by Socrates' behaviour after his trial;[165] the trial itself was sufficient evidence of the injustice of a city's laws. The advantage of obedience to the laws for both the community and the individual is, incidentally, the argument used by Socrates in the *Memorabilia* to support his contention that τὸ νόμιμον and τὸ δίκαιον are one and the same.

Cyrus tells Mandane that he is sufficiently schooled in justice, but adds that he can always turn to his grandfather if the need for further instruction arises. His mother is not reassured and hastens to explain to her son that Persian principles of justice are quite different from Median norms. Astyages has made himself master of everything in Media, whereas in Persia τὸ ἴσον ἔχειν δίκαιον νομίζεται, fair possession (i.e. due property rights) is considered just.[166] Cambyses, his wife points out, is a 'constitutional monarch', both ruling and ruled according to the precepts of his city,[167] with the law rather than his own desires as a guideline.[168] Astyages, on the other hand, is a tyrant

[164] See esp. the scathing remarks of Sinclair 1967: 90–1, 170 n. 3, and cf. Jones 1956: 11.

[165] Cf. Scharr 1919: 304–5 for a good discussion of this point.

[166] ἴσον should be understood as 'fair, just', rather than 'equal', and τὸ ἴσον ἔχειν, possessing one's fair share, is contrasted here with τὸ πλέον ἔχειν, claiming more than one's due—cf. *Cyr.* 2. 2. 20; Pl. *Gorg.* 483C, 508A; and especially Pl. *Rep.* 359C and Arist. *Nic. Eth.* 1129ᵃ32 ff. Cf. Vlastos 1981: 184–5 and Gutglueck 1988: 25–6 with n. 7, who terms the τὸ δίκαιον εἶναι = τὸ ἴσον ἔχειν equation 'the conventional Greek view of justice based on possession'.

[167] *Cyr.* 1. 3. 18 τὰ τεταγμένα μὲν ποιεῖ τῇ πόλει, τὰ τεταγμένα δὲ λαμβάνει; Xenophon describes the rule of Agesilaus (*Ages.* 2. 16) and Cyrus the Younger (*Anab.* 1. 9. 3–4) in similar fashion. Cf. Pl. *Laws* 643E, 715D and Arist. *Pol.* 1277ᵇ9, and compare Sinclair 1967: 38–9, 42, 234–5 on this ruling–ruled ideal.

[168] *Cyr.* 1. 3. 18 μέτρον δὲ αὐτῷ οὐχ ἡ ψυχὴ ἀλλ' ὁ νόμος ἐστίν. Nestle 1940–1: 32 thinks that the use of the word μέτρον here may be due to the influence of Protagoras, but for μέτρον as 'guideline' or 'measure' in Xenophon see *Lac. Pol.* 2. 1 and *Anab.* 3. 2. 21.

who rules by whim, is unfettered by laws, and is interested mainly in self-aggrandizement—or so we are led to understand, for Xenophon does not have Mandane condemn her father outright; instead she speaks in more general terms, contrasting tyranny with kingship.

We shall return to the differences between the Persian and Median constitutions below (ch. 5. 2), but the contrast drawn here between king and tyrant is, of course, hardly novel and appears elsewhere in Greek writings.[169] In a somewhat isolated passage of the *Memorabilia* (4. 6. 12) Socrates discusses various types of governments and notes that a king rules over willing subjects in accordance with the laws, while a tyrant rules without consent and according to whim. (Mandane, it should be noted, does not claim that her father's subjects are unwilling; she simply states that there are no laws to temper the tyrant's whims.) It is interesting that this discussion of justice, limited kingship, and tyranny is found in a Persian (or actually Median) setting, and we are reminded of the famous constitutional debate by three leading Persians in Herodotus (3. 80–2). The discussion between Xerxes and Demaratus, a tyrant and a (deposed) 'constitutional' monarch, in book 7 of Herodotus is an even closer parallel. Demaratus' Spartan compatriots, like the Persians of the *Cyropaedia*, are ruled by the law (Hdt. 7. 104 ἔπεστι γάρ σφι δεσπότης νόμος), while the subjects of the tyrant Xerxes, like the Medes, are under the control of a single man (7. 103 ὑπὸ μὲν γὰρ ἑνὸς ἀρχόμενοι).

It is noteworthy that it is Mandane, a Mede by birth and the daughter of the tyrant Astyages, who is so critical of her native regime. Mandane appears only in this chapter of the *Cyropaedia*, the description of her stay with Cyrus in Media, and she acts as a kind of Persian conscience, reminding Cyrus of his roots while tactfully refraining from open criticism of her father. In her very first words (1. 3. 2), she points out to her impressionable son that Median luxury is not necessarily better than Persian austerity. When young Cyrus exclaims over his grandfather's elaborate dress, coiffure, and make-up, she asks him who is more handsome, Astyages or Cambyses, and her question is meant to remind her son that Persian simplicity can be as effective as Median artifice.[170] She next speaks up at Astyages' dinner-party (1. 3. 11), diplomatically intervening after Cyrus has been too outspoken in his criticism of his grandfather's eating and

---

[169] Cf. e.g. Pl. *Pol.* 291 E; Arist. *Pol.* 1279ᵃ32 ff., 1285ᵃ18 ff., 1313ᵃ1 ff.

[170] Tatum 1989: 99–100 sees more sinister implications behind Mandane's question.

drinking habits. Cyrus' objections to Astyages' luxurious, lavish spread are those of a moderate, self-restrained Persian (see below, ch. 3. 2) and Mandane, it seems, intercedes not because she disagrees with her son's censorious attitude but because she is afraid of angering her tyrannical father. Perhaps this unspoken fear is what leads Mandane to object only mildly when her father asks for permission to have Cyrus extend his visit beyond her own (1. 3. 13); she saves her serious reservations for private discussion with her son. Even in this conversation with Cyrus, Mandane, as we have seen, praises Cambyses and his regime directly, but criticizes her father only in a roundabout way, using the impersonal expression τὸ τυραννικόν to characterize Astyages and his rule. None the less, the Mandane of the *Cyropaedia* does reject her father and his way of life, and this may be a lingering trace of her troubled relationship with Astyages in Herodotus. In Herodotus' version of the childhood of Cyrus, Mandane does not appear in the flesh and we never actually hear of her reaction to her unsuitable marriage and disappearing baby (Hdt. 1. 107–8; cf. 122), but one can well imagine her negative feelings towards her father. In the benign world of the *Cyropaedia* Mandane is married to a king and her child is separated from her here with her express permission,[171] but she none the less carefully avoids, placates, and ultimately repudiates her father, the Mede tyrant.

Young Cyrus dismisses his mother's fears that his grandfather will teach him to be excessively acquisitive.[172] Astyages, he notes, is an expert at teaching others to have less rather than more, for he has taught all the Medes to have less than himself. Mandane does not reply to her son's clever argument[173] and tacitly consents to his remaining in Media. Cyrus in fact turns out to be a good influence on his tyrannical grandfather, and curbs Astyages' tendency to trample upon the rights of others (cf. 1. 4. 14, 26).

This brief discussion between Mandane and Cyrus combines

---

[171] Cf. Due 1989: 121.

[172] *Cyr.* 1. 3. 18 τὸ πλέον οἴεσθαι χρῆναι πάντων ἔχειν; for πλεονεξία as the distinguishing feature of a tyrant, as opposed to a king, see Arist. *Pol.* 1279ᵃ32 ff., 1313ᵃ1–3; cf. Xen. *Lac. Pol.* 15. 8.

[173] Erasmus 1954: 114–15 thinks that the Cyrus of 1. 3. 18 (and throughout 1. 3) is meant to be a naïve 'Kulturkritiker', whose words were not taken seriously; he points to Xenophon's use of the word λαλεῖν, immediately after our dialogue, to characterize Cyrus' conversation (1. 4. 1 τοιαῦτα μὲν δὴ πολλὰ ἐλάλει ὁ Κῦρος). λαλεῖν need not, however, mean 'chatter', and young Cyrus, if clever and sophistic in our dialogue, does seem to be genuinely wise beyond his years at Astyages' dinner-party (below, ch. 3. 2).

several influences. The initial juxtaposition of martial prowess, horsemanship, and justice seems Persian, while Herodotus also leaves his mark on the proceedings, both in the delineation of Mandane's relationship with her father and in the comparison of constitutions. The topics of laws versus justice and kingship versus tyranny arise, as we have seen, in the *Memorabilia*, and there is in that work one further dialogue, an exchange between Alcibiades and Pericles (*Mem.* 1. 2. 40–6), which is reminiscent of *Cyr.* 1. 3. 15–18. Pericles and his ward discuss νόμος, its relation to βία, and the various kinds of constitution; young Alcibiades is argumentative and sophistic (cf. *Mem.* 1. 2. 46 ἐσοφιζόμεθα), just as young Cyrus is here. The Alcibiades–Pericles discussion is the only dialogue of the *Memorabilia* in which Socrates does not participate, and it is interesting to note that there is no real 'Socrates' or leading figure in our *Cyropaedia* dialogue: both mother and son voice didactic ideas and both echo notions attributed to Socrates in the *Memorabilia*.

4. THE ARMENIAN KING'S TRIAL: *CYR* 3. 1

In *Cyr.* 3. 1 we are told of the capture and trial of the Armenian king. The Armenians were neighbours of the Medes who were defeated in battle by Astyages, Cyrus' grandfather, and consequently had to pay tribute to the Medes, as well as supply them with troops on demand. Originally Cyaxares and Cyrus had relied upon the Armenians as allies against the Assyrian forces, but now the Armenian king, hearing of the many enemies gathering against the Medes, looks down upon Cyaxares and sends neither tribute nor troops. We learn all this from a discussion Cyrus holds with Cyaxares (*Cyr.* 2. 4. 9–17). The Persian leader, anxious to find sources of revenue, is reminded of the recalcitrant Armenians and the debt they owe. Cyrus thinks that he may be able to persuade the Armenian king to send the tribute and troops because of his childhood relationship with the Armenian's children. In addition, Cyrus hopes to win back the king's allegiance. After this conversation with Cyaxares, Cyrus takes his troops and a part of the Median cavalry to the Armenian border, pretending that they are engaged in a great hunting expedition. In this way the Persian

leader plans to catch the Armenians unawares; Cyaxares will be a
short distance away, waiting with back-up forces.[174]

Cyrus' plans proceed smoothly (*Cyr.* 2. 4. 18–23). At first he and
his men hunt near the Armenian border. He then reveals to his
officers that their real prey is the Armenian king and sends his trusted
lieutenant, Chrysantas, ahead with some of the infantry to capture
the king's mountain refuge. Cyrus himself proceeds with the rest of
the army towards the king's palace, prepared to fight and pursue the
Armenians if necessary. He sends a messenger to the Armenian king,
ordering him to send the tribute and men at once, thinking it more
friendly, we are told, to warn the king in advance before marching
against him (2. 4. 32).

The Armenian king is shocked, conscience-stricken, and frightened upon receipt of Cyrus' message. He hesitates and then rushes
about: gathering his forces, sending his family and precious possessions to the mountains, spying upon Cyrus' movements, and
organizing his men. His outburst of activity, emphasized by the
twice-repeated ἅμα μὲν . . . ἅμα δὲ . . . , is to no avail. His frightened
men scatter to their homes, his family and treasures are captured by
Chrysantas' troops in the mountains, and he himself, at a loss, flees to
a hill (3. 1. 4 ἀπορῶν ποῖ τράποιτο ἐπὶ λόφον τινὰ καταφεύγει), which
is then surrounded by Cyrus' army. The Persian leader, negotiating
through a messenger, asks the king to descend from the hill and
stand trial. Cyrus will act as judge: the gods have placed the
Armenian at his mercy to do with as he pleases (3. 1. 6 χρῆσθαί σοι ὅ
τι βούλοιτο). We are immediately reminded of an omen Cyrus saw
just as he left for Armenia: an eagle swooped down, seized a fleeing
hare, struck it, and carried it off to a hill to do with as he pleased
(2. 4. 19 ἐπὶ λόφον τινὰ . . . ἐχρῆτο τῇ ἄγρᾳ ὅ τι ἤθελεν).[175] The
Armenian is reluctant to face a trial in which the Persian leader will
be the judge, but he has no real choice. He descends from the hill and
is carried off by Cyrus' forces (*Cyr.* 3. 1. 1–6).

Tigranes, the elder son of the Armenian king and Cyrus' childhood companion, now opportunely arrives on the scene, returning
from a sojourn abroad. He is both brave—unlike most Armenians
(cf. e.g. 3. 2. 8)—and a loyal friend of Cyrus. Had he been present

[174] Cyrus, when formulating this plan, may have remembered an incident in his
youth, when the Assyrian prince turned a hunting expedition into a foray against the
Medes (*Cyr.* 1. 4. 17).
[175] Compare the famous omen of Aes. *Ag.* 111 ff. This is a rare instance in the *Cyr.* of
an omen foreshadowing a subsequent success of the Persians.

when Cyrus and his troops overran his country, Tigranes would have had to choose between fighting against an old friend in defence of his country and submitting meekly to the dictates of a (well-loved) outsider, but Xenophon neatly solves the dilemma by removing Tigranes from Armenia at the crucial time, thus dissociating the prince from his father's actions. Tigranes, when he learns of his family's fortune, bursts into tears, but Cyrus, preserving a façade of judicial impartiality, does not comfort or welcome his old friend: he simply notes that Tigranes has returned in time for the king's trial.

Cyrus now sets the scene for the trial itself, summoning Persian, Mede, and Armenian leaders to attend the proceedings. Even the women, seated in their carriages, are allowed to listen. When all is organized to the Persian leader's satisfaction, the trial begins: Cyrus deliberately arranges a dramatic setting, serving not only as judge but also as stage manager. Thus, while the trial was originally offered to the Armenian king as an alternative to being disposed of at Cyrus' pleasure, we begin to sense that the Persian is using the trial for that very purpose.

Cyrus is well qualified to serve as judge. Like all Persians who go through their country's educational curriculum, he has learnt justice from an early age, and as a boy practised bringing charges against his peers (1. 2. 6–7). We have already seen that the young Cyrus was considered an expert in justice and was appointed by his teacher to judge others. More generally, the exercise of judicial functions by a ruler was widespread among ancient peoples—Greeks, Persians, etc.[176] In Xenophon's time Athens had long gone over to a jury system, with a single magistrate found only in preliminary hearings, while in Persia we hear of a number of βασιλήιοι δικασταί sitting in judgement together;[177] but a local ruler, too, could mete out punishments single-handedly, as Xenophon himself testifies (*Anab.* 1. 9. 13).

The trial opens with Cyrus advising the king in very strong terms to tell the truth. Lying, he says, is most hateful, and if the Armenian is caught in a lie he will have only himself to blame for suffering the most dire consequences. Cyrus' opening words on truth place him

---

[176] See Bonner and Smith 1930: 30, who cite Hdt. 1. 14 (Phrygians), 1. 96–7 (Deioces the Mede, judge-turned-ruler), and 2. 129 (Egyptians) among the sources. For the early Greeks see MacDowell 1978: 13–16, 23.

[177] Cf. Lewis 1977: 22–3 with n. 126, who distinguishes between the king's (seven) counsellors and the various numbers of βασιλήιοι δικασταί mentioned in Hdt. 3. 14, 3. 31, 5. 25, 7. 194; Plut. *Art.* 29. 8–12; Aelian *VH* 1. 34; Diod. 15. 10–11.

squarely in the Persian tradition. Herodotus tells us that the Persians abhorred lying,[178] and this is corroborated by the hymns (*Gathas*) of Zoroaster himself, where *Asha* (Truth) and *Druj* (Lie) represent the two antithetical forces of good and evil, righteousness and impiety.[179] Darius in his *Res Gestae*, the Behistun Inscription, equates rebellion against his empire with Lie and states that he himself is a friend of Truth,[180] while in the *Anabasis* Xenophon describes the importance Cyrus the Younger attached to keeping his word (1. 9. 7; cf. *Cyr.* 8. 8. 2–3).

But Cyrus' emphasis on the need for truth may reflect another tradition as well—that of a solemn oath taken by the parties to a dispute on the overall truth of their statements. In ancient Greece the entire trial once consisted of an exculpatory or evidentiary oath taken by the accused, and this practice survived down to the classical period in Gortyn. In classical Athens litigants were required to take an oath at the preliminary hearing before a magistrate, the ἀνάκρισις, and at the trial itself witnesses could be required to confirm their statements by oath as well.[181] Darius claims in his tomb inscription that he always listens to both parties to an argument before passing judgement, and his son Xerxes echoes this claim, which has been taken as evidence that in Achaemenid judicial procedure litigants took a solemn oath before a verdict was delivered.[182] In effect the Armenian king is taking such an oath here. He knows that the penalty for lying will be extreme (3. 1. 9 τὰ ἔσχατα παθεῖν; cf. 3. 1. 12), and fatalistically promises to tell the truth, despite the likely consequences of his words.

The first part of the king's trial consists of a series of questions and replies, an interrogation of the Armenian king by Cyrus, who acts as prosecutor as well as judge. The Persian leader's first questions establish the facts of the case. The Armenian admits that he was defeated in battle by Astyages and promised to pay tribute, supply an army when required, and refrain from building fortifications; he

---

[178] Hdt. 1. 138 αἴσχιστον δὲ αὐτοῖσι τὸ ψεύδεσθαι νενόμισται. Truth-telling is, according to Herodotus' famous statement, one of the three things that Persian children are taught (1. 136).

[179] See Zaehner 1961: 36, 40, 60–1 and Hirsch 1985: 18–19 with nn. on 156–7.

[180] Behistun Inscription: DB 1. 30–5, 4. 4–31, 36–40. See also How and Wells on Hdt. 1. 136. 2; Zaehner 1961: 156; Frye 1976: 112–13.

[181] Cf. Jones 1956: 136; Bonner and Smith 1930: 128; Harrison 1971: 99, 139–40.

[182] DNb 21–4; XPl 23–6. The Xerxes inscription allows scholars to emend an error in the parallel Darius inscription, so that Kent's translation is revised by Gharib 1968: 56, 64–5 and Hinz 1976: 231–3; cf. Frye 1976: 113.

replies with a simple 'yes' to Cyrus' questions. When he is then asked why he has not kept his word, the Armenian's reply is longer: he longed for freedom both for himself and for his children (3. 1. 10).[183]

Cyrus does not care to discuss the joys of freedom with the king, but points out the duties of a vassal instead. (We can assume that the historical Cyrus, who rebelled against his Mede grandfather and gave the Persians their freedom, had rather different views on this subject.) The Armenian king himself—Cyrus suggests and the king immediately confirms—would punish a subject who had rebelled against him. The Armenian, questioned closely by his Persian judge, now admits point by point that he would replace a wrong-doing commander, deprive him of his fortune, and actually put him to death if he joined the king's enemies. κατακαίνω, the king declares, implicitly condemning himself to death: he is under oath and prefers to die telling the truth rather than being caught in a lie (3. 1. 11–12).

At this last admission the king's family, fearing all is lost, give way to their grief. The king's son—presumably the younger Sabaris rather than his older brother Tigranes—tears off his tiara and rends his robes, while the women present lament aloud and lacerate their cheeks. Cyrus orders them to be silent, again giving us the impression that he is carefully orchestrating this trial scene. The Persian judge has one final question to ask of his captive. How is Cyrus to apply the Armenian's verdict to the king's own situation (3. 1. 13 τὰ μὲν δὴ σὰ δίκαια ταῦτα ... ἡμῖν δὲ τί συμβουλεύεις ἐκ τούτων ποιεῖν;)? The Armenian is silent, at a loss (3. 1. 13 ἀπορῶν)[184] whether to advise Cyrus to put him to death or to be inconsistent and recommend a different course of action. From this moment on the king remains silent and his part in the trial is over.[185]

The similarities between Cyrus' cross-examination of the Armenian king and Socratic ἔλεγχος are apparent.[186] The exchange between the Persian and the Armenian is in the form of questions and answers, with Cyrus, the prosecutor, asking leading questions

---

[183] For the close association in Greek eyes between freedom and the ability to dominate others—which is how the Armenian king seems to understand freedom here—see Larsen 1962; cf. Avery 1972: 532–3.

[184] Such ἀπορία is an outstanding feature of the Armenian king from the very moment he appears on stage in the *Cyr.*—see 3. 1. 4, 6, 14, and cf. Tatum 1989: 136–8.

[185] The Armenian king's role in the subsequent discussion between Tigranes and Cyrus is like that of the silent, third parties found in some of the *Mem.* dialogues—cf. above, sect. 1 at n. 16.

[186] Cf. e.g. Hirzel 1895: 168; Luccioni 1947: 227 n. 162.

and holding the upper hand. His respondent answers briefly and virtually against his will, disliking the conclusions he is forced to draw: eventually, the captured king is reduced to a state of *aporia*. Cyrus also introduces a hypothetical case in order to have the Armenian judge himself, thus using the Socratic device of applied analogies found so frequently in the *Memorabilia*. Here, of course, the relation between the Persian leader's 'hypothetical' questions and the Armenian's immediate plight is apparent from the start. While the facts of the case and the king's excuse for his behaviour could have been set forth in speeches (by Cyrus and the Armenian king respectively), the most effective part of this scene, the Armenian's progressively harsher verdict on his own actions, could only have been achieved through a series of questions and answers.

Such Socratic methods of investigation are found in other cross-examinations in the *Cyropaedia* as well. Cyrus' reconciliation scene with Cyaxares (5. 5. 13 ff.; see below, sect. 5) is the most outstanding instance, but there are several other, less formal 'Socratic' interrogations in the *Cyropaedia*.[187] In general, the trial or cross-examination scenes found in Xenophon's non-Socratic works—such as Orontas' trial in the *Anabasis* (1. 6. 4–10) or Dercylidas' interrogation of Meidias in the *Hellenica* (3. 1. 25–6)—are usually those sections that strike commentators as being peculiarly Socratic.[188] A closer look at the trial scenes in Xenophon will help us to understand why this is so.

Beginning with the *Anabasis*, we find that the trial of the Persian traitor Orontas was conducted in a dramatic setting, with 3,000 Greek hoplites surrounding Cyrus the Younger's tent, where the proceedings were held in camera. Those present included Cyrus and his advisers—seven distinguished Persian nobles—and Clearchus, as representative of the Greeks (*Anab.* 1. 6. 4–7). Cyrus, the prosecutor and chief judge, opens the trial with a short speech, explaining that he wants to do justice to Orontas. He then reviews the facts of the case. Orontas, although under Cyrus' command, had, at the instigation of Artaxerxes, attacked him at Sardis. He was defeated there by Cyrus, and the two then exchanged pledges of friendship. Cyrus now turns to question Orontas directly (*Anab.* 1. 6. 7–8). The questions put by Cyrus are of the familiar 'question and reply' kind: they are

[187] See *Cyr.* 1. 6. 9, 2. 1. 2 ff., 8. 4. 9–10, and cf. 1. 6. 12–14.
[188] See e.g. Hirzel 1895: 161, 167–8, 172; Luccioni 1953: 135–6, 146; Hartmann 1889: 85.

brief, straightforward questions that can generally be answered with a simple 'yes' or 'no'. Orontas is made to admit[189] each of his past misdeeds, and further agrees, in response to the Persian ruler's questions, that he has not been wronged by Cyrus in any way but has himself sinned against him. Finally, in answer to Cyrus' last question ('Could you still possibly be my brother's enemy and my loyal friend?'), Orontas is, in essence, forced to condemn himself ('Even if I were to be your friend, you could not believe me'). Cyrus then turns to the others and asks Clearchus for his verdict. Clearchus recommends the death penalty and the others present concur: Orontas is taken by his belt and condemned to death. This sample of Persian justice,[190] in particular Cyrus the Younger's cross-examination, which uses short, sharp questions and elicits the interlocutor's agreement, step by step, is very much like a Socratic elenchus.

Another cross-examination in the *Anabasis* is conducted by Xenophon himself (*Anab.* 5. 8. 1 ff.). Xenophon has been accused of ὕβρις or, more specifically, of beating several men without due cause. The Athenian commander interrogates his first accuser, a mule-driver, interspersing a series of short, factual questions (cf. 5. 8. 2–6) into a longer description of the circumstances of the incident. The mule-driver retorts sharply to some of the questions (5. 8. 6, 11) and barely answers others (5. 8. 5), and is a more vocal opponent than either Orontas or the Armenian king (or, for that matter, a typical interlocutor of Xenophon's Socrates). None the less, it is interesting to find cross-examination as part of the judicial procedure here.[191] When Xenophon is called upon to defend himself on another occasion, he chooses to do so by means of a long continuous speech—perhaps because he faces a large body of accusers (5. 7. 1 ff.).[192]

Turning to the *Hellenica*, we find two trials which consist solely of a

---

[189] Cf. *Anab.* 1. 6. 7 ὡς αὐτὸς σὺ ὁμολογεῖς; 1. 6. 7 καὶ ταῦθ᾽ ὡμολόγει Ὀρόντας; 1. 6. 8. ὁμολογεῖς οὖν.

[190] If the *Anab.* account is indeed such a sample. Clearchus was Xenophon's (direct or indirect) source for the trial (*Anab.* 1. 6. 5), and one wonders how accurate Clearchus' own account could have been. Were the proceedings translated to him bit by bit or did Cyrus simply summarize the case for him at the end? In addition, Clearchus—or Xenophon—may have altered particulars of the trial considerably in the retelling.

[191] See Nussbaum 1967: 24–5 on judicial practices in the army of the *Anab.*

[192] In a third 'courtroom' scene in the *Anab.* (7. 2. 23–8) Xenophon interrogates Medosades, the emissary sent to him by the Thracian king Seuthes, in the presence of the king himself. Medosades is, for all intents and purposes, a witness whom Xenophon cross-examines, in friendly fashion, in order to establish his case.

speech by the accuser followed by a counter-speech or defence by the accused. These trials—the case of Critias vs. Theramenes (*Hell.* 2. 3. 24–34, 35–49) and that of the Theban officials against one of Euphron's murderers (7. 3. 6, 7–11)—do not include any interrogations or cross-examinations. Euryptolemus tried to arrange a proper, separate trial for each of the generals of Arginusae—with one third of the day set aside for the prosecution, one third for the defence, and one third for the deliberations of the jury—but the generals were condemned *en masse* with no real trial (*Hell.* 1. 7. 16 ff.). Another trial, that of the Spartan Cinadon, is reported only indirectly in the *Hellenica*, but the wording of the passage suggests that it was in essence an interrogation, in which Cinadon was forced to confess his crime and reveal his co-conspirators.[193] Xenophon does not report the proceedings of another famous trial at Sparta, that of Sphodrias, but since the accused was not present he could hardly have been interrogated (*Hell.* 5. 4. 24).

Dercylidas' cross-examination of Meidias (*Hell.* 3. 1. 24–8) takes place not in a courtroom setting, but while awaiting dinner. None the less, it is in fact a trial of one vanquished, at the hands of his conqueror (as with the Armenian king of the *Cyropaedia*). Dercylidas begins with the suggestion that he and Meidias examine the situation jointly in an attempt to do justice—ἐγὼ καὶ σὺ τὰ δίκαια πρὸς ἀλλήλους καὶ διασκεψώμεθα καὶ ποιήσωμεν (*Hell.* 3. 1. 24)—and this invitation to embark upon a joint investigation immediately reminds us of Socrates (cf. below, sect. 5). Dercylidas then begins to question Meidias, prefacing his first question with the request εἰπέ μοι (3. 1. 25; cf. 26), just as Xenophon often has Socrates open his interrogations: here too Meidias' replies will be used against him. Dercylidas' questions are short, factual ones meant to establish the limits of Meidias' property. When the interrogation turns to more uncomfortable topics (Meidias' illegitimate claims to property owned by Mania), Meidias evidently falls silent, for others present, the men of Scepsis, reply in his stead. Dercylidas' final verdict, termed by him δικαιότατον (cf. 3. 1. 22, 24), is based directly on the answers to his leading questions.

Why do these scenes of legal cross-examination in Xenophon seem especially influenced by Socrates? A brief comparison with

---

[193] *Hell.* 3. 3. 11 ὡς δ᾽ ἀνήχθη ὁ Κινάδων καὶ ἠλέγχετο καὶ ὡμολόγει πάντα καὶ τοὺς συνειδότας ἔλεγε, τέλος αὐτὸν ἤροντο . . . ὁ δ᾽ ἀπεκρίνατο; compare the summary of Ismenias' trial at *Hell.* 5. 2. 35–6.

Herodotus on this point is illuminating. Herodotus' history contains several scenes of investigation and cross-examination, and there is not a single instance of a trial involving speech and counter-speech.[194] Yet the interrogations in Herodotus do not remind us in the least of Socrates' questions in the *Memorabilia*. Generally the cross-examiner in Herodotus is a powerful figure, often a ruler (e.g. Astyages at 1. 115 and 1. 117, Darius at 3. 130, and Prexaspes at 3. 63), so that there is not even the pretence that the enquiry is a joint one between equals. Often, too, Herodotus' interrogator asks only one question, to which his respondent replies at some length, so that the exchanges are not of the 'question and reply' kind. These instances of interrogations in Herodotus show us that such cross-examinations are not necessarily, in themselves, particularly Socratic.

Why, then, do Xenophon's cross-examinations seem so Socratic? One explanation is that both Socrates' ἔλεγχοι or question-and-answer interrogations and the trial scenes in Xenophon share a common influence—the various kinds of legal questioning used in the courts of Socrates' time. A closer look at actual legal procedures will show us that Socrates' methods of investigation, particularly his use of 'question-and-reply' interrogations, strongly resemble the forensic questioning regularly found in Athenian legal processes.[195] Xenophon's cross-examinations, even if directly influenced by Socrates' methods of interrogation, probably reflect this legal influence as well.

There were three different types of forensic questioning practised in Socrates' Athens: (1) the magistrate's questioning of the plaintiff and defendant and their questioning of one another at the ἀνάκρισις, the pre-trial hearing; (2) the ἐρώτησις, i.e. the litigants' interrogation of one another at the actual trial; and (3) the examination of witnesses at the trial. Let us examine the evidence for each of these in turn.

At the ἀνάκρισις, the initial hearing of a case before a magistrate, proceedings were, it seems, entirely oral in Socrates' time.[196] The magistrate, in his attempt to clarify the issue at hand and determine

---

[194] There are, however, several instances of paired speeches in other contexts—cf. Hdt. 7. 9–10, 8. 140–2, 9. 26–7, and Heni 1976: 19–20.

[195] Scholars have not paid much attention to this similarity; cf., however, Lloyd 1979: 86, 252–4.

[196] On the ἀνάκρισις see Harrison 1971: 94–9; Bonner and Smith 1930: 289–93; Carawan 1983: 211–12. Written pleas had to be handed in by the litigants as part of the initial proceedings only later, in the second or third decade of the 4th cent., possibly starting in the year 378/7 BC; cf. Calhoun 1919 and Bonner and Smith 1930: 353 ff.

whether the case was admissible, would question both parties to a dispute, as the very name ἀνάκρισις implies.[197] The litigants would also question one another. There is no interrogation by a magistrate extant—possibly because the proceedings were oral—but we do have one sample of the questions put by a plaintiff to defendants at an ἀνάκρισις at Isaeus 6. 12–13. There the plaintiff asks who the mother of the two boys claiming an estate is.[198] The defendants cannot answer at first, but are then ordered to do so in accordance with the law καὶ τοῦ ἄρχοντος κελεύοντος ἀποκρίνασθαι κατὰ τὸν νόμον (6. 12). The plaintiff then continues to investigate the family background, asking further questions about the boys' maternal grandfather (who he is and whether he is alive or not).

Two main points emerge from this sample of an ἀνάκρισις: (1) the legal contestants are compelled to answer questions posed by their opponents (and the magistrate), and (2) the questions asked are short factual ones, requiring brief answers. The first of these points is confirmed by another passage from Isaeus, in which a litigant tells at his trial of a point (damaging to his case) which he was forced to concede at the pre-trial hearing: ἠνάγκασμαι μὲν οὖν, ὦ ἄνδρες ... ἐν τῇ ἀνακρίσει ... προσγράψασθαι (10. 2). A passage in Andocides which contains an imaginary cross-examination at an ἀνάκρισις serves to confirm the second of our points. The questions supposedly put to Andocides[199] are again short and circumstantial, and all but the final, rhetorical question is answered by Andocides with a simple 'no'.

The second form of questioning regularly found in fifth-century Athens was the ἐρώτησις or interrogation of one legal opponent by another at the trial itself.[200] Here too it is compulsory for the litigants to answer each other's questions,[201] and the short exchanges found in

---

[197] Cf. Isaeus 5. 32; Dem. 48. 31; Arist. *Ath. Pol.* 56. 6; Harpocration s.v. ἀνάκρισις, etc.

[198] Isaeus 6. 12 τίς εἴη αὐτῶν μήτηρ καὶ ὅτου θυγάτηρ;

[199] And. 1. 101 εἰπέ μοι, ὦ Ἀνδοκίδη, ἦλθες ... καὶ ἐπετείχισας ...;—οὐκ ἔγωγε.— τί δέ; ἔτεμες ... καὶ ἐλήσω ...;—οὐ δῆτα.—οὐδ' ἐναυμάχησας ... οὐδὲ συγκατέσκαψας ... οὐδὲ συγκατέλυσας ... οὐδὲ βίᾳ κατῆλθες ...;—οὐδὲ τούτων πεποίηκα οὐδέν.

[200] On the ἐρώτησις see Harrison 1971: 138, 162; Bonner and Smith 1938: 8, 122; Latte 1920: 16 n. 27. Carawan 1983 argues for widespread use of ἐρώτησις in 4th-cent. courts. Aristotle in the *Rhetoric* (1418^b39 ff.) includes advice on the conduct of an ἐρώτησις, and this would seem to show the 'importance attached to these interrogatories' (Bonner and Smith 1938: 122). Cf. too the discussion of ἐρώτησις in the *Rhetorica ad Alexandrum* attributed to Anaximenes (1444^b8 ff.; Spengel–Hammer i. 94–5).

[201] Dem. 46. 10 τοῖν ἀντιδίκοιν ἐπάναγκες εἶναι ἀποκρίνασθαι ἀλλήλοις τὸ ἐρωτώμενον; cf. Socrates' words to Meletus at Pl. *Apol.* 25 D: ἀπόκρινου ὦ ἀγαθέ. καὶ γὰρ ὁ νόμος κελεύει ἀποκρίνεσθαι.

Lysias 12. 25 and 22. 5 are perhaps the most authentic examples of
such interrogations to have survived. They indicate that the questions
asked were, again, generally brief, polar ('yes or no?', 'A or B?'), and
related to the facts of the case. The questions are leading ones and the
respondent is left very little scope for argument or elaboration in his
reply. Often the replies given are quite brief and echo phrases used in
the question.[202] The other instances of such interrogations in the
orators, while not actual ones—either because the speaker provides
both questions and answers[203] or because the opponent's answers are
not recorded[204]—also exhibit very similar features.

There are several more literary examples of an ἐρώτησις, such as
the interrogation of Meletus by Socrates in both Plato (Apol. 24 c ff.)
and Xenophon (Apol. 19–21), and the questioning of Orestes by the
Erinyes in Aeschylus (Eum. 585 ff.). In Plato some of Socrates' questions seem quite long because they include a lengthy preface, but the
actual questions posed by the philosopher are consistently polar and
concise, and Meletus' responses are correspondingly brief. It is interesting to note that this is not true of the ἐρώτησις in Xenophon. His
Socrates uses long rhetorical questions, which are not a choice
between alternatives, and his Meletus answers neither concisely nor
to the point. Similarly, in the mock beauty competition between
Socrates and Critobulus in Xenophon's Symposium (5. 1–10), which
is supposedly conducted along legal lines,[205] neither the philosopher's questions nor Critobulus' answers are of the spare legal kind.

The Erinyes' examination of Orestes in Aeschylus (Eum. 585 ff.) is,
on the other hand, very like a judicial ἐρώτησις. The Furies question
Orestes, point by point, on the circumstances of Clytemnestra's death,
and the line-by-line exchange between Orestes and the chorus—the
tragic stichomythia—is admirably suited to the question-and-reply
format of legal interrogation.[206] This is true of Athena's interrogation of

---

[202] Cf. e.g. Lysias 12. 25 ἦσθα . . .;—ἦν.—πότερον συνηγόρευες . . . ἢ ἀντέλεγες;—
ἀντέλεγον.—ἵνα μὴ ἀποθάνωμεν;—ἵνα μὴ ἀποθάνητε.

[203] See Dinarchus 1. 83 (ἔγραψας . . .;—ἔγραψας.—ἐγένετο . . .;—ἐγένετο.—τεθνᾶσι
. . .;—τεθνᾶσι.) and cf. Dem. 43. 48–9.

[204] Isaeus 11. 5; cf. Lysias 13. 30, 32.

[205] Cf. Symp. 5. 2 εἰς ἀνάκρισιν τοίνυν σε . . . πρῶτον τῆς δίκης καλοῦμαι and the
references to κριταί (5. 1, 9) and their votes (5. 10).

[206] Cf. Eum. 585–8:

> CHORUS: πολλαὶ μέν ἐσμεν, λέξομεν δὲ συντόμως.
> ἔπος δ' ἀμείβου πρὸς ἔπος ἐν μέρει τιθείς·
> τὴν μητέρ' εἰπὲ πρῶτον εἰ κατέκτονας.
> ORESTES: ἔκτεινα . . .

the chorus at the pre-trial ἀνάκρισις (*Eum.* 415 ff.) as well. Another literary interrogation, the questions put to Odysseus by Palamedes in Gorgias (*Pal.* 22–6), is another good instance of the kind of questions asked at an ἐρώτησις, for all that Odysseus' replies are missing and supplied rhetorically by his questioner. Finally, mention should be made of what is perhaps the shortest ἐρώτησις on record, the single life-and-death question put to the Plataeans by the Spartan judges at their trial: εἴ τι Λακεδαιμονίους καὶ τοὺς συμμάχους ἀγαθὸν ἐν τῷ πολέμῳ δεδρακότες εἰσίν (Thuc. 3. 68; cf. 3. 52). A negative response by the Plataeans led to their immediate execution.

The last of the three types of forensic questioning practised in Athens was the interrogation of witnesses at a trial. As with the proceedings at the ἀνάκρισις, written affidavits replaced the earlier oral testimony some time at the beginning of the fourth century.[207] In Socrates' time, however, witnesses at a trial were examined orally. There is only one instance of the cross-examination of a witness to be found in the Attic orators, Andocides 1. 14. The questions put by Andocides to Diognetus are again short, factual ones and the answers given are simple affirmations.[208] Literary sources provide further evidence for such 'question-and-reply' interrogation of witnesses. In Aristophanes' *Wasps* (962–6) the cheese-grater is examined in just this fashion by Bdelykleon in the dog trial scene,[209] and this is surely a parody of actual forensic practices. Sophocles' *Oedipus Rex*, while far removed from the courtroom, contains several cross-examinations: Creon (99 ff., 555 ff.), Jocasta (732 ff.), the Corinthian messenger (1017 ff.), and the shepherd (1115 ff.) are all questioned by Oedipus, and the king's interrogation of this last witness seems particularly influenced by forensic forms:

> OEDIPUS: δεῦρό μοι φώνει βλέπων
> ὅσ' ἄν σ' ἐρωτῶ. Λαΐου ποτ' ἦσθα σύ;
> SHEPHERD: ἦ . . .
>
> (1121–3)[210]

Witnesses were not always examined by means of leading questions;

---

[207] On witnesses in general see Harrison 1971: 136–44; Bonner and Smith 1930: 353–62; Bonner and Smith 1938: 123 ff.; MacDowell 1978: 242, 274 nn. 544–5. For the change-over from oral to written testimony see the references quoted above, n. 196.

[208] ἦσθα . . .;—ἦν.—οἶσθα . . .;—οἶδα . . .—ἔστι ταῦτα . . .;—ἔστι ταῦτα.

[209] ἀπόκριναι σαφῶς, εἰ μὴ κατέκνησας . . . φησὶ κατακνῆσαι.

[210] Cf. Knox 1957: 19, 91, 95, 231 nn. 180–2. Greiffenhagen 1966, esp. 162–3, has a more technical analysis of the legal aspects of the play.

they were allowed at times to testify freely, telling their stories at some length in their own words.[211] The stricter form of interrogation, using leading questions which required only 'yes' or 'no' for an answer, may have been used only when a litigant called upon a hostile witness to testify on his behalf: this would allow a legal contestant greater control over the evidence elicited, as with the questioning of an opponent at the ἀνάκρισις or trial.

In sum, both direct and indirect (i.e. literary) sources indicate that all three types of legal questioning regularly found in fifth-century Athens closely resemble—in form if not in content—the 'question-and-reply' interrogations particularly associated with Socrates. In all likelihood it is the converse that is true: that is, it is more correct to say that Socrates' questioning technique is very like—or actually modelled upon—such forensic interrogations.

While scholars generally overlook the relationship between legal questioning and Socrates' methods, they often mention the influence of sophistic eristic upon the philosopher,[212] and it is worth while to note the strong parallels between legal questioning and eristic contests. Plato's *Euthydemus* is the best illustration of what an eristic competition was like,[213] and it is probably not a coincidence that the brothers Euthydemus and Dionysodorus, who have only recently acquired their skill in eristic (Pl. *Euthyd.* 272 A), have long been known as experts in legal wrangling (272 A; 273 C). In an eristic contest, as in a legal one, the object is to win—in this case by refuting one's opponent (272 A; cf. 275 E) and reducing him to ἀπορία, to silence (275 D, 286 B). The practitioner of eristic always asks the questions, while his opponent always responds and they may not exchange roles (275 C, 287 C–D, 295 A–B, etc.); this is, of course, true of forensic cross-examinations as well. As in legal examinations, the questions asked in an eristic contest are framed in such a way that the respondent must choose between a pair of opposite alternatives, or simply answer 'yes' or 'no' (cf. Arist. *Soph. El.* 175[b]8–9); he may not add to or clarify his answer in any way (Pl. *Euthyd.* 296 A–B). In

---

[211] Cf. And. 1. 69 αὐτοὺς κάλει . . . ἄριστα γὰρ ἂν εἰδότες τὰ γενόμενα λέγοιεν εἰς τούτους . . . μέχρι τούτου ἀναβήσονται καὶ λέξουσιν ὑμῖν ἕως ἂν ἀκροᾶσθαι βούλησθε, and cf. Lysias 17. 2.

[212] For sophistic eristic vs. Socrates' methods see e.g. Guthrie 1975: 248, 275; Gulley 1968: 22–37; Kerferd 1981: 32 ff.; Thesleff 1967: 35–6.

[213] Keulen 1971: 62–73 has a very useful discussion of eristic; he considers the *Euthydemus* the 'Grundlage' for our knowledge of sophistic eristic and terms Aristotle's *Sophistici Elenchi* an 'Ergänzung und Korrektiv' (62); see too Hawtrey 1981.

addition, the eristic's partner is compelled to respond to his interrogator's questions (297 B; cf. 276 E), again reminding us of the
situation in a courtroom. The eristic contest, with its well-defined
rules, has, then, much in common with the procedures of forensic
questioning, and the development of its methods and regulations was
probably influenced by legal practice. Socrates, in his interrogations,
seems to incorporate both the legal and the eristic influences, while
Xenophon's courtroom scenes, in turn, probably owe something
both to Socrates' cross-examinations and to actual legal practices. In
other words, the trial or courtroom scenes in Xenophon seem
Socratic because of their forensic context: Socrates' own manner of
questioning has much in common with courtroom techniques.

Returning to the Armenian king's trial, we find that Tigranes asks
permission to speak in place of his father, who has been reduced to
silence by Cyrus' last question. Tigranes and Cyrus used to hunt
together as boys (*Cyr.* 3. 1. 7, 14; cf. 2. 4. 15), but the Persian leader
has not acknowledged their old bond so far. Now, however, recalling
that Tigranes used to spend time with a certain sophist whom he
admired (3. 1. 14 σοφιστήν τινα αὐτῷ συνόντα καὶ θαυμαζόμενον ὑπὸ
τοῦ Τιγράνου), Cyrus is very eager to hear what his Armenian friend
has to say and bids him speak freely. Thus, in the middle of a serious
trial of a captured rebellious subject, Cyrus is eager to engage in a bit
of sophistic argument; this is a hint of the Persian leader's real
attitude towards the court martial he arranges. Cyrus enters into this
discussion not because he needs advice, but out of curiosity and a
love of rhetorical argument.

It is rather unexpected to find a sophist and his enthusiastic pupil
here, and later (3. 1. 38–40) we learn even more surprising details
about Tigranes' teacher, who is, it seems, a kind of Socrates in
Armenia.[214] He was a noble man (3. 1. 38 καλὸς κἀγαθός), but, as
Tigranes tells Cyrus in the presence of his father, the Armenian king
had him put to death for corrupting his son (3. 1. 38 διαφθείρειν
αὐτὸν ἔφη ἐμέ). We are, of course, immediately reminded of the
execution of Socrates and the charge brought against the philosopher
(*Mem.* 1. 1. 1 ἀδικεῖ Σωκράτης ... τοὺς νέους διαφθείρων; cf. Pl.
Apol. 24 B). The Armenian king hastens to justify his action to Cyrus,
explaining that he was jealous of the sophist because Tigranes

[214] So e.g. Hirzel 1895: 168 calls the Armenian sophist 'eine Kopie des Sokrates'.
This identification goes back to a 1568 commentary on the *Cyr.* by Brodaeus; see
Gaiser 1977: 85.

regarded him more highly than his own father. The sophist had
alienated Tigranes' affections and had to be executed, the king
explains, just as a husband kills a man caught in adultery with his
wife, not because he has made her more lustful[215] but because he has
taken away her love for her husband (*Cyr.* 3. 1. 39). Socrates too is
accused of causing young people to admire him more than anyone
else (*Mem.* 1. 2. 52), and in Xenophon Meletus expressly says that
Socrates' νέων διαφθοραί consist of persuading young men to obey
him rather than their parents (Xen. *Apol.* 19–20; cf. *Mem.* 1. 2. 49).
(We shall see below that Cyrus is also made to face the same charge of
alienation of affections.)

In view of these points of resemblance between Socrates and
Tigranes' teacher, it is interesting to note the way Cyrus reacts to the
execution of the sophist. When he learns of his death, the Persian
exclaims φεῦ τοῦ ἀνδρός (*Cyr.* 3. 1. 39), but after hearing the king's
explanation Cyrus says to the Armenian ruler ὦ Ἀρμένιε, ἀνθρώπινά
μοι δοκεῖς ἁμαρτεῖν (3. 1. 40)[216] and urges Tigranes to forgive his
father. How are we to interpret Cyrus' remarks? Are they a reflection of
Xenophon's own attitude towards the death of Socrates, many years
after the event? One scholar suggests that the Persian leader's attitude
here indicates that Xenophon has now, at the time of the *Cyropaedia*'s
writing, pardoned the Athenians, while Tigranes is a fictional version
of his younger self.[217] Commentators see Cyrus' call for forgiveness as
an attempt on Xenophon's part to re-establish good relations with his
fellow Athenians at about the time that his banishment was revoked.[218]
Since we know neither the exact date of the composition of the
Cyropaedia nor the date of Xenophon's recall from exile (see above, ch.
1. 3), we cannot verify such an assumption. It is probably wrong simply
to identify Cyrus as the mouthpiece of his author here. Xenophon may
be demonstrating a greater understanding or forgiveness of Socrates'
execution, but, by introducing the Armenian sophist, he does not
allow any of his readers to forget the philosopher or his end.

[215] Reading ὡς ἀκρατεστέρας ποιοῦντας at 3. 1. 39 for the crux ἀμαθεστέρας in
Marchant's OCT edition; cf. Erbse 1960: 150–2 vs. Gaiser 1977: 79.
[216] Cf. the Persian leader's similar attitude towards human frailty elsewhere—*Cyr.*
5. 4. 19, 6. 1. 37.
[217] So Schwartz 1943: 69–70, who says (of the sophist, Tigranes, and the Armenian
king respectively): 'Jeder erkennt Sokrates, Xenophon und das attische Volk auf den
ersten Blick.' Schwartz thinks that the scene allows a rare glimpse into the soul 'des
jungen, des verbannten und des begnadigten Xenophon'.
[218] Thus Gaiser 1977: 88–92, who makes much of Xenophon's almost Christian
attitude of forgiveness. See too Chroust 1957: 260 n. 479 and Luccioni 1953: 146 n. 2.

The σοφιστής of the *Cyropaedia* shares not only Socrates' fate but some of the philosopher's vocabulary and concerns as well. Before he was executed, the sophist told Tigranes not to be angry with his father, for the king was acting out of ignorance, not maliciousness (οὐ γὰρ κακονοίᾳ . . . ἀλλ᾽ ἀγνοίᾳ). Since the Armenian king's wrong-doing was due to ignorance, it must be considered involuntary: ὁπόσα δὲ ἀγνοίᾳ ἄνθρωποι ἐξαμαρτάνουσι πάντ᾽ ἀκούσια ταῦτ᾽ ἔγωγε νομίζω (*Cyr.* 3. 1. 38). The sophist's statement sounds like a variation on—or misunderstanding of—the famous Socratic paradox that 'no one does wrong willingly'. For Socrates κακόνοια would be equivalent to, not contrasted with, ἄγνοια, and ὁπόσα δὲ ἀγνοίᾳ ἄνθρωποι ἐξαμαρτάνουσι would, in fact, be all wrongdoing. The Armenian sophist, while making use of the concepts associated with the paradox (ignorance, wrongdoing, involuntary acts), has not quite reproduced Socrates' famous statement. This may be because his author finds the paradox difficult as well: Xenophon's Socrates does state that 'virtue is knowledge', but only rarely and in rather vague terms.[219]

Tigranes' teacher, while bearing a resemblance to Socrates, is termed a σοφιστής: this is not a word Xenophon uses in relation to the real Socrates.[220] The term 'sophist' is not necessarily a pejorative one in Xenophon: at times he links σοφισταί closely with σοφοί or φιλόσοφοι or uses the word to describe natural philosophers.[221] Elsewhere the term has more negative connotations: Socrates attacks τοὺς σοφιστάς for prostituting their wisdom and selling it to anyone who can pay their fee, and in the *Cynegeticus*, a work of doubtful authenticity, there is a sweeping attack on sophists.[222] Antisthenes is called a sophist by Callias in the *Symposium* (4. 4; cf. 4. 2) when he tries to refute his host by cross-examination, and it is perhaps this meaning of σοφιστής—skilful debater or expert with words—which comes closest to what is meant in our dialogue. (We shall see that

[219] For the Socratic paradoxes in Plato see e.g. the references collected by Calogero 1957: 13 n. 11; cf. *Mem.* 3. 9. 4–5, 4. 6. 6. On Xenophon's understanding of Socratic doctrine see e.g. Irwin 1974: 412; O'Brien 1967: 81–2; Guthrie 1969: 455–7.

[220] See Classen 1984 for an analysis of all the uses of the word σοφιστής (and its cognates) in Xenophon. He concludes, correctly, that the word is not a *terminus technicus* in Xenophon and bears a wide range of meanings.

[221] Cf. *Mem.* 4. 2. 1, 8; *Poroi* 5. 4 (and cf. *Cyr.* 6. 1. 41 πεφιλοσόφηκα μετὰ τοῦ ἀδίκου σοφιστοῦ); *Mem.* 1. 1. 11.

[222] Cf. *Mem.* 1. 6. 13 and *Cyneg.* 13. 1–9. See Gray 1985 for a recent discussion of the authenticity of the *Cynegeticus*; cf. Breitenbach 1966: 1913–21 and the further references there.

Tigranes, the sophist's pupil, is a lively debater and his arguments
are clever, if specious at times.) In any event, Tigranes' Armenian
teacher is not meant to be an exact copy or double of Socrates, and it
is not by chance that he is termed a σοφιστής. His execution is
certainly intended to remind us of the last days of the Athenian philosopher, but the Armenian, who regularly accompanied his young
charge on hunting expeditions, does not seem to have lived the way
that Socrates did. More important, the sophist's teachings and
methods of argument, to judge by his pupil Tigranes, are not like
those of Socrates; they are more 'sophistic'.

At this stage of the trial the discussion between Cyrus and Tigranes
is not forensic (for all agree that the Armenian king is guilty as
charged) but deliberative (what should be done to him?). This
change in rhetorical category is significant, since, as Aristotle tells us,
forensic and deliberative discussions have different aims in mind: the
former are concerned with justice and the latter, expediency.[223]
Tigranes seems well aware of these rhetorical rules for, when requesting permission to speak, he indicates at once that he is going to
discuss Cyrus' interests (3. 1. 14 ἃ οἶμαί σοι βέλτιστα εἶναι) and his
arguments throughout are based on the Persian leader's self-interest
rather than the question of justice, even if at one stage he is forced to
take justice (or at least retribution) into account.[224] Cyrus, on the
other hand, seems at first to be interested in justice, but later concentrates solely on his own advantage: expediency wins the day. The
Armenian prince uses dialogue rather than a set speech to plead his
case here, and we should remember that the sophists also trained
their pupils to argue by means of questions and answers.[225] Normally
speeches were used when deciding affairs of state, and the closest
parallel to our deliberative dialogue is Thucydides' Melian Dialogue:
the Athenians too are interested in expediency rather than justice
(Thuc. 5. 84–113).[226]

Tigranes' first argument (Cyr. 3. 1. 15) is that Cyrus should imitate
his father (i.e. be guided by the death verdict the king has just
delivered against himself) only if he admires him. The Persian leader

[223] Arist. Rhet. 1358ᵇ13 ff. τέλος δὲ ... τῷ μὲν συμβουλεύοντι τὸ συμφέρον καὶ
βλαβερόν ... τοῖς δὲ δικαζομένοις τὸ δίκαιον καὶ τὸ ἄδικον.
[224] Cf. Cyr. 3. 1. 22 τοῦ δίκην διδόναι and cf. 3. 1. 15 τὰς τιμωρίας ποιεῖσθαι.
[225] See Kerferd 1981: 32–4.
[226] On the unusual form of the Melian Dialogue see Hudson-Williams 1950 and
Macleod 1974: 387–8 (= 1983: 54–5). For justice vs. expediency in Thucydides see e.g.
Macleod 1974: 389 (= 1983: 56) and Guthrie 1969: 84–8; cf. Finley 1967: 32–5, 39–40.

replies that by doing justice he would not be following in the foot-steps of the wrong-doing Armenian king, and Tigranes is forced to concede the point. Since it is just to punish unjust people, continues Cyrus, he must, according to Tigranes' own argument, punish the king.

Undaunted by Cyrus' victory in this first round, Tigranes now argues that it would be against Cyrus' interests to kill the defeated king (3. 1. 16 ff.). Since the Armenian king has been caught in a misdeed, he has been brought to his senses and has become σώφρων, and is now more valuable to the Persian leader than ever. All the other qualities that Cyrus may wish to make use of in a friend or subject—strength, bravery, wealth, or political power—are worth-less, claims Tigranes, without σωφροσύνη.[227] This stress on the importance of σωφροσύνη is reminiscent of Socrates' teachings in the *Memorabilia* (4. 3. 1; cf. 1. 2. 17, 4. 2. 34–5), but while Cyrus also appreciates the value of σωφροσύνη (see *Cyr.* 6. 1. 47, 8. 1. 30, and cf. 1. 2. 8–9), he does not believe that it is a quality that can be acquired overnight. The Persian leader holds the more traditional view that moral qualities are instilled slowly, by study and repeated practice.[228] Tigranes, says Cyrus, thinks that σωφροσύνη is an emotion (πάθημα) of the soul, akin to sorrow, but the Persian leader views it as a trait that must be learnt (μάθημα). This juxtaposition of πάθημα and μάθημα immediately reminds us of the proverbial πάθει μάθος, the idea that one learns through suffering.[229] Here, however, the two terms are taken as opposites, rather than cause and effect, and the very meaning of the word πάθημα has shifted from 'suffering' or 'experience' to 'emotion'.[230]

The Armenian prince now tries to demonstrate to Cyrus that σωφροσύνη can be acquired very rapidly, and brings two illustrations of defeat acting as a catalyst to bring men to their senses (3. 1. 20 σωφρονίζειν; cf. 2. 2. 14, 8. 4. 14). When the Persian leader objects that the Armenian king has not suffered any real defeat, Tigranes replies that his father's self-knowledge—the realization that he has

---

[227] Here the word σωφροσύνη seems to mean a realistic appraisal of one's powers; see North 1966: 131–2.

[228] Compare Cyrus' argument with Chrysantas at *Cyr.* 3. 3. 50 ff. (below, sect. 6) and Croesus' words at 7. 2. 20–5 (below, ch. 4. 4).

[229] See e.g. Aes. *Ag.* 177 and Croesus' statement in Herodotus: τὰ δέ μοι παθήματα ἐόντα ἀχάριτα μαθήματα γέγονε (Htd. 1. 207).

[230] See Dörrie 1956 for a survey of the use of παθεῖν with μαθεῖν. He compares (30–1) the use of πάθημα in our passage to Gorgias, *Hel.* 9.

lost all freedom and been foiled in every attempted move, while Cyrus has fooled him as completely as if he were blind, deaf, and a fool—is defeat enough. Cyrus is sceptical as to whether the knowledge that someone else is superior is indeed enough of a lesson, but Tigranes claims that such knowledge is a greater deterrent than actual physical defeat in battle. Men who have been overpowered by force may try to fight their opponents again on some later occasion, he argues, but they will readily obey those whom they believe are better. The claim that men will willingly listen to their superiors is, as we have seen, an argument used both by Cambyses and the Socrates of the *Memorabilia*, but here Cyrus takes exception to the idea and asks the Armenian prince if he really thinks that thieves, liars, and unjust men do not realize that other men are better. The Armenian king broke his word and violated his treaty with the Medes knowing full well that they had done no wrong (3. 1. 21). Tigranes is forced to concede that knowledge alone—without punishment—is not enough to bring his father to his senses. But, the Armenian prince adds almost immediately, the king *has* been punished, for he has been greatly afraid and the fear of suffering is worse than the actual suffering itself. Tigranes now waxes eloquent on the shattering effects of fear, but Cyrus remains unconvinced. He thinks that the Armenian king will be subdued for only a short time and will then regain his confidence and be up to mischief again.

Tigranes, admitting that Cyrus has good cause to be suspicious of the Armenian royal family, says that they will blame only themselves for any military restrictions that the Persian may choose to impose. (Here, for the first time, Tigranes identifies with his father's actions, probably in order to arouse his friend's sympathy.) If, however, Cyrus installs a new ruler in Armenia, he is likely either to arouse his enmity by being too suspicious, or allow him to cause even greater damage by being too lenient. When the Persian objects that he would like servants who are motivated by good will and not by constraint, Tigranes' reply reaches new heights of sophistry. Using a series of rhetorical questions, the Armenian prince argues that the king will be more friendly and more grateful to Cyrus than anyone else could possibly be. Another ruler, one who had done Cyrus no harm, will not appreciate it if the Persian does not kill him or his family, nor will he be made as grateful by having the kingdom handed over to him, for he has never lost it. The Armenian king, who has the most to lose, will be gaining the most, and his gratitude to Cyrus will be in direct proportion to the favours granted. Finally, turning again to Cyrus' immediate self-interest, Tigranes points out that his father is an experienced king and best acquainted with Armenia. Under his rule the country will be most stable, the greatest possible army will be raised, and all the country's hidden resources will be made available to Cyrus. Tigranes ends as he has begun, warning his friend that punishing the Armenians will lead to even greater damage for Cyrus himself (3. 1. 30; cf. 15).

Cyrus, Xenophon tells us, is extremely pleased to hear Tigranes' final plea, for by acceding to it he will achieve all that he has promised Cyaxares to accomplish. The Armenian king—so Tigranes has just promised and so it turns out—will be more of a friend than ever, besides furnishing the money and the troops. Tigranes has persuaded Cyrus, not by the twists and turns of his arguments, but by recommending the very course of action the Persian decided upon before leaving for Armenia. The whole of their debate has been no more than a diversion for Cyrus, for he had never intended to execute the Armenian king, despite his talk of justice, and he emerges from the discussion unconvinced perhaps, but with all his objectives offered to him.[231] Cyrus pardons the Armenian king, releases his family, and re-establishes him on his throne, as a willing ally (3. 1. 32–7).

Tigranes' chief appearance in the *Cyropaedia* is in this chapter (3. 1), and henceforth he plays a minor, fairly passive role as the leader of the Armenian contingent in Cyrus' army.[232] The Armenian prince is not a historical figure,[233] and his conversation with Cyrus is pure fiction, invented by Xenophon for his readers' delight. Tigranes has been taught by an Armenian version of Socrates and his debate with Cyrus has a dialectical quality only rarely found in Xenophon's dialogues; none the less, *Cyr.* 3. 1. 16 ff. is not very like the Socratic dialogues of the *Memorabilia*. The discussion includes 'Socratic' topics (the importance of σωφροσύνη, man's willingness to obey his betters) and methods of argument found in the *Memorabilia* (illustrations from everyday life, a series of rhetorical questions), but none of these features is exclusively Socratic and they may simply be seen as general rhetorical techniques. More than anything else it is the

[231] Cf. Tatum 1989: 138–45.
[232] Cf. e.g. *Cyr.* 4. 2. 9, 5. 1. 27, 8. 3. 25, 8. 4. 1 ff. (where, interestingly, Tigranes does not join in the lively sympotic banter).
[233] Cf. Breitenbach 1966: 1712–13.

casual attitude of the two opponents which makes this very dialectical conversation un-Socratic: Xenophon's Socrates is almost invariably too didactic and purposeful to argue for argument's sake. One would not guess from the casual, competitive tone of this conversation that Tigranes is fighting for his father's life and kingdom while Cyrus has a great deal at stake in his first major, independent foray, for neither can resist trading clever arguments and scoring points.[234] In addition, the Armenian and the Persian are too evenly matched—there is no one leading figure in the conversation, no 'Socrates'. At first Tigranes takes the offensive in their verbal duel, but almost immediately afterwards it is Cyrus who attacks and Tigranes who must parry, modifying his position in the light of the Persian's remarks. Tigranes may have been trained in dialectic, but Cyrus is the hero of the *Cyropaedia*, and as such is not easily rivalled. Both the Armenian and the Persian emerge victorious from their debate: Tigranes seemingly convinces Cyrus with his arguments, while Cyrus both gains his objectives and earns a reputation for benevolence and magnanimity. Perhaps the most interesting thing to be learnt from this discussion between Tigranes and Cyrus is how lively and sophistic Xenophon can be when he chooses to free himself from the constraints of the Socratic pattern of dialogue.

5. CYAXARES THE MEDE: *CYR.* 5. 5. 5-37

Cyr. 5. 5. 5–37 is a lengthy, dramatic conversation between Cyaxares and Cyrus. The Persian leader and his uncle meet on the Median–Syrian border, following a long separation during which Cyaxares has remained at home with a reduced Median force while Cyrus has conquered enemy strongholds, acquired many new allies, and established a Persian cavalry—all with the aid of Cyaxares' soldiers, who have volunteered to join him. The meeting between uncle and nephew follows two angry exchanges by messenger (4. 5. 9–11, 18)

---

[234] In the *Anab.* (2. 1. 7 ff.) we find a similar situation, in which the love of speculative argument seems to cause the leaders of the Ten Thousand to banish all thought of the dangerous situation in which they find themselves. After the death of Cyrus the Younger, Phalinus and a Persian contingent request that the Greeks surrender their arms to Artaxerxes, and the ensuing debate is surprisingly philosophical—cf. in particular Phalinus' laughing remark to young Theopompus ἀλλὰ φιλοσόφῳ μὲν ἔοικας, ὦ νεανίσκε, καὶ λέγεις οὐκ ἀχάριστα (*Anab.* 2. 1. 13).

and letter (4. 5. 27–33), in which Cyaxares requests the return of his men and Cyrus refuses him.

Cyrus now summons Cyaxares so that they can discuss future plans together. The Median king, accompanied only by a small retinue, rides out to join Cyrus, who awaits him with an elaborate display of the best-mounted and best-armed of his forces, including Cyaxares' own Median cavalry. The Median king feels slighted and is deeply distressed: he turns away from Cyrus' attempt to greet him with a customary embrace and openly cries. Cyrus then dismisses his entourage, draws his uncle aside to a nearby grove of palm-trees, and orders Median carpets to be spread on the ground: the scene is now set for a private discussion between the two. Xenophon uses this dramatic prelude to characterize the two interlocutors: we see Cyrus naïvely and thoughtlessly glorying in his newly won gains while Cyaxares reacts emotionally, almost childishly, to the sight. The Median rugs which Cyrus orders especially for his uncle are a particularly apt touch. Many commentators are reminded of the meeting between Agesilaus and Pharnabazus in the *Hellenica* (4. 1. 30), where Pharnabazus' servants spread soft carpets on the ground for their richly attired master.[235] There Pharnabazus is ashamed to sit on soft rugs while the Spartan leader and his men sit on the grass, but here Cyaxares seems somewhat mollified by Cyrus' gesture. The Median king's love of luxury and finery is repeatedly stressed in the *Cyropaedia*, and his nephew caters to it more than once.[236]

After they are seated, Cyrus asks his uncle why he is so angry with him. Cyaxares replies that he, the scion of a long line of royal ancestors, is ashamed to appear with such a lowly retinue at the same time that Cyrus uses Median forces to make a magnificent impression. The emphasis here on Cyaxares' ancient royal lineage (5. 5. 8 ἐφ᾽ ὅσον ἀνθρώπων μνήμη ἐφικνεῖται καὶ τῶν πάλαι προγόνων καὶ πατρὸς βασιλέως πεφυκέναι καὶ αὐτὸς βασιλεὺς νομιζόμενος εἶναι) is curious, for Cyrus of the *Cyropaedia* is also the son of a long-established royal house (cf. 7. 2. 24), so Xenophon may be hinting here at other versions of Cyrus' origins. According to Ctesias, Cyrus came from a lowly, far from regal background,[237] and this would

[235] See Gray 1981: 326 on the function of this narrative prelude in the *Hell.*, and cf. below, ch. 3. 4 at n. 113.

[236] For the Median king's love of finery see *Cyr.* 1. 6. 8, 2. 4. 5–6, 4. 1. 13, 18, 6. 1. 1, 6. Cyrus indulges him: 4. 5. 51–2, 5. 5. 2, 39–40, 8. 5. 17, 20, and esp. 4. 5. 21.

[237] For Ctesias' account of Cyrus see below, ch. 3. 2.

make the Median king's present plight all the more unpalatable. In this section of the *Cyropaedia* we are given, in fact, the strongest hints of the actual, historical sequence of events—the conquest of the Median empire by Cyrus. According to all the other (non-Xenophontic)[238] accounts of Cyrus' rise to power, the Persian leader took the Median empire by force, defeating the reigning king, Astyages. Our Cyaxares, the son of Astyages and Cyrus' maternal uncle,[239] is found only in the *Cyropaedia*, and one of his chief functions is to serve as a link in the quiet transfer of power. Cyaxares has no sons and Cyrus marries his only daughter, thus peaceably inheriting the Median empire.[240] Xenophon does, however, allow a few traces of the actual Median–Persian conflict to remain in the *Cyropaedia*.[241] His Cyrus detaches and 'borrows' most of Cyaxares' Median forces, refusing to release them when the Median king asks for their return, which leads to the present angry confrontation between the two. In the course of their joint campaign Cyrus gradually usurps Cyaxares' power and authority, taking charge of the expedition against the Assyrians in his stead. In our dialogue we hear of the Mede's angry reaction to this turn of events, and while Xenophon quickly reconciles the two, he does show his Persian hero overriding a hostile Median king.[242]

Cyaxares explains to his nephew that he feels humiliated, ridiculed,

[238] Xenophon knows, of course, that the Medes were conquered by the Persians; cf. *Anab.* 3. 4. 8, 11.

[239] See Bremmer 1983 on the significant role of maternal uncles in Greek literature; Cyaxares fits the pattern well.

[240] Interestingly, this process of 'claim by dowry' or inheritance through a wife may be an institution peculiar to Persian law and is at variance with the Greek law of Xenophon's time; see Atkinson 1956.

[241] It is interesting to compare Cyrus' reception of Cyaxares' delegate in the *Cyr.* (4. 5. 18 ff.) with the welcome extended by Cyrus to Astyages' messengers, according to Nicolaus of Damascus (*FGrH* 90 F 66. 26–7). (Nicolaus is probably reproducing the account found in Ctesias—cf. below, ch. 4 n. 24.) In the *Cyr.* Cyrus greets Cyaxares' messenger kindly and urges his ally, the Hyrcanian leader, to do his utmost to entertain the Mede and persuade him to stay. In Nicolaus' account Cyrus and his chief adviser, Oebares, welcome the Mede delegates warmly, inviting them to dinner and plying them with drink in order to detain them. So too the angry exchange of messages between Cyaxares and Cyrus before their meeting here (*Cyr.* 4. 5. 9–11, 18, 27–33) has a parallel in the harsh words exchanged between Astyages and Cyrus before they do battle, in Nicolaus' account (90 F 66. 33). In the *Cyr.*, once Cyrus has his way he is kindly and conciliatory towards Cyaxares, just as in other accounts the Persian leader behaves benevolently towards Astyages after he defeats him (Hdt. 1. 130; Ctesias, *FGrH* 688 F 9); cf. Hirsch 1985: 81–2.

[242] See Hirsch 1985: 81–2, with nn. 63–7 on 176–7, for further discussion of the 'coup' Cyrus stages against Cyaxares in the *Cyr.*.

and threatened by his own men and states that he would prefer
sinking to the ground ten times over to his present situation. He then
bursts into tears, and Cyrus too is led to cry. While some of the heroes
of the *Cyropaedia* do weep in sad or trying circumstances, tears are
normally the province of women, children, and weak or humiliated
men;[243] Cyaxares belongs in the latter category. Cyrus' tears are less
heartfelt: in any event, he is the first to recover from weeping. He
hastens to reassure his uncle that the Medes certainly intend their
king no harm. He will not defend them—for that will only serve to
anger Cyaxares yet further—but offers a general piece of advice: a
ruler should not constantly be angry with his subjects, for that will
only unite them against him. Cyrus explains that he was afraid to
have the Median soldiers face their king's anger on their own, and
indeed in the *Cyropaedia* Cyaxares' short temper is notorious (cf.
4. 5. 9, 18, 19). Interestingly, Herodotus' Cyaxares, grandfather of
our fictitious one, was also known for his difficult temper or ὀργή
(Hdt. 1. 73).

Cyrus now turns to the charges Cyaxares has levelled against him
(*Cyr.* 5. 5. 13–15). He suggests that they carefully examine together
the wrong he has done, rather than accuse one another at random.
The Persian leader also makes his uncle a proposal: if Cyaxares
concludes that his nephew has done him wrong, Cyrus will accept
the verdict without question. The Median king, on the other hand,
must agree that he has suffered no wrong if Cyrus is shown neither to
have done nor intended him any harm. If it appears that Cyrus has
actually benefited his uncle as much as possible, the Median king
must concede this point as well. Cyaxares agrees to these terms for
their joint investigation, and uncle and nephew are ready to examine
Cyrus' past actions one by one, in order to distinguish the good from
the bad.

The ground-rules Cyrus lays down for this discussion with
Cyaxares are reminiscent in many ways of the two theoretical
descriptions of Socrates' method of investigation found in the
Memorabilia (4. 5. 11–12, 4. 6. 13–15). Xenophon tells us that Socrates stresses that those examining a question must search jointly,
avoiding unclear or unproved assertions. The investigators, according to Socrates, must distinguish between deeds, classifying them
according to kind as good or bad. In addition, the philosopher always

---

[243] Heroes: *Cyr.* 3. 1. 7, 7. 3. 8–11; cf. 1. 4. 25–6 and 7. 5. 32. Women, children, and
weak men: 3. 1. 13, 1. 4. 2, 5. 4. 31, 6. 1. 35.

tries to proceed through agreed points when discussing a question.²⁴⁴ In the *Memorabilia* we only rarely see Socrates putting this method into practice—*Mem.* 4. 2 and 4. 6 are perhaps the only actual instances—so that it is interesting to find Cyrus applying these theoretical principles of discussion assigned by Xenophon to Socrates to an actual situation in the *Cyropaedia*.

The Persian's very invitation to his uncle to investigate the situation (5. 5. 15 ἄγε τοίνυν . . . σκοπῶμεν) seems an echo of many such addresses by Socrates to his interlocutors.²⁴⁵ Generally such a call for joint investigation introduces a series of questions by Socrates, and in fact Cyrus now begins to interrogate Cyaxares. In this joint investigation conducted by Cyrus and Cyaxares the Persian leader is in effect on trial, facing a charge of ἀδικία, for the question to be decided is whether or not Cyrus has done wrong.²⁴⁶ The first part of the investigation or trial takes the form of a 'question-and-reply' interrogation, so that once again, as with the Armenian king's trial (and the further examples discussed there), we find that Socratic methods of investigation are used in a legal context. Cyrus now reviews his past actions with Cyaxares, deed by deed (καθ' ἓν ἕκαστον),²⁴⁷ beginning with the Median king's original request for military aid. Cyaxares is led by Cyrus' questioning first to admit the facts—his nephew did indeed come to his aid with as large a force as possible—and then to classify Cyrus' action as good rather than bad. Next Cyaxares is made to acknowledge that his nephew did not shirk his duty in any way when in battle with the enemy. Cyrus' next two questions—on his plan to pursue the defeated enemy and Cyaxares' loan of the Median cavalry for that purpose—touch on more sensitive points, and his uncle does not reply. Cyrus, despairing of receiving

---

²⁴⁴ Joint search: *Mem.* 4. 5. 12 τοῦ συνιόντας κοινῇ βουλεύεσθαι; 4. 6. 14 τί οὖν . . . ἐπεσκεψάμεθα . . . ; see also *Mem.* 4. 6. 1, 4. 7. 8, and cf. Pl. *Crito* 48 D; *Prot.* 330 B; *Charm.* 158 D, etc. Classification of deeds: *Mem.* 4. 5. 12 διαλέγοντας κατὰ γένη τὰ πράγματα; cf. 4. 5. 11 διαλέγοντας κατὰ γένη τὰ μὲν ἀγαθὰ προαιρεῖσθαι, τῶν δὲ κακῶν ἀπέχεσθαι. Proceeding through agreed points: *Mem.* 4. 6. 15 διὰ τῶν μάλιστα ὁμολογουμένων ἐπορεύετο.

²⁴⁵ See *Mem.* 1. 6. 4, 2. 1. 1, 10, 3. 1. 10, 3. 4. 7, 3. 5. 1, 4. 6. 14, etc.; cf. *Oec.* 3. 14, 4. 5, 17. 7.

²⁴⁶ See *Cyr.* 5. 5. 12, 13, 17, 20, 21; cf. also 5. 5. 19 πλεονεξίαν κατηγορῆσαι and 5. 5. 22 αἰτίας ἄξιον.

²⁴⁷ Note the very similar use of καθ' ἓν ἕκαστον in Cyrus' point-by-point interrogation of the Armenian king at his trial (3. 1. 12); cf. also 1. 6. 22 and 6. 4. 5; *Hiero* 11. 1; *Oec.* 19. 14. In the Melian Dialogue the Athenians suggest to the Melians that their negotiations proceed in dialogue form (καθ' ἕκαστον . . . ὑπολαμβάνοντες) rather than by an exchange of continuous speeches (Thuc. 5. 85 συνεχεῖ ῥήσει . . . ἑνὶ λόγῳ).

answers to his questions, now abandons the cross-examination of his uncle and continues his defence in a speech (5. 5. 21 ff.). Any further questions put by Cyrus are purely rhetorical: his 'trial' takes the more usual form of speech and counter-speech.

The Persian leader briefly reviews the events leading up to his acquiring Mede volunteers for his campaign (5. 5. 21–2; cf. 4. 1. 13–24) and then stresses the importance of his subsequent victories for Cyaxares himself (cf. 5. 5. 23 τῶν ἐπὶ σὲ ἐλθόντων, χρήματα ... τὰ σά, τοὺς σοὺς φίλους, τὰ μὲν σοί, τὴν σὴν ἀρχήν, etc.).[248] Cyaxares, says Cyrus, has seen his territory increased and his enemy's diminished, and this is the greatest good of all (5. 5. 24).[249] Cyrus concludes his speech by saying that he cannot imagine that he has done anything but good for Cyaxares: none the less, he is willing to hear his uncle's point of view.

Cyaxares' reply is the most interesting and curious feature of our dialogue. The Median king, as we have seen, is not a historical figure and seems to have been invented by Xenophon. Normally he serves simply as a pallid and ineffectual contrast, a kind of counter-figure, to the hero of the work, Cyrus. From the very start of the *Cyropaedia* uncle and nephew are compared with one another, and Cyrus is consistently shown to be the better of the two.[250] When Cyrus and Cyaxares hold discussions or consult together, each has a regular role to play—the Persian is an ambitious but sensible leader, while the lazy, impulsive Mede displays poor judgement. Generally Cyaxares is made to accept proposals put forward by Cyrus (cf. e.g. 2. 4. 9–17, 3. 3. 13–20), and when he himself initiates a plan it is almost invariably misguided and has to be quashed by his nephew.[251] The readers of the *Cyropaedia* can count on Cyaxares to say the wrong thing or hold the wrong views: he thinks, for instance, that putting on showy, impressive clothing is more important than appearing

[248] Earlier (5. 5. 19), when describing his original plan that he and Cyaxares pursue the enemy together, Cyrus has repeatedly used the word κοινῇ.

[249] We shall see below (sect. 6) how Cyrus—in most un-Socratic fashion—often stresses the joys of victory.

[250] See *Cyr.* 1. 4. 5, 7, 9, 20–2, 1. 6. 8, 2. 4. 1–8, 3. 3. 24–5, 29–33, 46–7, 56, 4. 1. 13–24, 4. 5. 26–34, etc.; cf. Due 1989: 55–62.

[251] See e.g. 3. 3. 29–33, 46–8, where Cyrus rejects Cyaxares' plan to attack the Assyrians at once. The Persian leader finally gives in with bad grace at 3. 3. 56–7, but it is plain that Cyaxares can do no right; cf. Tatum 1989: 115–33, esp. 122–3. The only initiative undertaken by Cyaxares which Cyrus readily approves is his suggestion that the Persian leader marry his daughter and inherit his kingdom (8. 5. 17–20); here Cyrus has no counter-proposal to make.

promptly at councils (2. 4. 5–6, 6. 1. 1, 6) and he judges an army by
the quantity, rather than the quality, of its soldiers (2. 1. 8–10). Often
it seems that Xenophon has Cyaxares speak up simply in order to
have his words demolished by Cyrus. But there are two occasions
where the Mede has substantial differences of opinion with his
nephew and his point of view cannot be dismissed out of hand. Our
dialogue is one such occasion, while the other instance, their
exchange at 4. 1. 13–23, is directly related to, and precedes, this
present conflict.

At *Cyr.* 4. 1. 13–23 Cyrus approaches his uncle with a request for
Median assistance. The Persian leader and his men have decided to
pursue and plunder the Assyrians, who have just been routed, but
they need the assistance of the Median cavalry in order to do so.
When the Persians turn to the Mede ruler with their plan, Cyaxares—who is, Xenophon tells us, both jealous that the Persians
have taken the initiative and reluctant to face danger yet again—tries
to dissuade them from the mission. The Mede's arguments, even if
they do stem from laziness and jealousy, are surprisingly powerful
and persuasive.[252] Cyaxares believes that moderation is a wise policy
on the part of victors. He reminds Cyrus that the Persians (as
opposed to the Medes) do not generally over-indulge in any single
pleasure: consequently they should be especially self-controlled in
regard to the greatest pleasure of all, success. The Persians and
Medes can grow old in happiness and security, Cyaxares continues,
while repeated pursuit of further pleasures (i.e. victories) may lead to
the loss of everything. The Mede king then uses a second argument
against continuing the campaign: the enemy, who are much more
numerous than the Persians and their allies, will fight courageously
to defend their wives and children if they are compelled by Cyrus to
do so. Cyaxares concludes by saying that he does not wish to order
the merry-making Medes to go to battle once again.

Cyrus pays little attention to Cyaxares' arguments and simply asks
his uncle for permission to recruit volunteers among the Medes to
join him. He is by his very nature opposed to Cyaxares' quietism and
lack of ambition and states at the start of the campaign that he
believes in practising moderation and working hard, but only as a
means to achieve greater rewards (cf. 1. 5. 7–11). It is plain that Cyrus

---

[252] Cf. Breitenbach 1966: 1731, who points out that Cyaxares' arguments, an
'ernstzunehmender Gedankenblock', do not actually fit the motives attributed to him
by Xenophon.

thinks that all of Cyaxares' well-reasoned points are just window-dressing, meant to gloss over the fact that his uncle is afraid of continuing the campaign. Indeed, in our dialogue Cyrus flatly states that Cyaxares had rejected his plan out of fear of the dangers involved—ἐπεί σοι οὐκ ἀσφαλὲς ἐδόκει εἶναι τὸ διώκειν, σὲ μὲν αὐτὸν ἀφῆκα τοῦ κινδύνου τούτου μετέχειν (*Cyr.* 5. 5. 20).

None the less, the reasons that Cyaxares brings for ending the campaign against the enemy are substantial ones, regularly used by sober speakers in war debates.[253] Thus, for instance, the Mede ruler, when advising Cyrus not to undertake an ambitious campaign, is not unlike Artabanus in Herodotus, who warns Xerxes against attacking the Greeks (Hdt. 7. 10ff.).[254] Artabanus' fears prove justified, while those of Cyaxares do not, but that is not to say that the Mede's arguments are any less cogent. We find similar points raised by the Spartans in Thucydides (4. 17–20) and by two eminently respectable speakers in the *Hellenica*. Callistratus, arguing in favour of a peace agreement between the Athenians and the Spartans, contends that overweening ambition in war is bound to lead to a fall (*Hell.* 6. 3. 16), while Jason, when trying to dissuade the Thebans from fighting the Spartans, warns that the enemy, if compelled to fight, will struggle to the bitter end (*Hell.* 6. 4. 23).[255] Commonplace or not,[256] Cyaxares' words are not ridiculous and the stance he assumes here is a legitimate one: this is one of the rare instances where the author of the *Cyropaedia* allows us to see that serious, worthwhile objections can be made to a proposal put forward by Cyrus. Xenophon may have included Cyaxares' views because they were a standard topos, regularly found in war debates, but it is noteworthy that the hapless Cyaxares is the one to oppose his hero; one of Cyrus' trusty lieutenants, Chrysantas or Hystaspas, would be a more natural candidate for such a role.[257] There is a certain tension between the

---

[253] Cf. e.g. Hdt. 7. 10ε, 7. 16α, 8. 109, Thuc. 4. 17–20, and see Latham 1981 on the regular appearance at councils of war of a sober speaker who counsels against fighting.

[254] See Lattimore 1939: 24–6 and Bischoff 1932 (excerpted in Marg 1965: 302–19) for further instances of such 'tragic warners' in Herodotus.

[255] Breitenbach 1950: 136–9, who notes the resemblance between *Hell.* 6. 3. 15ff. and Thuc. 4. 17–20, thinks that the speakers' words in the two *Hell.* passages reflect Xenophon's own attitude in favour of moderation in war.

[256] The argument that over-ambitious victors are bound to fall is even recommended in a rhetorical handbook, *Rhet. ad Alex.* 1425ª36ff. Cf. Hornblower 1987: 47–50, who discusses the relation between Thuc. 4. 17–20 and the passage in the *Rhet. ad Alex.*

[257] Indeed Chrysantas plays just such a part in his debate with Cyrus at 3. 3. 48ff.; cf. below, sect. 6.

role of adviser and the Mede ruler's more usual function in the *Cyropaedia*, and Xenophon has not really resolved the contradiction between the two: while he *tells* us that Cyaxares is peevish and cowardly, he *shows* us that the Mede ruler has sober, moderate advice to offer.

In our dialogue, their next confrontation, Cyaxares again uses powerful arguments that are not answered by Cyrus, but here he presents his case in a way that reminds us of Socratic techniques in the *Memorabilia*. The Mede ruler begins his speech by conceding that it cannot be said that Cyrus has done anything bad. None the less, he would have much preferred being the one to confer such benefits, rather than being their passive recipient: having Cyrus shower such blessings upon him is somehow disgraceful (5. 5. 25–7). This is a point of view that the Persian should well understand, for he often expresses the desire to outdo his friends in granting favours and he too is ashamed to be on the receiving, and not the giving, end.[258] The regular scheme of values found in the *Cyropaedia* does in fact pose a problem: for every happy benefactor there must be a humiliated recipient.

Next Cyaxares turns to his chief complaint against Cyrus, the alienation of his soldiers' affections. The Mede states that he would have been less displeased to discover his subjects actually wronged by Cyrus than he is now, by seeing them so deeply indebted to his nephew. Realizing that this statement may sound unreasonable, Cyaxares suggests that Cyrus put himself in his place (5. 5. 28 μὴ ἐν ἐμοὶ αὐτὰ ἀλλ᾽ εἰς σὲ τρέψας πάντα καταθέασαι).[259] How would the Persian feel if another were to treat his dogs, attendants, wife,[260] or— the example most analogous to Cyaxares' own case (5. 5. 31 τὸ μάλιστα τῷ ἐμῷ πάθει ἐμφερές)—his Persian soldiers so well that they would love him more than Cyrus himself? Clearly, argues Cyaxares, Cyrus would not consider such a man his friend. Cyaxares' method of argument here is a variation on Socrates' technique of applied analogies in the *Memorabilia*. Socrates, as we have seen, asks his interlocutor to judge a series of hypothetical situations and only then applies the analogous verdict to the speaker himself, but here

---

[258] Cf. *Cyr.* 2. 3. 12, 5. 1. 1, 28–9, 5. 3. 2, 5. 4. 32, 8. 2. 7.

[259] Cf. *Hell.* 3. 4. 7–10, where the affronted Agesilaus actually puts Lysander in his place, having him experience the feelings of a slighted friend; cf. Gray 1989: 46–8.

[260] When justifying his conduct towards Tigranes' teacher, the Armenian king has also compared his situation to that of a husband whose wife becomes attached to another; cf. *Hiero* 3. 3–4.

the Median king announces at the very start that his hypothetical examples relate to their present situation. While Cyaxares' questions are plainly rhetorical and Cyrus is not actually meant to judge these analogous cases, there is a Socratic air to the interrogation.

The very issue raised by Cyaxares—the alienation of affections from their rightful recipient—also reminds us of Xenophon's Socrates. We have seen that in both the *Memorabilia* (1. 2. 49, 51) and the *Apology* (19–20) Socrates faces the charge of causing young people to regard him more highly than their parents and relatives.[261] (Since this is also the case with Tigranes' teacher, who is executed by the Armenian king because he is jealous of his son's greater admiration for the sophist, perhaps it is not too far-fetched to say that this is one charge brought against Socrates which genuinely troubled Xenophon.) In Xenophon Socrates' answer to this accusation is that in his field of professional competence, παιδεία (cf. *Apol.* 20–1), he is indeed more deserving of respect and attention than the young people's parents, just as other professionals (e.g. medical, legal, and military experts) are normally preferred to one's kin when specialist advice is required. Xenophon makes it quite plain that Cyrus has succeeded in attracting the Mede volunteers because he is a far more capable leader than his uncle,[262] but that is an argument that Cyrus cannot (and does not) use under the present circumstances, for he would only wound his uncle further. In this respect Xenophon's Cyrus is, perhaps, a better psychologist than his Socrates. The philosopher, at his trial, tells his accuser Meletus that he is considered the best educator to be had, while the Persian, after his initial showy appearance with Cyaxares' soldiers, does not flaunt his superiority before one who feels slighted by him.

Curiously, the weak and lackadaisical Cyaxares realizes what is really at stake in this power struggle—not the control of territory and wealth, but his good name and honour. The Median ruler knows that his sovereignty over the Medes depends upon their recognition of his overall superiority rather than any greater strength of arms: οὐ γάρ τοι ἐγὼ Μήδων ἦρχον διὰ τὸ κρείττων αὐτῶν πάντων εἶναι, ἀλλὰ μᾶλλον διὰ τὸ αὐτοὺς τούτους ἀξιοῦν ἡμᾶς αὐτῶν πάντα βελτίονας εἶναι (5. 5. 34). Cyaxares, like his father Astyages before him, is a

---

[261] See too Libanius, *Apol. Soc.* 102–3.

[262] Cyrus, unlike Cyaxares, is not afraid to approach the Mede soldiers in the midst of their merry-making (cf. 4. 1. 18, 5. 5. 21) and readily recruits volunteers for his initiative, thanks to his personality, past actions, and reputation (4. 2. 10–11).

tyrant and one would not have expected him to describe his rule in such terms. The Mede, in seeing excellence as the real source of his power, sounds like his brother-in-law Cambyses or, for that matter, Socrates.[263] Cyaxares makes another surprising statement as well. He complains that he has been put in a passive, womanlike position, while Cyrus appears thoroughly masculine, a true man (5. 5. 33 σὺ μὲν ἀνὴρ φαίνῃ). We would not expect Cyaxares to reject this feminine role so explicitly: elsewhere great stress is placed upon his love of luxury and finery. Croesus, another effete ruler in the *Cyropaedia*, who is made to present a sorry contrast with Cyrus, is more than happy to be treated as a woman, for he has always considered his wife's life of luxury without anxiety the happiest life possible (7. 2. 27–8). Cyaxares' moment of Socrates-like wisdom is short-lived—almost immediately after this discussion he returns to his old, frivolous ways, keeping all the allied leaders waiting while he puts on an elaborate costume (6. 1. 1–6)—but we should note that he is granted such a moment.

At this point Cyrus interrupts his uncle and allows him to continue no further. He does not argue with the Mede, and indeed Xenophon lets us see that Cyaxares' charge is true, for Cyrus certainly is foremost in the hearts of the Median soldiers.[264] Instead, Cyrus suggests that Cyaxares should end his reproofs and put his nephew's loyalty to the test. Cyaxares suddenly capitulates and agrees to his nephew's proposal; he allows Cyrus to embrace him as well. The two kiss and the Median and Persian soldiers, who are carefully following the proceedings from a distance, cheer. Uncle and nephew ride off together, with the Median soldiers falling behind Cyaxares (not spontaneously, as Xenophon points out, but because Cyrus has signalled to them to do so). Cyaxares is brought to the tent which has been set aside for him, and his soldiers come to him bearing gifts (partly, we are again told, at Cyrus' prompting). The reconciliation is complete, with the conclusion of the dialogue presented as vividly and dramatically as the opening.

What are we to make of this encounter between Cyrus and Cyaxares? In many ways the conversation is similar to Tigranes' exchange with Cyrus: it is a kind of trial, held in a dramatic setting,

---

[263] See *Cyr.* 1. 6. 21 ff. and above, sect. 2.

[264] Cf. e.g. 4. 5. 51, where Cyrus tells the Medes, who are dividing up war spoils, to set aside the pick of the booty for Cyaxares. When the Medes actually apportion the spoils they first give Cyrus the choicest bits and only then set aside for their king the second-best items (4. 6. 11 δεύτερον δὲ Κυαξάρῃ τὰ δεύτερα).

and the differences between the two parties are substantial. Both
sides put forward cogent arguments, but here too the conversation is
not very like the Socratic dialogues found in the *Memorabilia*, because
the two opponents are too evenly matched. None the less, both uncle
and nephew do have certain Socratic qualities. Cyrus tries to guide
the conversation in accordance with Socrates' methods of investigation and the Persian ruler is made to face an accusation—alienation
of affections—which is very similar to one levelled against Socrates
and his counterpart in the *Cyropaedia*, Tigranes' teacher. Cyaxares is
allotted a serious role in the conversation, a more substantial part
than that normally given to Socrates' interlocutors in the *Memorabilia*,
and he uses (albeit somewhat laboriously) Socratic techniques of
argument while presenting his case in a surprisingly forceful manner.
With both Tigranes and Cyaxares the outcome of their debate with
Cyrus is not actually determined by the course of the conversation.
Cyaxares' surrender at the close of our dialogue is not so much the
result of his nephew's persuasive powers as of the author's need to
end the impasse between the two. Similarly, Cyrus' capitulation to
Tigranes is not due to his being convinced by the Armenian. The
debate between Tigranes and Cyrus is no more than a diversion, but
here Xenophon shows us the darker side of Cyrus' rise to power, the
price that others must pay for the Persian leader's successes.[265] It is
noteworthy that Xenophon chose to make the normally wooden
figure of Cyaxares come alive for this debate: when it comes to a
power struggle, the Median ruler is at his least foolish and he
confronts Cyrus with real and, at times, unanswerable arguments.

6. EXHORTATIONS AND SILENCES: CYR. 3. 3. 48–56

Cyr. 3. 3. 48–56, a conversation between Cyrus and his chief aide
Chrysantas, takes place as the Persians and their allies are about to
do battle with the Assyrians for the first time. Chrysantas, along with
some of his fellow ὁμότιμοι, has brought several Assyrian deserters
up to Cyrus to be interrogated. These tell the Persian leader that the
forces on their side are already armed and arrayed for battle; the king
himself accompanies his troops as they set out, exhorting them
vigorously and at length (3. 3. 48 ἔλεγον ὅτι . . . αὐτὸς ὁ βασιλεὺς . . .
παρακελεύοιτο . . . πολλά τε καὶ ἰσχυρά). We have already been

---

[265] Cf. Tatum 1989: 115 ff. for this point.

given a sample of the Assyrian king's pre-battle oratory (3. 3. 43–5), in a rare glimpse behind enemy lines, and this report by the Assyrian defectors is probably meant to refer back to that speech. Chrysantas now suggests that Cyrus too gather up his forces and address them before battle in order to make the men better soldiers: this leads to a discussion between the two on the value of pre-battle exhortations.

Cyrus replies to his aide that no one speech, excellent though it may be, can turn bad men into good on the spot (3. 3. 50 αὐθημερόν; cf. 51). The soldiers will not become good archers, lancers, or cavalrymen if they have not practised their art in the past. Chrysantas then suggests that an exhortation by the Persian leader would improve the soldiers' souls, if not their physical prowess, but Cyrus again rejects the notion that a single oration can have a lasting effect on its audience. A speech is not the way to instil ideals—such as loyalty, honour, and courage—argues Cyrus, and oratory will not ensure that these values will abide, imprinted upon the fighters' hearts (3. 3. 50–2).

The objections Cyrus raises here to exhortations addressed to soldiers before a battle are surprising, to say the least; the Persian leader is being remarkably inconsistent. In this very section of the *Cyropaedia* Cyrus delivers two such orations, and there are many other pre-battle παρακελεύσεις or παρακλητικοὶ λόγοι delivered by him, scattered throughout the work.[266] Not only does Cyrus regularly address his soldiers before military engagements, he also encourages and exhorts them on a wide variety of occasions.[267] Cyrus, Cambyses, and Cyaxares all share the conviction that a soldier's state of mind when fighting is even more important than his physical fitness,[268] and very early on (1. 6. 19) Cyrus and his father have agreed that one of the chief tasks of a good general is to inspire his soldiers with enthusiasm. While the Persian king warns his son against raising his men's hopes too often, Cambyses does think that exhortation and encouragement (1. 6. 19 παρακέλευσιν) should be used by a leader in times of crisis. The forthcoming battle with the Assyrians is certainly one such critical occasion, as Cyrus himself is well aware. Only a short while before this exchange with Chrysantas, the Persian leader had summoned the ὁμότιμοι, his peers and companions from earliest youth (3. 3. 34 ff.). Cyrus tells these men that he would be ashamed to

---

[266] Cf. *Cyr.* 3. 2. 3–5, 4. 2. 21–6, 6. 2. 13–20, 6. 4. 12–20, 7. 5. 19–24, etc.
[267] Cf. *Cyr.* 2. 1. 14–18, 2. 3. 1–4, 3. 3. 7–8, 4. 1. 1–6, 7. 5. 71–86, 8. 6. 10–13.
[268] *Cyr.* 3. 3. 19; cf. 2. 1. 11, 5. 2. 33–4.

exhort them, for they have known, trained for, and practised the martial arts throughout their lives, just as he has. Instead, Cyrus would like the ὁμότιμοι to address those Persians who have only recently joined their ranks, in an attempt to make the new recruits fight more valiantly. The Persian leader recommends the use of exhortations, reminders, and advice to help these newcomers face the crucial test of valour awaiting them on the battlefield. Immediately after urging the ὁμότιμοι to speak to their forces, Cyrus himself exhorts and encourages other members of his army, the rearguard officers (3. 3. 40–3). Why then does he firmly reject Chrysantas' suggestion of yet another hortatory address?[269]

One reason seems to be Xenophon's desire to distinguish between, or contrast, Cyrus and his foe, the Assyrian king. Reports of the Assyrian's forceful address are what prompted Chrysantas to suggest a counter-exhortation, as it were, by Cyrus. Pairs of rousing speeches by the two opposing sides in a clash are found already in Homer[270] and appear several times in Thucydides.[271] While such paired speeches are not universal in Greek accounts of battles—Herodotus, for example, has very few military harangues and no pairs of exhortations by opposing leaders, and this is true of Xenophon's *Hellenica* as well[272]—it is perhaps this tradition of presenting the positions of both parties prior to a conflict which led Xenophon to deviate from his usual practice and allow his readers a look at the Assyrian side. Normally, events in the *Cyropaedia* are related strictly from the Persian perspective, and this is the only time that the old Assyrian king actually appears 'on stage' in the work. It is only natural to compare two such opposing speeches, and if Cyrus were to address his troops in the wake of the Assyrian king's exhortation (and Chrysantas' advice) we would expect his words to be a reply to—or a refutation of—the oration by the Assyrian. A closer look at the speech

[269] Breitenbach 1966: 1727–8, in an otherwise excellent discussion of our passage, suggests that Xenophon is expressing here the impatience felt by an experienced military man with useless speeches, but Xenophon allows himself many lengthy exhortations in the *Anab.*—cf. 3. 1. 15–25, 35–44, 3. 2. 7–32, 5. 4. 19–21, 6. 3. 11–18, 6. 5. 23–4.

[270] Cf. *Il.* 15. 485–500, 501–14 for addresses, in the midst of battle, by Hector and Ajax respectively. For military exhortations in classical literature see Albertus 1908, esp. 24–9.

[271] See Thuc. 2. 87, 89, 4. 92, 95, 7. 61–4, 66–8; see Luschnat 1942 and de Romilly 1956: 136–61 on the function of such speeches in Thucydides.

[272] See Hdt. 6. 11, 7. 53, 9. 17, and cf. 6. 109, 8. 78, 83. See also *Hell.* 2. 4. 13–17, 5. 1. 14–17, 7. 1. 30, and cf. 1. 6. 8–11, 7. 2. 20. Cf. Vorrenhagen 1926: 120, 129–31; Gray 1989: 99–101, 132–4.

by the enemy king will show us why Cyrus does not counter or contradict his enemy's words.

The Assyrian ruler begins his speech by urging his men to be brave, reminding them that the forthcoming struggle is for their very lives, land, homes, and families. If the Assyrians are the victors, their ruler tells them, they will continue to retain all these good things, but if they are defeated, all will go to the enemy. Consequently, the Assyrian forces must remain on the battlefield and fight to the last. Running away is foolish, stresses the king, for it will mean exposing their unseeing and unarmed flank to the enemy, making death even more likely than on the battlefield. Winners take all, the Assyrian states in conclusion, while the vanquished forfeit their lives and property (3. 3. 43–5).

The attitude towards victory, defeat, and flight displayed here by the Assyrian king differs in no way from Cyrus' own outlook. The Persian leader too stresses on various occasions that winners are entitled to all the spoils of victory while the defeated are left with nothing, and he also thinks that an enemy caught fleeing should be executed at once.[273] Cyrus often extols victory over one's enemies,[274] and in this very conversation tells Chrysantas that courage on the battlefield is the greatest virtue of all (3. 3. 54 τὴν μεγίστην τῶν ἐν ἀνθρώποις ἀρετήν). Cyrus, it seems, is no more humane or noble than his foe, and any exhortation of his would simply echo the sentiments expressed here by the Assyrian king: the two opponents, Assyrians and Persians, go to war according to the same rules and share the same values. These cold realities of wartime behaviour are presented as an immutable and just law in the *Cyropaedia*—it is not unjust to take away a defeated enemy's possessions, claims Cyrus, but humane to allow him to hold on to anything.[275] Such an attitude towards enemies is, of course, part and parcel of the more general precept of 'do good to your friends and harm to your enemies', which is often found in Xenophon's works.[276] It is interesting that these

[273] Winners take all: *Cyr.* 4. 2. 26, 7. 1. 13, 7. 5. 73; cf. 2. 3. 2. Execution of enemy: 3. 1. 3, 4. 2. 32, 4. 4. 6, 4. 5. 5–6.

[274] See *Cyr.* 5. 5. 24, 6. 1. 55, 7. 3. 11, 7. 5. 79; cf. 4. 2. 26 and 7. 1. 10, 13.

[275] Cf. *Cyr.* 7. 5. 73 νόμος γὰρ ἐν πᾶσιν ἀνθρώποις ἀίδιός ἐστιν ὅταν πολεμούντων πόλις ἁλῷ, τῶν ἑλόντων εἶναι καὶ τὰ σώματα τῶν ἐν τῇ πόλει καὶ τὰ χρήματα. οὔκουν ἀδικίᾳ γε ἕξετε ὅ τι ἂν ἔχητε, ἀλλὰ φιλανθρωπίᾳ οὐκ ἀφαιρήσεσθε, ἤν τι ἐᾶτε ἔχειν αὐτούς.

[276] See e.g. *Mem.* 4. 5. 10; *Hiero* 2. 15; *Hell.* 2. 4. 17, 5. 1. 16–17 (on the joys of defeating foes), and *Hiero* 2. 2; *Hell.* 4. 1. 8, 10; *Mem.* 2. 3. 14; *Anab.* 1. 3. 6, 1. 9. 11 (on the desire to benefit friends and harm enemies).

principles need to be *stated* by the Persian leader (and his enemy): if
this viewpoint were thoroughly taken for granted by all the characters
of the *Cyropaedia*, we would not expect it to be mentioned so
frequently and so explicitly. Xenophon is, perhaps, slightly uneasy
with these simplistic black-and-white maxims: while it is not surprising to find such sentiments uttered by the conqueror of a great
empire, this scheme of values can hardly be called Socratic, and at
times Xenophon seems aware of other, more generous, approaches
to foes. His Socrates appears to accept the 'help friends, harm
enemies' maxim, but Xenophon notes that the philosopher himself
benefits his friends and does no harm to anyone.[277] When Socrates in
the *Memorabilia* points out to Euthydemus that it is just to capture
and enslave an enemy's city, he is careful to add the proviso that the
hostile city is also an unjust one (*Mem.* 4. 2. 15; cf. 2. 2. 2).[278] In the
Cyropaedia too Cyrus always wages war against evil, unjust aggres-
sors: we are never given a hint of the expansionist nature of the
historical Cyrus' conquests.

The Assyrian king's speech is not a bad example of pre-battle
exhortation—it is rhetorical,[279] appeals to the deepest emotions of his
audience, and resembles to a great extent the kind of speeches Cyrus
normally makes; but it is to no avail. The king has repeatedly urged
his men not to flee from the battlefield, stressing how foolish such a
move would be, but great numbers of the Assyrians and their allies
do in fact run away from the Persians, during and after the battle,
leading to their disastrous defeat (3. 3. 63, 66, 4. 1. 8). Thus Cyrus'
contention that a single, well-spoken speech is of no real use is
manifestly true: the Assyrian's exhortation has proven worthless
when his forces were actually put to the test. Cyrus' men, on the other
hand, fight valiantly and are victorious, without having been
addressed or exhorted at the last moment. The most effective
counter-exhortation by Cyrus has been, in this case, his silence, and
this is probably why Xenophon allows the Assyrian king, one of the
villains of the *Cyropaedia*, to have his say in the first place—in order to

---

[277] *Mem.* 4. 8. 11; contrast 2. 3. 14, 2. 6. 35, 3. 9. 8. Plato's Socrates, of course, does
not believe in returning injury for injury—see e.g. *Crito* 49 B–C with Burnet's note *ad*
49 B 10 and Adam on Pl. *Rep.* 331 E ff. See also Scharr 1919: 217–18; Tatum 1989: 39;
Due 1989: 158–63, 196–7. Blundell 1989: 26–59 has a wide-ranging survey of Greek
popular thought on helping friends and harming enemies; she notes (56 with n. 146)
that active disapproval of the idea of harming enemies is not found before Socrates.
[278] Cf. Dover 1974: 180–4, 313–16; Ducrey 1968: 232.
[279] Cf. in particular 3. 3. 45 μῶρον γὰρ . . . μῶρος δὲ . . . μῶρος δὲ . . .

show how little his forceful words have meant. The Persian's rejection of discourse in favour of action, training, and practice is, incidentally, almost a topos in pre-battle exhortations.[280]

Cyrus, while denying that a single exhortation can bring about abiding virtues, suggests to his aide how such qualities as courage and honour can be acquired and retained. If men are to be virtuous, states the Persian leader, there must be laws to reward the good and punish the bad, as well as teachers to instruct and accustom their pupils to good behaviour. This method of instilling virtue, a combination of laws and instruction, conforms to the Persian system of education outlined by Xenophon at the beginning of the *Cyropaedia* (1. 2. 2–14) and is reminiscent of Protagoras' more elaborate description of how virtue is taught in Plato's *Protagoras* (325 C–326 E). Cyrus emphasizes the need to reinforce concepts of right and wrong until they become a very part of men (3. 3. 53 ἔστ' ἂν ἐγγένηται αὐτοῖς), thereby restating the claim he has made when debating with Tigranes: virtue—be it courage in battle or σωφροσύνη—cannot be acquired instantly, for it is the product of instruction, time, and practice.[281] Chrysantas would like instant results from a speech, notes Cyrus, but his aide is foolish to think that an extempore declamation, a kind of rhapsodical flourish (cf. 3. 3. 54 ἀπορραψῳδήσας),[282] will suffice to produce courage on the battlefield. Cyrus' rejection of oratory here reminds us of the negative attitude towards rhetoric held by Socrates.[283] Xenophon's philosopher does, however, take it for granted that a general must exhort his army (*Oec.* 5. 16; cf. *Mem.* 3. 3. 10–11), and in practice neither the Socrates of the *Memorabilia* nor the Persian leader of the *Cyropaedia* is at all averse to exhorting others at length in an attempt to make them more virtuous. Cyrus' words here are as empty as those of the Assyrian king, for his arguments against exhortations do not match his customary deeds: when the Persian leader rejects rhetoric, he is actually condemning his own behaviour throughout the *Cyropaedia*.

[280] See e.g. Thuc. 5. 69, 6. 68, and the further references in Latham 1981: 64–5 n. 21.

[281] For 'the familiar triad of nature, training, and knowledge' associated with the acquisition of virtue see O'Brien 1967: 144–6 n. 27.

[282] The word ἀπορραψῳδήσας used here by Cyrus is meant to be scornful, for rhapsodists were generally agreed to be the least intelligent of men—cf. *Mem.* 4. 2. 10; *Symp.* 3. 6; and Ion in Plato's dialogue of that name.

[283] This negative attitude towards rhetoric is more frequently associated with Plato's Socrates, who disapproved of the sophists' attempts to turn young men into professional orators almost overnight, while ignoring the moral qualities of their pupils (cf. e.g. the *Gorgias*), but see *Mem.* 1. 6. 11–14, 4. 2. 6–7, 11.

This conversation between Cyrus and Chrysantas is very like many of the dialogues of the *Memorabilia*, both in structure and in content. Cyrus, who clearly is the 'Socrates' of our conversation, does most of the talking, uses an analogy (delivering a splendid speech on courage to those untaught in ἀρετή is as useful as singing a fine song to the unmusical, 3. 3. 55), and ends the exchange with a long speech (3. 3. 51–5), just as the philosopher does so often in the *Memorabilia*. Chrysantas, the 'pupil', resembles the second category of Socrates' interlocutors described above, i.e. he contributes something to the conversation, but is an amenable, non-contentious partner, for after his initial suggestion of a hortatory address by his commander[284] he has little to add. The ideas espoused by the Persian leader in our conversation—his talk of acquiring virtue and his disdain for empty rhetoric—if not very original, sound Socratic, and in fact arise in the *Memorabilia*.[285] While this is one of the most *Memorabilia*-like exchanges in the *Cyropaedia*, it is also one of the more disappointing. Xenophon writes here with a heavy hand and Cyrus merely serves as a mouthpiece for his author's ideas, at the price of his own consistency as a character. It is perhaps not a coincidence that Xenophon deviates least from the basic 'mould' of a *Memorabilia* dialogue when he is at his most didactic: it seems that this pattern or vehicle automatically came to mind when he had a particular moralistic message to convey.[286]

7. THE DEATH OF A HERO: *CYR.* 8. 7

According to most Greek sources, Cyrus the Great died a sudden and violent death on the battlefield, after having ruled for some thirty years,[287] but in the *Cyropaedia* he dies peacefully in his bed, old and content. The Persian king, in Xenophon's version, has reached a ripe

---

[284] In the *Mem.* only rarely does a friendly interlocutor initiate a conversation with Socrates, as Chrysantas does here. *Mem.* 4. 8 is the closest parallel; there Socrates rejects Hermogenes' unsolicited advice, just as Cyrus turns down Chrysantas' suggestion here.

[285] Virtue: *Mem.* 3. 9. 1–3 (a discussion of whether courage can be taught or is a natural gift); cf. 2. 1. 6, 4. 1. 4. Empty rhetoric: 1. 6. 11–14, 3. 6, 4. 2. 6–7, 11.

[286] *Cyr.* 8. 2. 15–23, discussed below (ch. 4. 4), is another instance of a didactic dialogue constructed strictly according to the standard pattern found in the *Mem.*, where a character, Croesus, is presented in an inconsistent way.

[287] See e.g. Hdt. 1. 204–14 and Ctesias, *FGrH* 688 F 9. 7–8; for a complete collection of the Greek sources on Cyrus' death see Weissbach 1924: 1156ff.

old age (8. 7. 1 μάλα . . . πρεσβύτης ὤν), and is paying a state visit to Persia when, asleep in the royal palace, he is warned of his forthcoming end in a dream. Cyrus immediately offers prayers and sacrifices to the gods and then takes to his bed. Three days later he gathers his family and friends round his bedside for a long farewell address. In this final speech he delivers his political testament, appointing his older son, Cambyses, king and his younger son, Tanaoxares, satrap of various territories, and cautioning the brothers at length on the importance of fraternal devotion. Cyrus also reflects on the nature of the soul and asks to be buried simply. Finally, bidding those at his bedside farewell, the Persian ruler covers himself and dies (8. 7. 1–28). Such is the dignified and calm departure from life which Xenophon allots to his hero.

The Persian king's death is in many ways a philosophic one: the presence of his family and friends, his calm acceptance of impending death, the brief review of his own life, and his reflections on the soul and immortality all remind us of Socrates in his last days (as described by both Xenophon and Plato).[288] There is little doubt that these Socratic echoes are deliberate, but *Cyr.* 8. 7 has a Persian cast as well. In fact this farewell scene is particularly interesting because it intertwines Persian and Greek influences so closely together; at times it is a challenge to disentangle the various strands.[289]

We have already discussed above (ch. 1. 2) the arguments put forward by the Iranian scholar Christensen for the direct use of Persian epic traditions by Xenophon. According to Christensen, *Cyr.* 8. 7 furnishes the strongest evidence for such use of—or dependence upon—Persian epic. Christensen bases his argument upon a recurring scene found in the *Shahnamah*, the carefully arranged death of model kings. In the *Shahnamah*—which, claims Christensen, preserves patterns already formulated by ancient Persian epic—the exemplary king, before dying, arranges his succession, makes his last wishes known, delivers his political testament, and presents a few well-chosen reflections; naturally, not all these elements are present in every such scene.[290] It is true that Cyrus in the *Cyropaedia* conforms

---

[288] See Luccioni 1953: 148–9 for a comparison between *Cyr.* 8. 7 and various passages in the *Mem.*, Plato's *Apol.*, and the *Phaedo.* (Xenophon's *Apol.*, especially 26 ff., should be borne in mind as well.)

[289] Perhaps the best characterization of Cyrus' deathbed speech is that of Knauth 1975: 53, who terms it 'ein Musterbeispiel der gräko-iranischen Synthese'.

[290] Cf. Christensen 1936: 126–34. Knauth 1975: 53–63 expands upon, but does not really improve, Christensen's arguments; cf. Due 1989: 142–3.

to this model, and specific details of his departure from life—the message from the gods about his approaching death, the naming of his successors, the call for unity rather than friction between the brothers, and the short review of his own life—have fairly close parallels in different episodes of the *Shahnamah*.[291] None the less, Christensen's claims are ultimately unconvincing: while Xenophon *may* have been acquainted with such Persian material at first hand, the Persian elements found in the description of Cyrus' death could be due to an intermediary source, Ctesias. In his *Persica* Ctesias also describes the death of Cyrus the Great, and his account includes most of the Persian themes or elements outlined by Christensen. Since Xenophon was acquainted with the *Persica*,[292] Ctesias' work, rather than Persian oral traditions, may account for any Persian elements to be found in *Cyr.* 8. 7.

According to Ctesias (*FGrH* 688 F 9. 7–8), Cyrus the Great was wounded in battle in the thirtieth year of his rule, and died only three days later. Before dying, the Persian king appoints his older son, Cambyses, king and gives his younger son, Tanyoxarkes, command of various territories; his stepsons are allotted satrapies as well. Cyrus bids his sons obey their mother at all times and enjoins them to be loyal to one another. He also has his children pledge friendship with his enemy-turned-counsellor, Amorges. Finally, he blesses those of his family and friends who will remain loyal to one another and lays a curse upon any who will disrupt this unity. Only then does Cyrus die: ταῦτα εἴπας ἐτελεύτησε. Even though Ctesias' tale has reached us in abridged form, via Photius, the similarities between his account of Cyrus' dying words and the later version by Xenophon are plain: these correspondences are above and beyond the more general Persian pattern noted by Christensen. Both writers have Cyrus linger on for three days before delivering his final address, both call Cyrus' younger son by virtually the same name, Tanaoxares or Tanyoxarkes,[293] and both assign the two brothers very similar shares of Cyrus' kingdom. Finally, both Xenophon and Ctesias convey the

---

[291] Dream, last wishes, and appointment of successor: Kay Khosrow (Levy 1967: 177 ff.). Appointment of successor, call for unity: Vishtaspa (Levy 1967: 218). Review of life: Manuchehr (Levy 1967: 49). See too the further parallels in Christensen 1936: 126–34.

[292] For the relative chronology of the *Persica* and the *Cyr.* and Xenophon's acquaintance with Ctesias' work, cf. below, ch. 4. 1 at n. 16.

[293] In other Greek sources this son of Cyrus is known by a variety of names—Bardiya, Smerdis, etc.; cf. Hirsch 1985: 178 n. 72.

dying king's great concern with preserving family unity. Thus while Persian elements are plainly present in Cyrus' death scene in the *Cyropaedia*, we cannot determine the nature of Xenophon's sources for this material.

Returning to the *Cyropaedia*, we find that in Cyrus' dream a figure larger than life (8. 7. 2 κρείττων τις ἢ κατὰ ἄνθρωπον) approaches him and bids him make ready, for he is about to depart to the gods. This dream, with its straightforward rather prosaic revelation of forthcoming events (i.e. that Cyrus is close to death), is of a kind classified as a χρηματισμός or 'oracle' dream by ancient writers on dreams.[294] In Plato Socrates dreams a similarly uncomplicated dream only three days before his death. He too is warned (by a beautiful woman who quotes Homeric verse) of his imminent demise, or, to be more exact, of the precise date on which he will be executed (Pl. *Crito* 44 A–B).[295] Herodotus, of course, has a very different version of Cyrus' end—with the queen of the Massagetae dipping the Persian king's severed head in a pool of blood after his defeat at her hands[296]—but his Cyrus is also told in a dream of his impending death (Hdt. 1. 209). In Herodotus the Persian king's dream is opaque and allusive, and includes a further element, a symbolic indication that Darius will eventually succeed Cyrus as ruler of the empire.[297] It is interesting to note that Xenophon's own dreams, as reported in the *Anabasis* (3. 1. 11–13, 4. 3. 8), are closer in kind to the indirect, symbolic dream Cyrus has in Herodotus than to the straightforward revelation Xenophon allows his hero in the *Cyropaedia*.

[294] See Macrobius, *Somn. Scip.* 1. 3. 8, and cf. Dodds 1951: 107–10 with nn. on 124–5.

[295] Another noble figure who receives a supernatural summons before he dies is Sophocles' Oedipus (*OC* 1621 ff.). Oedipus hears this divine voice while awake, and the message he receives from the gods is, as in the case of our Cyrus, in plain, unadorned language (1627–8 ὢ οὗτος οὗτος Οἰδίπους τί μέλλομεν | χωρεῖν; πάλαι δὴ τἀπὸ σοῦ βραδύνεται; cf. *Cyr.* 8. 7. 2 Συσκευάζου ὢ Κῦρε· ἤδη γὰρ εἰς θεοὺς ἄπει). Oedipus, like Cyrus, dies quietly and painlessly, following this divine summons (*OC* 1663–5).

[296] Herodotus tells us that he chooses this gory version from several traditions related to the Persian king's death known to him (cf. Hdt. 1. 214 πολλῶν λόγων λεγομένων). See Sancisi-Weerdenburg 1985 for an interesting discussion of the three versions—in Herodotus, Ctesias, and Xenophon—of the death of Cyrus; her attempt to find parallels between Cyrus' farewell address in the *Cyr.* and Darius' Behistun Inscription is unconvincing. Hirsch 1985: 82–4, with nn. on 177–8, and Due 1989: 131–7, 142–4 also have analyses of Cyrus' death as reported by Herodotus, Xenophon, Ctesias, etc.

[297] Croesus (1. 34), Astyages (1. 107–8), and Cambyses (3. 30; cf. 64–5) are other figures in Herodotus who have such dreams telling of the end of a dynasty and the accession of a new ruler to the throne.

Cyrus' immediate reaction upon being informed that he is to die is to sacrifice to the gods on the heights, Persian fashion.[298] He presents the gods with thank-offerings in gratitude for their having indicated to him throughout his life what he should and should not do (8. 7. 3 ἅ τ' ἐχρῆν ποιεῖν καὶ ἃ οὐκ ἐχρῆν), and this final summons to the Persian king, telling him to ready himself, is perhaps one last instance of a message from the gods ἃ χρὴ ποιεῖν. Once again a comparison with the Persian king's death in Herodotus is illuminating: the Herodotean Cyrus also states before his death that the gods care for him and send him signs about the future—ἐμεῦ θεοὶ κήδονται καί μοι πάντα προδεικνύουσι τὰ ἐπιφερόμενα, he boasts to Hystaspas (Hdt. 1. 209)—but, ironically, he fails to interpret these signs, the dream sent him by the gods, correctly.[299] Our Cyrus tells the gods that despite their constant solicitude he has never forgotten his limitations as a mortal being (8. 7. 3).[300] He then petitions the gods for happiness for his family, friends, and country; for himself, Cyrus requests an end in harmony with the life the gods have given him (8. 7. 3). This interplay of ideas—an appreciation of mortal limitations, concern for the happiness of one's family and homeland, and the desire for a death as noble and untroubled as the life one has lived—immediately brings to mind Solon's famous discussion with Croesus in Herodotus (1. 30–3); these Solonian echoes are continued and elaborated in Cyrus' farewell address below.

After offering these prayers and sacrifices, Cyrus retires to his bed in the palace, accepting only drink but no food. On the third day after his dream he summons his sons, friends, and the Persian magistrates to his bedside. He informs those gathered round him that his end is near and, in a brief review of his life, explains why he should be considered happy. The Persian ruler has reaped the benefits of each of the four stages of life—childhood, youth, adulthood, and old age[301]—to the full and has always attained what he has desired. The aged Cyrus emphasizes that he has not found old age a burden and has sensed no lessening of his powers (8. 7. 6). When Xenophon's Socrates reviews his life in a similar situation, towards

---

[298] Cf. Hdt. 1. 131 and see Boyce 1982: 179–80, 216, who thinks that Xenophon may have been influenced here by Herodotus.

[299] Cf. Due 1989: 133 and cf. Hdt. 3. 64, where Cyrus' son, Cambyses, also fails to understand an oracle warning him of (the place of) his death.

[300] Compare Xenophon's words in praise of Agesilaus at *Ages.* 11. 2; cf. 11. 8.

[301] This division into four stages is in accordance with the Persian way of life, as outlined by Xenophon at the beginning of the *Cyr.* (1. 2. 4–14).

the very end (*Apol.* 5–6, 14–18; cf. *Mem.* 4. 8. 4–10), he concentrates on matters of the spirit, describing his own character and moral accomplishments and telling of the moral benefits his friends reap from his presence. (Cyrus, not surprisingly, is more concerned with practical or material attainments.) Socrates also stresses that he will be fortunate to die while his faculties are still intact, before old age and its infirmities set in. In fact the Athenian embraces death as an escape from the decrepitude and debility of old age, and this is the reason Xenophon gives for the philosopher not offering any real defence at his trial. When Socrates and Cyrus sum up their own achievements they are, in effect, eulogizing themselves, thus leaving the reader with an uncomfortable impression of their smugness. In the encomium *Agesilaus* Xenophon is more adept at presenting and praising a favourite personality because it is he, rather than his hero, who produces the kind words and flattering descriptions of the Spartan king's deeds and character. Agesilaus, incidentally, is like neither Cyrus nor Socrates in his attitude towards old age: Xenophon praises him for continuing to battle on even though he is old and infirm. His fighting spirit made the Spartan king even more formidable in old age than in his prime, contends his encomiast.[302]

Cyrus, continuing to sum up his own accomplishments in his farewell address, notes that he has aided his friends and harmed his enemies. (The Persian king will return to this point later on, at the very end of his speech.) He has also transformed his country into the foremost land of Asia, besides preserving all that he originally inherited. This desire to retain one's inheritance and acquire new holdings as well is perhaps universal—we hear of it in relation to both Greeks and Persians. In Athens the ephebes take an oath to preserve and increase their city's territory: καὶ οὐκ ἐλάττω παραδώσω τὴν πατρίδα, πλείω δὲ καὶ ἀρείω κατά τε ἐμαυτὸν καὶ μετὰ ἀπάντων.[303] On the Persian side, Herodotus' Xerxes explains that he intends to attack Athens so as not to lag behind his predecessors on the throne in adding to the Persian empire (Hdt. 7. 8a). In their famous bedroom scene Atossa encourages Darius to attack Greece, pointing out that he sits back on the throne idle without increasing the power

---

[302] Cf. *Ages.* 11. 14 ἡ μὲν τοῦ σώματος ἰσχὺς γηράσκει, ἡ δὲ τῆς ψυχῆς ῥώμη τῶν ἀγαθῶν ἀνδρῶν ἀγήρατός ἐστιν, and cf. 11. 15.

[303] See Robert 1938 (= Tod 1948, No. 204) for the text of this 4th-cent. inscription. Siewert 1977: 104 finds a deliberate echo of this oath in Thuc. 1. 144. 4 and notes (cf. his references in n. 18) that the concept of bequeathing something undiminished or enlarged was a topos in Greek speeches.

of the Persians (Hdt. 3. 134). Cyrus, of course, cannot be accused of such idleness (cf. *Cyr.* 1. 1. 4).

The Persian king now returns to the Herodotean themes of the mutability of human fortune and the meaning of true happiness, explaining that the ever-present fear of a mishap of some kind has saved him from arrogance and immoderate happiness. Now that he is about to die, Cyrus feels that he should indeed be considered blessed (8. 7. 9 μακαριζόμενος), since his children survive him and his homeland and friends are prospering. The Persian king's oblique definition of happiness here is very similar to the description of happy men provided by Herodotus' Solon. In fact Cyrus' life sounds like that of Tellus the Athenian, the man whom Solon designates as happiest of all in his conversation with Croesus (Hdt. 1. 30).[304] Tellus, like Cyrus, has led a good life, and when he dies he leaves behind a prosperous city and children (not to mention grandchildren) who survive him. There is, however, one significant difference between Cyrus and Tellus: the aged Persian king dies peaceably in bed, while Tellus dies a valiant death on the battlefield, defending his city. Cyrus' painless departure from life is more like that of Cleobis and Biton, the next pair of fortunate men mentioned by Solon; the two die quietly in their sleep (Hdt. 1. 31). Echoes of this famous exchange between Solon and Croesus are found elsewhere in the *Cyropaedia*,[305] and it is interesting that Xenophon chooses to have two wise figures—Solon and Socrates—cast their shadow over Cyrus' farewell address. Socrates dies swiftly,[306] amidst friends, with great dignity and calm—just as Xenophon has Cyrus pass away—but he was, of course, executed. The philosopher did not have what could be described as a fitting or—despite the arguments he produces in Xenophon—timely death, and if his life is judged according to Solon's precept of 'looking to the end' (Hdt. 1. 32 σκοπέειν . . . τὴν τελευτήν), Socrates cannot be considered truly fortunate.[307] This disturbing dissonance between Socrates' dignity and fortitude in the face of death and the actual fact of his execution may have been what

---

[304] See Keller 1911: 255–6 for a detailed comparison of the two passages, and cf. Lefèvre 1971: 295–6.

[305] i.e. at *Cyr.* 7. 2—cf. below, ch. 4. 4.

[306] It has been suggested that Plato prettifies or idealizes Socrates' death, minimizing the painful physical effects that the hemlock would have had on the philosopher; see Gill 1973 and Ober 1982.

[307] In the *Apol.* Xenophon *does* present Socrates' death as ideal—ἐμοὶ μὲν οὖν δοκεῖ θεοφιλοῦς μοίρας τετυχηκέναι· τοῦ μὲν γὰρ βίου τὸ χαλεπώτατον ἀπέλιπε, τῶν δὲ θανάτων τοῦ ῥᾴστου ἔτυχεν (*Apol.* 32)—but this is clearly apologetic.

led Xenophon to introduce echoes of Solon into our scene as well.
When he is told that he is about to die, Cyrus prays to the gods for a
death consonant with his way of life: αἰτοῦμαι ... ἐμοὶ δὲ οἰόνπερ
αἰῶνα δεδώκατε, τοιαύτην καὶ τελευτὴν δοῦναι (8. 7. 3). In other
words, the Persian king looks to his own 'end' and Xenophon, who,
as we have seen, did not feel bound by the actual historical facts, acts
in lieu of the gods here and grants his hero such a felicitous end. It is
interesting that Xenophon chooses a peaceful, philosophical passing
as most appropriate for his hero: one might have thought that a
courageous death on the battlefield—a death like that of Tellus,
Cyrus the Younger, Agesilaus,[308] and the Cyruses of both Herodotus
and Ctesias—would have best suited the outstanding conqueror of
the *Cyropaedia*. Xenophon's Cyrus is, however, not only a successful
military leader but an ideal ruler of an empire, and in this death
scene his author chooses to stress this side of his character, presenting
the Persian as a kind of philosopher king.[309]

The dying Persian king now turns to the question of succession to
the throne, and here he addresses his two sons, Cambyses and
Tanaoxares, directly. (This is the Persian princes' first, and last,
appearance in the *Cyropaedia*.) We have already seen that the delivery
of a political testament by a moribund king is a regular feature of late
Persian epic and that this may reflect genuine early Persian tradition,
but it is worth noticing that Socrates' last words in Plato's *Apology*
(41 E–42 A) also concern *his* sons. Socrates asks his followers to carry
on their education, scolding and exhorting them in emulation of his
own manner.[310] Herodotus' Cyrus, arrogant though he may be,
realizes that he may die in his forthcoming clash with the Massagetae. Hence he too bequeaths a moral testament of sorts: the
Persian king entrusts his wise counsellor Croesus into Cambyses'
hands, enjoining his son to behave properly towards the Lydian
monarch (Hdt. 1. 208).[311] In any event, here—as well as in the
versions of both Herodotus and Ctesias—Cyrus, before dying,

[308] The 83-year-old Agesilaus did not actually die on the battlefield, but on the
homeward voyage from Egypt.

[309] Anderson 1974: 37–9 suggests that Xenophon was thinking about his own death
as well.

[310] More generally, 'Dying king names successor' and 'wise words of dying father'
are both common folk motifs; one is reminded, for example, of the patriarch Jacob's
final words to his sons (Gen. 34). See Thompson 1955–8: P 17. 3 and J 154.

[311] Cf. Sancisi-Weerdenburg 1985: 467; she points out that Cambyses' last words in
Herodotus (3. 64–5)—the exhortations, blessings, and curses—are even more of a
spiritual testament and resemble Cyrus' farewell address in Ctesias.

appoints Cambyses king. There are several instances of Achaemenid kings appointing their successors—the dying Darius II summons his two sons, Artaxerxes and Cyrus the Younger, to his bedside and appoints his heir at the opening of the *Anabasis* (1. 1–4), and in Herodotus Darius is asked to name his heir before setting out on a dangerous campaign, in accordance with Persian practice (7. 2 κατὰ τὸν Περσέων νόμον)—but we cannot be certain that there was indeed such a custom or law.[312] Our Cyrus explains that he must bequeath his throne in unambiguous fashion in order to prevent strife: while he loves both his sons equally, the crown will go to his older son Cambyses, for the young must give way to their more experienced elders. Such yielding to elders is, Cyrus points out, the ancient, established Persian custom (cf. 8. 7. 10 παλαιὰ καὶ εἰθισμένα καὶ ἔννομα), which the king himself and his sons have been taught to honour.[313] Succession according to primogeniture was not, in fact, an absolute rule in Achaemenid Persia. Xerxes, for example, was not Darius' eldest child, but the first born after his father ascended to the throne, and Parysatis, according to Ctesias, tried to persuade Darius to make use of this criterion and leave his kingdom to her favourite, Cyrus the Younger.[314] Our Cyrus tries to reconcile his younger son to being second in command, explaining to Tanaoxares that his life will be happier and less care-ridden than that of his older brother. Cambyses, as king, will need to spend a great deal of time and energy attempting to match his father's great deeds, besides plotting and being plotted against (8. 7. 12 καὶ τὸ ἐπιβουλεύειν καὶ τὸ ἐπιβουλεύεσθαι).[315]

Next Cyrus reminds his older son that loyal friends are the best guardians of royal power, and no friend can be more trustworthy than a brother: this leads the dying king to a discussion of the virtues of fraternal devotion. Children born of the same parents, who are raised together, notes the Persian king, are bound by the very nature of things to be close to one another. We find this same claim made by Socrates when he tries to reconcile two brothers who have quarrelled (*Mem.* 2. 3. 4). Both Socrates and Cyrus also contend that other

---

[312] Cf. How and Wells on Hdt. 7. 2. 1: 'There is no hint of any such rule or law when Cambyses invaded Egypt . . . Darius Scythia . . . or Xerxes Greece.'

[313] Cf. *Mem.* 2. 3. 15–16.

[314] *FGrH* 688 F 17. 2. 4; cf. Hdt. 7. 2–3.

[315] See Soph. *OR* 583–99 and Eur. *Hipp.* 1016–20 for similar appreciations (by Creon and Hippolytus respectively) of the advantages of being second in command, and cf. *Cyr.* 7. 2. 27–9.

people, outsiders, respect and fear brothers who are allies (*Mem.* 2. 3. 4; *Cyr.* 8. 7. 15–17, 23).[316] Interestingly, Cyrus does not make use of a notable argument concerning the value of a brother, found in a Persian context: the famous statement by Intaphrenes' wife that a brother, unlike a spouse or children, is irreplaceable once one's parents are gone (Hdt. 3. 119).[317] The Persian king's next argument for good relations between the brothers leads him to speak of death, the soul, and immortality: Cyrus warns his sons that his soul may be able to observe and supervise them even after he dies. It is in this section of Cyrus' farewell address that we are most strongly reminded of the dying Socrates, but the Persian's thoughts on the question of an afterlife are, in essence, a digression and subsequently he returns to his main concern, the relationship between his sons.

Here, then, we find Xenophon at his most apologetic, explaining away the awkward historical facts without actually referring to them in any way. Whatever the exact course of events—Cambyses may have murdered his brother and his motive may have been the latter's attempt to usurp his throne[318]—it is clear that Cyrus' two sons were at violent odds with one another. His Persian hero, the author of the *Cyropaedia* tells us insistently but indirectly, is not to be blamed for this unfortunate turn of events: Cyrus' very last words to his sons are a clarion call for love and loyalty between the brothers.

Brotherly love was not, of course, an outstanding quality of the Achaemenid royal families. From the death of Cyrus the Great down to Xenophon's own day the Persian kingdom was plagued by the problem of fraternal strife, and on several occasions one brother assassinated another in order to succeed to the throne. Xerxes and Artobazanes settled their succession dispute peaceably (Hdt. 7. 2–3), but Darius II (Ochos) killed his half-brother Sogdianos, who had earlier assassinated another half-brother, Xerxes II; the latter was the only legitimate heir to the throne of Artaxerxes. Xenophon, of course, was involved in the Persian fraternal conflict of his own day, that between Artaxerxes II and Cyrus the Younger. Not only did he support the younger brother, Cyrus, but he actually fought at the

[316] Cyrus' very presentation of this argument—by means of a series of rhetorical questions—is reminiscent of Socrates' hortative methods of persuasion in the *Mem.* Socrates includes a further argument not mentioned by Cyrus: brothers are even better suited to work together and help one another than other objects which come in pairs (*Mem.* 2. 3. 19 τἆλλα ὅσα ἀδελφὰ ἔφυσεν ἀνθρώποις), such as hands, feet, and eyes.

[317] Cf. Soph. *Ant.* 905–12.

[318] See Cook 1983: 48–54.

usurper's side against the older, legitimate heir: this makes Cyrus the Great's words here particularly interesting. Why does Xenophon have his hero speak in favour of the ancient, established law of primogeniture and expound upon the merits of fraternal devotion when he could have ignored these questions altogether?

One reason may be that Xenophon wishes to counter an argument frequently used against political leaders in Plato, that they do not educate their sons and transmit to them their ἀρετή. The statesmen Themistocles, Aristides, Thucydides, and particularly Pericles are criticized by the Platonic Socrates for their inability to educate their sons in matters of virtue. At times Socrates implies that these politicians are not, in fact, wise and this is the reason that they are unable to teach others (e.g. *Alc. I* 118c–119A); elsewhere his argument is that the unsuccessful sons of statesmen are proof of the fact that virtue cannot be taught (e.g. *Prot.* 319E–320B).[319] Cyrus the Great is another conspicuous instance of a political leader who did not—or could not—transmit his good qualities to his sons, but, Xenophon shows us here, it was not for lack of trying. Cyrus' words here anticipate (and virtually refute in advance) a criticism of the Persian king found in a chronologically later composition, Plato's *Laws* (694c–695B). The Athenian stranger of the *Laws* claims that Cyrus had left the education of his sons to women and eunuchs and suggests that this is why Cambyses was such a notorious failure. In our chapter of the *Cyropaedia* Xenophon demonstrates that Cyrus *did* devote time and energy to the moral instruction of his sons and consequently should not be held responsible for subsequent events.[320]

The next section of Cyrus' farewell address, the dying king's thoughts on immortality (8. 7. 17–22), was translated and adapted by Cicero in the *Cato Maior* (79–81; cf. 30).[321] The Persian king begins by warning his sons that they cannot be certain that his soul will not remain alive even after he dies. While he himself believes that his soul will continue to exist after leaving his body, the Persian king is undogmatic and sees immortality as a possibility, no more;[322]

---

[319] Cf. Protagoras' reply at 326c–328B, and see Pl. *Meno* 93B–94E. In the *Laches* (179c–D) it is the sons of two of these famous statesmen, rather than Socrates, who complain that their accomplished fathers have neglected their education.

[320] Cf. Tatum 1989: 227–34.

[321] For a detailed comparison of the two texts, with a rich collection of further parallels, see Powell 1988: 256–61. Cf. also Krömer 1977; Tatum 1989: 210–12.

[322] Cf. *Cyr.* 8. 7. 22 εἰ μὲν οὖν οὕτως ἔχει ταῦτα ὥσπερ ἐγὼ οἴομαι . . . εἰ δὲ μὴ οὕτως and 27 ἢν μετὰ τοῦ θείου γένωμαι . . . ἢν μηδὲν ἔτι ὦ.

Socrates is similarly open-minded in Plato's *Apology* (29 A–B, 40 C).[323]
One argument in favour of an afterlife adduced by Cyrus is that the
soul is invisible, not seen even in the living: we recognize its presence
only through its effect on its surroundings. Xenophon's Socrates
makes a similar claim in the *Memorabilia* (1. 4. 9, 4. 3. 13). A second
point raised by the Persian ruler is that the unjust are haunted by the
souls of their victims. Here Cyrus comes closest to threatening his
sons, hinting that he will haunt them if they misbehave,[324] and we are
reminded of the blessings and curses attributed to Ctesias' dying
Cyrus.[325] In both Plato and Xenophon Socrates identifies with those,
such as Palamedes, who have been unjustly condemned, but the
philosopher does not speak of haunting his accusers after his death
(Pl. *Apol.* 41 B; Xen. *Apol.* 26): Plato's Socrates thinks that his revenge
will come from the young men who will continue to practise his
methods in less restrained fashion (*Apol.* 39 C–D), while Xenophon's
philosopher thinks that time will vindicate him (*Apol.* 26, 29).

The Persian ruler's next two arguments concerning the immortality of the soul have interesting echoes of the *Phaedo*. Cyrus contends
that the soul is the vital life-giving force in human beings and the
body is alive as long as the soul remains in it: we can conclude that
there is no reason why a soul should die when separated from a body
(*Cyr.* 8. 7. 19; cf. *Phaedo* 105 C–D). A second *Phaedo*-like argument
adduced by Cyrus is that the soul is wisest when it is on its own, away
from the body, separate and pure (*Cyr.* 8. 7. 20 ἄκρατος καὶ καθαρός;
cf. *Phaedo* 64 C–67 B); the Persian's use of the word καθαρός is particularly reminiscent of the Orphic influence which is so prominent in
Plato's dialogue.

Cyrus' final argument—after stating that a dead body is resolved
into its component elements, with every part returning to its kindred
matter except for the soul[326]—is that death is very like sleep (cf. Pl.
Apol. 40 D). In sleep, states the Persian king, the soul is most divine
and is able to see something of the future (i.e. in dreams); in death,
we can assume, the soul will be even more god-like. Cyrus' words

[323] For a sensible discussion of Socrates' views on the soul and immortality see
Guthrie 1969: 477–84.

[324] It is significant that Cicero does not translate this sentence (*Cyr.* 8. 7. 18) in his
more benign version of Cyrus' speech in the *Cato Maior*; cf. Krömer 1977: 96–8; Powell
1988: 258.

[325] Cf. *FGrH* 688 F 9. 8 καὶ τοῖς μὲν ἐμμένουσι ταῖς πρὸς ἀλλήλους εὐνοίαις ἀγαθὰ
ηὔχετο, ἐπηρᾶτο δὲ τοῖς χειρῶν ἄρξουσιν ἀδίκων.

[326] See the parallels collected by Powell 1988: 259.

here are particularly interesting as evidence for a new outlook developing among Greeks. In this view man has a hidden self of divine origin and this self—the soul—is the source of dreams, rather than an outside figure.[327] Socrates in both *Apology*s mentions the fact that men often prophesy on the verge of death, and in each work the philosopher offers a prediction of his own (Pl. *Apol.* 39 c; Xen. *Apol.* 30). Cyrus, however, offers no such view into the future—for what can he predict other than the ruin that will result from his sons' quarrel?[328]—but turns to the gods.

Since the Persian king does not insist upon immortality, he bolsters his plea for good relations between the brothers by reminding them that if he will not oversee their relationship, the all-powerful gods will. The gods, states Cyrus, are eternal, all-seeing, and omnipotent. They keep the universe—indescribable in its beauty and grandeur—in order and his sons should fear and respect them. There is a very close parallel to Cyrus' words in the *Memorabilia* (4. 3. 13), where Socrates discusses religion with Euthydemus,[329] and this strong similarity demonstrates once again how Greek or Socratic, rather than Persian, Cyrus' religion generally is.

When the Persian king finally finishes exhorting his sons—again warning them that others will not trust them if they quarrel and urging them to consider the fate of warring brothers in the past—he turns to the question of his mortal remains. Cyrus asks for a simple burial with no gold or silver trappings: he, a lover of men, will be happy to mingle with a great benefactor to mankind, the earth.[330] His request raises several interesting questions. In actual fact the Persian monarch was laid to rest in a gold coffin amidst a collection of gold, precious stones, and rich carpets, as we know from the fourth-century eyewitness report of Aristobulus.[331] Furthermore, a request for a lavish tomb with trappings of silver and gold may have been a

[327] See Dodds 1951: 135–40, with nn. on 156–7. Cyrus' actual dream in the *Cyr.*, announcing his death, is none the less of the old-fashioned 'external' kind.

[328] Cf. the epilogue of the *Cyr.* (8. 8. 2): ἐπεὶ μέντοι Κῦρος ἐτελεύτησεν, εὐθὺς μὲν αὐτοῦ οἱ παῖδες ἐστασίαζον.

[329] Compare *Cyr.* 8. 7. 22 θεοὺς ... οἳ καὶ τήνδε τὴν τῶν ὅλων τάξιν συνέχουσιν ἀτριβῆ καὶ ἀγήρατον καὶ ἀναμάρτητον καὶ ὑπὸ κάλλους καὶ μεγέθους ἀδιήγητον and *Mem.* 4. 3. 13 καὶ ὁ τὸν ὅλον κόσμον συντάττων τε καὶ συνέχων, ἐν ᾧ πάντα καλὰ καὶ ἀγαθά ἐστι, καὶ ἀεὶ μὲν χρωμένοις ἀτριβῆ τε καὶ ὑγιᾶ καὶ ἀγήρατα παρέχων. For a discussion of Xenophon's sources for the interesting, teleological arguments of *Mem.* 4. 3 see Breitenbach 1966: 1827–30.

[330] On the 'just earth' see Powell 1988: 208–9; contrast Pheraulas the commoner's attitude to the earth—*Cyr.* 8. 3. 38.

[331] Cf. Arrian, *Anab.* 6. 29. 4–11 and Strabo 15. 3. 7 (who cites Onesicritus as well).

recurring theme in Persian epic tradition, a regular feature in the farewell addresses of dying kings.[332] Here Cyrus rejects both historical verisimilitude and (possibly) Persian tradition, and Xenophon transforms the dying king's request for an elaborate burial into a Socratic desire for simplicity.[333] It should be noted that the question of Cyrus' burial is also rather tricky if we accept Herodotus' version of the death of the Persian king, the version which is often considered closest to the historical truth. The Persians, according to Herodotus, would have had to recover Cyrus' mutilated body, transport it back to Pasargadae, and then erect a tomb there for his remains.[334]

A further problem raised by the Persian king's desire to be buried in the earth is the question of Cyrus' Zoroastrianism.[335] If Cyrus were indeed a full-fledged Zoroastrian, one might at first sight expect his body to be exposed rather than immediately inhumed, with Xenophon tactfully avoiding the subject. Herodotus knows that the Magi practise the funerary rite of exposure (Hdt. 1. 140), but this may not have been an absolute religious ordinance of Zoroastrianism in Achaemenid times.[336] The purpose behind this rite of exposure is to avoid polluting the elements—earth, fire, and water. The historical Achaemenid rulers may have made some concessions to the precepts of Zoroastrianism even while having elaborate tombs erected, since Cyrus' body, like that of Darius and his successors, was first embalmed and then placed in a gold coffin inside a tomb of stone: both stone and metal were considered impermeable and acted as barriers to impurity. These impressive kingly tombs were meant, it seems, to serve as reminders of the power and mystique of royalty

---

[332] Christensen 1936: 132–5 points out that there are two such requests by a dying monarch for an elaborate burial in the *Shahnamah*—'Alexander' asks to be buried in a gold coffin and Kasra Nashirvan gives detailed instructions concerning his tomb, which is to resemble the one built for the historical Cyrus. This tradition, contends Christensen, began with Cyrus the Great.

[333] Thus Christensen (see previous n.), who believes that Xenophon was acquainted with this feature of Persian epic; in essence, Christensen tries to demonstrate Persian influence here by its very absence. But Xenophon may simply have been transforming what he knew of Cyrus the Great's actual tomb. It seems likely that descriptions of the impressive monument at Pasargadae would have reached Xenophon's ears from his contemporaries, either Greek or Persian, particularly if, as is now conjectured, a smaller replica of the tomb was built for Cyrus the Younger at Buzpar in south-western Fars. See Hirsch 1985: 84, 173–4 n. 43; Boyce 1988: 27.

[334] See Hirsch 1985: 84 (with nn. on 170). For the present-day identification of Cyrus' tomb at the archaeological excavations of Pasargadae see Cook 1983: 35–6 (with nn. on 235) and Stronach 1985: 838–41.

[335] See above, sect. 2 at n. 113.

[336] See the sensible remarks of Frye 1984: 123, 134.

and to encourage an attitude of veneration towards the dead kings.[337] Despite his request for a simple burial, our Cyrus is interested in having the Persians and their allies come to his graveside, and he asks his sons to provide rewards for those who will so honour him (8. 7. 27).

Cyrus, sensing that death is near, now takes his leave of those present at his bedside. The Persian king's last words to his sons are both a plea for unity between the brothers and a conventional, un-Socratic piece of Greek morality: by being kind to their friends his sons will be able to punish their enemies, Cyrus states.[338] The Persian ruler then asks his sons to bid their mother farewell on his behalf, shakes hands with those at his bedside, covers himself, and immediately dies.

It is instructive to compare the quiet, restrained departure of Cyrus with the final moments of Socrates, as described by Plato in the *Phaedo* (115 B–118). (Xenophon, of course, does not depict the actual death of Socrates.) We have already noted that on their deathbeds both Socrates and Cyrus are surrounded by friends and both accept their imminent death with great dignity and calm, sharing their thoughts on immortality. The philosopher is not, however, interested in the details of his burial, and his very last words (on the cock owed to Asclepius—*Phaedo* 118) are enigmatic, as opposed to Cyrus' final statement, which sums up the credo of a lifetime. In the *Phaedo* the tone is more emotional: Socrates' friends openly cry after he drinks the hemlock (117 C–E) and the distressed Xanthippe has to be escorted home (60 A–B). The Persian king's family and friends are remarkably dry-eyed and restrained. There are no tearful women present, and Cyrus seems to think of his wife only in her role as mother of his sons; there is no emotional parting like that between Panthea and Abradatas. Cyrus does not even have a maudlin, weeping companion—Gadatas would be a good candidate—akin to Socrates' disciple Apollodorus. The Persian king demonstrates great fortitude, of course, in the face of death, and Xenophon is more understated than usual, portraying Cyrus in this manner without

---

[337] See Boyce 1982: 54–7, 70. She points out (1988: 27–8) that the fire-holders found at Cyrus' tomb at Pasargadae—objects whose workmanship indicate that they date from the time of Cyrus—are further evidence for the practice of Zoroastrianism by the Achaemenid ruler.

[338] *Cyr.* 8. 7. 28 καὶ τοῦτο . . . μέμνησθέ μου τελευταῖον, τοὺς φίλους εὐεργετοῦντες καὶ τοὺς ἐχθροὺς δυνήσεσθε κολάζειν; compare Cyrus the Younger's prayer at *Anab.* 1. 9. 11, and see above, sect. 6.

actually underlining for his readers how brave and noble his hero is. Elsewhere Xenophon pointedly admires Socrates (*Apol.* 27–8) and Theramenes (*Hell.* 2. 3. 56) for confronting death with wit and courage. All in all, Cyrus' passing, while quiet and dignified, is—unlike Socrates' death in the *Phaedo*—rather bloodless, and this· farewell scene is a low-key finale to the *Cyropaedia*.[339]

In this section of the *Cyropaedia* Xenophon has set himself a complex task: he has his hero Cyrus sum up the accomplishments of a lifetime and die a quiet, philosophical death, while at the same time dissociating himself from the future misdemeanours of his sons without actually acknowledging them. Xenophon blends a variety of influences—Greek and Persian literary sources, historical occurrences in the Achaemenid empire, and the death of a well-loved contemporary figure—in order to accomplish this task. More specifically, Cyrus' farewell scene is a curious amalgam of three main ingredients: the story of Cyrus' death as found in Persian sources, the musings of Herodotus' Solon on the true meaning of happiness, and the description of Socrates' final days in both Plato and Xenophon. These influences have proved surprisingly compatible, and many specific features of *Cyr.* 8. 7—Cyrus' dream announcing his death, his death exactly three days later, his pride in increasing his patrimony, the delivery of a last will and testament—cannot be attributed to any one particular source, either Greek or Persian. The wide range of sources combined by Xenophon in this chapter and the several, diverse aims he has in mind make this farewell scene a kind of *Cyropaedia* within a *Cyropaedia*, a microcosm of the entire work.

Before concluding this chapter, it is worth noticing just how many different candidates for the role of Socrates can be found in the *Cyropaedia*. At first sight one would expect that the part of leading, didactic figure would be reserved exclusively for the hero of the work, Cyrus: normally Xenophon is as eager to glorify the Persian leader as he is to extol the Athenian philosopher. Indeed, at times Cyrus is very clearly 'Socrates': in the farewell scene which we have just seen, in his conversations with Astyages and with the Armenian king, and in his discussion with Chrysantas, where the Persian leader plays a part very like that of the philosopher of the *Memorabilia*. The *Cyropaedia*, however, unlike the *Memorabilia*, is not an apologetic work, and Xenophon can give free rein to his imagination and ingenuity when

[339] For the problematic epilogue of the *Cyr.*, 8. 8, see below, ch. 5. 3.

constructing didactic dialogues: Cyrus need not be the teaching figure in every one of these conversations. Thus Cambyses, in his long talk with his son, is plainly meant to be 'Socrates' (with Cyrus cast in the role of pupil), while the Armenian sophist is a third figure who cannot but remind us of the Athenian philosopher. In other encounters—with Mandane, Tigranes, and Cyaxares—neither Cyrus nor his fellow conversationalist can be termed a 'Socrates', despite the Socratic tone of these conversations: these exchanges are more fluid and livelier than the majority of the dialogues of the *Memorabilia*. Often Socratic influence is at its best or most interesting in the *Cyropaedia* when Xenophon alters the basic pattern of the *Memorabilia* in some way, either making the conversations more dialectical or blending in other—most notably Persian and Herodotean—elements. If Xenophon allows himself a freer hand in the *Cyropaedia* than in the *Memorabilia*, he uses that freedom well.

3

The Symposia of the *Cyropaedia*

I. INTRODUCTION

Only one gathering in the *Cyropaedia*, a celebration after the conquest of Babylon (8. 4. 1–27), is actually termed a symposium,[1] but several relaxed, semi-serious conversations which take place round the dinner table are found in the work. These parties are, as a rule, lively interludes meant to charm and instruct the reader rather than advance the plot of the work in any substantial way. Astyages arranges a banquet for Mandane and young Cyrus during their visit to Media (1. 3. 4–12), Cyrus invites several of his Persian officers to join him at mess in his tent (2. 2. 1–2. 3. 1), Gobryas joins his new ally, Cyrus, at dinner on the grounds of his estate (5. 2. 5–22), and Pheraulas and a Sacian rearrange their future in a tête-à-tête over dinner (8. 3. 35–50).[2] These parties, besides lending vivacity and colour to the work, are an interesting blend of Greek and Persian customs, while the influence of Socratic symposia is never far in the background. All of these banquets share a number of recurrent themes, and a closer look at *Cyr.* 8. 4. 1–27, the longest and most varied symposium in the work, is perhaps the easiest way to identify these characteristic topics.

At this symposium Cyrus celebrates his victory in the races following his inaugural royal procession. The Persian's most loyal friends (Chrysantas and Hystaspas) and the leaders of his allies (Artabazus, Tigranes, Gobryas, and the Hyrcanian chief) have been invited. Gadatas is in charge of the arrangements for the party, including the seating plan (8. 4. 1–2). The guests, we are told, are not seated at random, but according to merit, with those most loyal to Cyrus in closest proximity to their host (8. 4. 3–5): Cyrus encourages his men

---

[1] 8. 4. 13 προϊόντος δὲ τοῦ συμποσίου.

[2] There are in the *Cyr.* three additional conversations which take place over dinner: the exchange between Cyrus, Tigranes, and the Armenian king on the fate of 'Socrates' (3. 1. 38–40; see above, ch. 2. 4), and two short conversations between Cyrus and his soldiers at mess (2. 3. 19–20, 2. 3. 22–4), which are too brief to be considered symposia.

to compete for his favour.[3] This theme of rivalry or competition among the guests at a symposium, introduced here even before the party actually begins, is one that is found in almost all the symposia of the *Cyropaedia*. Likewise, the careful attention paid to the physical arrangements of the party is not unusual, and will be found in the other banquets of this group.

The conversation at this symposium—a series of loosely connected exchanges between Cyrus and his guests—begins only after dinner. Gobryas opens in a serious vein, admiring Cyrus' generosity in distributing leftovers from the meal to absent friends. Cyrus, says Gobryas, is even more outstanding as a philanthropist than as a general. His host accepts the compliment and adds didactically that he prefers benefiting people to harming them (8. 4. 6–8). This opening exchange is plainly meant to be edifying, and there is, as we shall see, a pronounced didactic tendency in all the symposia of the *Cyropaedia*.

The drinking continues and Hystaspas is the next one to address Cyrus. He is hurt that Chrystantas has been seated in a more honoured position and he cross-examines the Persian leader in order to discover why he has been relegated to an inferior place. Cyrus explains that Chrysantas has frequently taken the initiative in furthering his aims, besides executing the actual orders he receives. Often, adds Cyrus, Chrysantas rejoices in his leader's good fortune more than Cyrus does himself. Hystaspas accepts this explanation but is puzzled by one thing: how is he meant to demonstrate his great joy at Cyrus' successes? By clapping his hands or laughing? Artabazus suggests that he dance the Persian dance and the party dissolves into laughter (8. 4. 9–12). While the humour of this last remark is lost upon modern readers, its overall purpose is not. The guests at this symposium are rivals and Artabazus' jest helps to relieve the tension and lighten the party's atmosphere. Such alternation between serious and light-hearted matters is found throughout this party, and it is a key feature of the symposia of the *Cyropaedia*.

The next exchange at the banquet (8. 4. 13–23) is also semi-serious in tone. Gobryas admits that he is much happier now at the prospect of his daughter marrying one of Cyrus' men than he was when he originally made the offer (cf. *Cyr.* 5. 2. 7 ff.). The Persians have now shown that they know how to bear good fortune, explains Gobryas,

[3] Compare Xerxes' conference before Salamis, where he seats his allies according to rank (Hdt. 8. 67).

and this is a task even more difficult than their earlier one of bearing hardships with good cheer. The Persian leader claims to be much impressed with Gobryas' words of wisdom, and Hystaspas states that Gobryas' present display of profundity is an even greater incentive towards marrying his daughter than his earlier display of drinking-cups was (see again 5. 2. 7 ff.). This talk of marriage leads Cyrus to offer his services as an expert matchmaker, and he then demonstrates his skill by showing, in comic fashion, what sort of wife would best suit Chrysantas. Once again the other symposiasts burst into laughter: Cyrus' wit and urbanity are the envy of his guests.

Several new themes common to most of the symposia of the *Cyropaedia* are introduced in this section. Gobryas' opening words and Hystaspas' choice of wisdom rather than drinking-cups are in essence a commentary on what constitutes true wealth. Material riches and their pitfalls are contrasted with spiritual treasure here; similar discussions of real and apparent wealth are found in several other of the dinner-parties. Cyrus' matchmaking in fun (and in earnest—see immediately below, 8. 4. 24–6) is another sympotic pastime that should be noted. Finally, this exchange reflects the symposiasts' desire to appear wise or witty in the eyes of their fellow guests. Such attempts to outshine table companions in conversation is again a regular feature of symposia, and is, of course, one facet of the competition normally found among party guests.

In the last section of this dialogue (8. 4. 24–7) Cyrus distributes gifts to his guests: a robe, a golden cup, a horse, etc. Cyrus' present to Gobryas is a husband for his daughter—Hystaspas—and he has the two men shake hands to confirm the betrothal. Hystaspas then receives from Cyrus many gifts to send on to his prospective bride. Chrysantas is awarded a kiss and this arouses the envy of Artabazus, a long-standing admirer of Cyrus (cf. 1. 4. 27–8). Artabazus too will receive an embrace, promises the Persian leader, thirty years from now. Artabazus declares that he will wait and the party ends on this light note.

The distribution of gifts found here (like Cyrus' distribution of titbits from his table to absent friends, at the beginning of the symposium) is a Persian feature rather than a Greek one, and the actual gifts presented seem particularly Persian. The reference to kissing at the very end of the party, with its homosexual overtones, seems, on the other hand, more Greek than Persian.[4] Both features are found in most of the dinner-parties of the *Cyropaedia*.

The following themes are found, then, in this symposium: competition among the guests, a blending of the serious with the frivolous (σπουδαιογέλοιον), edifying or didactic remarks, a discussion of poverty versus wealth, matchmaking (or, more generally, heterosexual love), an allusion to homosexual love, and a presentation of gifts. Finally, there is a wealth of background detail devoted both to the physical setting of the party and the reactions and thoughts of its participants. Not all of the themes and features listed here are found in all the remaining symposia of the *Cyropaedia*, but several of these motifs are found in each of the parties: on the whole, the symposia of the *Cyropaedia* form a well-defined group. What is the relationship between these parties and other literary symposia? More specifically, how do they resemble other banquets found elsewhere in Xenophon? A look at Xenophon's *Symposium* would be the most useful place to start since it provides the clearest indication of what Xenophon thought should—and should not—be found in a symposium.[5] His drinking-party is one of the most fully elaborated and realistic[6] depictions of a symposium found in classical literature.

The *Symposium* tells of a party given by Callias in honour of the young athlete Autolycus. In addition to Autolycus, his father Lycon, and Niceratus, Callias also invites Socrates and a group of his friends—Critobulus, Hermogenes, Antisthenes, and Charmides—to the celebration (*Symp.* 1. 1–10). During dinner Philippus, a comedian, appears uninvited (1. 11–16) and after dinner a Syracusan impresario and his troupe provide entertainment. This leads to a discussion of the virtues of perfume, women, dance, and drink (2. 1–3. 1). Thereafter the party consists of a series of exchanges between the guests, interrupted at intervals by the performances of the Syracusan band.[7] In the

[4] For Persians' kissing as a sign of social rank see Hdt. 1. 134 and cf. *Cyr.* 1. 4. 27. See also *Ages.* 5. 4; Arrian, *Anab.* 4. 12; and Tuplin 1990: 23.

[5] Although Xenophon repeatedly calls Callias' party a symposium (*Symp.* 6. 5, 7. 3, 7. 5, 9. 7), it seems unlikely that he actually gave the title Συμπόσιον to the work (*pace* Breitenbach 1966: 1871). There is little evidence that authors assigned titles to their compositions at the time that the *Symp.* was written; see Griffith 1977: 242–3.

[6] Xenophon's *Symp.* seems true to life despite the author's chronologically untenable claim to have been present at the party he describes (1. 1 παραγενόμενος ... γιγνώσκω). The dramatic date of the *Symp.* is 422 BC, and Xenophon would have been a child then—cf. already Athen. 216D and e.g. Breitenbach 1966: 1874–5.

[7] See Körte 1927: 7 ff. for an analysis of the artistic way in which Xenophon uses these entertainments to break up one topic of conversation and introduce another, in a natural fashion.

central section of the *Symposium* Callias and his guests take turns
describing the quality or asset they most pride themselves on and
then give the reasons for their choice (3. 2–4. 64). Next comes a mock
beauty contest between Socrates and Critobulus (5. 1–10), which is
followed by some lively, even raucous, exchanges among the other
guests (6. 1–10). Socrates then asks the Syracusan for a quiet and
pleasing entertainment, and while this is being readied he discourses
at length on love, providing an ἐρωτικὸς λόγος (8. 1–43). The party
breaks up after a moving dance, depicting the love of Dionysus and
Ariadne, is performed by two of the Syracusan troupe (9. 1–7).

Xenophon provides a full and varied dramatic backdrop in the
Symposium: he describes in detail the events leading up to the party,
the setting of the symposium, its seating arrangements, and entertainments—the sights and sounds (2. 2 θεάματα καὶ ἀκροάματα).
The reactions, expressions, and thoughts of the symposiasts are also
frequently mentioned.[8] We have already seen that the symposia of
the *Cyropaedia* are similarly rich in background detail. All of the
themes or motifs we have noted in the parties of the *Cyropaedia*—save
the distribution of gifts—are present in Xenophon's *Symposium* as
well, and we shall now see how these features appear in the work, one
by one.

Let us begin with σπουδαιογέλοιον, the combination of serious
and frivolous themes, or alternatively, the presentation of weighty
ideas in a playful manner. At the very outset Xenophon announces
his intention to present a picture of worthy men in a light, rather than
serious, mood (*Symp*. 1. 1).[9] This half-playful, half-serious atmosphere is a key feature of Xenophon's *Symposium*,[10] and σπουδαιογέλοιον was, in fact, particularly associated with Socratic symposia in
ancient times.[11] Plutarch, for example, describes both Plato and
Xenophon as combining playfulness and seriousness in their *Symposia* (*Mor.* 686 D; cf. 708 D, 614 A).[12] In the *Memorabilia* too Xenophon

---

[8] Reactions of symposiasts: *Symp*. 2. 11, 17, 3. 10, 13, 4. 62, etc.; expressions: 3. 10,
12, 4. 2–3, 8. 4; thoughts: 1. 12, 6. 6.

[9] δοκεῖ τῶν καλῶν κἀγαθῶν ἀνδρῶν ἔργα οὐ μόνον τὰ μετὰ σπουδῆς πραττόμενα
ἀξιομνημόνευτα εἶναι, ἀλλὰ καὶ τὰ ἐν ταῖς παιδιαῖς.

[10] See von Fritz 1935: 24 ff. for an illuminating discussion of the role of παιδιά in
Xenophon's *Symp*.

[11] The question of an actual genre of Socratic symposia (with or without Socrates as
one of the symposiasts) need not concern us here. See Hirzel 1895: 359; Ullrich 1908: 8,
22–3, 47–9; and Martin 1931: 1–5.

[12] See Martin 1931: 1–32, esp. 4 n. 1, 5 n. 3, and 7 n. 1, for a useful collection of
ancient critics' pronouncements on literary symposia. Particularly noteworthy is the

points out how Socrates helped his companions in his lighter moods just as much as when he was serious, immediately after relating a series of anecdotes on Socrates' behaviour at dinner (*Mem.* 4. 1. 1; cf. 1. 3. 8).

In his *Symposium* Xenophon often uses the very words σπουδή and γέλως in close juxtaposition in order to underline for his reader the fact that he is blending the two elements. Philippus' loud, raucous entrance into the silent symposium, where all present are entranced by the beauty of Autolycus, is the first instance of such a juxtaposition (1. 13).[13] Subsequently Socrates talks earnestly to a laughing audience of the virtues of dance and of his own dancing efforts (2. 15–20). So too Socrates' claim to be an expert procurer (3. 10; 4. 56–64) is, of course, only semi-serious. Socrates assumes a serious expression before putting forth his paradoxical boast; none the less his listeners immediately laugh (3. 10). The discussion of Socrates' erotic interest in Critobulus and the dangers of physical contact (4. 27–8) is also half-playful, half-earnest, as Xenophon hastens to remind us. Sometimes the blend of serious and light-hearted attitudes in the *Symposium* is implicit rather than explicit. The beauty contest between Critobulus and Socrates (5. 1–10) is pure fun, but the teleological or utilitarian arguments used by Socrates are not. Hermogenes notices how Socrates guides and teaches Callias in his conduct and manages to please him at the same time (8. 12). Finally, the closing performance of the Syracusan troupe, the Ariadne–Dionysus dance, is perhaps another instance of σπουδαιογέλοιον, for the two young performers seem to be expressing their real feelings (9. 6) and the effect of this light entertainment on its audience is a powerful one.

Straightforward didactic passages, with Socrates as teacher, are also found in the *Symposium* (e.g. 2. 3–5, 24–6, 7. 2–5). There is a great deal of competition at Callias' party as well. The guests vie with one another in presenting and justifying their proudest possession or quality (3. 2–4. 64), while Antisthenes tries to disprove or minimize some of their claims (3. 5–6, 4. 1–5). Socrates and Critobulus compete for kisses in their playful beauty contest (4. 18–20, 5. 1–10) and the Syracusan impresario feels that Socrates is a serious rival in attracting the guests' attention (6. 6–8).

remark of 'Hermogenes' that this combination of light and serious features is a key characteristic of Socratic symposia: Συμποσίου Σωκρατικοῦ πλοκὴ σπουδαῖα καὶ γελοῖα καὶ πρόσωπα καὶ πράγματα (περὶ μεθόδου δεινότητος 36, p. 454 Rabe).

[13] Cf. Callias' words καὶ γὰρ οἱ παρόντες σπουδῆς μὲν . . . μεστοί, γέλωτος δὲ ἴσως ἐνδεέστεροι.

There are several references to matchmaking (e.g. Socrates' expertise in procuring: 3. 10, 4. 56–64) and heterosexual love. Niceratus, we are told, loves and is loved in return by his wife (8. 3). The closing scene of the *Symposium* (9. 2–7), where the two young dancers who play Ariadne and Dionysus seem to be in love themselves, is a powerful evocation of marital love and causes most of the symposiasts to think at once of their own (present or intended) wives. None the less, the theme of homosexual love is even more prominent. The pairs Autolycus–Callias (1. 8–12, 8. 7, 11, 37, 42), Cleinias–Critobulus (4. 10–26), Syracusan producer–boy dancer (4. 52–4) are all discussed at some length, along with more joking references to Socrates' supposed relationship with Critobulus (4. 27–8) and Antisthenes (8. 4–6). So too the bulk of Socrates' ἐρωτικὸς λόγος (8. 1–43) is addressed to Callias, as Autolycus' *erastēs*, so that in the speech love is, in essence, homosexual love.

Finally, another topic which appears in several symposia of the *Cyropaedia*, a discussion of real (as opposed to apparent) poverty and wealth, is also found in the *Symposium*. Both Antisthenes and Charmides have some paradoxical things to say about the virtues of riches and poverty (3. 8–9, 4. 29–44; see below, sect. 5). Only one of the themes of the *Cyropaedia* is missing in the *Symposium*: there is no presentation of gifts by Callias—or anyone else—at the party.

Almost all of the motifs or themes that we have found in the symposia of the *Cyropaedia* are present in Xenophon's full-scale treatment of a banquet as well: Xenophon seems to have considered these features particularly suitable for symposia. But there is not a complete correspondence between our group of parties in the *Cyropaedia* and the *Symposium*, for the latter includes a number of features which do not appear in any of the *Cyropaedia* symposia (a variety of entertainments, an uninvited guest, a discourse on love, etc.). This partial correspondence leads to two different lines of enquiry: first we shall look at the themes common to the *Cyropaedia* group and Xenophon's *Symposium* in order to see whether these motifs were particularly associated with literary symposia even before Xenophon. Next we shall turn to those features of the *Symposium* which are not found in the dinner-parties of the *Cyropaedia* and attempt to understand why Xenophon omitted them.

The first objective is, then, to see how traditionally sympotic the recurring themes of the *Cyropaedia* dinner-parties are—that is to say, to see which of these features appear in earlier depictions of drinking-parties in Greek literature. It should be stated at the outset that our purpose here is *not* to trace the 'shadowy phenomenon' of early sympotic literature[14] or to postulate the existence of a full-fledged literary genre of symposia prior to Xenophon, but simply to look at the Greek background to, and possible influences on, Xenophon's symposia in the *Cyropaedia*.

Naturally Plato's *Symposium* immediately comes to mind as one such possible influence. The question of whether Plato's *Symposium* came before Xenophon's work of the same name has long been debated,[15] but it is sufficient for our purposes to note that Plato's *Symposium* was, in all likelihood, composed before the *Cyropaedia*.[16] Plato's *Symposium*, like Xenophon's composition of that name, contains all the motifs that we have found in the *Cyropaedia* group of dinner-parties, other than the giving of gifts, but the emphasis placed on several of the themes is noticeably different.

It is not surprising to find that in Plato's narrated-dialogue-within-a-narrated-dialogue there is a great deal of background description. As in many of Plato's earlier dialogues, there are lively dramatic episodes, such as Aristophanes' hiccups (Pl. *Symp.* 185c–e) and Alcibiades joining Agathon and Socrates on their couch (213a–b), but Plato also pays special attention to the details related to the symposium *per se*. Thus we hear of Socrates' careful grooming before the party (174a), the seating arrangements at the banquet (175a–c), the libations after the meal (176a), the discussion of the amount of wine to be drunk (176a–e), etc.

The doctor Eryximachus is perhaps the only didactic figure in Plato's work, as his words on the dangers of drinking (176d) and the cure for hiccups (185d–e) illustrate. The instruction given by Socrates in his central speech (201d–212c) and in his questioning of Agathon (199c–201c) is of a different order entirely.

σπουδαιογέλοιον—the combination or juxtaposition of serious and light elements—is a prominent feature of Plato's *Symposium*.[17] Agathon, for instance, terms his encomium of Eros half-serious, half-

---

[14] The expression is that of Guthrie 1969: 344–5 n. 2.

[15] See e.g. Thesleff 1978 for an airing of the question; Breitenbach 1966: 1872 has further references.

[16] The *Cyr.*, as has been argued above (ch. 1. 3), was probably written after 371, while Plato's *Symp.* is plausibly dated to 384–379 by Dover 1965 (= 1988: 86–101) or more generally to several years before Plato's second visit to Sicily in 367—cf. Guthrie 1975: 53.

[17] For a general discussion of play and earnest in Plato see Guthrie 1975: 56–65.

playful,[18] while the comic poet Aristophanes is cautioned by Eryximachus to speak seriously (189A–C; cf. 193B, D). (In his speech Aristophanes demonstrates, of course, that he is perfectly capable of being serious and funny at the same time.)[19] In more general terms, Alcibiades' noisy entrance (Pl. *Symp.* 212Cff.), which follows immediately upon Socrates' lofty discussion of spiritual love, is the harshest (and most effective) juxtaposition of the frivolous and the serious in Plato's work.[20] Alcibiades' subsequent encomium of Socrates (215A–222B) interweaves these two qualities, perhaps because Socrates himself combines gravity and playfulness in his person, as Alcibiades points out (216E). Finally, the very close of the *Symposium*, where Socrates tries to persuade the nodding Agathon and Aristophanes that the same man is capable of writing tragedies and comedies, should be noted in this context.

The round of speeches on love undertaken by the guests is, of course, a form of competition or contest among them—as Socrates' compliment to Eryximachus on his successful efforts (194A καλῶς . . . ἠγώνισαι) indicates—but the real rivalry at the party seems to be between Socrates and Agathon. Early on Agathon challenges Socrates to a contest of wisdom (175E) and the latter apparently takes up the challenge with his two cross-examinations of Agathon (194A–C, 199C–201C). Eventually Alcibiades crowns Socrates the victor (213E). As in Xenophon, there are also allusions to sexual rivalry and jealousy, particularly concerning the supposed relationship between Socrates and Alcibiades (213C–D, 214C–E, 222C–223A).

This brings us to another central theme, homosexual love. Most of the discourses on ἔρως in the *Symposium* use love as meaning love between males: Pausanias' speech (180C–185C, esp. 181B–C) is the outstanding instance. The presence of the pair Agathon and Pausanias (177D, 193B) and the tale of Alcibiades' attempt to seduce Socrates (217A–219D) only underline this motif of παιδικά. Heterosexual love, on the other hand, plays a very small part in Plato's *Symposium*—we find only Phaedrus' words on Alcestis (179B–D) and Aristophanes' description of the male and female halves of the

---

[18] 197E τὰ μὲν παιδιᾶς, τὰ δὲ σπουδῆς μετρίας . . . μετέχων. Agathon is, it seems, following in the footsteps of his teacher Gorgias, who terms his encomium of Helen Ἑλένης μὲν ἐγκώμιον, ἐμὸν δὲ παίγνιον (DK 82 B 11. 21).

[19] Cf. *Frogs* 389–90 καὶ πολλὰ μὲν γέλοιά μ' εἰπεῖν πολλὰ δὲ σπουδαῖα.

[20] The similarity between Alcibiades' entrance here and Philippus' entrance in Xenophon's *Symp.* (1. 11) is apparent; cf. Gorgias' statement δεῖ . . . τὴν μὲν σπουδὴν διαφθείρειν τῶν ἐναντίων γέλωτι, τὸν δὲ γέλωτα σπουδῇ (DK 82 B 12).

androgyne searching for one another (191 D–E)—and this is an important difference between Plato and Xenophon.[21]

The last topic (other than the missing one of the presentation of gifts) is that of real, as opposed to apparent, wealth. There is, perhaps, a suggestion of this motif in Diotima's depiction of Eros as the son of Poverty (Πενία) and Resource (Πόρος)—but not Wealth (Πλοῦτος)—who has features of both parents and constantly moves from one state to another (203 B–E). Alcibiades also mentions Socrates' total disregard for wealth (216 D–E), but there is no real discussion of the theme.

What of earlier symposia? In what way do they resemble the dinner-parties of the *Cyropaedia*? Let us begin with Homer.[22] As Athenaeus points out (186 D–E),[23] Homer is careful to supply the time, persons, and occasions (χρόνους, πρόσωπα, αἰτίας), i.e. the dramatic setting, of his feasts. We are given, for instance, the list of guests invited to Agamemnon's banquet (*Il.* 2. 402–8) and a description of the double marriage celebration in Menelaus' house (*Od.* 4. 1–19). So too Homer provides descriptions of the physical setting—the food, furnishings, dishes, and drinking-cups—at these gatherings as well as their entertainments, singing and dancing.[24] Homer also notes at times the symposiasts' thoughts or reactions. We hear, for example, of Odysseus' tears while listening to Demodocus: these, we are told, pass unnoticed by all except Alcinous (*Od.* 8. 83–95, 521–34; cf. *Od.* 4. 113–20).

There are several instances of didacticism or moralizing in Homeric symposia, such as Menelaus' words to Telemachus on wealth (*Od.* 4. 78 ff.) or Athena's remarks to Telemachus on the arrogant behaviour of the suitors (*Od.* 1. 224–9). So too Eteoneus (*Od.* 4. 30–6) and Alcinous (*Od.* 7. 155–66) are reproved for not extending hospitality to unexpected guests. Often the symposiasts are concerned that their party should be conducted properly. Telemachus both scolds his mother for trying to dictate to Phemius which songs should be sung (*Od.* 1. 336–60) and calls the unruly suitors to

---

[21] See on this point Flacelière 1961, who perhaps exaggerates the strength of the feminist convictions held by Xenophon (and Antisthenes and Aeschines).

[22] See Murray 1983: 196–8 for an excellent discussion of the role and significance of feasts in Homeric society, and cf. Slater 1990.

[23] See Athen. 186E–193C (including 177A–182C) for an entertaining, if not always illuminating, analysis of Homeric symposia.

[24] Physical setting: *Od.* 1. 126–43, 4. 49–58, 7. 85–102, etc. Entertainments: *Od.* 1. 151–5, 4. 17–19, 8. 72 ff., etc.

order (*Od.* 1. 365–71). Alcinous, disturbed by Odysseus' tears, calls
for his guests to enjoy themselves (*Od.* 8. 533–45; cf. 9. 1–13) and
Hephaestus is afraid that Hera's quarrel with Zeus will spoil the
gods' feasts (*Il.* 1. 575–9). So too Peisistratus, Menelaus, and Helen
all make an effort to dispel the sadness which has overtaken their
party by means of drink, potions, and story-telling (*Od.* 4. 183 ff.).

Such transitions from tears to tales, songs, and drink remind us of
the combination of jest and earnest found in later symposia. Even
more noteworthy in this context are those occasions where feasting
and drinking serve as a prelude to serious discussions and war
councils. In the *Iliad* Nestor advises the Achaean leaders several
times after they have sacrificed, eaten, and drunk (*Il.* 2. 402 ff.,
7. 313 ff.). In book 9 the embassy to Achilles is sent as a result of post-
prandial deliberations. After the Achaean leaders have made their
sacrifices, feasted, and drunk (*Il.* 9. 89–92), Nestor advises Agamemnon to make peace with Achilles. Agamemnon agrees and a delegation is chosen (9. 93–170). The party then pours libations and drinks
together once again (9. 171–7). Here, then, a serious discussion takes
place over wine-cups, and, as Athenaeus points out (192 c), this is
reminiscent of the Persian custom of sympotic councils (see below,
sect. 3). In the *Odyssey* weighty matters are sometimes raised in the
midst of a banquet, such as Athena's conversation with Telemachus
(*Od.* 1. 156 ff.).

Before leaving Homer it should be noted that gifts are sometimes
presented in conjunction with a banquet, if not actually at the feast
itself. Menelaus offers Telemachus first horses and then a gold wine-
bowl the morning after their party together (*Od.* 4. 589–619), and
Odysseus is presented with clothes, gold, a sword, and a cup by
Alcinous and the Phaeacians after one festive meal and before the
next (8. 389–432).[25] Finally, two more of our themes, competition
and matchmaking, also feature in the many banquets held by the
suitors at Odysseus' house, for these men are, of course, all rivals for
Penelope's hand.

Turning to sympotic poetry, we again find at times careful elaboration of the setting of the drinking-party: Xenophanes' depiction of
the floor, table, cups, wine, wreaths, perfume, bread, cheese, and
honey at such a gathering (1. 1–12)[26] is particularly noteworthy.

[25] On the role and function of gifts in Homer see Finley 1972: 73–5, 111–13, 140–3.
[26] The numbering of the poems is according to West 1971–2, unless otherwise
noted.

Other poets also seem to enjoy dwelling on the symposium's setting, surroundings, and entertainments: Phocylides' two-line sympotic poem (fr. 14 Diehl), for instance, is almost entirely devoted to painting the backdrop of a drinking-party.[27]

It is not surprising that almost all of these poems, which seem to have been written to introduce the rounds of drinking at a party,[28] are somewhat didactic in tone and tell the symposiasts what form their celebration should (and should not) take.[29] Symposiasts are told, for example, to drink in moderation, avoid tales of ancient strife, and talk of pleasant matters, χοὖτως συμπόσιον γίνεται οὐκ ἄχαρι (Theognis 496).[30] Sometimes the guests are instructed to put their own quarrels aside (Theognis 494; Dionysius Chalcus 2. 2), so we can conclude that strife or rivalry among the symposiasts was not unknown. Dionysius Chalcus tells us of one mild form of competition among the guests, the capping of one another's verses (1. 1–5); there were, of course, other party games as well.

Some poets recommend to their fellow symposiasts a blend of frivolity and high-mindedness: πίνειν καὶ παίζειν καὶ τὰ δίκαια φρονεῖν (Ion 26. 15–16).[31] Others place more stress on the gaiety (Phocylides 14. 1–2) or the solemnity (Xenophanes 1. 13–24; Theognis 563–6) of the occasion. Theognis 309–12 is a particularly interesting instance of σπουδαιογέλοιον: the wise symposiast, we are told, while seeming to join in the party fun, can unobtrusively observe the other merrymakers and later make use of his observations.[32] One final theme found in several of the sympotic poems is

[27] See also Theognis 487–91; Ion of Chios 27. 3–4; Critias 6. 1–7; Dionysius Chalcus 1. 1–3 and 3. 1–6.

[28] It is generally agreed that symposia were the occasion of a considerable amount of extant elegy (and archaic poetry in general), but opinions vary as to whether elegies were composed for other occasions as well. See Reitzenstein 1893: 45 ff.; Bowie 1986, 1990; Rösler 1990; Pellizer 1990: 179–80 and the further references there. West 1974: 10–13 argues for a wider variety of occasions.

[29] See Bowra 1953: 1–14 for a good discussion of the hortatory character of sympotic elegy in general and Xenophanes' fr. 1 in particular. See also West 1974: 15; Slater 1990: 213–16.

[30] Cf. also Anacreon eleg. 2. 1–4; Xenophanes 1. 13–24; Phocylides 14. 1–2; Theognis 211–12 (509–10), 309–12, 467–96; Dionysius Chalcus 2. 1–3; Critias 6. 8–27.

[31] Cf. Ion 27. 5–7, Critias 6. 14–16, Theognis 491–6, and Anacreon fr. eleg. 2.

[32]
ἐν μὲν συσσίτοισιν ἀνὴρ πεπνυμένος εἶναι,
πάντα δέ μιν λήθειν ὡς ἀπεόντα δοκοῖ
εἰς δὲ φέροι τὰ γελοῖα· θύρηφι δὲ καρτερὸς εἴη
γινώσκων ὀργὴν ἥντιν᾿ ἕκαστος ἔχει.

See West's commentary ad loc.

that of love or the pleasures of Aphrodite: ἀγλαὰ δῶρ᾽ Ἀφροδίτης (Anacreon eleg. 2. 3; cf. Ion 27. 9–10; Critias 6. 18–19).

Sympotic poetry is, then, particularly notable for its didactic tendency, i.e. for the instruction given to guests on how a symposium should be conducted, but several other of our motifs—a description of the physical surroundings of the party, rivalry among the guests, a combination of playfulness and seriousness, and references to sexual pleasure—are also found in some of the poems.[33]

The symposia of comedy are generally quite different in tone.[34] The outstanding feature of these banquets is, it seems, the lavish descriptions of the various delicacies that were served: Epicharmus' ῞Ηβας γάμος (41–75 Kai.) is a particularly good example.[35] Gluttony (Eupolis 166, 187, 190 K.–A.) and heavy drinking (Epicharmus 34 Kai.; Eupolis 165 K.–A.) are also regularly mentioned.[36] Entertainments too are often described, and we hear of singing, dancing, riddles, and comparisons and counter-comparisons at comic symposia.[37] Most of these party games were, of course, competitive, with guests taking pains to demonstrate their skill and unsuccessful participants having to pay a forfeit (cf. Antiphanes 74 K.). Thus one of our themes, that of rivalry among the guests at a symposium, is frequently found in comedy.

Aristophanes' *Wasps* and the fragments of Eupolis' Κόλακες are the two comedies which are closest in feeling to the symposia of the *Cyropaedia*. In Aristophanes Bdelycleon is giving his father a detailed lesson in how to behave at a symposium. He rapidly outlines the normal course of events at a party—reclining on couches, washing, dining, washing again, libations, flute-girl, etc. (*Wasps* 1212–19)[38]—

---

[33] The later elegy *Adesp. Eleg.* 27 (= *P. Berol.* 13270), which is generally dated to the end of the 4th cent. BC, is worth noting in this context. The poem recommends combining laughter and seriousness at symposia, mentions the guests speaking in turn (ἐν μέρει), and is generally didactic in tone. See Ullrich 1908: 17–18 and West 1974: 11–12, 15.

[34] The survey in Ullrich 1908: 23–7 is most useful; see too Körte 1927: 44–8 and Martin 1931: 126–7, 138–9.

[35] See also Eupolis 160, 174 K.–A. The emphasis on food and drink in comedy may well reflect the particular interests of Athenaeus, our chief source for these comic fragments.

[36] Cf. also Sophocles' satyr play Σύνδειπνοι (esp. frr. 563, 564 Radt). Sutton 1989: 100 notes that comical banqueting scenes were not uncommon in satyr plays.

[37] Singing: Aristoph. *Wasps* 1219ff.; *Clouds* 1354ff.; Eupolis 395 K.–A. Dancing: Epicharmus 75 Kai. Riddles: Epicharmus 87 Kai.; Aristoph. *Wasps* 20–3; Antiphanes 74, 124 K.; cf. Athen. 448B–459B. Comparisons and counter-comparisons: Aristoph. *Wasps* 1308–14; Epicharmus 87, 90 Kai.

[38] Cf. Plato Comicus 71 K.–A. for a similar outline of a symposium's proceedings.

and places particular emphasis on the setting of the symposium. Philocleon, Bdelycleon insists, must pay careful attention to his surroundings and compliment his host on the bronzeware, ceiling, and tapestries (*Wasps* 1214–15; contrast Diphilus 61 K.). Bdelycleon then turns to the singing of σκόλια: he wants to be sure that his father will know how to hold his own in exchanging lines of song with the other guests. The old man is, if anything, over-prepared to chime in with lines of verse, and Bdelycleon's instructions end (*Wasps* 1222–49).

Eupolis' play *Κόλακες* tells of a symposium at Callias' house, with Protagoras as the guest of honour (157–8 K.–A.). Other symposiasts included Chaerephon the Socratic and, possibly, Alcibiades (180 and 171; cf. 177–9). As is to be expected, we hear of the flatterers' greedy and lustful behaviour (162, 166, 171, 172, 174, 175, 187, and 190), but there are also hints of talk of a somewhat more serious nature. Thus Protagoras addresses Callias in pedantic fashion, telling him to drink in order to clear his lung (158; cf. 157). Callias' flatterers are said to have received rewards or prizes from their host (τῆς κολακείας τὸ ἆθλον)—wine-cups, hetairai, and other luxuries (Max. Tyr. 14. 7)— so that once again gifts are presented in conjunction with a Greek symposium.

There are several prose descriptions of symposia which were written before Xenophon. Sophron's mimes may have included a description or representation of one,[39] but the fragments do not yield any real evidence of anything other than references to food (14–16, 24–31 Kai.) and drink (e.g. 99). Ion of Chios, whose sympotic poetry has already been mentioned, is a more valuable source for our purposes. His prose composition Ἐπιδημίαι—a series of anecdotes relating to famous men of his time whom he had met—was mentioned in ch. 1. 1. The work may have contained a section devoted to party wit or parties:[40] in any event, two[41] descriptions of symposia are extant.

One banquet was given by Laomedon in Athens, with Cimon as guest of honour (Plut. *Cimon* 9. 1–6 = *FGrH* 392 F 13). At this party Cimon, we are told, sings in a pleasant manner and is praised by the other guests for being more accomplished (musically) than Themistocles. The members of the party discuss some of Cimon's great

---

[39] See Ullrich 1908: 28 and Hirzel 1895: 156.

[40] See Dover 1986: 34 (= 1988: 8).

[41] Mattingly 1977: 237 thinks that Ion's remarks on Pericles (*FGrH* 392 F 15, F 16) also come from the description of a banquet.

exploits, leading the general himself to tell of a clever stratagem he once used when dividing up booty. Thus two of our sympotic themes—competition and didactic instruction—are found at this gathering. The atmosphere at the symposium is relaxed, with Cimon handling the compliments he receives gracefully, and the conversation seems to have been a blend of serious and lighter topics.

The second symposium described by Ion is a gathering in Chios in honour of Sophocles (Athen. 603E–604D = *FGrH* 392 F 6). Ion's account here, even if it is abridged,[42] is especially interesting, for it contains many of our sympotic motifs. At the party Sophocles manages to kiss a handsome young cupbearer, while parrying a pedantic schoolmaster's remarks on literary matters. Ion describes the setting and dramatic background of the symposium in detail, mentioning the fire, the cupbearer's blushes, the downcast schoolmaster, Sophocles' laughter, etc. Sophocles himself is both playful and clever (παιδιώδει παρ' οἴνον καὶ δεξιῷ) when devising his 'stratagem' to steal a kiss from the boy, and his remarks on Pericles' criticism of him are semi-serious, an excellent example of σπουδαιογέλοιον. The pedantic Eretrian schoolmaster, on the other hand, provides, in his attempts to correct Sophocles, both the didactic and competitive elements we have learnt to look for. The whole of the tale is, of course, a παιδικὸς λόγος, and is used by Athenaeus to illustrate the fact that Sophocles was an admirer of young boys. The bulk of Ion's Ἐπιδημίαι is lost, but these surviving fragments do seem to be close in spirit to Xenophon's literary symposia.[43]

Our next author is Herodotus, who describes several dinner-parties. Most of these banquets (5. 18–20, 9. 15–16, 9. 110–11; cf. 1. 118–19 and 7. 135) involve Persians and will be discussed below. One gathering, a party given by Cleisthenes of Sicyon before announcing which suitor is to marry his daughter Agariste (Hdt. 6. 129–30), is well worth attention. The suitors, who remind us of the Homeric μνηστῆρες,[44]

---

[42] Jacoby 1947: 16 (= 1956a: 167–8) argues that Ion's original versions of both dinner-parties were longer and included a detailed guest-list at the beginning, in addition to a description of the setting. See also his commentary on *FGrH* 392 F 6 and n. 18 to his introduction there on Ion (iiib Text, 197; iiib Notes, 126–7). Two other fragments of the Ἐπιδημίαι mention dinner-party delicacies (392 F 4 and F 5; cf. F 19 on wine-cups), so there may have been a description of the menu as well.

[43] See the cogent remarks of Dover 1986: 33–5 (= 1988: 6–9) on the relation between Ion's style of composition in the Ἐπιδημίαι and Xenophon's style in the *Mem.* (and Socratic dialogue in general); cf. West 1985: 75–6.

[44] Murray 1980: 203 thinks that the suitors are 'self-consciously aware of Homeric precedent'.

are, of course, all rivals for Agariste's hand, so that two of our themes—competition and matchmaking—are very much in evidence at the party. The suitors also compete, Herodotus tells us, in music-making and speaking before the party as a whole (6. 129. 2 οἱ μνηστῆρες ἔριν εἶχον ἀμφί τε μουσικῇ καὶ τῷ λεγομένῳ ἐς τὸ μέσον). These speeches may have contained some edifying pronouncements, for the matter at hand is a serious one, the culmination of a year's trial of the suitors. None the less, the atmosphere at the party is generally light, with the guests drinking, singing, and dancing until the carefree Hippocleides dances his prospects away: once again we find the serious and the frivolous juxtaposed. It is also worth noting that the host, Cleisthenes, presents all the disappointed suitors with a talent of silver as compensation at the close of the party. Herodotus' story here is clearly a blend of fact and fiction, but it is generally agreed that his source is an Alcmaeonid one,[45] so that certain features of this symposium may have been recast in Athenian form.

Most of the sympotic themes of the *Cyropaedia* can, then, be found in Greek literature from Homer onwards. The influence of certain authors (Homer, several sympotic poets, Ion of Chios), or at least a certain similarity in tone and content between their banquets and those of the *Cyropaedia*, is apparent. (This is *not* to postulate a series or chain of literary banquets which ultimately led to Xenophon's symposia in the *Cyropaedia*.) The most prominent features or motifs of these earlier symposia are emphasis on the setting and background of the party, competition among the guests, didactic pronouncements, and σπουδαιογέλοιον.

Before leaving the question of the relation between the symposia of the *Cyropaedia* and earlier Greek literary tradition concerning banquets, it is worth while to take a brief look at the vestiges of early, lost literary symposia. Plato may refer to one such composition in his own *Symposium*, for we are told that Phoenix, son of Philippus (who is otherwise unknown), has given a different version of a banquet which numbered Socrates, Alcibiades, and Agathon among the participants (Pl. *Symp.* 172 B; 173 B);[46] no trace of any such work is extant. Plutarch (*Mor.* 823 D) seems to know of a

---

[45] See Griffin 1982: 55–6; Burn 1960: 205–6; Legrand's notes ad loc. in the Budé edition; cf. Fehr 1990: 191–2.

[46] See Bury's discussion in the introduction to his edition of Pl. *Symp.*, pp. xvii–xix; he suggests that what is really meant here is a lost work by Polycrates.

symposium where Alcibiades was host and Socrates the chief guest: this has been taken by one scholar as a reference to Aeschines' *Alcibiades*, whose setting was, he argues, a symposium.[47] Alcibiades also appears as an inebriated guest at a party in Anytus' house (Plut. *Alcib.* 4. 5; cf. Athen. 534 E–F), and again this story is thought to come from a literary symposium,[48] although a historical source is equally likely. Another precursor of Plato and Xenophon in the writing of symposia[49] may have been Antisthenes and his (almost entirely lost) Προτρεπτικός. This work, according to one commentator, included two symposia—a meeting of sophists at Callias' house and a gathering of the seven wise men at Periander's—but there is no real evidence for this.[50] There *is* an elusive tradition of some sort of meeting or banquet of the seven wise men at Periander's or Croesus' house,[51] but Plutarch's *Banquet of the Seven Sages* may have been the first literary representation of a discussion (or wisdom contest) among these sages over wine.[52] Finally, in the pages of Athenaeus (427 F–428 A) Xenophon himself makes an appearance at a symposium at the court of Dionysius of Sicily, and justifies his moderate drinking to the tyrant in didactic fashion. This anecdote too is assigned to a lost symposium.[53] All in all, these bits and pieces of what may have been symposia are not very helpful and will be ignored in the following discussion.

Let us turn now to those ways in which the dinner-parties of the *Cyropaedia* are *unlike* other symposia in Xenophon (and elsewhere).

[47] The scholar is Martin 1931: 301–8, who points out that Aeschines' dialogue deals with the theme of love as a means to achieve political ἀρετή (as does Xenophon's *Symp.*); the context of Plutarch's remarks—on statesmen—also suits this theme. See also Hirzel 1895: 359 n. 1 and Ullrich 1908: 48–9 n. 1 (who thinks 'Alcibiades' is a slip of the pen for Agathon).

[48] See Martin 1931: 198 n. 1 and Joël 1901: 725–6.

[49] Thesleff 1978: 158 argues on the basis of Athen. 216F that the Hellenistic critic Herodicus knew of no close parallel to Plato's *Symp.* other than Xenophon, but the passage simply demonstrates that Herodicus knew of no other speech on love by Pausanias (outside of Plato) and no other appearance by Pausanias in a literary symposium.

[50] See Joël 1901: 708 ff.; his misguided attempts to see Antisthenes' influence everywhere lead to some interesting byways. Cf. Ullrich 1908: 28–30 n. 5 for a brief refutation of this view and see also Woldinga 1938–9: 7 with nn.

[51] See Pl. *Prot.* 343 A and Ephorus, *FGrH* 70 F 181–2; cf. Diog. Laert. 1. 40.

[52] See the further references in Joël 1901: 763–5 and cf. Martin 1931: 269–70, 292; Ullrich 1908: 28–30 n. 5; Barkowski 1923: 2252–4; Ziegler 1964: 247–8. Snell 1966 states on the basis of the opening lines of *PSI* 9. 1093 (= Pack², No. 2292) that a tale (in verse) of a meeting of the seven wise men already existed in the 5th cent. BC; Fehling 1985: 9–18 argues on the basis of Pl. *Prot.* 342 A ff. that Plato was the first to invent the canon of the seven sages.

[53] See Hirzel 1895: 359 n. 1 and the objections of Ullrich 1908: 48–9 n. 1.

One minor feature missing from those in the *Cyropaedia* is the appearance of an uninvited guest (ἄκλητος).[54] Menelaus is the earliest self-invited guest on record (*Il.* 2. 408; cf. Pl. *Symp.* 174B–C). Subsequently the parasite who comes of his own accord to banquets was a regular figure in comedy,[55] and Xenophon's Philippus is an example of this stereotype. Plato has two uninvited symposiasts put in an appearance at Agathon's house—Aristodemus and Alcibiades—and later writers of symposia continued with this topos,[56] but there are no such figures in the *Cyropaedia*. Another item missing from the parties of the *Cyropaedia* is that of *organized* competitions or contests. While the symposiasts of the *Cyropaedia* often vie with one another, there are no series of exhibitions of any kind—be it σκόλια, dances, toasts, or riddles—with each member of the party taking his turn, such as are often found in other symposia.[57] More specifically, there are no rounds of speeches on a set theme, where each symposiast holds forth in turn (as in the *Symposium* of Plato or Xenophon).[58] In Plato the series of speeches is on ἔρως, and a theoretical analysis of the power and effect of love, an ἐρωτικὸς λόγος, is often associated with symposia.[59] Besides Plato's *Symposium*, which consists largely of a series of ἐρωτικοὶ λόγοι,[60] Xenophon's *Symposium* also has two long passages on the effect of love (4. 10–28, 8. 1–43). In the

[54] Cf. Fehr 1990.

[55] Cf. e.g. Epicharmus frr. 34, 35, 37 Kai., and see Ullrich 1908: 25, together with Bury's note on Pl. *Symp.* 174B; Woldinga 1938–9: 50–1; Körte 1927: 44–6.

[56] Cf. Martin 1931: 64ff.

[57] σκόλια and capping verses: Eupolis fr. 395 K.–A.; Aristoph. *Wasps* 1219ff.; Dionysius Chalcus 1. 1–5. Dance: *Anab.* 6. 1. 5ff. Toasts: Critias 6. 6–7. Riddles: Athen. 457C–459B; see also the references in n. 37 above. Theognis 495, Hdt. 6. 129, and *Adesp. Eleg.* 27. 7–8 (cf. above, n. 33) use the expressions εἰς τὸ μέσον and ἐν μέρει respectively. Martin 1931: 127–39, esp. 136ff., Woldinga 1938–9: 147–9, Reitzenstein 1893: 26ff., and Hug–Schöne's introduction to their third edition of Pl. *Symp.*, pp. vi–vii, all include discussions of the role of an ἀγών in symposia.

[58] See Xen. *Symp.* 3. 3–4. 64, where Callias' promise to display his wisdom (ἐπιδείξειν τὴν αὑτοῦ σοφίαν) becomes the occasion for everyone to speak εἰς μέσον (3. 3). The round of speeches is termed by Xenophon ἡ περίοδος τῶν λόγων (4. 64). In Plato's *Symp.* the series of encomia on ἔρως are spoken from left to right (177D ἐπὶ δεξιά), in turn (198C ἐν τῷ μέρει), except for the hiccuping Aristophanes (185D); cf. also 214B–C. Alcibiades is meant to initiate another round of speeches in which each man praises the guest on his right (214C; cf. 222E), but his is the only speech made. There are in the *Cyr.* two such series or rounds of speeches, in which each man expresses his opinion (*Cyr.* 5. 1. 19–29, 6. 1. 6–18), but these are councils where plans for the future are discussed.

[59] See Lasserre 1944, who argues that this 'genre mineur de la prose littéraire' first began at the end of the 5th cent.; he collects all the evidence for early ἐρωτικοὶ λόγοι. Cf. also Hug–Schöne's third edition of Pl. *Symp.*, pp. x–xv.

[60] Cf. Pl. *Symp.* 172B and Arist. *Pol.* 1262[b]11.

Memorabilia there are three conversations dealing with ἔρως and all three have close links with symposia.[61] There are, as it happens, two deliberations on the nature of love in the *Cyropaedia* (5. 1. 8–18 and 6. 1. 36–44; cf. below, ch. 4. 2), but neither takes place at a symposium.

The most outstanding feature of the *Cyropaedia*'s parties in relation to other symposia is their unusual sobriety. There is next to no mention of any wine-drinking, let alone drunkenness (see only *Cyr.* 1. 3. 9 and 8. 4. 9).[62] The banqueters of the *Cyropaedia* do not find it necessary to regulate or limit their drinking in any way, and there is no formal decision by a symposiarch on the amount of wine to be imbibed, such as is often found elsewhere: it seems taken for granted that all will drink moderately. In the *Cyropaedia* it is only the Medes (1. 3. 10–11, 4. 5. 7–8), along with the Babylonians (7. 5. 15, 25, 27) and latter-day Persians (8. 8. 10), who are intemperate and become intoxicated. A related omission in the *Cyropaedia*'s symposia is that of entertainments. We have seen that music and dance, performances by comedians, and party games such as riddles and the casting of likenesses, were a regular part of most banquets. Xenophon's full-length *Symposium*, for instance, has an abundance of such pastimes.[63] In the symposia of the *Cyropaedia*, however, there are no formal entertainments whatsoever—no song, music, dance, or party games. (There is, of course, a great deal of light-hearted banter.) Singing-girls and musicians are certainly not unknown in the *Cyropaedia* (cf. 4. 6. 11, 5. 1. 1, 5. 5. 2, etc.), and singing and dancing are mentioned in passing at the symposia themselves (1. 3. 10, 8. 4. 12), but Cyrus and his friends do not indulge in these pastimes at their parties. Once again, it is the Medes who are described as celebrating in this way (1. 3. 10, 4. 5. 7).

[61] *Mem.* 1. 3. 8–15, 2. 6. 28–39, 3. 11. The first of these passages, in which Socrates warns Critobulus (indirectly) about the dangers of kissing, not only has a close parallel in *Symp.* 4. 10ff., but also comes immediately after a brief depiction of Socrates at a symposium. *Mem.* 2. 6. 28ff. is yet another version of Socrates lecturing Critobulus on love, and it too shows traces of 'eine farbenreiche symposiastische Szene' (Gigon 1956: 153). The setting of *Mem.* 3. 11, Socrates' conversation with the courtesan Theodote, is very like a symposium and its tone is semi-serious. Cf. Breitenbach 1966: 1820–1 and Joël 1901: 710. Von Fritz 1935: 31–9 also discusses all three passages; he thinks Xenophon was strongly influenced by Aeschines' *Aspasia*.

[62] ὑπέπινον at *Cyr.* 8. 4. 9 should be understood as drinking after a meal, at dessert (see LSJ s.v. ὑποπίνω), and not as drinking to excess. Hystaspas, Cyrus' close friend and cohort throughout, does not need to become intoxicated in order to summon up his courage and address Cyrus—*pace* L. Breitenbach (in his commentary ad loc.) and Sturz (s.v. ὑποπίνειν).

[63] Cf. 2. 1–2, 8, 11, 21–2, 3. 1, 6. 8–10, and 9. 2–6.

The symposia of the *Cyropaedia* are, then, particularly puritanical and subdued. It is illuminating to compare for a moment the *Cyropaedia* group of banquets with two parties described in the *Anabasis*. Both these parties are gatherings of military leaders and thus in occasion, at least, resemble two of the symposia of the *Cyropaedia* (5. 2. 5–22 and 8. 4. 1–27). These real-life parties could easily have served as models for those in the *Cyropaedia*, but in fact the symposia in the two works are quite dissimilar.

In the first symposium of the *Anabasis* (6. 1. 3–13) the generals of the Ten Thousand are hosts to Paphlagonian envoys. The party turns into a dancing exhibition by the various Greek contingents, once the formalities of sacrifice, libations, and paeans are over. The dancing is lively, even rowdy, and the humour plain, with the Greeks joking that it is their women (dancers) who do the real fighting (*Anab.* 6. 1. 13). Only two of the *Cyropaedia*'s sympotic themes are found here—an elaborate narrative background and competition among the guests.

The second party (*Anab.* 7. 3. 15–39) is given by Seuthes, the Thracian king, with the leaders of the Ten Thousand among the guests. On their way in to dinner the guests are stopped by Seuthes' agent, Heracleides, who solicits rich gifts for the king, promising various benefactions in return. The banqueters then dine in a circle and Seuthes distributes bread and meat from his plate to select guests. After the meal the most distinguished guests toast the king, one by one, and present him with various valuable gifts—a horse, a servant, a rug, a silver cup, etc. Xenophon is drunk, empty-handed, and embarrassed, since he is seated in the position of honour next to Seuthes. He offers himself and his men as a present, expressing the hope that they will enable the king to acquire other, more tangible gifts. After a final toast by Xenophon and Seuthes there is entertainment: music, jesters, and a mime by the host. The party ends with a practical discussion of military arrangements. Here again, although several of our sympotic motifs can be discerned—a careful description of the surroundings, the presentation of gifts,[64] and even one semi-serious speech by the drunken Xenophon—the overall rough-

---

[64] Here the gifts are presented by the guests rather than their host; Seuthes does, however, distribute food at the party to those whom he favours. At the other party in the *Anab.* the guests also arrive bearing gifts, probably as a gesture of good will (*Anab.* 6. 1. 2). See Thuc. 2. 97. 4 on the Thracian custom of soliciting rather than presenting gifts, and compare Theopompus (*FGrH* 115 F 263) on gifts presented to the Persian king.

and-tumble atmosphere is notably different from that of the parties in the *Cyropaedia*

Why does Xenophon present his Persian party-goers in this manner? Surely this portrait of Cyrus and his sober symposiasts is not meant to reflect reality: Xenophon, of course, was well aware that banqueters often become intoxicated, and we have just seen that in the *Anabasis* he refers gracefully to his own inebriated state at Seuthes' party (*Anab.* 7. 3. 29). Real-life Persians were considered fond of wine, and they normally enjoyed music and dancing at their symposia as well.[65] Even at more philosophical gatherings, drink is very much part of the proceedings. In Plato's *Symposium* the symposiasts decide to limit their drinking, but we are specifically told (and shown) that Socrates himself is capable of downing a great deal of wine with no ill effect (*Symp.* 176C, 220A, 223C–D). Alcibiades, when he appears at the party, is plainly drunk (212D) and Aristophanes and Agathon, who apparently continue to drink with Socrates all night long, also succumb, in the end, to the influence of alcohol (223C–D).[66] It is perhaps characteristic of Xenophon's more didactic approach that in his *Symposium* Socrates' drinking capacity is not mentioned and none of Callias' guests becomes intoxicated. So too it is Xenophon's Socrates who suggests that the symposiasts limit their drinking after Philippus, the buffoon, calls for huge wine-goblets. (In Plato the suggestion to drink moderately comes from Pausanias.) None the less, despite these restrictions, wine-drinking is an integral part of the banquet in Xenophon's *Symposium* as well.

Why are the symposia of the *Cyropaedia* so puritanical? It seems very likely that Xenophon excludes (excessive) wine-drinking and entertainments from the dinner-parties in this work for didactic reasons: he wishes to portray model symposia of sensible and temperate men. Xenophon's desire to educate and edify is, as we shall see, apparent in each of the *Cyropaedia*'s symposia, and is particularly prominent in the description of young Cyrus' criticisms of Median party habits (1. 3. 4–12) and the depiction of the dinner held outside Gobryas' fortress (5. 2. 5–22). This desire to paint an idealized picture prevails, perhaps, over a more realistic depiction of men relaxing in their cups. In the *Cyropaedia* entertainments go hand in

---

[65] Wine: Hdt. 1. 133, 5. 18–19; Esther 1: 7; *FGrH* 689 F 2, etc. Music and dance: *FGrH* 76 F 5, 689 F 2. See also Tuplin 1990: 26 and the further references there.

[66] For Plato's (changing) attitude towards wine-drinking and symposia cf. *Laws* 636E ff. and see Tecuşan 1990.

hand with excessive drinking,[67] and this is probably why Xenophon also omits entertainments at his symposia. A link between party pastimes and drink is found elsewhere as well. In Plato's *Symposium*, for example, the type of entertainment to be provided seems to be related to the amount of wine to be imbibed, for Eryximachus' suggestion that the flute-girl be dismissed and the guests entertain one another by speaking on Eros comes immediately after all have agreed to drink in moderation (Pl. *Symp.* 176E). A passage in the *Protagoras* (347C–D) dealing with the question of party amusements (and drink) is worth noting in this context. Socrates contrasts the behaviour of low and common men with that of educated, well-bred symposiasts. The former, says Socrates, are unable to amuse themselves or converse with one another at symposia and are obliged to introduce outside voices (i.e. of singers and musical instruments). Gentlemen, on the other hand, are sufficient unto themselves at parties: they speak and listen to one another in turn, in orderly fashion, even if they have drunk a great deal of wine. In Xenophon's *Symposium*, even though the Syracusan troupe of entertainers performs several times in the course of the evening, the question of the proper way for gentlemen to amuse themselves at a party also arises. Socrates states that it would be a disgrace if he and his fellow banqueters, who consider themselves superior to the band of entertainers, were to prove incapable of improving or amusing one another. The guests then turn immediately to a semi-serious discussion of each symposiast's special virtues (*Symp.* 3. 2 ff.).[68] At another point (7. 2–5) Socrates advises the Syracusan impresario that daredevil exhibitions by his group would be inappropriate and suggests that they dance to the flute instead. In other words, only certain kinds of entertainments are found in Xenophon's *Symposium*, and these pastimes do not serve as a substitute for the guests diverting one another by means of their own conversation. It is probably this sentiment, that men of culture have no real need for flautists or dancers (see Pl. *Theaet.* 173D)—let alone much drink—which leads Xenophon to omit entertainments altogether in the model celebrations of the *Cyropaedia*. If this is indeed the case, it is rather surprising that Xenophon makes the point only indirectly. One would

[67] See *Cyr.* 1. 3. 10 and 4. 5. 7; cf. Athen. 434 E–F.

[68] The similarity between Pl. *Prot.* 347 C–E and Xen. *Symp.* 3. 2 has led some scholars to argue for Xenophon's dependence on Plato here, but such reflections on the proper pastimes at symposia may have been a commonplace. See Dittmar 1912: 210–12 and Woldinga 1938–9, 58–60.

have expected to find at one of the banquets of the *Cyropaedia* a
comment akin to the remarks of Socrates (at Pl. *Prot.* 347 c–e or Xen.
Symp. 3. 2): we could well imagine Xenophon contriving a situation
in which a guest, for instance, would suggest bringing in a singer or
dancer and Cyrus would then advise the symposiasts that they, as
men of culture, amuse one another by conversing instead. Xenophon
does have young Cyrus speak out against excessive wine-drinking,
but he does not explain (or excuse) the lack of party entertainments
in any way.[69]

In conclusion, the omissions and restrictions of the *Cyropaedia*'s
symposia, as well as their general uniformity in tone, must have been
deliberately planned by Xenophon, for he was acquainted with very
different types of symposia, both actual and literary. It is only in his
Symposium that the widest possible range of characters, themes, and
activities is presented: the themes and motifs of the *Cyropaedia* group
of parties are a conscious selection, chosen from a wider range of
possibilities.

Before turning to a commentary on the individual parties of the
Cyropaedia, one further influence should be borne in mind, Persian
party practices.[70] In Herodotus (9. 15–16) we hear of a banquet in
Thebes, where each one of the fifty Greeks present shares a couch
with a Persian guest. The two nationalities feast, pour libations, and
drink together (and even confide in one another): this would seem to
show that Persian and Greek sympotic customs were not altogether
alien. None the less, the Persians did have customs of their own—
their habit of holding serious deliberations over wine (below, sect. 3)
is perhaps the most famous one—and these play a part in the
banquets of the *Cyropaedia*. These Persian features will be noted as
they arise.

2. ASTYAGES' FEAST: CYR. I. 3. 4–12

The first party found in the *Cyropaedia* is a banquet given by Astyages
for his daughter Mandane and grandson Cyrus, who have recently

---

[69] Another possible explanation for the lack of entertainments at the banquets of the
Cyr. is that Cyrus and his men are too busy with their conquests and empire-building
to indulge in making music, just as Themistocles was (cf. Plut. *Them.* 2. 3; *Cim.* 9. 1).
Again, one would have expected Xenophon to make this point directly.

[70] See the surveys in Olmstead 1948: 179–83 and Cook 1983: 139–42 (with nn. on
250–1).

arrived in Media on a visit. Astyages has invited the two to Media in order to make his grandson's acquaintance. The occasion of this dinner-party—a feast served up by Astyages, shortly after he becomes acquainted with the young Cyrus—has rather sinister associations, at least for readers of Herodotus: one is immediately reminded of the Thyestean feast Astyages arranges for Harpagus after the Mede despot discovers that his grandson is still alive (cf. Hdt. 1. 114ff., esp. 119).[71] It is interesting, then, that Xenophon also chooses to have his Astyages preside over a dinner-party. Astyages is, of course, a benign figure in the *Cyropaedia* and has never attempted to harm his grandson in any way; Xenophon does not allow the memory of Harpagus and son to cast a pall over his proceedings. Astyages' dinner-party in the *Cyropaedia* is a cheerful affair, touching upon both serious and light topics, in the sympotic tradition of σπουδαιογέλοιον: Xenophon counters Herodotus' account only indirectly.

In one respect, none the less, Xenophon's young Cyrus is very like his Herodotean counterpart: in both writers the Persian lad (he is aged ten in Herodotus, about twelve in the *Cyropaedia*) addresses his despotic grandfather freely and without fear.[72] Our Cyrus' outspokenness becomes apparent in his very first exchange with the Mede ruler over dinner. Astyages has taken pains to please the boy, offering him a rich and varied meal, with several side dishes, sauces, and meats. Cyrus is used to plain Persian fare (cf. *Cyr.* 1. 2. 8, 11) and does not understand why Astyages takes such a long and circuitous route, through so many dishes, on his way to satiety, instead of eating bread and meat the way the Persians do. When his grandfather explains that this method of dining is a pleasing one, Cyrus retorts that Astyages himself seems disgusted by these rich dishes, for he always wipes his hands after touching one of them (1. 3. 4–5).

In this exchange—the first of a series of reproofs delivered didactically by young Cyrus to his grandfather—Persian simplicity is contrasted with Median luxury, a comparison regularly found in the *Cyropaedia*.[73] Elsewhere, of course, it is the Persians who are fond of dainty dishes while the Greeks (or more specifically the Spartans) eat

---

[71] See Cizek 1975: 550 with n. 53.
[72] Compare Hdt. 1. 116. 1 ἐδόκεε . . . καὶ ἡ ὑπόκρισις [sc. τοῦ Κύρου] ἐλευθεριωτέρη εἶναι and *Cyr.* 1. 3. 8 καὶ τὸν Κῦρον ἐπερέσθαι προπετῶς ὡς ἂν παῖς μηδέπω ὑποπτήσσων, and see Höistad 1948: 82–4.
[73] See *Cyr.* 1. 3. 2–3, 1. 5. 1, 1. 6. 8, 2. 4. 1, 5–6, 4. 5. 54, etc.

simple repasts. Herodotus' story of how Pausanias arranged for a
Persian meal and a Spartan one to be set side by side and then laughingly pointed out the Persians' folly in coming to rob the Greeks of
their poverty (Hdt. 9. 82) is perhaps the most vivid illustration of this
commonplace.[74] The contrast here between Cyrus and Astyages not
only establishes the Medes as the luxury-loving 'Persians' of the
Cyropaedia but also assigns to the hero of the work a trait much
favoured by his author, modest eating habits. Xenophon's heroes
often emphasize the importance of eating moderately,[75] and Cyrus
himself will return to this theme many times throughout the *Cyropaedia*.[76] Astyages, in any event, evidently takes Cyrus' words to
heart, for later, when offering his grandson all sorts of treats as an
incentive to staying on in Media, he promises him *simple* meals
(1. 3. 14).

Cyrus then accepts several cuts of meat from Astyages, only to
distribute them to attendants present at the meal, in return for
various services they have rendered him. Here we are reminded of the
Persian practice of paying subordinates—be they nobles, soldiers, or
servants—in food and rations rather than with money. Persian
satraps and nobles, as well as the king, all had, apparently, an
entourage of underlings who shared their table and were dependent
upon them for the very food they ate (cf. *Cyr.* 8. 2. 2–4).[77]

Only Sacas, Astyages' handsome cupbearer, does not receive any
meat from Cyrus, and Astyages asks why his most honoured servant,
who has the power to decide who shall be admitted to the royal
presence, has been passed over. Cyrus, who is, as Xenophon points
out, too young to be shy, immediately demands to know why his
grandfather is so fond of Sacas. Astyages jokingly replies that it is
because his servant pours the wine so gracefully, and this leads Cyrus
to demonstrate that he too makes a skilful cupbearer. He then
performs the service with such a serious expression that he causes his
mother and grandfather to laugh (1. 3. 9).

Cyrus' turn here as a cupbearer is particularly interesting, for it
seems to be a variation on—if not an explanation of—one part of

[74] See also Hdt. 1. 133 (but cf. 1. 71); *Ages.* 9. 3, etc.
[75] e.g. Socrates—*Mem.* 1. 3. 5–8, 3. 14. 5–6; Agesilaus—*Ages.* 9. 3; cf. *Hiero* 1. 17–19
and see above, ch. 2. 1, at n. 3.
[76] Cf. *Cyr.* 1. 5. 12, 4. 5. 4, 7. 5. 80, etc., and cf. Due 1989: 175–9.
[77] Heraclides of Cyme (*FGrH* 689 F 2) is our main source for this practice, along with
some recently discovered Persepolis tablets. See Hornblower 1982: 147, 151, 155–6
with nn.; Cook 1983: 139–40; cf. Lewis 1984: 595–6.

Ctesias' version of how Cyrus rose to power.[78] According to Ctesias,[79] Cyrus came from very lowly origins—his father was a brigand and his mother a goatherd. Cyrus attached himself to the Median court in order to earn his living and performed various menial functions there. At first he worked outdoors in the palace grounds and subsequently he was employed in the palace itself. The Persian lad served as a lamp-carrier and then worked under Astyages' chief cupbearer, who poured wine for the king himself. Young Cyrus poured the wine so skilfully[80] that he caught Astyages' eye and eventually replaced the chief cupbearer upon the latter's death. Cyrus' influence over the king grew, Ctesias tells us, and he and his family became wealthy and powerful. Eventually Cyrus rebelled against the Median despot and captured his kingdom. In the *Cyropaedia* Cyrus, of course, comes from royal stock and is on the best possible terms with his Mede relations. By having his young Cyrus only play at pouring wine, Xenophon is, perhaps, referring obliquely to the Ctesian tale, demonstrating how such a (false) story could have arisen: since Cyrus once jestingly poured wine for his grandfather Astyages, he was later thought to be the king's cupbearer. If this is the case, then Xenophon is once again using Astyages' lively dinner-party to establish the 'true' relationship between the Mede despot and his grandson and to counter or explain away other versions of the Astyages–Cyrus tale.

Cyrus, although he carefully imitates Sacas' other movements when pouring wine, does not actually taste the wine, and Astyages asks him why he refrains from doing so. Cyrus explains that he is afraid that there is some sort of drug in the wine-bowl, because he is certain that Sacas had placed a drug in the wine he served to the king and his friends at Astyages' birthday celebration. That group of revellers, says Cyrus, were unsteady in mind and body and more badly behaved than children: they all spoke at the same time, sang off tune, and danced out of rhythm. All the guests seemed to have forgotten that Astyages was their king, and they demonstrated Median freedom of speech (ἰσηγορία) by never keeping silent. Astyages asks Cyrus whether his own father ever becomes intoxicated

---

[78] See for this point Höistad 1948: 87 n. 1.

[79] Or, to be more exact, the summary of Ctesias found in Nicolaus of Damascus (*FGrH* 90 F 66); see below, ch. 4 n. 24.

[80] *FGrH* 90 F 66. 5 καὶ τὴν φιάλην εὐσχημόνως ἐπιδιδόντα; compare our passage: εὐσχημόνως πως προσενεγκεῖν καὶ ἐνδοῦναι τὴν φιάλην (*Cyr.* 1. 3. 9).

and his grandson replies that Cambyses drinks moderately, for he has no Sacas to pour wine for him (1. 3. 10–11).

Once again young Cyrus lectures his grandfather on a favourite theme of Xenophon's, the ill effects of excessive drinking. The phrase Cyrus uses to describe the revellers' confusion of mind and body— ταῖς γνώμαις καὶ τοῖς σώμασι σφαλλομένους (1. 3. 10)—is used by Xenophon several times to describe the effects of drink: Socrates (*Symp.* 2. 26), Lycurgus (*Lac. Pol.* 5. 4), and the ancient Persians (*Cyr.* 8. 8. 10) all think this condition should be avoided. We have seen that in the *Cyropaedia* the Persians are exceptionally sober, even at their drinking-parties, while the Medes, Babylonians, etc. are more inclined to become intoxicated: here young Cyrus is quick to point out to his grandfather this contrast between Medes and Persians. In Ctesias' tale Astyages' inclination towards drink leads, in a way, to his downfall. At first, according to Ctesias, Cyrus worms his way into Astyages' confidence while serving as his cupbearer. Later, when Ctesias' Cyrus requests permission to go to Persia—ostensibly to visit his sick father, but actually to set the wheels of a Persian rebellion in motion—Astyages wisely refuses to let him go. It is only when Astyages is relaxed and in his cups (*FGrH* 90 F 66. 22 βασιλέα ἐν πολλῇ ὄντα παιδιᾷ τε καὶ μέθῃ) that the Mede ruler relents and allows the visit, with its disastrous consequences.

Our Cyrus was disturbed by the sudden sense of equality between Astyages and his subjects at the despot's birthday celebration: all alike seemed to have forgotten that he was their king and this led to everyone talking at once. Cyrus ironically terms this free-for-all ἰσηγορία, Median freedom of speech. His remark is a two-edged one, for in the *Cyropaedia* Astyages is a tyrant, subject to no law but his own, and his subjects would not normally speak freely in front of him: in fact Cyrus often acts as an intermediary in relaying the requests of the Mede nobles (*Cyr.* 1. 4. 1–2).[81] Hence Cyrus, who is used to the freedom granted to Persian citizens (cf. 1. 2. 13–15), can mock Median ἰσηγορία, saying in effect that Medes can speak freely only when they are drunk. On the other hand, Cyrus objects to the fact that Astyages was not held in awe by his fellow symposiasts and was treated as an equal, not a king. In the *Hiero* the fact that a tyrant can never really enjoy himself with his subjects but must always be on his guard is considered a heavy burden that the ruler must bear

---

[81] Compare the fear that Cyaxares, Astyages' son and heir, arouses in his subjects as king (*Cyr.* 4. 5. 18–19).

(*Hiero* 6. 2–3), so that Astyages' relaxed behaviour can be considered reassuring, an indication of how secure he feels amongst his subjects. Does Cyrus disapprove because he thinks Astyages must be more cautious, or simply more dignified? Xenophon's Socrates, like young Cyrus, is also displeased by excessive rowdiness at a symposium: he restores order by starting a song (*Symp.* 7. 1).

Astyages' drunken party took place on his birthday. It seems that all Persians celebrated their birthdays (Hdt. 1. 133), and naturally the king's birthday was an especially important occasion (cf. Hdt. 9. 110–11; [Pl.] *Alc. I* 121 c);[82] this was probably true of the Medes as well. At the party described by young Cyrus, Astyages and his guests sing and dance, but in other Greek sources we hear of more professional entertainment at Astyages' court, with minstrels and dancers performing at the king's symposia. The most famous song sung to the Mede ruler was an allegorical one, warning him of a beast (i.e. Cyrus) which is about to attack.[83]

Returning to Astyages' party for young Cyrus in the *Cyropaedia*, we find that Mandane speaks up for the first time. Mandane, anxious perhaps to blunt Cyrus' criticisms of her father, asks Cyrus why he dislikes Sacas so much. Her son explains that he is angry at the cupbearer because he frequently forbids him to disturb Astyages. Cyrus then jokingly demonstrates how—if he were allowed to rule over Sacas—he would keep the cupbearer away from his meals, using the same pretexts that Sacas now uses to deny Cyrus access to his grandfather. On this light note (1. 3. 12 τοσαύτας . . . εὐθυμίας) the banquet ends.

The role assigned here to Sacas is an unusual one, for he combines two separate functions: cupbearer and chief usher to the king. The latter role of εἰσαγγελεύς (or chiliarch or hazarapatish),[84] controller of the king's audience, was clearly a most important one, and Sacas seems to have been Astyages' right-hand man—as the despot's own words (1. 3. 8 ὃν ἐγὼ μάλιστα τιμῶ) attest. Cupbearers, who were sometimes eunuchs, generally had a less important role at court.[85] It

---

[82] It is not altogether clear whether the occasion of Xerxes' celebration in Herodotus (9. 110ff.) is his birthday or coronation day; the Greek ἐν ἡμέρῃ τῇ ἐγένετο βασιλεύς (Hdt. 9. 110) is ambiguous.

[83] See Ctesias ap. Nicolaus of Damascus (*FGrH* 90 F 66. 26) and Deinon (*FGrH* 690 F 9); the latter is apparently a variation on the former. See too above, ch. 1. 2.

[84] See Lewis 1977: 16–19; Cook 1983: 143–4 (with nn. on 251–2); and Chaumont 1973: 139–41, for the history and meaning of the terms; cf. Tuplin 1990: 22 with n. 7.

[85] For cupbearers as eunuchs see Artembares, Cyrus' patron according to Ctesias (*FGrH* 90 F 66. 5–7), and the variant reading εὐνοῦχος for οἰνοχόος at

is interesting that Sacas' beauty is mentioned (1. 3. 8); the cupbearer is, it seems, a Ganymedes-type figure, and perhaps this is why Astyages so favours Sacas.[86]

In *Cyr.* 1. 3. 4–12 Xenophon does not restrict himself to Greek sympotic motifs, but introduces other elements from very different worlds: Median and Persian customs and functions, oblique allusions to Herodotus and Ctesias, and several pet themes of the author all play a part in Astyages' feast.

3. CYRUS' OFFICERS AT MESS: CYR. 2. 2. 1–2. 3. 1

Cyr. 2. 2. 1–2. 3. 1 tells of a dinner-party Cyrus gives while camping out in Media with his Persian army. The Persians have arrived in Media at Cyaxares' request, in order to aid him in the impending conflict with the Assyrians and their allies. After setting up camp, the Persian forces practise military manœuvres, readying themselves for the battle ahead. Cyrus, Xenophon tells us, regularly invites select officers (and soldiers) to dinner in his tent in the camp, and makes a point of serving all those present the same food. The author of the *Cyropaedia* then plunges immediately into a description of one such meal hosted by Cyrus, telling us nothing of the menu, guest-list, or preparations for the dinner. This reticence about the setting of the party is uncharacteristic,[87] but Xenophon's chief interest here lies in describing the conversation that took place at the meal. Cyrus, we are told at the very start, always took pains to ensure that conversation at dinner was both entertaining and conducive to good (2. 2. 1); at the close of the party Xenophon is again careful to characterize the proceedings—τοιαῦτα μὲν δὴ καὶ γελοῖα καὶ σπουδαῖα καὶ ἐλέγετο καὶ ἐπράττετο ἐν τῇ σκηνῇ (2. 3. 1)—underlining for his reader the half-serious, half-playful atmosphere at the meal.[88]

Cyrus opens the conversation by questioning his officers about the

Neh. 1: 11. According to Hdt. (3. 34), Prexaspas is Cambyses' audience-master, while his son serves as the king's cupbearer; cf. Lewis 1977: 20.

[86] Cf. Bremmer 1990.

[87] Cf. Due 1989: 46–8.

[88] We have already seen that according to 'Hermogenes' this combination of light and serious features is an important characteristic of Socratic symposia (περὶ μεθόδου δεινότητος 36, p. 454 Rabe; cf. above, n. 12). Immediately after describing Socratic symposia, 'Hermogenes' goes on to quote the opening sentence introducing our party, ἀλλὰ καὶ ἐν τῇ Κύρου παιδείᾳ φησὶ Ξενοφῶν ἀεὶ μὲν οὖν ἐπεμέλετο κ.τ.λ. (*Cyr.* 2. 2. 1), indicating just how 'Socratic' our symposium is.

Persian commoners, who have recently been invited to fight in the ranks of the upper-class ὁμότιμοι (cf. 2. 1. 11–19). The Persian leader asks whether these commoners, who have not had the benefit of an upper-class Persian education, are proving themselves equal to the ὁμότιμοι, both in social and in military matters. While the question appears at first sight to invite a theoretical discussion concerning the value of education, of the kind made popular by sophists, it is actually designed to let the ὁμότιμοι complain openly about the new soldiers. The sudden promotion of these men has, naturally enough, caused a great deal of tension among the original ὁμότιμοι. In fact, only one of Cyrus' officers, Sambaulas, has anything good to say about the new recruits at our party (below, 2. 2. 28–31); all the other officers criticize them.

Hystaspas, Cyrus' close companion, is the first to respond to the Persian leader's question, telling of a commoner who is certainly inferior to the ὁμότιμοι in social graces. This commoner, termed a δύσκολος (2. 2. 2, 6), complains because he is never allowed first go at portions of meat passed round to the soldiers at their meal. Hystaspas finally arranges for the disgruntled man to help himself first, but since the commoner is over-excited and greedy he ends up with no food at all. At the time, Hystaspas could barely control his laughter at the man's discomfiture, and the listeners at Cyrus' party naturally laugh at the tale as well (2. 2. 1–5). This anecdote of a greedy soldier reminds us of two other gluttonous party-goers in Xenophon: a nameless dinner companion of Socrates who concentrates almost exclusively on his ὄψον and is mockingly termed an ὀψοφάγος (*Mem.* 3. 14. 2–4), and an Arcadian at Seuthes' party in the *Anabasis* who is so busy eating that he passes the wine along to Xenophon for safe-keeping and causes all those present, including his host, to burst into laughter (*Anab.* 7. 3. 25). The loud, gluttonous Persian commoner is also reminiscent of the boorish παράσιτοι or κόλακες found in the symposia of comedy.[89] It is well in line with the didactic nature of this symposium that the greedy Persian does not actually appear at the party but is only mentioned: Cyrus' select officers—the actual guests in his tent—do not behave in this way. The nameless δύσκολος is the first of a series of character types, akin to those described in Theophrastus' *Characters*, found in this symposium.

---

[89] See above, sect. 1. For the influence of Old Comedy on Xenophon's *Symp.* see Körte 1927: 44–8. Breitenbach 1966: 1824, thinks that the comic figure of the ὀψοφάγος also appeared in Socratic dialogues, such as Aeschines' *Callias.*

An unnamed taxiarch is the next of Cyrus' guests to address himself to the question of the new recruits, and he tells of their drill practice. After being reprimanded for advancing in disorderly fashion, a platoon of fifty men follow their leader's orders too punctiliously and end up serving as an armed guard to a . . . letter. A second stock figure, the over-obedient, literal-minded man, is introduced here. Once again Cyrus and his guests laugh at the tale and the Persian leader ironically praises the new recruits' responsiveness and discipline (*Cyr.* 2. 2. 6–11).

Another taxiarch, an austere Persian named Aglaitadas, is not as amused by these tales of the new recruits as Cyrus and the others are: he accuses the two previous speakers of making up their stories or dissembling (ἀλαζονεύονται) in order to please Cyrus. Aglaitadas, a stern and humourless man (2. 2. 11), appears only here in the *Cyropaedia*, and he is the third character type to appear in our dinner-party—the ill-humoured symposiast.[90] Hermogenes in Xenophon's *Symposium* is another such unsociable figure:[91] he is criticized by Socrates for disturbing the other guests by his excessive silence and gravity (*Symp.* 6. 1–5; cf. 4. 50, 8. 3). Aglaitadas' fellow diners consider his seriousness a challenge: they do not rest until they manage to make him smile (*Cyr.* 2. 2. 16).

The Persian leader will not, in any event, have his men called dissemblers, and Cyrus goes on to define the term ἀλαζών with almost Aristotelian precision: the symposiasts are not pretending to possess a certain quality in order to gain something by their posturings,[92] but are simply trying to amuse their companions. Aglaitadas, continues another taxiarch, would surely object if his fellow officers

---

[90] See Demetrius, *De Eloc.* 134–5, for an appreciation of the charming use Xenophon makes of this grim character.

[91] Woldinga 1938–9: 30 n. 1 calls Aglaitadas a 'dubbelganger' of Hermogenes. Xenophon's own attitude towards his symposiast Hermogenes is difficult to pin down. Hermogenes' views on a most important topic—the gods—seem close to those of his author (*Symp.* 4. 46–50), but Socrates reprimands Hermogenes rather pointedly (6. 1–5) and his praise of the latter's serious brow, calm countenance, and cheerful disposition (8. 3) seems somewhat ironic, *pace* Bruns 1896: 401 and 407. Elsewhere in Xenophon Hermogenes is mentioned as one of Socrates' close companions (*Mem.* 1. 2. 48), and he serves as Xenophon's source for Socrates' last days (*Mem.* 4. 8. 4 ff.; cf. *Apol.* 2 ff.). In the *Mem.* Socrates praises Hermogenes as a useful, loyal friend (*Mem.* 2. 10. 3), and there the praise rings true.

[92] ἀλαζονεία is one of the character traits defined by Theophrastus: see *Char.* 23. 1 ἡ ἀλαζονεία δόξει εἶναι προσποίησίς τις ἀγαθῶν οὐκ ὄντων and cf. *Cyr.* 2. 2. 12 ὁ μὲν γὰρ ἀλαζὼν ἔμοιγε δοκεῖ ὄνομα κεῖσθαι ἐπὶ τοῖς προσποιουμένοις καὶ πλουσιωτέροις εἶναι ἢ εἰσί κ.τ.λ.; see also Arist. *Nic. Eth.* 1127ᵃ20–2 δοκεῖ δὴ ὁ μὲν ἀλαζὼν προσποιητικὸς τῶν ἐνδόξων εἶναι καὶ μὴ ὑπαρχόντων καὶ μειζόνων ἢ ὑπάρχει, and cf. MacDowell 1990.

were to move him to tears by means of pitiful songs and tales the way writers do (2. 2. 13 ὥσπερ ἔνιοι καὶ ἐν ᾠδαῖς καὶ ἐν λόγοις οἰκτρὰ ἄττα λογοποιοῦντες εἰς δάκρυα πειρῶνται ἄγειν), but why reproach them for trying to entertain him? This brief venture into poetics, with its vague echoes of the words of Ion the rhapsode (Pl. *Ion* 535 c), Gorgias (*Helen* 9 ff.), and, of course, Aristotle (*Poetics* 1449ᵇ24 ff.), is a particularly Greek contribution to the Persian party, but Aglaitadas is not without reply. He says that causing others to weep is often a beneficial act, particularly as a means to teach moderation, justice, or obedience to laws, but there is no good to be had from arousing laughter. The stern Aglaitadas is none the less finally made to smile himself when he is told by Hystaspas that it is easier to rub fire out of him than to make him laugh.[93] Cyrus then teasingly accuses his men of corrupting his most serious officer with laughter and their discussion περὶ γέλωτος ends.

In Xenophon's *Symposium* Philippus, the jester, also discusses the relative merits of tears and laughter. Philippus is almost the exact antithesis of both Aglaitadas and Hermogenes, his fellow symposiast; he is as incapable of being serious as the other two are of being lighthearted (*Symp.* 1. 15). Philippus prides himself on his γελωτοποιία and considers himself far superior to those (such as actors) who can cause many others to weep—the very opposite of Aglaitadas' position here.[94] At one point in the symposium Philippus is made to cry (*Symp.* 1. 15), just as Aglaitadas is made to laugh at our party (and Hermogenes is prodded into joining the general banter at Callias' house). Perhaps this is Xenophon's way of showing that the jester's excessive buffoonery, like the excessive gravity of Aglaitadas and Hermogenes, should be rejected: a blend of the two—σπουδαιογέλοιον—is to be preferred.

The next topic of conversation (2. 2. 17–22) is introduced by Chrysantas, Cyrus' right-hand man. He is concerned that the new recruits will think that all soldiers, whether deserving or not, should have an equal share of any booty that the Persians may capture. Nothing, says Chrysantas, is more unequal or unfair (ἀνισώτερον) than equal awards for good and bad men alike; he favours another kind of equality, that of equal awards for those whose merit is equal.

---

[93] There is a pun here in the Greek—on Aglaitadas being the butt of a joke rather than laughing himself; cf. οὐ παρεκτέον σοι ἡμῖν γέλωτα and οἴει . . . γέλωτα περιποιεῖν ἐξ ἐμοῦ (*Cyr.* 2. 2. 15).

[94] Compare *Symp.* 3. 11 πολλοὺς κλαίοντας καθίζειν and *Cyr.* 2. 2. 14 τοῦ κλαίοντας καθίζειν.

This is known elsewhere as proportionate or geometrical equality,[95] as opposed to arithmetic equality, or equal shares for all. Geometric equality was often associated with oligarchic or aristocratic regimes, while arithmetic equality was favoured by democracies. Although Chrysantas does not use this mathematical terminology, our passage is Xenophon's contribution to the contemporary discussion of the 'two equalities', an issue also touched upon by Isocrates (*Aerop.* 21–2; cf. *Nic.* 14–15) and Plato (*Laws* 757 A–758 A). All three writers are in favour of rewards according to merit, or geometric equality.[96]

Cyrus suggests putting the question of allotment of spoils before the army as a whole, at an assembly. Chrysantas is sceptical as to whether the commoners will vote for rewards according to merit, but the Persian leader thinks that given the proper encouragement, these men will indeed realize that good men deserve more. All the party-goers then agree to try to persuade others to vote for an unequal allotment of spoils. The very next day an assembly is held, and it is decided there that war prizes will be awarded unequally, according to valour (2. 3. 1–16). In this symposium we find, then, an instance of an important proposal which is first discussed over dinner and then reconsidered the following day under more formal circumstances. Here we come fairly close to the Persian custom of holding deliberations over wine and then re-evaluating the result when sober. Herodotus (1. 133), Plutarch (*Mor.* 714 A–C), Strabo (15. 3. 20), Athenaeus (192 C), and Maximus of Tyre (22. 4 C–F) all tell us of this practice,[97] while in the book of Esther (3: 15, 5: 6) we find two instances of King Ahasuerus actually considering critical matters in his cups.[98] We have seen above (sect. 1) that in Homer too serious discussions take place over wine, and this practice of combining wine and decision-making is perhaps a Persian version of—or variation on—Greek σπουδαιογέλοιον: it is, in effect, a juxtaposition of the serious and the frivolous.

At the dinner-party another taxiarch now laughingly tells of at least one commoner who does not believe in sharing all things

[95] Pl. *Gorg.* 508 A ἡ ἰσότης ἡ γεωμετρική. See Dodds ad loc. for the Pythagorean origins of the expression 'geometric equality' and cf. Arist. *Pol.* 1301ᵇ29 ff. for an explanation of the mathematical terminology.

[96] For the 'two equalities' see the discussion in Scharr 1919: 221–9; Guthrie 1969: 151; Vlastos 1981: 188 n. 89 and 195–6 with nn.

[97] Cf. Tuplin 1990: 26 on the role of drink in Persian assassination plots.

[98] See Hoschander 1923: 181–2, 218–19. These Persian deliberations over wine are attested down to Sasanian times; cf. Shaked 1982: 294.

equally, for he tries to have a larger portion of everything except work (2. 2. 22–8). Here a fourth character type, the lazy and selfish man, is introduced. Cyrus says at once that such men must be expelled from the army: lazy men are like drones (κηφῆνες) and are harmful only inasmuch as others must support them, but men who are both idle and intent on self-aggrandizement are dangerous, for they seem to demonstrate that vice does pay.[99] Base men are often more persuasive than good ones, continues Cyrus, for they offer immediate pleasures and satisfactions while the way to virtue is arduous and steep (2. 2. 24). Cyrus' words here immediately bring to mind Prodicus' tale of Heracles at the crossroads (as reported by Socrates, *Mem.* 2. 1. 20 ff.) and its precursor, Hesiod, *Works and Days* 287 ff. The Persian commoners play the role of Heracles here, while their officers have the same function as the beautiful and modest Arete.

Cyrus' didactic speech here is very like many of Socrates' pronouncements in the *Memorabilia*, and he now continues with a series of *Memorabilia*-like analogies, comparing the army and its soldiers to a chariot and its horses, and to a household and its servants.[100] The speech also contains a surprising note of cosmopolitanism: Cyrus tells his officers to choose new soldiers according to their ability and not because they are compatriots (2. 2. 26 ἐκ τῶν πολιτῶν . . . πατριῶται).[101] This generosity of mind is in fact selfish, for Cyrus is interested above all in an army which is as large and powerful as possible and he is willing to concede that others besides the Persians may suit his aims. In Xenophon's own time Cyrus the Younger puts this idea into practice when he enlists Greek troops in the campaign against his brother, and specifically tells the Greeks that he prefers them to the barbarians (i.e. Cyrus' own Persian troops) because of their superior fighting ability (*Anab.* 1. 7. 2–3). Usefulness makes for tolerance, as we shall see immediately below.

In the last exchange of this dinner-party (2. 2. 28–31) the Persian leader calls attention to an extremely ugly and hairy man who shares a couch with his commanding officer, Sambaulas. Cyrus, teasing Sambaulas (who appears only here in the *Cyropaedia*), asks him if he

[99] This is perhaps reminiscent of Plato's drones with and without stings in the *Rep.* (552 C–D; cf. *Oec.* 17. 14 and Hes. *WD* 303–6). Cyrus is called a 'king' bee in the *Cyr.*, for all his men wish to be ruled by him (5. 1. 24; contrast Pl. *Pol.* 301 D–E).

[100] See e.g. *Mem.* 2. 3. 7, 2. 4. 5, 4. 1. 3–4; cf. 4. 4. 5.

[101] Scharr 1919: 294–6 contrasts Pericles' law of 451/50 (re-enacted in 404/3), which restricted Athenian citizenship to children of two free Athenian parents, and points out that Xenophon had 'einen weiteren historischen Horizont' (296).

has brought the lad along, in Greek fashion (κατὰ τὸν Ἑλληνικὸν τρόπον), because of his good looks. When Sambaulas replies that he very much enjoys the sight of his companion, the others laugh and demand to know why. He explains that he admires the recruit's instant obedience to any request and adds that his good example has influenced Sambaulas' whole squad of ten men. One of the symposiasts then suggests that Sambaulas kiss his friend and the ugly commoner himself rejoins that this would be a task equivalent to any military drill (compare Critobulus at *Mem.* 2. 6. 32–3). On this note of rough humour the party ends, after prayers and libations are offered to the gods (2. 3. 1).

Sambaulas and his friend present us with a rather pallid παιδικὸς λόγος or homosexual love interest: they are the last of the stock figures in our symposium—the pair of lovers.[102] Sambaulas' intimacy with the ugly recruit is presented as the Persian version of Greek homosexuality, for while Sambaulas is much pleased with the young soldier and goes about everywhere with him, their relationship is not a sexual one but simply Sambaulas' way of rewarding his most loyal and useful soldier. In the *Symposium* of both Plato and Xenophon it is argued that true love between men, the proper kind of ἔρως, inspires them to excel and, more specifically, to be courageous in battle;[103] this argument may have appeared in Aeschines' *Aspasia* as well.[104] In actual practice there was the Theban Sacred Band,[105] while in the *Anabasis* (7. 4. 8) we hear of a successful military company recruited solely on the basis of the participants' good looks. Here, however, the commoner's excellence in military matters has led to his being admired or loved, and not vice versa.

In Xenophon's *Symposium* (8. 9 ff.), while Socrates distinguishes between love of the soul and love of the body (Ἀφροδίτη Οὐρανία τε καὶ Πάνδημος) and tries to show the advantages the former has over the latter, he does not totally separate the two. In our passage the dichotomy between these two kinds of love is complete, since the relationship between Sambaulas and his soldier is not at all physical. The relations between Artabazus and Cyrus, the only other male 'pair' in the *Cyropaedia*, are equally chaste. While Artabazus does

---

[102] See Martin 1931: 113–16 on this topos of 'Liebespaar' in symposia.

[103] Pl. *Symp.* 178 D–179 B (Phaedrus speaking), 184 C–185 C (Pausanias); Xen. *Symp.* 8. 26 ff. (Socrates).

[104] See Ehlers 1966: 88 ff., 104 ff.

[105] See Plut. *Pel.* 18–19; *Mor.* 760 D–761 D; cf. Xen. *Symp.* 8. 34 and Woldinga 1938–9: 471–2.

seem interested in physical contact with Cyrus (1. 4. 27–8, 8. 4. 26–7), the Persian leader playfully rejects these advances. None the less, he manages to put Artabazus' feelings towards him to good use, having him enlist Median support for his plans in times of crisis (see 4. 1. 22–4, 5. 1. 24–6, 6. 1. 9–10). Homosexual relationships in the *Cyropaedia* are almost exclusively utilitarian: while there are joking references to sexual contact, such contact is in fact minimal and the main emphasis is on the pragmatic benefits one (or both) of the partners derives from their intimacy. If the ugliness of Plato's Socrates only emphasizes his inner, spiritual beauty, the displeasing looks of Sambaulas' recruit serve as a foil to his practical usefulness in military matters.

Before leaving *Cyr.* 2. 2 it is worth looking more closely at the various personalities who participate in the gathering. Two of the guests at the party are Cyrus' closest aides—Hystaspas and Chrysantas—and both make their first appearance in the *Cyropaedia* here. Xenophon has the two speak up without describing them in any way: each is formally introduced only later (Chrysantas at 2. 3. 5; Hystaspas at 4. 2. 46). None the less, both behave in characteristic fashion: Hystaspas is the first to take up the conversational gauntlet thrown by Cyrus, replying to his question about the commoners, and he sets the tone of the comments that follow from the other officers—playful, but critical. Chrysantas is more concerned with fundamental issues of prestige and power, i.e. the division of booty, and he may have discussed this problem with Cyrus in advance (see below, sect. 6). Both Hystaspas and Chrysantas have, in any event, well-defined personalities of their own. The other participants in the symposium are more shadowy figures. Several symposiasts are identified only by their military function, rather than by name (e.g. 2. 2. 22 τῶν ταξιάρχων τις; cf. 2. 2. 6, 29) and, as is to be expected, these anonymous men have no character of their own; it is only their words that count. A third group of guests at the dinner—Aglaitadas, Sambaulas, and the ugly commoner—appear only here in the *Cyropaedia*, and it is probably not a coincidence that the three represent stock figures of a kind often found in symposia. Xenophon probably invented these three characters solely in order to have them play a specific role in this symposium; consequently he discards them immediately afterwards.[106] It is illuminating to compare Aglaitadas

---

[106] Cf. Tatum 1989: 199–201, and see Bassett 1917: 571–3 on Xenophon's use of the stock characters of the humorist.

or Sambaulas and the ugly commoner with their counterparts in
Xenophon's *Symposium*. The solemn Hermogenes (and joking
Philippus) and the pair of lovers Callias and Autolycus are all real
personalities with qualities and characters of their own in addition to
their 'stock' roles. The other character types described at our party—
the gluttonous commoner and the over-obedient one—have even less
of an independent existence. These anonymous figures do not
actually participate in the symposium and are introduced only
indirectly through the anecdotes of Cyrus' officers. It seems clear that
Xenophon was interested in displaying a variety of character types at
this party—characters he thought appropriate for a semi-serious
gathering—but was less concerned with portraying real, full-fledged
personalities.

Finally, once again the blend of Greek and Persian ingredients in
this symposium should be noted. Cyrus' distribution of food from his
table and the political deliberations over wine are Persian features of
the party, while the analysis of tears and laughter, the discussion of
the uphill path to virtue, and the presence of a 'homosexual' pair are
more in line with Greek sympotic traditions.

4. AT GOBRYAS' ESTATE: *CYR.* 5. 2. 5–22

Our next symposium, *Cyr.* 5. 2. 5–22, takes place at Gobryas' estate.
Cyrus and his soldiers have come to the estate for a first visit, shortly
after the Persians have forged an alliance with Gobryas, in order to
become acquainted with their new ally, his forces, and his land.
Gobryas' men bring out wine, barley, flour, and various meats in
order to feed the whole of Cyrus' army outdoors, while the Persian
leader and a small company enter inside the fortress for a tour of
inspection. The Assyrian presents Cyrus with various gold ornaments, a countless number of darics,[107] and, last of all, his daughter.
The girl is of exceptional beauty and stature but of sad countenance,
since she grieves for her dead brother, who was killed by the young
Assyrian king (4. 6. 2–5; see below, ch. 4. 3). Cyrus, Gobryas pro-
claims, is to do with her (and the gifts) as he likes: all the Assyrian and
his daughter ask in return is the Persian's help in exacting revenge
from the young Assyrian king (5. 2. 5–7).

[107] This mention of darics, generally thought to be named after Darius, is an
anachronism; see Cook 1983: 70.

Gobryas' beautiful, sad daughter reminds us of Panthea, who has just been introduced in the previous chapter. Both Assyrian women are unusually beautiful and tall, both are distressed, both have been harmed by the young Assyrian king, and both are intended for Cyrus, only to be rejected, albeit gently, by him.[108] Panthea, of course, plays an active role in the *Cyropaedia*, while Gobryas' daughter is seen, if not actually heard, only here. She has been mentioned by her father earlier (4. 6. 9) and is referred to once more in the *Cyropaedia*, when Hystaspas offers himself—and is accepted— as her husband (8. 4. 13–16, 24–6). Her situation here is also similar to that of Cyaxares' daughter, who first appears towards the close of the *Cyropaedia* (8. 5. 18–20). The two women are presented to Cyrus by their fathers, along with valuable gifts, in the hope that a marriage will cement the alliance between the Persian leader and the pro- spective father-in-law. We know from the *Anabasis* (7. 2. 38) that a similar proposal was made to Xenophon in real life, for Seuthes offers his daughter to Xenophon—and would be happy to accept a (non- existent) daughter of Xenophon's in return—in order to strengthen the bond between them. Cyrus, of course, chooses Cyaxares' daughter. Neither Gobryas' daughter nor Cyaxares' is named and neither woman is portrayed at any length or given a character of her own: both are simply their powerful fathers' daughters.[109]

Cyrus responds to Gobryas' plea for vengeance by promising once again to do his utmost to punish the young Assyrian king. He will keep Gobryas' gifts in trust for the man who will wed the Assyrian's daughter, but Cyrus himself wishes for only one gift from his new ally—a gift worth more than all the wealth of Babylon. Gobryas, Xenophon tells us, suspects that Cyrus means his daughter, but in fact the Persian prince is more concerned with his good reputation. Many men, Cyrus explains to Gobryas, do not wish to do wrong but are unable to demonstrate their true worth, since they are never given the opportunity to (mis)use wealth and power. Gobryas, by placing his fortress, wealth, forces, and daugh- ter at Cyrus' disposal, has put him to the test and the Persian

---

[108] Beautiful and tall: *Cyr.* 5. 2. 7, 5. 1. 5, 7; distressed: 4. 6. 9 and 5. 2. 7, 5. 1. 6; harmed by the Assyrian: 4. 6. 9 and 5. 2. 7, 6. 1. 45; intended for Cyrus: 4. 6. 9 and 5. 2. 7, 5. 1. 6; rejected: 5. 2. 8, 12, 5. 1. 8.

[109] This is more surprising in the case of Cyaxares' daughter, for Cyrus does, after all, marry her. There is a hint that the two enjoyed a close relationship during Cyrus' childhood visit to Media (8. 5. 19), but this is a retroactive reference, for we first hear of her only minutes before her betrothal to Cyrus (8. 5. 18–20; cf. 28).

wishes both to be and to seem just.[110] The distinction between
seeming and being, or character and reputation, is often a prob-
lematical one,[111] but for Cyrus there is no such dichotomy between
actual and apparent virtue: good behaviour and a good name go
hand in hand. Early on the Persian prince has been taught by his
father that the quickest way to seeming wise or well-versed in any
area is to become so (*Cyr.* 1. 6. 22–3). A reputation with no sound
basis is in fact worthless, Cambyses warns, for impostors are soon
unmasked.[112] Cyrus seems to think that the converse is also true—to
be virtuous without enjoying the esteem of others is worth very
little—and he is proud of being praised and emulated (5. 2. 11–12).

Gobryas considers his daughter the most valuable gift being
offered to Cyrus: one wonders how he views the Persian's rejection of
the girl, by way of a diatribe on virtue. Cyrus, in any event, promises
to find a husband for her: his men are not rich, he concedes, but their
qualities of loyalty and steadfastness are worth more than all the
wealth of Assyria and Babylon, as Gobryas will soon witness for
himself (5. 2. 12–13). The Persian leader then rises to depart with his
men and invites Gobryas to join them for a meal outside, after
turning down the Assyrian's invitation to dine in the fortress. It is
only now that the symposium proper begins. The two eat their meal
outdoors, reclining on straw mats, and this leads Cyrus to ask
Gobryas who, in his opinion, has more coverings (στρώματα)—
Gobryas or each one of Cyrus' men? The Assyrian replies that the
Persians have a bigger house than his, since they use the heavens and
earth as a dwelling-place. So too they have as many couches as there
are places to sleep on the ground, and their covers come not from
sheep, but from the mountains and plains (5. 2. 15).

This exchange between the two new allies is a surprising one.
Costly carpets, coverings, and couches were a regular feature, almost
a symbol, of Persian (or Oriental) luxurious living. In the epilogue of
the *Cyropaedia* the Persians of Xenophon's day are condemned for
over-indulging in these trappings (8. 8. 16), while Cyrus especially

[110] Cf. *Cyr.* 5. 2. 11 ἕως ἂν ἀνὴρ δίκαιος ὦ καὶ δοκῶν εἶναι τοιοῦτος; 5. 2. 12 ἀρετῆς
καὶ δόξης ἀγαθῆς; cf. *Ages.* 3. 5.

[111] Aeschylus' line οὐ γὰρ δοκεῖν ἄριστος ἀλλ' εἶναι θέλει (*Sept.* 592) is perhaps the
most famous statement of the problem. For a discussion of the discrepancy between
character and reputation see e.g. Glaucon's words in Plato's *Rep.* (360 D–362 D); cf. Pl.
Gorg. 527 B.

[112] Compare *Mem.* 1. 7. 2 and 2. 6. 38, where Socrates speaks in very similar fashion;
cf. Gigon 1953: 166 and 1956: 158.

provides Median carpets for the spoilt Cyaxares to sit on when trying
to appease him (5. 5. 7). When Cyrus' forces organize the equipment
to be taken along on a long and arduous march, blankets are jet-
tisoned in favour of provisions, for, as Cyrus reassuringly explains,
the men will be able to sleep well even without them (6. 2. 30). Elsewhere in Xenophon we find Pharnabazus ashamed to make use of
the soft rugs spread out for him when he finds Agesilaus and his men
sitting on the ground (*Hell.* 4. 1. 30). Agesilaus, we are told, falls
asleep easily on the simplest kind of bedding, in contrast to the
Persian king (*Ages.* 5. 2, 9. 3). So too Heracles at the crossroads is
warned by Arete about the soft blankets and mattresses that are part
of Kakia's corrupting lifestyle (*Mem.* 2. 1. 30).[113] In short, the point
made here—that plain mats are more than adequate—is a favourite
one of Xenophon's, part of his general approval of simplicity and
moderation. What is unusual is the fact that Gobryas, rather than
Cyrus, is Xenophon's spokesman here, with the Persian's question
only a 'feed'. Gobryas is exceedingly wealthy—he has a storehouse
with enough supplies for a generation of men (*Cyr.* 5. 2. 4)—and is
used to rich trappings and furnishings. It is only natural for him to
look down upon poor people with few possessions, and indeed we are
told almost immediately afterwards that Gobryas, seeing the Persians' simple provisions, thinks that his men are more refined than
the Persians (5. 2. 16; cf. 5. 3. 3). Hence one would expect Cyrus to
be the one to demonstrate how heaven and earth, the mountains and
the plains, are enough to satisfy his men's needs, with Gobryas,
perhaps, offering to supply them with carpeting and bedding. In any
event, Gobryas' pantheistic perception of heaven and earth as a
dwelling-place for the Persians is the outdoors counterpart of Antisthenes' description of his house in the *Symposium* (4. 38). The walls of
his home, Antisthenes says, are like a warm tunic and the roof is a
thick cloak, so that he has little need of other clothes. Antisthenes too
is more than satisfied with his (presumably non-existent) bed-covers
(*Symp.* 4. 38 στρωμνὴν . . . ἀρκοῦσαν ἔχω).

The rest of the symposium held in front of Gobryas' castle is not
presented to us in direct dramatic form, but only indirectly, through
the Assyrian's reaction to the proceedings. Xenophon only rarely
describes the thoughts of his characters (other than Cyrus) in the

---

[113] Joël 1901: 485–7 thinks that many of these passages in Xenophon are influenced
by a 'Ponoslobschrift' by Antisthenes; see the additional references collected by him
there.

Cyropaedia, and hardly ever at the length allotted here to Gobryas.
The Assyrian's reflections are intended, of course, to present Xenophon's own views on what a convivial gathering of educated, well-
bred men should be like. Gobryas, who, as we have seen, at first
thinks poorly of Cyrus' men because of their simple fare, quickly
learns to appreciate the table manners of these educated Persians
(5. 2. 17 τῶν πεπαιδευμένων).[114] They do not become over-engrossed
in their food and drink, for they consider such behaviour bestial, and
they are moderate, sensible, and attentive to their surroundings. In
fact, Cyrus' educated Persians at dinner are very like the Spartans at
their communal meals. In his *Lac. Pol.* Xenophon notes that the
Spartans eat and drink with restraint at their συσσίτια and usually
speak of important political deeds, so that there is little room for
insolence, drunkenness, or unseemly conduct or talk.[115] These noble
Persians remind Gobryas (or, in all likelihood, the author of Περὶ
ἱππικῆς and Ἱππαρχικός) of horsemen who can ride their mounts
and look, listen, or talk at the same time. Their conversation, the
Assyrian notes, is playful but not at all offensive, and the questions
and repartee are of a kind that is more pleasant to hear than not
(5. 2. 16–18). In his other symposia Xenophon depicts actual
instances of such conversation and then, at times, underlines or
explains what he is doing (cf. e.g. 2. 3. 1). Here we are not provided
with any samples of the table-talk, and Plutarch in fact devotes a
section of his *Quaestiones Conviviales* (629E–635A) to illustrating the
type of pleasant questions to which Gobryas is probably referring.
Similarly, instead of being presented with a greedy eater who gets his
just deserts (as in *Cyr.* 2. 2. 2–5), we are simply told that the Persians
are not excessively interested in their food and drink. This device of
describing the symposium by means of general observations, with no
enlivening examples to attract the reader, makes Xenophon's didactic aims all too apparent. The other symposia of the *Cyropaedia*,
despite the 'gentlemanly' absence of music, dance, and spirits (see
above, sect. 1), are lively, colourful parties, and as such are more
successful models of civilized, well-bred celebrations.

Gobryas is especially impressed by the Persian rationing system:

[114] These men are the ὁμότιμοι—cf. *Cyr.* 2. 3. 13, 3. 3. 59, 70.

[115] *Lac. Pol.* 5. 6 ὥστ' ἐκεῖ ἥκιστα μὲν ὕβριν, ἥκιστα δὲ παροινίαν, ἥκιστα δὲ
αἰσχουργίαν καὶ αἰσχρολογίαν ἐγγίγνεσθαι; cf. our passage: ὡς πολὺ μὲν ὕβρεως ἀπῆν,
πολὺ δὲ τοῦ αἰσχρόν τι ποιεῖν, πολὺ δὲ τοῦ χαλεπαίνεσθαι πρὸς ἀλλήλους (*Cyr.* 5. 2. 18).
Plutarch (*Lyc.* 12. 4) and Critias (6. 14–16 West) also mention the Spartans' gentle,
harmless banter at their gatherings.

all of Cyrus' men—officers, regular soldiers, and possibly camp-followers as well—receive equal portions of food (cf. 2. 1. 25, 30, 4. 2. 38), for they think that the most enjoyable feast is to make their fellow soldiers as strong as possible. From the Assyrian's reaction it would seem that this system of equal rations for all is an innovative one and was not the usual practice in Xenophon's own time, but the evidence for this is not clear-cut.[116]

The symposium ends with one final direct exchange between Cyrus and Gobryas. The Assyrian expresses his admiration for the Persians, who are bent on self-improvement, unlike his own men, whose chief interest lies in accumulating possessions. Cyrus does not respond directly to this observation by his new ally but turns rather abruptly to practical plans and instructions for the next day; there is a similar transition from polite dinner-party conversation to more mundane military matters at the close of Seuthes' party in the *Anabasis* (7. 3. 34–9). *Cyr.* 5. 2. 5–22, the most didactic of our symposia, ends on this practical note: ἀπῆλθον ἑκάτερος ἐπὶ τὰ προσήκοντα.

5. PHERAULAS AND THE SACIAN: *CYR.* 8. 3. 35–50

Our next symposium, *Cyr.* 8. 3. 35–50, is an intimate dinner-party for two, the Persian commoner Pheraulas and an unnamed Sacian; they are one of the most curious pairs in the *Cyropaedia*. Pheraulas, an old friend of Cyrus, is a most gentleman-like commoner (2. 3. 7) who has just helped Cyrus arrange the inaugural royal procession in Babylon to be as impressive as possible (8. 3. 5ff.). The Sacian is a rank-and-file member (8. 3. 25 ἰδιώτης ἀνήρ) of his tribe's forces, who has met Pheraulas thanks to his swift horse. Immediately after the royal procession and sacrifices Cyrus organized a series of horse-races, with each nationality competing separately. Cyrus won the Persians' race, Artabazus was the first of the Medes, Tigranes was the best Armenian rider, etc.: in other words, the leaders of each national group won their respective races. The only exception

---

[116] In Sparta the hoplites' servants, the Helots, apparently received half the rations that their masters did (cf. Thuc. 4. 16), while Athenian hoplites and their attendants received equal shares (Thuc. 3. 17). Different kinds of soldiers received, in some cases, different sizes of rations (see Thuc. 5. 47. 6 and Dem. 4. 28). See Anderson 1970: 46–52 with nn. and Pritchett 1971: 3ff., esp. the charts on 16 and 51.

to this rule[117] is the young, ordinary Sacian who comes out far ahead in the contest with his compatriots, presumably because of the quality of his steed. Cyrus then asks him whether he would accept a kingdom for his horse and the Sacian replies that he is not interested in a kingdom, but would like to earn the gratitude of a good man (i.e. he would give the horse to a good man in the hope of reaping some benefit in return). The Persian leader then tells the Sacian that there are so many good men surrounding him, he is bound to hit one, even with his eyes shut, if he throws a clod of mud in a certain direction. The Sacian closes his eyes, throws a lump of mud, and hits Pheraulas, who continues to ride on as if nothing has happened because he is in the midst of performing an errand for Cyrus. The Sacian is puzzled by Pheraulas' behaviour and Cyrus does not help much, suggesting that Pheraulas may be mad. The Sacian then rides up to the Persian commoner, who is bleeding from the blow he has received, gives him his horse, and explains what has happened. Pheraulas accepts the horse, giving his own mount to the Sacian in return, and prays that his new friend will not regret the gift, even though, he adds, the Sacian would have been wiser to choose a richer man (8. 3. 25–32). This, then, is how Pheraulas and the Sacian become acquainted; the dinner-party at the Persian's quarters is their second meeting.

This story of the first encounter between the two is puzzling, even intriguing. Horses played an important part in the life of the Persians, as Darius' inscriptions telling of his 'kingdom great possessed of good horses, possessed of good men' indicate.[118] So too in the Avestan hymns to deities, or *Yashts*, various heroes pray for swift horses and for victory on the race-course, since horse- and chariot-races seemed to have been a regular test of bravery among the ancient Iranians.[119] On the Greek side, in the *Anabasis* the Ten Thousand, after arriving at Trapezus, first perform sacrifices and then organize various games, including horse-races (*Anab.* 4. 8. 25 ff.; cf. 5. 5. 5). Thus it is quite natural to find Cyrus, who likes to have his men compete (cf. e.g.

---

[117] Rhatines, the winner of the Cadusian competition, is mentioned only here (8. 3. 32), but it seems likely that he is in fact the anonymous new leader chosen by the Cadusians after their military fiasco (5. 4. 15–23).

[118] DSf lines 8–12 = DSm lines 3–5; see also DSp and DSs. The text of these inscriptions is in Kent 1953: 142–4, 146.

[119] See Schwartz 1985: 659–60, who refers to *Yashts* 5. 50, 86, 98, and 19. 777 in this context, and cf. Hdt. 7. 196. Kuhrt 1987: 52–3 points out how *Cyr.* 8. 3–4 reflects both elements of the Babylonian new year festival and Iranian practices.

Cyr. 2. 1. 22), organizing a series of horse-races; natural too is his desire to obtain the Sacian's remarkably swift horse. What is odd is Cyrus' abrupt 'kingdom for a horse' question: what does the Persian leader mean by his offer? There are certain Indo-European traditions which indicate that there were strong links between a ruler and his horse(s). The king in India, as well as in Iran, carried out a great ritual horse sacrifice, and in India a new king was allotted the amount of territory that a special horse covered when allowed to roam freely. In Achaemenid Persia we know of at least one ruler who owed his kingdom to his horse—Darius I (Hdt. 3. 84–6; cf. Ctesias, *FGrH* 688 F 13. 17).[120] None the less, these links between a kingdom and a horse do not prepare us for Cyrus' question, which is introduced both suddenly and indirectly.[121]

Puzzling too is Cyrus' suggestion that the Sacian choose the man who is to receive his steed by throwing a clod of earth with his eyes closed. This random method of selection is obviously meant to show that good men in Cyrus' company are thick and fast and can be found almost everywhere—elsewhere Xenophon uses the same 'can't be missed' idiom to describe the enemy (*Anab.* 3. 4. 15; *Hell.* 2. 4. 16)—but blindly throwing clumps of earth does seem an extravagant way of proving this point. Similarly, the fact that Pheraulas carries on with his duties and ignores the blow is meant to demonstrate the Persian commoner's worth, but why does Cyrus mislead the Sacian and imply that Pheraulas is unbalanced, instead of praising his friend? It is tempting to conjecture that Xenophon is reworking and possibly compressing another, somewhat longer tale.

Finally, it should be noted that Pheraulas and the Sacian exchange horses (8. 3. 32). It is perhaps not too fanciful to be reminded of two exchanges of gifts in the *Iliad*.[122] In their exchange of armour Glaucus presents Diomedes with a far more valuable present (*Il.* 6. 230–6), just as here the Sacian's horse is far better than

---

[120] On these Indo-European traditions see Sancisi-Weerdenburg 1980: 200–3 with nn.; Widengren 1959: 244, 251–2. On Darius' rise to power see Cook 1983: 54–5 and 238 n. 20, with the various interpretations he quotes there. For a more general survey of horsemanship in Iranian tradition see Knauth 1975: 97–104.

[121] Cf. 8. 3. 26 ἔνθα δὴ λέγεται ὁ Κῦρος ἐρέσθαι τὸν νεανίσκον. Xenophon normally presents the framework of the dialogues of the *Cyr.*—the identification of speakers, attribution of their words, etc.—directly and only rarely uses oblique forms such as λέγεται or φασί. Does his use of λέγεται here indicate that he is recalling a tale he has encountered elsewhere?

[122] For a good discussion of the role of gift exchanges in Homer (and in primitive societies in general) see Finley 1972: 73–6.

Pheraulas' mount. The exchange of presents between Hector and Ajax (*Il.* 7. 299–305) leads to grave, even fatal, consequences for each, at least according to post-Homeric tradition (cf. S. *Aj.* 1028–35); in our passage the exchange also has far-reaching (but not tragic) results for both parties.

Pheraulas initiates the next meeting with the Sacian, inviting him to dine. After dinner Pheraulas fills their wine-cups, toasts his guest, and then presents him with the goblets. The Sacian, who is impressed by the rich furnishings of Pheraulas' house and the many servants at his disposal, asks his host if he was a rich man back in Persia. (Here Xenophon uses the conventional, almost obligatory description of the physical setting of a symposium in order to lead up to his main theme—the true value of wealth.) Pheraulas explains that he comes from a poor family and was forced to forgo his education from an early age, working the small family plot by himself. All the Sacian sees is, in fact, a gift from Cyrus.[123]

The Sacian's curiosity about the source of Pheraulas' riches reminds us of Socrates' opening questions to the courtesan Theodote in the *Memorabilia* (3. 11. 4), when he visits her in her house. Both visitors are impressed and perhaps surprised by the luxuriousness of their surroundings and both immediately try to find out the source of this affluence; their questions serve as a smooth, natural transition to the main topic at hand. Socrates puts his questions to Theodote with tongue in cheek; the Sacian, on the other hand, really knows nothing of his host.

We have already learnt something of Pheraulas' background earlier in the *Cyropaedia*: he is a Persian commoner (2. 3. 7 Πέρσης τῶν δημοτῶν). The commoners are, apparently, those Persian citizens who cannot afford to attend the lifelong educational curriculum sponsored by the state (cf. 1. 2. 3–15) but must work for their living, just as Pheraulas describes himself doing here (8. 3. 37; cf. 2. 1. 15).[124] Although a commoner, Pheraulas is very much a gentleman in body and spirit (2. 3. 7) and he is an old acquaintance of Cyrus. At the assembly convened to discuss whether booty should be distributed according to merit or equally to all, Pheraulas speaks out in favour of rewarding men according to their actions and urges his

[123] Even the goblets presented by Pheraulas to the Sacian are, as Xenophon is careful to tell us, a present from Cyrus (8. 3. 33, 35).

[124] On the relationship between the ὁμότιμοι and δημόται in the *Cyr.* see Scharr 1919: 291–4; cf. Tuplin 1990: 18–20.

fellow commoners to compete with the ὁμότιμοι on equal terms
(2. 3. 8–15). In this earlier speech Pheraulas touches upon the
arduous and unhonoured (2. 3. 11 ἐπίπονον μέν, ἄτιμον δέ) life of the
commoners and points out that the commoners, like the ὁμότιμοι,
have been rigorously trained to withstand hunger, thirst, and cold
and to bear heavy burdens, but theirs was the best teacher of all—
necessity (2. 3. 13–14). This kind of gruff irony is characteristic of
Pheraulas and comes to play in all three of his appearances in the
Cyropaedia. When some of Cyrus' officers, who resent Pheraulas
being put in charge of them to organize the inaugural procession,
sarcastically term the commoner a great man (8. 3. 7 μέγας δὴ σύγε,
ὦ Φεραύλα), he replies 'not only that . . . I also serve as a porter', for
he is carrying with him robes—gifts that are meant to smooth their
ruffled feathers. Pheraulas, in a clever ploy (which may have been
Cyrus' idea—cf. the ambiguous οὕτω διαδοὺς ᾗ ἐτάχθη, 8. 3. 8), then
has each one of these leading Persians choose the 'better' of two
garments, seemingly granting each officer a special favour. In our
passage Pheraulas ironically praises his 'very just' (δικαιότατον) plot
of land, which in strict fairness gives back produce more or less equal
to the amount of seed it takes in, with little interest. Occasionally,
adds the commoner, the land returns double the amount it receives
out of 'nobility' (8. 3. 38 ὑπὸ γενναιότητος).[125] It is interesting to
compare Pheraulas' sarcastic remarks about his land with two
passages in the *Oeconomicus,* praising the earth and agriculture: the
same two qualities—justice and nobility—are mentioned there as
well. In the *Oeconomicus* Socrates tells Critobulus that the earth
teaches justice (δικαιοσύνην διδάσκει), for those who tend her best
receive the most in return (5. 12). Ischomachus praises the art of
farming as philanthropic and noble (γενναῖον): it is beneficial and
pleasant to work at, he states (*Oec.* 15. 4). Later Ischomachus reveals
the secret of his success at farming, a secret he has learnt from his
father: he diligently cultivates fallow, unplanted land which he has
bought cheaply until it becomes fertile, and then sells it off at a profit
(*Oec.* 20. 22 ff.). Pheraulas has not learnt these tricks of lucrative
farming, and his appreciation of the earth's finer qualities differs
radically from that of Ischomachus and Socrates; it is much more
akin to the slave's praise of his master's field in Menanders Γεωργός

---

[125] Nestle 1940–1: 44–5 (= 1948: 443–4) thinks that Pheraulas values the modest and
contented lot of the farmer and speaks in praise of agriculture here, but it seems clear
that Pheraulas' words are ironic.

(35–9). The field, says the slave, is most pious for it produces myrtle, ivy, and flowers. If one sows anything else, the land gives only a just and fair return, no surplus.

The two symposiasts now turn to a discussion of the pleasures (and pains) of wealth (8. 3. 39–48). The Sacian begins by congratulating Pheraulas on his newly acquired riches and adds that the Persian's pleasure in his affluence must be all the greater for his having been poor once. Pheraulas replies that he finds wealth more worrisome than poverty since he eats, drinks, and sleeps with no greater pleasure than before, but now has many more responsibilities. He must feed, clothe, and care for many servants and is often troubled by mishaps involving his sheep, oxen, and cattle. The joy of possessing wealth is not equal to the pain of losing it, continues the Persian commoner,[126] and while rich people do not stay awake at night for joy, those who lose their property do miss sleep in their grief. When the Sacian rejoins that people who have acquired wealth do stay awake because they are happy, Pheraulas concedes the point but stresses that possessing wealth is much less enjoyable than acquiring it. The rich man must expend great amounts on the gods, on friends, and on guests, and one who is very happy with his riches will be equally sorry to part with them. The Sacian then states that *he* would be happy both having and spending large sums of money. This is the second time that the Sacian has introduced himself into this discussion of Pheraulas' finances and feelings—cf. 8. 3. 42 πολλὰ ὁρῶν πολλαπλάσια ἐμοῦ εὐφραίνῃ—and he may be reminding the Persian that he has not yet received full recompense for his remarkable horse. Pheraulas, in any event, now suggests that the Sacian take over his fortune and do with it as he likes, treating the Persian as a mere guest in the household. The Sacian suspects that Pheraulas is joking (παίζεις) but the Persian is in earnest (8. 3. 47 σπουδῇ). He offers to ask Cyrus to release his friend from military and court duties so that he can stay at home and tend to Pheraulas' wealth. In this way Pheraulas will be able to devote himself wholeheartedly to Cyrus and his companions; any further wealth he may acquire will be handed over to his new steward. The two agree to the arrangement and each one considers himself most fortunate (8. 3. 48).

Pheraulas' exchange with the Sacian is one of several discussions of the relative value of wealth found in Xenophon. The two most interesting passages for our purposes are *Symp.* 4. 29–44 and *Cyr.*

---

[126] Compare *Cyr.* 7. 5. 82 and *Anab.* 7. 7. 28.

8. 2. 15–23.[127] *Symp.* 4. 29–44 is a pair of speeches by Charmides and
Antisthenes: Charmides explains why he is proud of his poverty
(4. 29–33), while Antisthenes gives his reasons for priding himself on
his (spiritual) riches (4. 34–44). Charmides contrasts his present life
as a poor man favourably with his former wealthy state: then he was a
slave, now he is a tyrant. As a rich man Charmides had to appease
sycophants and worry about losing his fortune. He was often called
upon to spend money on civic projects, but his loyalty was frequently
questioned and his movements restricted. Now that he is poor,
Charmides is able to come and go as he pleases, associate with
whomever he likes, and he is considered a threat by rich men even
while receiving financial support from the state. Thus the poverty-
stricken Charmides now sleeps content and relaxed.[128] The similarities between Pheraulas and Charmides are clear: both find riches
a heavy burden, entailing great worry and expense, and both feel
freer to pursue their own interests and inclinations when unencum-
bered by wealth. Under these circumstances Pheraulas' move to
divest himself of the responsibility of his wealth is a logical one and
Callias is perhaps right to wonder why Charmides does not turn his
back on every opportunity to acquire money (*Symp.* 4. 33).

Although Antisthenes is poor, he prides himself on his fortune, for
he thinks that poverty and wealth are related to spiritual rather than
physical acquisitons (*Symp.* 4. 34 οὐκ ἐν τῷ οἴκῳ . . . ἀλλ' ἐν ταῖς
ψυχαῖς). In his speech Antisthenes points out that the same income
can be more than enough for one person but insufficient for another:
he is easily able to satisfy his own modest needs and yet considers
himself as well provided for as Callias. The luxuries Antisthenes
desires are those of the mind and he enjoys the greatest delicacy of
all—leisure to spend his time as he likes, in the company of Socrates
(*Symp.* 4. 34–44). Antisthenes, unlike Pheraulas, positively embraces
poverty, but the Persian agrees with the Greek that being rich does

[127] For other passages in Xenophon condemning or depreciating wealth see the
references collected by Scharr 1919: 265 n. 837. Socrates' charming anecdote about the
encouraging example of Nicias' penniless, but noble, horse (*Oec.* 11. 3–6) is particularly noteworthy. For a brief general survey of changing attitudes towards wealth in the
late 5th and early 4th cents., see Bell 1978: 48–50 with nn.

[128] *Symp.* 4. 31 ἡδέως μὲν καθεύδω ἐκτεταμένος; cf. *Cyr.* 3. 1. 24. Aristotle in his
Χρεῖαι (cf. Stob. 4. 31. 91) tells of Anacreon rejecting the gold talent offered to him by
the tyrant Polycrates because of his dislike of presents that keep one awake. Cf.
Trenkner 1958: 122–6, who considers both the tale of Anacreon and our story of
Pheraulas and the Sacian illustrations of a prevalent theme in novellas—the poor man
whose life is upset by an unexpected treasure.

not cause one to eat, drink, or sleep better (*Cyr.* 8. 3. 40; cf. *Symp.* 4. 37).[129] Both Antisthenes and Pheraulas are interested in the leisure time which the rich cannot seem to afford, but Antisthenes devotes himself to Socrates and the pursuit of philosophy (as does Charmides to a certain extent), while Pheraulas intends to spend his time with Cyrus, helping him consolidate his rule over an empire. Thus Antisthenes' rejection of wealth in favour of the pursuit of wisdom—a favourite protreptic theme (cf. e.g. Pl. *Euthyd.* 278 E ff.)—becomes something very different in the *Cyropaedia*: one wonders if Pheraulas' goals are equally worthy in Xenophon's eyes.[130]

In our second passage, *Cyr.* 8. 2. 15–23, it is Cyrus who speaks out against wealth or, to be more precise, against accumulating riches. When Croesus chides Cyrus for distributing much of his fortune to friends and allies instead of storing it in treasuries, Cyrus demonstrates to the Lydian king that his friends act as treasurers and are always willing to put their funds at his disposal.[131] Cyrus himself is, as he admits, as avaricious as the next man, and is always after more possessions, but he does not choose to bury his money (cf. *Cyr.* 3. 3. 3), nor does he count, measure, or guard his hoard. Instead, the Persian leader distributes his wealth, acquiring both security—in the form of trusty, willing 'treasure-houses'—and a good reputation. He who acquires the most money by honest means and uses it well—and not one who possesses and guards the most—should be considered happiest, Cyrus concludes.

Pheraulas has found in the Sacian a loyal, trustworthy treasurer of the kind Cyrus acquires by means of his generous gifts. The Persian leader defines happiness in terms of the proper use of wealth, and the happiness of both Pheraulas and the Sacian does in fact depend upon their financial arrangements: Xenophon uses a great many expressions meaning happiness, joy, or good fortune in the course of our

[129] The tyrant Hiero is another character in Xenophon who shares this viewpoint (*Hiero* 1. 17–25).

[130] Another passage, *Oec.* 2. 2–9, in which Socrates paradoxically claims that Critobulus is to be pitied for his poverty, although the latter has a fortune a hundred times the size of his own, should also be mentioned in this context. Socrates points out that he manages satisfactorily with the little that he has, while Critobulus, who must sacrifice lavishly to the gods, entertain foreigners and fellow citizens, and expend great sums on civic enterprises, would scarcely manage if his present fortune were to be trebled. So too Critobulus wastes his time on childish pursuits, and if in need would not be helped by his supposed friends, while Socrates can always count upon the support of others. Cf. Woldinga 1938–9: 71–3.

[131] Agesilaus too is able to borrow money quickly from others—cf. *Ages.* 4. 3–4.

symposium.[132] According to Cyrus, the Sacian, who is made happy by controlling great sums of money, should be considered the less fortunate of the two, while Pheraulas makes good use of his fortune. Although Pheraulas continues to bring in additional revenues to the household, he seems much less acquisitive than either Cyrus or the Sacian. The Persian commoner does not really expect anything in return from his steward, other than leisure for his own concerns: his aim is to devote himself to his friends (8. 3. 50). Cyrus, on the other hand, expects—and receives—a great deal in return for his contributions: good will and friendship, security, and a good name (8. 2. 22 εὔνοιαν . . . καὶ φιλίαν . . . ἀσφάλειαν καὶ εὔκλειαν). This is characteristic of Cyrus' quid pro quo attitude: throughout the *Cyropaedia* we hear of Cyrus' gift-giving, but the mention of the Persian leader's benefactions is almost always coupled with a description of the advantages he obtains through his gifts.[133]

In essence, neither Cyrus nor Pheraulas actually parts with his wealth: they simply hand it over to reliable caretakers for safekeeping. While both partners benefit from such owner–steward relationships, it is the actual owner who derives the greater advantage from the arrangement. In the *Memorabilia* there are two depictions of owner–caretaker arrangements. The agreement between Crito and his 'watchdog' Archedemus (*Mem.* 2. 9. 1–8) seems to be of equal satisfaction to both sides, as with Pheraulas and the Sacian, but the other partnership (*Mem.* 2. 8. 1–6) presents a more negative view of the caretaker's role. Eutherus, when urged by Socrates to earn his living by acting as a steward to another man's estate, objects to the bondage (2. 8. 4 δουλείαν) and accountability to another (2. 8. 5 τὸ ὑπαίτιον εἶναι) that go with the job. The Sacian, who is freed from other duties and stays at home tending Pheraulas' fortune, is neither watchdog nor servant: he is somewhat like Croesus' wife, who, as her envious husband notes, leads a most blissful life, sharing in all of Croesus' wealth and luxuries, with no part in the wars, battles, and efforts to acquire further riches (*Cyr.* 7. 2. 27–8). The Sacian does, of course, have to manage the Persian's estate.

Xenophon concludes his account of Pheraulas' dinner-party with a description of the Persian commoner. Pheraulas, he tells us, has a

---

[132] ὢ μακάριε σύ (8. 3. 39), εὐφραίνῃ (8. 3. 42), εὐδαιμονία (8. 3. 44, 45), εὐδαίμων (8. 3. 46, 48), μακαριώτατος (8. 3. 48), and ὑπερήδετο (8. 3. 50).

[133] See 1. 3. 6–7, 1. 4. 10, 26, 1. 6. 3–4, 2. 4. 9–11, 5. 1. 1, 28–9, 5. 3. 2, 8. 2. 7 ff., and cf. 5. 4. 32 and 5. 5. 26.

friendly, loyal nature and likes nothing better than being useful to his fellow men. He finds men far superior to other creatures, for men, unlike animals, are eager to return any praise, favours, or affection they receive; this is especially apparent in human beings' loving devotion to their parents.[134] Pheraulas is, in a sense, describing himself here. The commoner, a pleasing man (2. 3. 7 ἀρεστὸς ἀνήρ), has been chosen by Cyrus to organize the inaugural procession because of this quality (cf. 8. 3. 5 τοῦ χαρίζεσθαι αὐτῷ οὐκ ἀμελῆ). The Persians of the Cyropaedia are instructed from earliest youth to reciprocate favours and beware ingratitude (cf. 1. 2. 7),[135] and this is a lesson that Pheraulas, who has only attended school as a boy, has absorbed well. He is a devoted son and tells the Sacian how after being cared for by his father as a child, he supported him in return (8. 3. 37–8). In sum, Pheraulas, with his loyal, grateful nature, ironic manner of speaking, and tendency to compare men to animals (cf. 2. 3. 9, 14, 8. 3. 49), has a voice and character of his own in the Cyropaedia; the same cannot be said of his new partner, the unnamed Sacian.

This symposium is unusual in several respects. The party has only two participants and consequently is not a lively gathering of celebrants, but a quite private meeting.[136] There is no competition or matchmaking at the party, nor is there any homosexual love interest. While the two partners regard one another with great affection (8. 3. 50 ἐφίλει δὲ ὁ μὲν Σάκας τὸν Φεραύλαν . . . ὁ δὲ τὸν Σάκαν), it is because each finds the other eminently useful; theirs is not a sexual relationship. Most of the conversation between Pheraulas and the Sacian deals with only one of our sympotic motifs—poverty and riches—and Xenophon seems to have been particularly interested in presenting to his readers these views on poverty and wealth. There are several indications that he especially fashioned this symposium as a vehicle for the discussion. To begin with, Xenophon takes his hero off-stage: this is the longest conversation in the Cyropaedia in which Cyrus has no part (and there are very few such conversations

[134] Elsewhere living creatures, in particular birds, are thought to be very devoted to their parents—cf. Soph. El. 1058–62; Aristoph. Birds 1355–7.

[135] Knauth 1975: 181–3 argues, chiefly on the basis of Cyr. 1. 2. 7 and the story of Darius and Syloson's red cloak at Hdt. 3. 139–41, that gratitude was 'eine speziell iranische Tugend'.

[136] Cyr. 3. 1. 38–40, where a private, rather painful conversation takes place between Cyrus, Tigranes, and the Armenian king after dinner, is perhaps the closest parallel to our symposium.

altogether). Cyrus, a Persian prince, could not convincingly rid himself of his riches in the straightforward way that Pheraulas does. The Sacian, on the other hand, appears only here in the *Cyropaedia* and he (not to mention his swift horse) was introduced, it seems, solely in order to have him take over the Persian commoner's household. In addition, Pheraulas' worries over his property, many servants, and great herds of livestock are contrived at this stage: Babylon has only recently been captured, Cyrus has just been inaugurated as king, and although the Persian leader has already distributed houses and servants to his friends (cf. 7. 5. 35–6, 56, 8. 3. 34), there has scarcely been time for Pheraulas to turn into a harassed estate-owner. This is, in any event, Pheraulas' last appearance in the *Cyropaedia*: the Persian commoner has fulfilled his function.

6. BANQUETERS IN BABYLON: *CYR.* 8. 4. 1–27

Let us return now to *Cyr.* 8. 4. 1–27, the symposium with which this chapter began. Cyrus' party celebrating his victory in the chariot-races, with its large group of symposiasts and plentiful, varied topics of conversation, presents an interesting contrast to Pheraulas' intimate and somewhat serious dinner-party: the symposium form is, it seems, flexible enough to encompass both sorts of occasions. The difference between the two banquets is especially noteworthy in view of the fact that they are held at virtually the same time, immediately after the horse- and chariot-races. Cyrus' victory banquet has already been described and its full complement of characteristic sympotic motifs has been noted (above, sect. 1); it remains now to comment upon several interesting features of the symposium.

When Cyrus states that he prefers the positive deeds of philanthropy to the harmful acts of a military commander (8. 4. 8; cf. Agesilaus' words at *Hell.* 4. 1. 10), he demonstrates a certain change in his scale of values. The Persian leader has never objected to the deeds of war in the past and has often emphasized that victory over the enemy is the greatest good, the chief source of happiness in life.[137] Although φιλανθρωπία is a character trait often associated with Cyrus in the *Cyropaedia*,[138] his interpretation of the quality is not

---

[137] See *Cyr.* 4. 2. 26, 5. 5. 24, 6. 1. 55, 7. 1. 10, 13, 7. 3. 11, 7. 5. 79, etc. and cf. above, ch. 2. 6.

[138] See *Cyr.* 1. 2. 1, 1. 4. 1, 4. 2. 10, 8. 2. 1, and cf. Due 1989: 163–70.

always as benevolent as it is here: earlier the Persian prince has stated that it is far from wrong to conquer and plunder hostile forces, while allowing the enemy to possess anything at all is an act of generosity (7. 5. 73 φιλανθρωπίᾳ).

Hystaspas, when asking Cyrus why Chrysantas has been seated in a more honoured position (8. 4. 9–12), first requests permission to speak his mind freely: he is afraid that Cyrus may be displeased. The Persian leader, when replying, is afraid in turn that the truth may hurt Hystaspas' feelings. This issue of speaking freely and truthfully arises yet a third time soon afterwards (8. 4. 13), when Gobryas is urged by Cyrus to reply honestly to a question. It is, of course, only natural for a speaker to think twice before saying something that is not likely to please his listener,[139] but such hesitancy before speaking up has—until now—been very rare. Cyrus' men have always approached him with their ideas and proposals. It is true that the Persian leader often rejects or alters in some way plans initiated by his companions, but neither party makes any polite disclaimers before stating his views.[140] Here, the old free-and-easy relationship between the Persian leader and his associates has changed, and this is probably the result of Cyrus' new position as master of a great empire. All concerned—Cyrus and his friends—are learning to adjust to the new reality.

Cyrus tells Hystaspas that he values Chrysantas because he does not simply obey every order, but actually anticipates Cyrus' wishes.[141] In addition, Chrysantas delights in Cyrus' successes more than the Persian leader himself. Often Chrysantas serves as the enthusiastic 'seconder' of new proposals put forward by Cyrus—e.g. to establish a Persian cavalry (4. 3. 3–21),[142] divide war booty according to merit (2. 3. 2–6), and live in Babylon in accordance with the customs and practices established in Persia (7. 5. 71 ff.)—but he also initiates several moves on his own. He suggests that Cyrus move into the royal Babylonian palace (7. 5. 55–6), recommends that the Persians attend Cyrus at his court in Babylon (8. 1. 1–5), and raises the question of distribution of spoils in the first place (2. 2. 17–21). In

---

[139] Compare, for instance, the exchanges between Pharnabazus and Agesilaus at *Hell.* 4. 1. 37 and Demaratus and Xerxes at Hdt. 7. 101. 3; cf. Gray 1989: 54.

[140] See below, ch. 5. 1 with n. 8.

[141] In the *Mem.* Socrates recommends Hermogenes in very similar terms (2. 10. 3; cf. 2. 6. 35).

[142] Chrysantas' speech here (4. 3. 15–21)—on the joys of being a centaur—is surprisingly light-hearted and fanciful.

his most Machiavellian address (6. 2. 21–2), spoken before the final offensive against Babylon to an assembly badly frightened by reports of enemy strength, Chrysantas, under the guise of explaining to Cyrus the soldiers' true feelings, makes pointed references to the rich and varied plunder to be had: he calms the soldiers by appealing to their sense of greed. The Persian leader tells Hystaspas that Chrysantas sometimes puts forward Cyrus' views as if they were his own, when it is inconvenient for him to express himself directly (8. 4. 11). This admission casts an interesting and somewhat sinister light on Chrysantas' acts of initiative. Who originally thought of having Cyrus move into the royal Babylonian palace? Whose idea was it to have the Persian nobles attend Cyrus' court? Chrysantas may have been no more than Cyrus' agent, generating 'spontaneous' enthusiasm for plans conceived by the Persian leader. If this is the case, the two men must work in close collusion and Hystaspas, an outsider to plots of this kind, does not stand a chance of replacing Chrysantas in Cyrus' affections.[143] Hystaspas, in any event, professes himself delighted with the results of his questioning, but the oath he uses—νὴ τὴν "Ηραν (8. 4. 12)—can be ironic and serves, at times, to express feigned admiration.[144]

Gobryas confesses that he is now more pleased than before to have his daughter wed one of Cyrus' men, since the Persians, after having cheerfully borne adversity, now succeed in an even more rigorous test of character, living with success and prosperity (8. 4. 13–14). The Assyrian's statement impresses Cyrus and Hystaspas a great deal, but the idea is, of course, far from novel. We have already encountered the contention that punishment or hardship brings a person to his senses and causes him to be level-headed (σώφρων) several times in the *Cyropaedia*,[145] while the view that hubris is the besetting sin of the rich and that soft living makes for idleness and cowardice is a commonplace.[146] Perhaps it is the Gorgianic phrasing

---

[143] Cf. Tatum 1989: 205–6.

[144] See e.g. *Mem.* 3. 11. 5, 4. 2. 9, 4. 4. 8; *Symp.* 4. 54 (feigned admiration), and compare *Symp.* 8. 12, 9. 1; *Mem.* 3. 10. 9 (genuine appreciation). The oath 'by Hera' is normally considered a woman's one and seems to have been used frequently by the historical Socrates. In Plato the oath is almost always used ironically, simulating admiration—see e.g. *Apol.* 24 E; *Gorg.* 449 D—and compare Calder 1983. The oath appears one more time (in a variant reading) in the *Cyr.* (1. 4. 12), and there its use is straightforward.

[145] Cf. Aglaitadas at 2. 2. 14 and Tigranes at 3. 1. 16 ff.

[146] See e.g. Solon fr. 6 West; Theognis 153–4; Hdt. 9. 122; and the further references in Dover 1974: 110–11.

of Gobryas' maxim (ῥῆμα), with its balanced, antithetical clauses—
τὰ μὲν [sc. ἀγαθὰ] γὰρ ὕβριν τοῖς πολλοῖς, τὰ δὲ [sc. κακὰ]
σωφροσύνην τοῖς πᾶσιν ἐμποιεῖ (8. 4. 14)—that impresses the Persians. The Assyrian has a whole collection of such statements written
down, and this collection will be part of his daughter's dowry
(8. 4. 16). It seems that Gobryas has carefully assembled an an-
thology of the sayings of wise men; in the *Memorabilia* Socrates
(1. 6. 14; cf. 1. 2. 56) and Euthydemus (4. 2. 1; cf. 4. 2. 8–9) have
similar collections. Such anthologies may well have been popular in
Xenophon's day,[147] but it is unexpected, even incongruous, to find
this doughty Assyrian commander, wise though he may be, sifting
through others' writings and painstakingly writing down their
maxims. Hystaspas finds Gobryas' collection a great attraction, even
more alluring than his collection of gold cups, and he now considers
becoming a suitor of Gobryas' daughter (8. 4. 15 τῆς θυγατρὸς
μνηστῆρα).[148] Euthydemus of the *Memorabilia* earns Socrates' praise
for similarly choosing wisdom over treasures of silver and gold
(4. 2. 9), but despite his extensive collection of learned sayings,
Euthydemus still has much to learn. Socrates himself plainly has an
ambivalent attitude towards such collections, for although he has his
own selection of the writings of wise men, he seems to view Euthydemus' pride in *his* collection as an added incentive to show the
youngster how little he really knows (4. 2. 1, 8–9). Are we meant to
think that Gobryas' treasure trove of writings is as valuable as
Hystaspas finds it?

Cyrus now (8. 4. 18) offers his services as a matchmaker; he
professes to be an expert in the art and claims to know what sort of
match would suit each of his friends. He then jestingly describes the
kind of wife that Chrystantas needs: his reasoning, while playful, is
also practical and functional. Chrystantas, being short, needs a short
wife (or else he will have to jump up in order to kiss her), and since his
nose is hooked and his stomach curves out his spouse should have a
concave stomach and a snub nose, if they are to be well matched.
This functional approach towards a person's physical appearance,
concentrating on utility rather than aesthetics, is reminiscent of
Socrates' attitude in his light-hearted 'beauty contest' with Crito-

---

[147] See Isoc. *Ad Nic.* 44 and the further references cited by Hudson-Williams 1910:
17.
[148] Here too the old-fashioned Homeric word is used; cf. Hdt. 6. 129–30 and see
above, sect. 1 with n. 44.

bulus in the *Symposium* (5. 1–10).[149] There Socrates points out,
feature by feature, how his prominent eyes, flat nose (compare the
discussion of noses in the *Cyropaedia*), and thick lips are better
adapted to their natural function of seeing, smelling, etc. than
Critobulus' classical, handsome features. Beauty, Critobulus readily
agrees, is found in anything that is well constructed or well endowed
to serve its function, and by these standards Socrates is, he concedes,
more beautiful. The competition betwen Critobulus and Socrates,
like Cyrus' attempt to find Chrysantas a suitable wife, is frivolous, but
both make use of a serious yardstick—utilitarianism. In the *Memorabilia* Socrates again discusses beauty in terms of fitness for function,
but there he is in earnest (*Mem.* 3. 8. 4–7, 4. 6. 9).[150]

Cyrus' unexpected espousal of the art of matchmaking calls to
mind Socrates' surprising claim, in Xenophon's *Symposium*, that the
skill he most prides himself upon is that of procurer (*Symp.* 3. 10 ἐπὶ
μαστροπείᾳ; cf. 4. 56–64). A good procurer, Socrates explains to his
fellow symposiasts, will be able to make his client agreeable to a great
many people, and the best procurer of all is capable of attracting an
entire city to his protégé, i.e. can transform him into a political
leader. Socrates' disreputable calling and his talk of love and sexual
union stem, of course, from his desire to educate and improve those
whom he matches together (cf. 8. 27).[151] Indeed, after hearing the
ἐρωτικὸς λόγος addressed to him by Socrates Callias understands
that this talk of love is meant to 'seduce' him into political activity,
once he has cultivated virtue out of his desire to win Autolycus' love
(*Symp.* 8. 42). In the *Cyropaedia*, on the other hand, Cyrus' matchmaking is down-to-earth and practical. Socrates' expertise as a

---

[149] For an excellent discussion of this beauty competition see Guthrie 1969: 387–9.

[150] Compare the 'teleological' argument at *Mem.* 1. 4. 6, and see Dickermann 1909
for further discussion of teleological arguments found in Xenophon. Woodruff 1982:
183–7 discusses the utilitarianism of the historical Socrates; see also Guthrie 1969:
462–7.

[151] In the *Mem.* (2. 6. 28–39) the question of fostering and encouraging relationships
between people arises again: Socrates tries to use Critobulus' desire for love (or friendship) to persuade him to become a better person. Socrates claims there to have learnt
about matchmaking from Aspasia (cf. *Oec.* 3. 14), and in Aeschines' dialogue *Aspasia*
(fr. 31 D. = Cic. *De Inv.* 51–2) we actually see this skilled matchmaker at work. At an
anachronistic meeting—Xenophon is already married in Socrates' lifetime (cf. Dittmar
1912: 32 n. 118)—Aspasia tries to reconcile Xenophon and his wife. She demonstrates
to the couple that if their marriage is to be a happy one, each must try to be the best
spouse possible, i.e. their love must lead to ἀρετή. For further discussion of Aeschines'
Aspasia and its likely influence on *Mem.* 2. 6. 28ff. and *Symp.* 4. 56ff. see Dittmar 1912:
1–39, esp. 36 n. 125; Ehlers 1966: 31ff., 101–23; Woldinga 1938–9: 78–86. Tomin 1987:
100–2 is more sceptical about the link between Aeschines and the Xenophon passages.

procurer is, no doubt, the literary precursor of Cyrus' matchmaking efforts in our symposium, but the theme of matchmaking and love is 'lowered' here and we hear nothing of the spiritual side of love. In the *Symposium* Socrates also goes on to say that his fellow guest Antisthenes is a procurer, unexpectedly transferring his special skill to another,[152] and he adds that Antisthenes has also perfected the art that follows upon procuring—pandering (4. 61 τὴν προαγωγείαν). Socrates hastens to explain to the indignant Antisthenes that a good pander is someone who pairs up people who can benefit one another, arousing in each the desire to be with the other. Antisthenes has, for example, brought together the needy sophist Prodicus and the rich, wisdom-seeking Callias, and has also introduced Socrates to various visitors to Athens after awakening his interest in them. There is a certain similarity between Antisthenes' pairing of Prodicus and Callias, who have complementary needs and qualities, and Cyrus' joking suggestion that Chrysantas with his hooked nose and convex stomach needs a wife with a snub nose and concave stomach. The Persian concentrates on physical characteristics while the Athenian is more interested in personality, but both pair up people according to the same principle of matching opposite (or complementary) qualities.

Cyrus, besides finding an ideal, imaginary wife for Chrysantas, arranges an actual match betwen Hystaspas and Gobryas' daughter. Here he is concerned with the property settlement—rather than the appearance of the bride and groom—and he reminds us of another matchmaker in Xenophon, Agesilaus. In the *Hellenica* (4. 1. 4–15) Agesilaus arranges a marriage between the daughter of Spithridates, a poor but noble Persian exile, and Otys, king of the Paphlagonians, using his considerable powers of persuasion and deviousness to do so.[153] Cyrus' dealings with Hystaspas and Gobryas are more straightforward than Agesilaus' handling of Spithridates and Otys, but both rulers arrange an unequal alliance between a rich man and a poor one—an alliance which should have its uses for the ruler himself—and both have the two men pledge the betrothal in their presence. Thus Cyrus, when acting as a matchmaker in our symposium, betrays two very different kinds of influence—that of Socrates and that of Agesilaus.

---

[152] Why he does this is something of a puzzle. None of the explanations offered (Ehlers 1966: 113; Körte 1927: 37–8; von Fritz 1935: 25–7) is especially convincing.

[153] For an excellent analysis of Agesilaus' deviousness (and Xenophon's use of the dialogue form) at *Hell.* 4. 1. 4–15 see Gray 1981: 321–4; cf. Gray 1989: 49–52.

At the close of his party Cyrus distributes presents to his guests. Persian rulers were well known for their lavish gift-giving or πολυ-δωρία, and favourite presents were robes, gold necklaces and bracelets, horses with golden bridles, drinking-cups, and swords[154] or the kind of gifts we find here.[155] The only unusual gift that the Persian leader awards at our symposium is the kiss he gives to Chrysantas—a kiss which arouses the envy of Cyrus' very first admirer, Artabazus. Chrysantas, with his hooked nose and rounded stomach, is in all likelihood not very attractive: once again, as with Sambaulas and the ugly soldier (above, sect. 3), it is usefulness rather than beauty which underlies 'erotic' relationships.

Before leaving the question of gifts given at symposia it is worth looking at two other Persian parties where we find such presentations. Herodotus (9. 110–11) tells us that at his royal dinner Xerxes gave gifts to the Persians. In addition, reluctant though he was, he handed over Masistes' wife to Amestris, compelled by the law (9. 111 ὑπὸ τοῦ νόμου ἐξεργόμενος) that no one may be refused a request at the king's royal feast. In the *Hellenica* (1. 5. 4–7) we again find a host granting a petition at a banquet, against his better judgement. Cyrus the Younger rejects, at first, the Spartans' request that he raise their sailors' pay, but he changes his mind over dinner with Lysander. When Cyrus toasts Lysander and asks what he can do to please him, the Spartan again asks for a raise in pay and this time Cyrus agrees.[156] A Persian host, it seems, not only gives presents but also fulfils requests at his parties. Perhaps this is why Cyrus does not refuse Artabazus' playful plea for a kiss (*Cyr.* 8. 4. 27) but merely puts him off for thirty years.

The short closing scene of our symposium, in which Artabazus, a

---

[154] On Persians' favourite gifts in general see Hdt. 3. 20–1; Xen. *Anab.* 1. 2. 27; *Cyr.* 8. 2. 7–9. Robes and clothing: *Cyr.* 1. 3. 3, 1. 4. 26, 8. 3. 3; Plut. *Artax.* 5; Esther 6: 8. Gold jewellery: *Cyr.* 1. 3. 3; *Anab.* 1. 9. 23; Plut. *Artax.* 4. Swords: Hdt. 8. 120; *Anab.* 1. 9. 23. Cf. Knauth 1975: 189–95; Sancisi-Weerdenburg 1980: 165–71; Tuplin 1990: 25 with n. 16.

[155] Sancisi-Weerdenburg 1980: 207 suggests that the γυναικεῖον κόσμον given to Tigranes as a present for his steadfast wife is, in fact, one of the gold bracelets and necklaces normally presented to Persian men. Xenophon, she argues, has changed the jewellery into a woman's gift because he finds such ornaments effeminate. She thinks that our symposium is a blend of two parties: one for the victors of the horse-races (Artabazus, the Hyrcanian, and Tigranes), who are by and large silent, and another party made up of more philosophical minds (Gobryas, Hystaspas, and Chrysantas). In fact only Tigranes' silence at the symposium is surprising, since Artabazus does speak up and the Hyrcanian is a cardboard figure throughout the *Cyr.*.

[156] Cf. Gray 1989: 14–17, who also compares Hdt. 6. 62.

long-time admirer of Cyrus, is jealous of the kiss Chrysantas has received and has his advances teasingly rejected by Cyrus, is again reminiscent of a scene in Xenophon's *Symposium*, Socrates' playful rejection of his admirer Antisthenes (8. 4–6). This exchange, in which Antisthenes claims to be in love with Socrates, only to have the philosopher coyly put him off, may in turn have been influenced by Socrates' mock complaints about Alcibiades' jealousy in Plato's *Symposium* (213c–d).[157] Such scenes involving an admirer's semi-serious jealousy combine, in fact, three of our sympotic themes: σπουδαιογέλοιον, competition among the symposiasts, and a homosexual love interest. In Socrates' symposium-like meeting with the courtesan Theodote there is yet another variation on this type of exchange, when Socrates lightly turns down Theodote's advances, claiming that he is too busy, partly because of his many female friends who do not leave his side (*Mem.* 3. 11. 15–18). Our symposium in the *Cyropaedia* ends on a light note, with Artabazus promising to stay alive for the next thirty years, if only to collect the kiss Cyrus has promised him. The guests then rise and depart.

Cyrus' banquet in Babylon, the last of the symposia of the *Cyropaedia*, is in many ways the most 'sympotic' of all the dinner-parties, and is closest in spirit to Xenophon's full-fledged *Symposium*. Two of its scenes—Cyrus' matchmaking efforts and Artabazus' jealous remarks—seem to be variations on or adaptations of episodes in the philosophical work. We have already seen that two figures in an earlier symposium, Aglaitadas and Sambaulas of *Cyr.* 2. 2, also have more fully fleshed counterparts in Xenophon's *Symposium* (above, sect. 3). Did the *Symposium* come before the symposia of the *Cyropaedia*? It is notoriously difficult to arrange Xenophon's works in chronological order; he often reworks his material, and the fullest treatment of a theme is not necessarily the earliest one. None the less, it is worth noting that the parallel episodes of the *Symposium*— Socrates' disapproval of the silent Hermogenes, the beauty competition between Socrates and Critobulus, and Antisthenes' jealous passion for Socrates—are well motivated, worked out in detail, and skilfully integrated into the work as a whole. These scenes are also

---

[157] Note in particular how in each case Socrates' admirer can barely restrain himself from physical violence: Xen. *Symp.* 8. 6 μόνον μὴ συγκόψῃς με; Pl. *Symp.* 213D τὼ χεῖρε μόγις ἀπέχεται. Most commentators agree that Xenophon in his *Symp.* is (rather unsuccessfully) adapting Plato's scene—see Körte 1927: 40–1; von Fritz 1935: 29–31; Woldinga 1938–9: 100; Martin 1931: 113–17, 131–2.

directly related to the characters and personalities involved; in the *Cyropaedia* this is only true of the exchange involving Artabazus, Cyrus' jealous admirer. All in all, it does seem as if the *Symposium* was earlier and left its mark upon the banquets of the *Cyropaedia*

4

Romance, Revenge, and Pathos
The Novellas of the *Cyropaedia*

I. INTRODUCTION

The colourful, romantic episodes of the *Cyropaedia*—the stories of
Panthea, Croesus, Gobryas, and Gadatas—are the subject of this
chapter. These dramatic tales, often referred to as the novellas of the
Cyropaedia,[1] are highly compelling in themselves; they also raise
interesting questions about Xenophon's sources. Did he invent these
stories? Rework them? Lift them whole from other sources? We shall
first look briefly at the content and form of these tales in order to see
just how unusual and colourful the stories of the *Cyropaedia* are. Next
comes an investigation of possible sources or influences, and the final
portion of the chapter is devoted to a detailed commentary on the
individual tales.

Three of the four main novellas of the *Cyropaedia* concern 'Assyrians', i.e. Babylonians,[2] who for one reason or another have joined
Cyrus in his military campaign against their former king; the fourth
tells of the Lydian monarch Croesus, who is an ally of the Assyrian
king. Panthea, the fairest woman in Asia, is the leading character in
the most famous story of the *Cyropaedia*. She is a beautiful and noble
woman who is taken prisoner of war (along with her maidservants,
eunuchs, and nurse) by the Persians and is allotted to Cyrus as war
booty. Cyrus asks his childhood friend from Media, Araspas, to

---

[1] The term novella, which seems to have been first used in contexts like our own by
Rohde 1914: 578 ff., is not, of course, one that Xenophon would have recognized. It is
difficult to define the term precisely—see Trenkner 1958: xiii; de Vries 1963; Aly 1936:
1171–2; Barigazzi 1957: 371–2. We may, following Trenkner 1958: xiii, define a novella
as 'a . . . story of limited length, intended to entertain, and describing an event in which
the interest arises from the change in the fortunes of the leading characters . . . an event
concerned with real-life people in a real-life setting'. This is meant to be no more than a
working definition of a novella, and the term is used here as a convenient shorthand
method of referring to dramatic tales of the kind found in the *Cyr.*

[2] See Hirsch 1985: 175 n. 52 on this Greek practice of terming Babylonians 'Assyrians'.

guard Panthea for him, and the impetuous Mede falls in love with the fair lady of Susa against his will. Panthea resists Araspas' advances and reports his attempts at seduction to Cyrus. The Persian leader sends another Mede, Artabazus, to scold his shamefaced friend and then secretly dispatches Araspas, now instructed to feign disaffection with Cyrus, to spy upon the enemy. Panthea now summons her husband Abradatas, who pledges allegiance to the Persian leader and volunteers to fight at Cyrus' side. Abradatas, decked out in golden armour that his wife has fashioned for him, fights valiantly at the battle of Thymbrara and dies on the battlefield. His grief-stricken widow then commits suicide, hugging Abradatas' mutilated corpse, and three of Panthea's eunuchs immediately follow suit, killing themselves in the wake of their masters.[3]

In this novella we find a variety of colourful characters: a beautiful and virtuous woman, a disappointed suitor, loyal servants, and a brave and noble spouse. Several more formal aspects of the story also merit attention. Panthea's story is presented in several instalments, in a series of episodes scattered over Books 5, 6, and 7 of the *Cyropaedia*. All of these episodes are carefully integrated into the main story-line of these books: Cyrus' preparations for the battle of Thymbrara—his second and decisive confrontation with the Assyrians—the battle itself, and its aftermath. Araspas, Panthea's love-stricken guardian, who is sent to spy upon the enemy because he makes a most plausible defector, is a good example of the strong links between the 'inner' workings of the novella and the 'outer' plot of the *Cyropaedia*. A second noticeable feature of the Panthea novella is that the story is told, by and large, by means of dialogues. Narrated portions of the novella are almost always found in the immediate vicinity of a dialogue, coming either before or after a conversation or in between two such conversations.[4]

A third characteristic of the Panthea novella is the brevity or economy with which the tale is told. Xenophon does not wring every last drop of pathos from his tale, and there are many incidents which

---

[3] Cf. *Cyr.* 4. 6. 11, 5. 1. 2–18, 6. 1. 31–51, 6. 3. 14–21, 35–7, 6. 4. 2–11, 7. 1. 15–18, 29–32, 7. 3. 2–16.

[4] Narrative introducing a conversation: *Cyr.* 5. 1. 2–3, 6. 1. 31–5; after a conversation: 5. 1. 18, 6. 1. 50–1, 7. 3. 15–16; in between two dialogues: 6. 1. 46, 7. 3. 6–7. The only exception to this rule is the narration of Abradatas' death on the battlefield (7. 1. 29–32), which appears as part of Xenophon's running description of the battle of Thymbrara; it is interesting to note that Abradatas' end is described a second time, briefly, in a dialogue (7. 3. 3).

could have been more fully elaborated, such as Araspas' attempts to seduce Panthea, Artabazus' reproachful speech to Araspas, or the attempt made by Panthea's nurse to dissuade her mistress from killing herself.[5] One final point to be noted (and this will be seen in more detail in the running commentary below) is that Xenophon's language here is at times poetic and the diction is grander than the usual style of the *Cyropaedia*.

The next two novellas, the stories of the two Assyrian nobles Gobryas and Gadatas, who go over to Cyrus' side, are closely related. Both men become allies of the Persian leader and play an active role in the conquest and consolidation of Cyrus' empire, and hence both appear fairly frequently in the pages of the *Cyropaedia*. Here our interest is in the dramatic side of their stories, i.e. the account of each one's relationship with the young Assyrian king.

Gobryas, an elderly Assyrian noble, was a loyal and highly respected subject of the old Assyrian king; their children were to have been married. The new Assyrian ruler, son of the former king, is, however, his sworn enemy, for he has murdered Gobryas' only son. The Assyrian prince's motive for killing Gobryas' son was jealousy, pure and simple: when the two young men were out hunting together, Gobryas' son proved to be the more successful of the two. Gobryas, bent on avenging the death of his only son, offers to aid Cyrus in his campaign against the Assyrians if the Persian leader will help him exact retribution from the young Assyrian ruler. He also offers Cyrus his daughter as a prospective wife. She is a beautiful but grief-stricken young woman, who was originally to have been the bride of the young Assyrian king. Cyrus accepts Gobryas' offer of an alliance and travels with his forces to his new ally's estate. Shortly afterwards Gobryas confronts his arch-enemy, the Assyrian ruler, speaking to him through a messenger on Cyrus' behalf. The young king jeers at Gobryas and refuses to do battle with Cyrus' forces. In Babylon Gobryas and the Assyrian king meet face to face for one final time: Gobryas, together with his fellow countryman Gadatas, kills the young king inside his palace. After the deed is done, the two Assyrians cry for joy and embrace Cyrus in deep gratitude.[6]

In Gobryas' novella we hear of a cruel young despot, a bereaved father, and a lovely but sorrowful young maiden. The story of Gobryas' dealings with the young Assyrian king is, like the tale of

[5] Cf. 6. 1. 31, 33, 6. 1. 35, 7. 3. 14.
[6] Cf. *Cyr*. 4. 6. 1–10, 5. 2. 1–22, 5. 3. 5–7, 7. 5. 26–32.

Panthea, presented in several episodes in more than one book of the *Cyropaedia*. These instalments are carefully woven into the main fabric of the work, for they explain and motivate the appearance of a powerful Assyrian noble at Cyrus' side. Gobryas' brief exchange with the Assyrian ruler (5. 3. 5–7), in which he both relays a message from Cyrus and comments on his own personal tragedy, is perhaps the best example of the links between the particular details of Gobryas' story and the overall plot of the *Cyropaedia*. Most of the Gobryas novella is presented through dialogues, but its finale, the execution of the young Assyrian king, is narrated.[7] As with the Panthea novella, Xenophon's language is at times unusually high-flown and poetic, but Gobryas' tale is presented with considerable restraint. Several scenes could have been more fully embroidered—with, for example, the daughter of Gobryas actually lamenting her dead brother, or Gobryas vilifying the Assyrian despot before killing him—but Xenophon avoids excessive pathos.

Our third novella is the story of Gadatas, a young Assyrian noble who joins Cyrus' forces. We first hear of Gadatas from Gobryas. Cyrus, while trying to recruit more allies in his campaign against the Assyrians, asks Gobryas if he knows of any other victims of the young Assyrian king. Gobryas tells him of the son of an Assyrian noble even more powerful than himself, who was a friend and drinking companion of the Assyrian crown prince. This young man, Gadatas, was castrated by the Assyrian prince because the prince's mistress praised his beauty. Gadatas, adds Gobryas, lives at the very gates of Babylon. After Gobryas fails to induce the Assyrian despot to confront the Persians, Cyrus asks Gobryas to meet Gadatas and recruit the eunuch to their cause. Gadatas agrees to enter an Assyrian fortress under false pretences and then help Cyrus, from within, to capture the stronghold. After the fortress is captured the Persian and the eunuch meet for the first time and confirm their alliance. Almost immediately afterwards Gadatas and his men are attacked by the angry Assyrian ruler and Cyrus comes to their rescue. Cyrus invites the frightened eunuch to join him on his campaign, and during the conquest of Babylon Gadatas, together with Gobryas, kills the Assyrian despot in his palace.[8]

The Gadatas novella, the story of the eunuch's treatment at the hands of the Assyrian king and his subsequent quest for vengeance,

[7] See 4. 6. 1–10, 5. 2. 7 ff., 5. 3. 5–7 vs. 7. 5. 26–32.
[8] *Cyr.* 5. 2. 23–30, 5. 3. 8–14, 15–19, 26–34, 5. 4. 1–14, 29–40, 7. 5. 26–32.

ends with the king's death, but Gadatas, like Gobryas, appears elsewhere in the *Cyropaedia* as Cyrus' guide and household manager. His
tale, like those of Panthea and Gobryas, is closely tied to the main
action of the work: Gadatas' role in capturing the enemy's fortress
and his assassination of the Assyrian ruler are the two strongest links
to the central plot. Here too the novella unfolds mainly through
dialogues, with straightforward passages of narrative coming before,
between, or after conversations.[9] The eunuch's adventures are,
however, concentrated in a relatively small section of the *Cyropaedia*,
and his story is not narrated as concisely and economically as the
novellas of Panthea and Gobryas. Gadatas refers several times to his
sorry state and Xenophon seems less concerned to avoid pathos in
this tale. At times Gadatas' diction is high-flown.

The last of our four tales deals with Croesus, the proud and
pampered ruler of Lydia. Croesus, as we have seen, is the only non-
Assyrian to be the hero of a novella, and his story differs from the
other three in other respects as well. In the *Cyropaedia* Croesus is an
ally of the Assyrians in their campaign against the Medes from the
very start. After the first defeat of the Assyrian forces and the death of
the old Assyrian king, Croesus is appointed commander-in-chief. In
the second confrontation between the Assyrian and Persian armies
Croesus is again defeated by Cyrus. The Lydian monarch escapes to
Sardis, but the Persians and their allies subsequently take the city by
storm. Cyrus summons Croesus and the Lydian monarch appears on
stage, so to speak, for the first time: this conversation between the two
is the core of the Croesus novella (7. 2. 9–29). All of the Lydian's past
history is narrated in this opening conversation, and the account of
Croesus' past activities is clearly influenced by Herodotus. In their
discussion the Persian leader asks for, and receives, advice from
Croesus on how to divide the spoils of Sardis without destroying the
city. The Lydian monarch also relates to Cyrus the history of his
dealings with the Delphic oracle and states that only now, after his
defeat at the hands of the Persians, has he finally learnt to obey the
entreaty of the oracle and know himself. At the end of their conversation Cyrus offers to restore to the captive monarch his family,
servants, and former luxuries, but forbids him to engage in further
military activities. The Persian leader also arranges to have Croesus
constantly at his side, considering him either too useful or too
dangerous to be left behind. We encounter Croesus on two later

[9] Cf. 5. 3. 15–17, 5. 4. 1–9.

occasions in the *Cyropaedia* (7. 4. 12–13, 8. 2. 15–23), and in both episodes the Lydian king again advises Cyrus on how best to guard his treasures.

The tale of Croesus, unlike our other three stories, is essentially contained in one single dialogue, the first conversation between Cyrus and the Lydian monarch. Croesus' story could have been broken up into several dramatic episodes, with, for example, a direct account of Croesus' election as commander-in-chief of the enemy's forces or a discussion between Croesus and a confidante on the meaning of the oracles. But the Lydian is not presented to us in the flesh, as it were, until he comes under Cyrus' control; this may be due to the fact that in the *Cyropaedia* we are hardly ever given a glimpse of scenes behind enemy lines. Croesus' story is presented in fairly restrained and unemotional language. Neither the account of Croesus' earlier history nor the story of his relationship with Cyrus after the conquest of Sardis advances the plot of the *Cyropaedia* in any real way, and Xenophon may have included the Lydian's tale simply because the story of Croesus and his downfall was so well known in the Greek world that any narrative of Cyrus' conquests would be incomplete without it.

Two other episodes in the *Cyropaedia* should be mentioned here, although both are too slight to qualify as full-fledged novellas.[10] The first story is a παιδικὸς λόγος, telling how the Mede Artabazus becomes enamoured of young Cyrus, who is visiting Media. When Cyrus, about to return to Persia, kisses his Mede relatives goodbye, Artabazus manages to steal several kisses, pretending to be another relative. Artabazus tells Cyrus that he begrudges even the time spent blinking when he cannot see his handsome Persian 'relative' (1. 4. 27–8). This playful incident has more serious consequences later on, for Cyrus' admirer Artabazus plays a key role in persuading Cyaxares' officers to continue with the campaign against the Assyrians. We have already seen that Artabazus also plays a part in the Panthea novella, and the Mede is an important and loyal ally of Cyrus throughout.

The second story is also a romantic one, involving in this instance newly-weds. Cyrus has just pardoned the Armenians for transgressing

---

[10] See the passages relating to 'das novellistische Element' of the *Cyr.* collected by Breitenbach 1966: 1717–18. De Vries 1963: 40 is right to term the stories of the new Persian recruits (*Cyr.* 2. 2. 2–10) 'illustrative anecdotes rather than novellas'; cf. Trenkner 1958: 153.

the terms of their treaty with the Medes, and all admire the Persian's beauty, wisdom, and kindness. Tigranes asks his wife if she too thinks Cyrus handsome, and she replies that she has eyes only for the man who promised to give his very soul to save her from servitude, i.e. Tigranes.[11] Unlike our previous anecdote, this brief tale has no further ramifications later on in the *Cyropaedia*. We hear of Tigranes' wife, who accompanies her husband throughout the campaign, only one more time, when Cyrus presents Tigranes with a gift for her (8. 4. 24). None the less, the depiction of the pair's marital devotion has left its mark upon many readers of the *Cyropaedia*, both ancient and modern.[12]

These, then, are the novellas of the *Cyropaedia*: their form and, of course, content are unusual and effective. All four stories have several structural features in common. (1) The tales are presented in several stages or episodes, which are fitted into wider sections of the *Cyropaedia*. (2) There are strong links between these stories and the main thread of the work—the novellas are not digressions. (3) Dialogues form the core of each tale, with related narrative passages coming in close juxtaposition to the conversations. (4) The stories, although generally narrated with considerable brevity and restraint, contain several emotional, grandiloquent passages. Xenophon presents these tales effectively, enlivening his didactic, pseudo-historical narrative with colourful characters and deeds, without digressing from the main story-line. We do not know whether Xenophon himself invented this useful means of animating long battle-ridden stretches of narrative or if he learnt the technique from others.

The question of sources or influences is even more interesting in relation to the content of the *Cyropaedia*'s novellas. The kinds of characters found here—a beautiful and virtuous woman, loyal servants, an impulsive but courageous young man, a brave warrior, a cruel and wilful young despot, a bereaved father, a frightened eunuch, a pampered king—are exotic. Emotions such as love, loyalty, lust, revenge, and jealousy run high and the deeds, including murder, bravery on the battlefield, mutilation of corpses, castration, and suicide, are bold and bloody. What is the source of these melo-

---

[11] *Cyr.* 3. 1. 41; cf. 3. 1. 36. Other bits of this chapter (3. 1), such as the Armenian king's rebellion, trial, and reprieve, and the sad end of 'Socrates', Tigranes' sophistic teacher, are equally colourful and dramatic; cf. above, ch. 2. 4.

[12] See Hermogenes, περὶ ἰδεῶν β (405, 406 Rabe), and cf. Plut. *Mor.* 634 B. Schwartz 1943: 70 thinks that Xenophon uses the Armenian princess to pay tribute to his own wife.

dramatic and romantic stories? Where does the lovely Panthea, so different from that Athenian paragon of virtue, Ischomachus' wife,[13] come from? Were she and the other characters in these lively tales simply invented by Xenophon or was he influenced by others in the writing of these stories? One possibility is that Xenophon makes use of Persian material in the novellas of the *Cyropaedia*, particularly in the stories of Panthea and Gobryas, but we have already seen that the little we know of Persian sources does not allow us either to prove or disprove this hypothesis.[14]

When we turn to Greek authors who may have influenced or inspired Xenophon when writing these colourful episodes set in the East in a (pseudo-)historical framework, the first writer who comes to mind is Xenophon's contemporary, Ctesias.[15] Ctesias, the physician from Cnidus who spent the years 404–398/7 BC at the court of Artaxerxes II, wrote a twenty-three-volume *Persica* or history of Persia. This work, which begins with the reign of Ninus in Assyria and ends with the final events of Ctesias' own stay in Persia, in 398/7 BC, first appeared in the 390s.[16] We know from the *Anabasis* that Xenophon was acquainted with the *Persica*,[17] so that it is possible, at the very least, that Ctesias influenced the *Cyropaedia*, which appeared much later. The *Persica* did not, of course, survive in direct transmission, but enough has been preserved indirectly, particularly in the epitomes of Diodorus and Photius, to give us a fairly good notion of the original form and content of the work. Diodorus gives us a summary of books 1–6, the history of the Assyrian and Median empires from Ninus to Astyages, while Photius provides a briefer précis of books 7–23, which told of the Persian empire from the time

---

[13] If Ischomachus' wife is indeed such a paragon of virtue—see Harvey 1984.

[14] Cf. above, ch. 1. 2.

[15] Hirzel 1895: 166 and Trenkner 1958: 26 both mention the likelihood that the *Cyr.* was influenced by Ctesias, but neither scholar discusses the question in detail. Schwartz 1943: 75, 84–8, points out the similarity between the Stryangaeus–Zarinaea episode of Ctesias and the Panthea novella, and notes the tremendous impact Ctesias' brand of Ionian romantic history had on its readers. Ctesias and the novellas of the *Cyr.* are often linked together in discussions of the origins of the Greek novel; see e.g. Lavagnini 1922: 53–4 n. 1 (= Gärtner 1984: 88–9 n. 1). For Ctesias as a source for the more 'historical' aspects of the *Cyr.* see Breitenbach 1966: 1709–12.

[16] For the dates of Ctesias' stay in Persia and the publication of his *Persica*, as well as his vita in general, see Jacoby 1922: 2032–6 (= 1956*b*: 311–13); Brown 1978 is speculative. Jacoby argues that Diodorus' statement that Ctesias spent 17 years in Persia (*FGrH* 688 T 3) is wrong, while Ctesias' own reference to the 8-year-old palm-trees on Clearchus' grave (*FGrH* 688 F 27. 71), which, if correct, would yield a date of 393/2 for his visit to the tomb, is pure fiction.

[17] *Anab.* 1. 8. 26 = *FGrH* 688 F 21; cf. T 15.

of Cyrus the Great to Artaxerxes II. The ancients testify—and the fragments themselves indicate—that Ctesias' history was picturesque and sensational, filled with dramatic, incredible tales.[18]

How far do the novellas of the *Cyropaedia* resemble stories found in the *Persica*? Let us begin with Panthea. Almost all the females to be found in the pages of Ctesias are cruel and strong-willed, and we can, generally speaking, distinguish two different kinds of women. The first type, best exemplified by Semiramis, are brave, beautiful, and strong-minded queens, who govern and at times do battle alongside their husbands, and then rule on their own after their husbands are gone. Other members of this group are Zarinaea, Sparetra, and, to a certain extent, Roxane.[19] The second category of women, of whom Parysatis is the most outstanding example,[20] are also wives or daughters of kings, but they themselves play a more passive role. They scheme at home behind the scenes and persuade their consorts, often unreasonably, either to punish their enemies or pardon their friends. These powers behind the throne also frequently torture their opponents in horrible fashion. Amytis (daughter of Astyages), Neitatis, Amestris, and Amytis (wife of Megabyxus) all belong to this category.[21] Panthea is like the women in this second group in that she exercises considerable power and influence in private, arranging an alliance between Cyrus and Abradatas behind the scenes, but in her noble character and behaviour Panthea does not, of course, resemble this company of vengeful, plotting women in the least.

The lady of Susa has certain features in common with the first group of Ctesian heroines as well. She does not actually take to the battlefield as these women do, but she is none the less closely involved in the wars of the *Cyropaedia*. Panthea's place is not at home (as with Ischomachus' wife) nor in the harem (as with Parysatis, Amytis, etc.), but in close proximity to the battlefield. Two of Ctesias' women, Semiramis and Zarinaea, are exceptionally beautiful besides being outstandingly brave, and they, like Panthea, find themselves at the centre of a romantic conflict which ends tragi-

[18] Cf. *FGrH* 688 T 11, T 13, T 19.

[19] Zarinaea: *FGrH* 688 F 5 34. 1–5, F 7, F 8a–b; cf. 90 F 5. Sparetra: 688 F 9. 3. Roxane: 688 F 15. 55.

[20] Cf. *FGrH* 688 F 15 and F 16 *passim*, F 17, F 24–F 29.

[21] Amytis, daughter of Astyages: 688 F 9. 1, 6, F 13. 12, 13. Neitatis: F 13a. Amestris: F 14. 39, 42–5. Amytis, wife of Megabyxus: F 13. 32, F 14. 34, 42–4.

cally.[22] According to Ctesias,[23] Semiramis first meets Ninus when she joins her husband Onnes, one of Ninus' lieutenants, at Bactra, which is being besieged by the Assyrian army. Semiramis ascends to the citadel of the city and captures it, thus bringing about the surrender of Bactra. Ninus rewards her for her courage and then, swayed by her beauty, falls in love with her. The Assyrian king tries to persuade Onnes to relinquish Semiramis and marry his daughter instead. When Onnes refuses, Ninus threatens to blind him and the miserable Onnes, frightened and in love, kills himself. Thus Semiramis becomes Ninus' queen, bears him a child, and later succeeds to his throne. In Ctesias it is the husband, rather than the importuning lover, who is rejected, but both triangles, Abradatas–Panthea–Araspas and Onnes–Semiramis–Ninus, involve the suicide of a loyal spouse.

Zarinaea, our second beautiful warrior, is a Sacian queen.[24] She encounters the Mede Stryangaeus in battle; he spares her, after unseating her from her horse, because she is so lovely. Later, Zarinaea's husband takes the Mede commander prisoner and intends to execute him. Instead, he himself is killed by Stryangaeus and his men, who have been set free by Zarinaea. Stryangaeus falls in love with the Sacian queen and, encouraged by his eunuch, declares his love for her. Zarinaea, despite her love for the Mede, rejects his advances gently, pointing out that he is married to an even more beautiful woman and asking him to be as manly in love as he is in war. Stryangaeus composes a farewell letter to Zarinaea in which he reflects on the workings of love, and then commits suicide. The affinities between Panthea and Zarinaea are apparent: both lovely women refuse would-be lovers because involvement with them

---

[22] Of the two other women in this group, Sparetra the Sacian queen—whom Jacoby 1922: 2059 (= 1956*b*: 325) calls 'eine Doppelgängerin der Zarinaia'—is presented only as a warrior, while in Roxane's case the emphasis is on the dire results of the passion she arouses in her half-brother.

[23] *FGrH* 688 F 1b 6. 4–10.

[24] The account here is compiled from two sources, Ctesias (*FGrH* 688 F 5 34. 1–5, F 7, F 8a–b) and Nicolaus of Damascus (*FGrH* 90 F 5). It is generally believed that Nicolaus made extensive, direct use of Ctesias' *Persica* when compiling his universal history, copying or slightly revising the Cnidian's work. The fragments *FGrH* 90 F 1, F 2, F 3, F 4, F 5, and F 66 all seem to stem directly from the *Persica*, and can be used to supplement our knowledge of Ctesias' original work—cf. Jacoby on *FGrH* 90 F 1–102, F 66 (iic. 233–5, 251); Drews 1973: 104 with n. 32 and the further references there. Toher 1989 argues that Nicolaus often alters his sources for his own purposes, but agrees that Ctesias was the basis for 90 F 5, Nicolaus' version of the Zarinaea tale; see also Gilmore 1888: 107.

would lead to a breach of marital fidelity. Both stories also include
lovers who commit suicide because they cannot bear living without
their beloved. Zarinaea does not, however, behave as impeccably as
Panthea: she seems to have colluded in the death of her own husband
and she is in love with Stryangaeus, so that her rejection of the Mede
is puzzling. It is also interesting to note that Ctesias' account of the
Zarinaea–Stryangaeus affair included reflections on the power of
ἔρως and the need for restraint in love, just as we find in the discussions between Araspas and Cyrus in the Panthea novella.[25]

Panthea, then, bears a certain resemblance to the kind of women
found in Ctesias' *Persica*. She is beautiful, strong-minded, and closely
involved—if not an actual participant—in scenes of military conflict.
Her loveliness brings about a romantic entanglement and her own
strong passions lead ultimately to suicide. The lady of Susa is instru-
mental in bringing about an alliance, between Abradatas and Cyrus,
and causing a (feigned) rift between two former allies, Cyrus and
Araspas. All of these qualities or characteristics can be found in one
or both types of women described by Ctesias. None the less, we
cannot 'explain' the Panthea of the *Cyropaedia* by reference to Ctesias,
nor can we trace all of the elements of her story back to the *Persica*. In
particular, Panthea is a noble wife, loyal and chaste, and no such
virtuous woman appears in the surviving fragments of Ctesias.

We should note in this context the two powerful and beautiful
Oriental women, Thargelia and Rhodogyne, who appear in Aeschines' Socratic dialogue *Aspasia*.[26] Rhodogyne is a brave and lovely
warrior queen of the Persians, similar to the Semiramis-type ruler we
have already encountered in Ctesias.[27] When she is informed of a
sudden rebellion in her empire, Rhodogyne goes off to conquer the
Armenians with her hair only half-braided. Later a gold statue,
portraying her with her hair partially arranged, is erected in her
honour. The beautiful Rhodogyne disdains men and has no interest

[25] See Stryangaeus' letter (688 F 8b) and the words of Zarinaea (90 F 5); cf. *Cyr.*
5. 1. 8–17, 6. 1. 36, 41.

[26] The *Aspasia* was probably written several years before the *Cyr.* Dittmar 1912: 55
dates the *Aspasia* to *c.*386 on the basis of its relationship to Plato's *Menexenus* and
Ctesias' *Persica*. (Dittmar believes that Aeschines was influenced by the *Persica*; see also
Ehlers 1966: 50.) Gigon 1947: 308 arrives at a date of before 380 for the *Aspasia* (and
most of Aeschines' works), since it seems likely that Lysias, who died *c.*380 BC, referred
to the dialogue in his speech against Aeschines (Athen. 611 Dff. = Lysias fr. 1 Thalheim;
cf. Harpocration s.v. Ἀσπασία). See also Jebb 1893: 152–5, 310–11.

[27] Ehlers 1966: 48 n. 51 is certainly right to link Rhodogyne, rather than Thargelia,
with Semiramis; contrast Dittmar 1912: 28–9.

in love, but this is not the case with Thargelia of Miletus. Thargelia, who succeeds her husband as ruler of the Thargelians, actively pursues men in order to win them over to the Persian cause. The Persian king, we are told, treats her as an equal.[28] Panthea does not particularly resemble either of these two women, but it is interesting none the less to note how depictions of outstanding Eastern women make their way into various literary forms, including Socratic dialogue.

Returning to Ctesias, we find that one feature of the novellas of the *Cyropaedia* which can be attributed with some assurance to the influence of the *Persica* is the prominent role played by eunuchs. One eunuch, the young Assyrian noble Gadatas, is the hero of one novella of the *Cyropaedia*, while in another tale, the story of Panthea, eunuchs play an important part—delivering messages, escorting their mistress, preparing Abradatas' grave, and in the end committing suicide upon the fresh grave of their master and mistress.[29] Eunuchs are key figures throughout Ctesias' *Persica*.[30] Often when a new king comes to power we are told at once (in Photius' summary, at any rate) who his chief eunuchs were, and their names are recorded in nearly formulaic fashion ($\mu\acute{\epsilon}\gamma\alpha$ $\pi\alpha\rho$' $\alpha\dot{\upsilon}\tau\hat{\omega}$ $\delta\upsilon\nu\acute{\alpha}\mu\epsilon\nu\sigma$).[31] This prominent position allotted to the eunuchs in Ctesias' narrative reflects their importance. Over two dozen individual eunuchs appear in the *Persica*,[32] and they perform a variety of functions. Some deliver messages or plead their master's cause in front of another. Such are the two eunuchs sent to influence Artaeus in the Nanarus–Parsondes affair and Artoxares, who helps reconcile

---

[28] The main sources for Aeschines' version of the story of Rhodogyne are *De Mul.* 8 and Philostratus, *Imag.* 2. 5 (= fr. 18 Dittmar). For Aeschines' Thargelia see Plut. *Per.* 24; *De Mul.* 11; Philostratus, *Epist.* 73; *Suda* and Hesychius s.v. (= frr. 21 and 22 Dittmar). Hippias apparently wrote of Thargelia even before Aeschines did—cf. Athen. 608 F (= *FGrH* 6 F 3). For reconstructions of the *Aspasia* see Dittmar 1912: 1–59 and Ehlers 1966; the latter's interpretation is more convincing.

[29] *Cyr.* 6. 1. 33–4, 6. 4. 11, 7. 3. 5, 7. 3. 15. There is also an original and curious passage in the *Cyr.* (7. 5. 58–65) in which Cyrus reflects that eunuchs are the most loyal servants to be had and are no less courageous than other men; cf. below, ch. 5. 2.

[30] See Guyot 1980: 78–87 for a survey of the eunuchs who appear in the fragments of Ctesias; Guyot's interest in the eunuchs is historical, and his main objective is to glean information on the various functions they perform.

[31] *FGrH* 688 F 9. 6, F 13. 9, F 13. 24, F 13. 33, F 15. 51; cf. F 15. 49 and F 15. 54 and see Jacoby 1922: 2047 (= 1956*b*: 319).

[32] Some 26 eunuchs, named and unnamed, can be found in the fragments of the *Persica*, together with the Ctesian fragments of Nicolaus of Damascus (cf. above, n. 24). For a prosopographical list of the eunuchs in Ctesias (and elsewhere) see Guyot 1980: 181 ff.

Megabyxus and Artaxerxes.[33] Other eunuchs perform more complex services, both good—e.g. escorting a dead master home for burial—and bad, such as Petasacas starving Astyages to death at Oebares' bidding or Matacas plundering Delphi under orders from Xerxes.[34] The eunuchs' most frequent activity in Ctesias seems to be plotting and conspiring against their masters. Thus we find eunuchs conspiring against Semiramis, Sardanapallus, the Magus pretender to the throne, Amyrtaeus, king of Egypt, Xerxes I, Artaxerxes I, Xerxes II, and Darius II.[35] (In the last instance Darius' eunuch Artoxares plots to become king himself and is caught ordering a false moustache and beard for the occasion!) As a result of their conspiratorial activities these eunuchs often die horribly, after cruel tortures.[36] Thus Gadatas in the *Cyropaedia*, who, together with Gobryas, kills the Assyrian king within the palace walls, follows the Ctesian pattern to a certain extent; we shall see below that the brief depiction of the assassination in the *Cyropaedia* has fairly close parallels in the *Persica*. Gadatas is not, however, altogether like the eunuchs in Ctesias, for he is an Assyrian noble, a member of an important family who was castrated by his ruler, certainly not meant to be a servant or court eunuch from the start. There are no stories of a noble castrated by a king in the surviving fragments of Ctesias.[37] Gadatas, while a sworn enemy of the Assyrian king, transfers his loyalty to Cyrus, whom he serves faithfully, thus demonstrating another, diametrically opposed, characteristic of eunuchs, their loyalty to their masters. Panthea's eunuchs, of course, provide an extreme example of this kind of loyal devotion when they kill themselves immediately after their mistress's suicide. In Ctesias too there are several tales of faithful eunuchs, such as Artoxares, who is exiled by Artaxerxes for speaking too freely on Megabyxus' behalf, Bagapatas, who lives by and guards Darius' tomb, and Parsicas, who

[33] *FGrH* 90 F 4, 688 F 14. 42, 43 (for Artoxares cf. Lewis 1977: 20–1, 75–6, 81–2). See also *FGrH* 90 F 5, F 66. 23, and 688 F 8b for more errands of this nature performed by eunuchs.

[34] Escorting dead master: *FGrH* 688 F 13. 9, F 13. 23, F 15. 47. Petasacas: F 9. 6; Matacas: F 13. 31.

[35] *FGrH* 688 F 1b 20. 1; F 1b 24. 4, F 1p; F 13. 13, 15, 16; F 13. 10; F 13. 33; F 14. 34; F 15. 48, 52; F 15. 54.

[36] 688 F 9. 6, F 13. 15, F 14. 34, F 15. 52, F 15. 54; cf. F 16. 66 and F 26.

[37] The Persian Parsondes (*FGrH* 90 F 4) is castrated metaphorically. Devereux 1973: 43 points out that for the Greeks blinding symbolizes castration; perhaps, then, Ninus' threat to blind Semiramis' husband should be considered such an instance. See also Maxwell-Stuart 1976.

grieves for Cyrus the Younger.[38] The eunuchs of the *Persica* sometimes die with their masters—as do Sardanapallus' eunuchs, who
join him on the funeral pyre—or in their stead, as in the case of
Parysatis' eunuchs, who are killed by Artaxerxes as a punishment for
his mother's misdeeds,[39] so that while there is no tale in Ctesias of
eunuchs stabbing themselves to death in the wake of their master's
demise, such a scene is not far removed from the world of the *Persica*.

The young Assyrian king of the *Cyropaedia* is, as we have seen, the
villain of the work; he is a harsh, jealous, and arrogant despot. None
of the leading figures in Ctesias seems quite as unrelievedly cruel and
vindictive as the Assyrian, but several perform deeds similar to his.
Ninus, for example, drives Onnes to suicide when he threatens to
blind him for refusing to part with his wife, Semiramis. Oebares,
Cyrus' right-hand man, is similarly ruthless. He kills the Babylonian
seer who predicts Cyrus' rise to power in order to guarantee his
silence, and also has Astyages starved to death long after the Mede
king has been subdued. Darius I chops off the heads of forty bearers
after his parents have been killed as a result of their negligence, while
Artaxerxes I condemns Megabyxus to death and then exiles him
instead, as a punishment for being more successful in a hunting
expedition; the parallel with Gobryas' son and the young Assyrian
king is apparent.[40] Several women in Ctesias, in particular Amestris
and Parysatis, are even better examples of cruel and vengeful figures.
Amestris persuades Artaxerxes to betray his word and hand Inarus,
her son's killer, over to her for punishment. She also tortures her
grandson's killer and Apollonides, the Greek doctor who seduced her
daughter.[41] Parysatis' list of victims is even longer and includes a
pretender to the throne, the entire family of her treacherous son-in-
law Terituchmes (including, in the end, Artaxerxes' wife Stateira),
and all those involved in the death of Cyrus the Younger at Cunaxa.[42]
Thus the young Assyrian king of the *Cyropaedia* would not be out of
place in the pages of the *Persica*. We should also remember that while
both Gadatas and Gobryas are presented as positive figures in the
Cyropaedia, their actions are motivated to a large extent by a desire for
revenge.

[38] 688 F 14. 43, F 13. 23, F 20. 12. 1–2.
[39] 688 F 1b 27. 2, F 27. 70.
[40] See *FGrH* 688 F 1b 6. 9–10, 90 F 66. 18–19, 688 F 9. 6, F 13. 19, F 14. 43 respectively.
[41] 688 F 14. 39, 45, 44.
[42] 688 F 15. 54; F 15. 56, F 16. 61; F 27. 70, F 29b; F 16. 66–7, F 26.

The story of Croesus in the *Cyropaedia* is closely linked to Herodotus' account of the Lydian king and bears little resemblance to
Ctesias' version.[43] None the less, one particular aspect of Xenophon's
account—Croesus' desire to be like his wife and lead the happiest of
lives, enjoying luxuries with no cares about acquiring them (7. 2. 26–
8)—is reminiscent of another favourite theme in the *Persica*, the
pampered, effeminate monarch. In Ctesias' work we meet several
such rulers who prefer to spend their time in the harem, leading a life
of ease. These include Ninyas, son of Ninus and Semiramis,
Sardanapallus with his philosophy of 'eat, drink, and be merry', and
Nanarus, the effete Babylonian satrap who turns his opponent
Parsondes into a music-girl.[44] Xenophon's Croesus is delighted to
join the ranks of such rulers, and the Mede ruler Cyaxares is, of
course, another such effeminate despot found in the *Cyropaedia*. In
the *Persica* these indolent, effete kings are often found alongside
ruthless warrior queens; Semiramis and her son Ninyas are the best
instance of this stark contrast. In the *Cyropaedia* the courageous
Panthea is perhaps meant to be such a counter-figure to the spoilt
Lydian monarch, even if no direct comparison is drawn between the
two.[45]

In sum, many of the themes and characters of the novellas of the
Cyropaedia are similar to those found in Ctesias, and it is not
unreasonable to assume that Ctesias influenced Xenophon in the
writing of the more colourful episodes of the work. Xenophon does
not, however, simply imitate Ctesias: for example, Panthea does not
take to the battlefield and Cyrus and the Assyrian king do not engage
in a face-to-face duel, as they would if they were merely copies of
figures in the *Persica*. The novellas of the *Cyropaedia* are more than
reworkings of, or variations on, stories of the *Persica*.

What of the form of the *Persica*? We have seen that Xenophon's
novellas are narrated mainly by means of dialogues: how does
Ctesias use conversations in his work? The two epitomes of Diodorus
and Photius which comprise the bulk of the fragments of the *Persica*
contain next to no direct speech, but there are several clear indications that 'speeches and dialogues ... were without doubt an

[43] Cf. 688 F 9. 4–5, F 9b–c.
[44] Ninyas: 688 F 1b 21. 1–2, F 1n; Sardanapallus: F 1b 23. 1–3, 24. 4, F 1p; Nanarus
and Parsondes: 688 F 6, 90 F 4.
[45] See Higgins 1977: 53. For the Greek view of Oriental culture and rulers as 'female'
with effeminate kings and strong women, see Sancisi-Weerdenburg 1983.

important (and effective) ingredient' in the original work.[46] Our first piece of evidence concerning dialogue in the *Persica* comes from Demetrius (*De Eloc.* 216 = 688 F 24), who quotes with approval the way Ctesias has a messenger gently break the news of Cyrus the Younger's death to Parysatis. In the exchange between the two the queen asks a series of questions and the messenger replies little by little, step by step (κατὰ μικρὸν καὶ κατὰ βραχύ), with the evil tidings of her son's demise. In this passage, as Demetrius notes, Ctesias uses dialogue effectively and dramatically. A second piece of evidence comes from a papyrus (*P. Oxy.* 2330 = 688 F 8b) generally believed to contain Ctesias' *ipsissima verba*.[47] The bulk of the papyrus contains Stryangaeus' farewell letter to Zarinaea before his suicide,[48] but more interesting for our purposes is the beginning of the papyrus (lines 1–5), which contains an exchange between the Mede Stryangaeus and his eunuch. The opening of their conversation is obscure, but Stryangaeus' prosaic final sentence ('come, first I'll write to Zarinaea': φέρε τὸ γοῦν πρῶτον γράμματα γράψω πρὸς Ζαρειεναίαν) would seem to indicate that Ctesias, like Xenophon, used dialogue in more commonplace situations as well, i.e. fairly regularly.[49]

Photius includes direct speech very rarely in his epitome of Ctesias, and there is only one exchange in *oratio recta* in the whole of his summary (*FGrH* 688 F 13. 13; cf. F 15. 52). None the less, there are several places in Photius' very succinct summary which seem to hint at speeches or conversations which appeared in the original full-scale *Persica*.[50] In those passages of Plutarch which stem from Ctesias and supplement Photius' brief account of the battle of Cunaxa and its aftermath, there is a great deal of direct speech.[51] Thus we find conversations between Cyrus and Clearchus, Artaxerxes' 'eye'

---

[46] Bigwood 1976: 5. She has an excellent analysis of the relation of Photius' summary to the original *Persica*.

[47] See Roberts 1954 for the original publication of the papyrus. Demetrius (*De Eloc.* 213 = 688 F 8a) contains an almost exact quotation of the opening of Stryangaeus' letter as found in the papyrus, while Nicolaus of Damascus (90 F 5) paraphrases the papyrus passage. For Ctesias as author of the papyrus see Bigwood 1986 (and the further references there) vs. Giangrande 1976.

[48] Gray 1989: 5 (with n. 14) notes the similarity between the opening of this letter and Tomyris' final address to the dead Cyrus in Herodotus (Hdt. 1. 214).

[49] Compare the version of Nicolaus of Damascus (*FGrH* 90 F 5), which does not include any direct speech here.

[50] See *FGrH* 688 F 9. 8, F 13. 32, F 14. 44, F 16. 63, F 16. 67.

[51] See 688 F 18, F 19, F 20 (11. 4, 12. 1, 12. 6), F 26 (14. 5, 6, 9, 15. 2, 3, 4, 6, 7, 17. 8), and cf. F 16. For Plutarch's direct use of the *Persica* see Bigwood 1983: 344 n. 18; cf. Jacoby 1922: 2070 (= 1956*b*: 330).

Artasuras and Cyrus' eunuchs, Artaxerxes and Parysatis, etc., and these dialogues probably appeared, if in slightly different form, in Ctesias' original work. The two versions of the story of Mithradatas are, perhaps, the best illustration of the way in which a fully elaborated dialogue, which appeared in all likelihood in the *Persica* and was preserved by Plutarch, was shortened by Photius. Mithradatas is egged on by Parysatis' eunuch to boast that he was the one to wound Cyrus the Younger fatally. In Plutarch the two meet at a dinner-party and their thoughts, reactions, and words are reported in a lively, dramatic dialogue (*FGrH* 688 F 26 = Plut. *Artax.* 15. 1–7). In the parallel passage in Photius, which corresponds closely to Plutarch's account, we are simply told that Mithradatas was handed over to Parysatis for punishment after he bragged at dinner of having killed Cyrus (F 16. 67 ἐπὶ τραπέζης μεγαλαυχήσαντα ἀποκτεῖναι Κῦρον).

In Diodorus' summary of the *Persica* (688 F 1b, F 5) there is not a single instance of direct speech, but there are several places in the narrative where it seems more than likely that the original did include either speeches or dialogues. Ninus' confrontation with Onnes over Semiramis, the exchange of messages between Semiramis and the Indian king before their battle, the council of war held by Arbaces, Belosus, and their allies, and Arbaces' magnanimous attitude towards Belosus at his trial—all seem to require, even demand, oratio recta.[52] Fortunately, using a fragment of Nicolaus of Damascus which is based on the lost *Persica* and supplements the epitome of Diodorus (90 F 3),[53] we are in a position to recover one such dialogue. Diodorus (688 F 1b 24. 2–3) tells us briefly of the friendship between the Mede Arbaces and the Babylonian seer Belosus, who meet at Babylon. Belosus, Diodorus relates, predicts that Arbaces will take over Sardanapallus' empire and the Mede promises him the satrapy of Babylonia in return. In Nicolaus' account (90 F 3) we are first told of the vision the Babylonian seer has concerning Arbaces' rise to power—a vision which includes a con-

[52] See *FGrH* 688 F 1b: 6. 9–10, 18. 1–2, 25. 4–5, 28. 5 respectively.

[53] For Nicolaus' use of Ctesias see above, n. 24. Wacholder 1962: 68–9, 123–4, argues that Nicolaus, who wrote tragedies in addition to history, dramatized Ctesias' account in the *Persica*-based fragments (90 F 1–F 5, F 66) and added the dialogues found there. He is convincingly refuted by Biltcliffe 1969, who points out that (1) dialogue is rarely found elsewhere in Nicolaus and (2) in the one fragment where we have sufficient evidence to judge, 688 F 8b = *P. Oxy.* 2330, Nicolaus turns the dialogue preceding Stryangaeus' letter into indirect speech, both shortening and toning down the whole passage; cf. Toher 1989: 169–72.

versation between two horses—and are then shown how Belosus slowly and gently informs Arbaces that he will become ruler of the Assyrian empire. Belosus asks his friend a series of questions ('What will you give me if I tell you that you will rule over territory *x*?') and thus gradually leads Arbaces to realize that he will become king. The technique used here is very similar to that used by the messenger to inform Parysatis of Cyrus the Younger's death, in the passage of Ctesias praised by Demetrius (688 F 24), and this exchange between Belosus and Arbaces must surely come from Ctesias himself.[54]

The other Ctesian fragments of Nicolaus also contain several dialogues and speeches which were, in all likelihood, simply copied or excerpted from the *Persica*.[55] We can assume, then, that Ctesias made frequent use of dialogues in his history and that the Cnidian may have influenced Xenophon in matters of form as well as content in the novellas of the *Cyropaedia*, i.e. in the regular use of conversations to present these dramatic tales. We have seen that the novellas of the *Cyropaedia* are an integral part of the work, not mere digressions. Ctesias too seems to have avoided digressions:[56] the *Persica* is, in fact, a chain of novellas, arranged in chronological order and interspersed into descriptions of lands, customs, battles, and the concrete achievements of each noteworthy monarch. We do not know if the novellas of the *Persica* were narrated continuously or were broken up into several episodes, as with the colourful tales of the *Cyropaedia*, since the nature of our sources for most of the fragments—epitomes by Diodorus and Photius—makes this point difficult to judge. It is worth noting that Parysatis' continuing vendetta against the family of her son-in-law Terituchmes is presented in several stages, and that there are several scattered episodes featuring Megabyxus, but this may well be Photius, and not Ctesias, at work.[57]

One further feature of the novellas of the *Cyropaedia* is the restraint and economy with which these stories are presented. It can safely be said that such brevity and moderation are not due to the influence of

[54] Cf. Biltcliffe 1969: 87 n. 16. Compare too the conversation between Oebares and Cyrus in Nicolaus, in which the former urges the latter, slowly and step by step, to rebel against Astyages (90 F 66. 15).

[55] Cf. 90 F 2, F 4, F 5, and F 66, and see above, n. 24. Jacoby *ad* 90 F 2–3 (iic. 235) notes how these fragments of Nicolaus give us 'einen Begriff von Ktesias' schriftstellerischer Art'.

[56] Cf. 688 T 13 οὐδὲ πρὸς ἐκτροπὰς δέ τινας ἀκαίρους, ὥσπερ ἐκεῖνος [sc. Herodotus], ἀπάγει τὸν λόγον.

[57] Parysatis: 688 F 15. 55–6, F 16. 58, 61. Megabyxus: F 13. 26, 31, 32, F 14. 34, 37–9, 40–4; cf. Bigwood 1976: 3 n. 9.

the *Persica*, for Ctesias was considered by the ancients to be long-winded, repetitive, and diffuse.[58] These qualities are not always apparent in the straightforward summaries of Diodorus and Photius, but certain fragments do reflect the Cnidian's prolixity. One such section of the *Persica* is the complicated, drawn-out affair of Cyrus' death at Cunaxa, in which, as Plutarch aptly remarks, Ctesias slowly finishes off the Persian prince 'as if with a blunt sword'.[59] Ctesias was not especially well known for his low-key presentation either: sensationalism, pathos, surprise, and incredible tales were his trademarks as a writer.[60]

We can assume, then, that Xenophon was influenced by the *Persica* when writing the novellas of the *Cyropaedia*. His characters and their stories belong to the Oriental world of court intrigues, harsh despots, and strong-minded women so beloved of Ctesias, and there are, as we shall see, several specific correspondences between the two works. Ctesias' history seems to have contained many speeches and conversations, and this too may have influenced Xenophon in the presentation of his tales. It is clear, on the other hand, that Ctesias was not Xenophon's sole source of inspiration for these spicy stories, and the *Cyropaedia*, even at its most colourful, is without doubt less sensational and melodramatic than the *Persica* was.

This postulated influence of the *Persica* on the dramatic tales of the *Cyropaedia* is particularly interesting in view of how little Ctesias has influenced Xenophon elsewhere, whether in this or in his other works: Ctesias' influence on the *Cyropaedia* is apparent only in relation to the work's novellas.[61] Xenophon's version of the life of Cyrus the Great, the main thread of the *Cyropaedia*, differs in almost every respect from the account found in Ctesias. We have already seen how in the *Persica* Cyrus is the son of a Persian brigand who works his way up from a lowly position at the Median court to become Astyages' chief adviser.[62] After wresting control of the

---

[58] Cf. 688 T 13, T 14a–b.

[59] 688 T 14b καθάπερ ἀμβλεῖ ξιφιδίῳ; cf. F 16. 63–4, F 19–F 21.

[60] Cf. 688 T 11, T 13, T 19.

[61] There is one curious passage in Diodorus' epitome of Ctesias (688 F 1b 21. 3–7) which is reminiscent of an entirely different aspect of the *Cyr.*—Cyrus' reflections on the best way to rule the people of his empire. In Ctesias we find an explanation of why Ninyas chose a new royal guard each year. The passage includes observations on the way armies react, the reasons why subjects rebel, etc., or what seem to be the Cnidian's thoughts on the governing of an empire. One wonders if this passage is unique or if the *Persica* included other such remarks.

[62] See above, ch. 3. 2.

Median empire away from Astyages, with the aid of Oebares and a Babylonian seer, Cyrus marries Astyages' daughter and expands his empire, warring with the Bactrians, Sacians, and Lydians, but not the Babylonians. Ctesias' Persian leader is fatally wounded in a conflict with a Scythian tribe, and delivers his last will and testament before dying. It is only in this farewell scene, as we have already seen, that one can find any real resemblance between the Cyrus of the *Persica* and Xenophon's hero.[63] Ctesias' Cyrus does not seem to have been the upstanding didactic figure that our Cyrus is, as can be seen, for instance, from his decision to torture Astyages' family (*FGrH* 688 F 9. 1). In general there are very few good or moral characters in Ctesias' work: only Memnon, a participant in the Trojan war, Sardanapallus' supplanter Arbaces, and Amorges, Cyrus' enemy-turned-ally, would seem to qualify.[64]

Another work which betrays very little of the Cnidian's influence is the *Anabasis*, even though Xenophon does once refer there to the *Persica*.[65] The *Anabasis* covers some of the same ground as the *Persica*—the preparations leading to the battle of Cunaxa, the battle itself, and its consequences—but the two compositions are very dissimilar, both in their factual account of the battle[66] and in their literary presentation of the conflict between Cyrus the Younger and his brother Artaxerxes II. Ctesias' account of the original feud between the two brothers is much more detailed than that of Xenophon[67] and includes such melodramatic scenes as Parysatis wrapping her arms and tresses of hair around Cyrus and clinging to his neck, while begging Artaxerxes to spare him. Xenophon's version of the same scene is ἡ δὲ μήτηρ ἐξαιτησαμένη αὐτὸν ἀποπέμπει πάλιν ... (*Anab.* 1. 1. 3), and this brief, low-key approach is characteristic of his narrative throughout. Both writers include a description of the face-to-face confrontation between Cyrus and Artaxerxes on the battlefield, with Cyrus wounding his brother, but in Xenophon Cyrus is then quickly dispatched to his demise, while Ctesias relates a complicated, protracted sequence of events which is so long (even in

---

[63] See above, ch. 2. 7, and cf. Jacoby 1922: 2067–8 (= 1956*b*: 329); Breitenbach 1966: 1709–12, 1719.

[64] Memnon: 688 F 1b 22. 3. Arbaces: 90 F 2–3; 688 F 1b 24–8, esp. 24. 1 and 28. 5–6. Amorges: 688 F 9. 3, 7, 8.

[65] *Anab.* 1. 8. 26–7.

[66] For a detailed comparison of the two versions see Bigwood 1983 and Cawkwell 1972: 38–43.

[67] *FGrH* 688 F 16. 59, F 17 vs. *Anab.* 1. 1. 3–5.

Plutarch's abridged version) that the reader greets Cyrus' death with considerable relief. The Cnidian then goes on to describe Artaxerxes' exultation—and the eunuchs' and Parysatis' grief—over Cyrus' corpse, but Xenophon includes no such emotional outbursts, lingering only over a description of Artapates, Cyrus' most loyal sceptre-bearer, who is killed near his dead master.[68] (Xenophon does, of course, eulogize Cyrus in the following chapter of the *Anabasis*.) Ctesias also seems to have dwelt on the mutilation of Cyrus' body in long and loving detail, while Xenophon handles the matter in a few words.[69] The only episode found both in Ctesias and in Xenophon which seems to have been presented in more sensational detail by the Athenian is the account of Meno's end. Ctesias, as far as we can glean from Photius and Plutarch, simply tells us that Meno was not killed along with Clearchus and the other captured Greek generals, while Xenophon, after a defamatory description of Meno's character and sexual misdemeanours, goes on to say that Meno died slowly and painfully, a year after the other Greek generals.[70] Xenophon could be as melodramatic and sensational as the Cnidian when he so chose.[71] On the whole, though, Xenophon's style and presentation in the *Anabasis* are rarely reminiscent of Ctesias, and it is difficult to detect the latter's influence upon him when he recounts the events surrounding Cunaxa.

What of the novellas of the *Anabasis*? For a start, there are next to none in that work, although there are many places where Xenophon hints at colourful tales that could have been further elaborated. Our interest is aroused by Cyrus the Younger's relationship with Epyaxa, wife of the king of Cilicia, Syennesis. We know that she supported Cyrus and persuaded her husband to meet him; Xenophon then discreetly adds ἐλέγετο δὲ καὶ συγγενέσθαι Κῦρον τῇ Κιλίσσῃ (*Anab.* 1. 2. 12).[72] Similarly, Cyrus' Ionian mistress, captured by Artaxerxes' forces, is simply dismissed as τὴν σοφὴν καὶ καλὴν λεγομένην εἶναι (*Anab.* 1. 10. 2), and we must turn to other writers for further details of this 'Aspasia'.[73] In all likelihood Xenophon could have (and

[68] *FGrH* 688 F 16. 64, 66, F 20, F 24, F 25; *Anab.* 1. 8. 26–9. See Higgins 1977: 85–6 for a thoughtful attempt to explain Xenophon's 'pause . . . in a narrative otherwise remarkably swift'.

[69] 688 F 16. 64, 66, F 20 vs. *Anab.* 1. 10. 1.

[70] 688 F 27. 69 (Photius), F 28. 5 (Plutarch), *Anab.* 2. 6. 21–9; cf. Diod. 14. 27. 2.

[71] See also *Anab.* 2. 5. 33, 4. 7. 13–14, and cf. 5. 4. 12–17, 32–4.

[72] See also *Anab.* 1. 2. 14–18, 26; cf. 688 F 16. 63.

[73] Cf. Plut. *Artax.* 26. 3–5; *Per.* 24. 7; Athen. 576 D; and cf. 'Aspasia's' half-clad Milesian colleague described at *Anab.* 1. 10. 3.

Ctesias would have) told us more about these women.[74] There are
other stories in the *Anabasis* which contain brief, somewhat tantaliz-
ing references to dramatic episodes and characters, but these are not
developed into full-fledged novellas of the kind we find in the *Cyropaedia*. We hear, for instance, of the family of the headman of an
occupied village in Armenia, including a newly married daughter, a
son-in-law away hunting, and a handsome son who catches a Greek
soldiers' fancy, but these figures are sketched only in outline.[75] The
Spartan Dracontius, who was exiled for accidentally killing a boy in
his youth, and Dexippus, a troublemaker who eventually received his
just deserts, are two other characters in the *Anabasis* whose background stories are alluded to, but not supplied.[76] Two other passages
in the *Anabasis* are more novella-like: Seuthes' story of his father's
exile and his own life as an orphan at another king's court (7. 2. 32–
4), and a charming encounter in which Xenophon persuades Seuthes
to allow Episthenes, a παιδεραστής who once recruited a company of
soldiers solely on the basis of their good looks, to spare the life of a
handsome Thracian lad (7. 4. 7–11). These two tales, like the longer,
episodic novellas of the *Cyropaedia*, are presented largely through dialogues. But Xenophon does not generally include romantic or melodramatic tales in the *Anabasis*, and his account of the Ten Thousand
is (perhaps deliberately) very unlike Ctesias' *Persica*.

Turning to the *Hellenica*, we find several colourful, dramatic tales
in this (more or less) straightforward historical composition. Such are
the description of Agesilaus' slightly devious matchmaking between
Otys and the daughter of Spithridates (*Hell.* 4. 1. 4–15), the tale of
the love affair between Sphodrias' son Cleonymus and Archidamus,
son of Agesilaus, which led to the acquittal of Sphodrias (5. 4. 25–33),
and the peace negotiations on the grass between Pharnabazus and
Agesilaus, with the charming exchange between Agesilaus and
Pharnabazus' son at their end (4. 1. 29–40).[77] These tales are all told
largely through dialogues, but two of the most dramatic stories of the

---

[74] Neuhaus 1901 argues that Ctesias is in fact Plutarch's source for the story of
Cyrus' 'Aspasia', but Deinon is another possible candidate. See Aelian *VH* 12. 1 for a
richly embroidered version of Aspasia's adventures.

[75] *Anab.* 4. 5. 24–4. 6. 3. The characters of this story and their awkward situation
recall the Armenian family of the *Cyr.*—the king, Tigranes, and their wives—at the
king's trial (*Cyr.* 3. 1).

[76] Dracontius: *Anab.* 4. 8. 25; Dexippus: 5. 1. 15, 6. 6. 5–34.

[77] For an excellent discussion of these episodes in the *Hell.* see Gray 1981, who
discusses novellas (but not under that name) at 330–1; cf. Gray 1989: 49–63.

Hellenica—Phillidas' nearly single-handed liberation of Thebes
(5. 4. 2–9) and the murder of Alexander, ruler of Thessaly, instigated
by his wife and perpetrated by her brothers (6. 4. 35–7)—are told
without any use of direct speech.[78] Both these accounts include vivid
background detail, such as Phillidas finding the unsuspecting
Leonidas lying down after dinner, with his wife working wool at his
side (5. 4. 7), or Alexander's wife holding the door tightly shut while
her husband is being murdered (6. 4. 36). Yet another novella in the
Hellenica is the story of Mania, the close friend and adviser of
Pharnabazus, who takes over her husband's satrapy and is later
murdered by her treacherous son-in-law Meidias. Meidias subsequently receives his just deserts at the hands of Dercylidas
(3. 1. 10–28); in this tale Xenophon uses a certain amount of direct
speech. Perhaps the most outstanding feature of the novellas of the
Hellenica is the important role assigned to love affairs between men.
While there are a few key women in the work—we have already
encountered Mania, Alexander's wife, and the more passive daughter of Spithridates, beneficiary of Agesilaus' matchmaking—men or,
to be more precise, romantic relations between men are the prime
factor in many of the stories. The outstanding example is the pair
Cleonymus and Archidamus, whose intimacy, Xenophon implies, is
responsible for Sphodrias' surprising acquittal. In addition, Alcestas'
παιδικά causes him to lose the acropolis of Oreus, Anaxibius'
beloved dies fighting at his side, and Alexander's mistreatment of his
boyfriend leads to his own death. The son of Pharnabazus charms
Agesilaus, and two other handsome young men, the sons of Mania
and of Spithridates, are also mentioned, if only briefly.[79] The
colourful stories of the *Hellenica* are not particularly like those of the
Cyropaedia (or those found in Ctesias): Artabazus the Mede, who is
enamoured of Cyrus and supports the Persian leader throughout, is
the figure who would feel most at home in the pages of the *Hellenica*.
Xenophon's technique for narrating novellas in the *Hellenica* is also
different from his method in the *Cyropaedia*: the tales in the *Hellenica*
are often digressions, or at best are of minor importance in relation

---

[78] Cf. Gray 1989: 65–72.

[79] See *Hell.* 5. 4. 25–33, 5. 4. 57, 4. 8. 39, 6. 4. 37, 4. 1. 39–40, 3. 1. 14, 4. 1. 6. Elsewhere in Xenophon (*Ages.* 5. 4–6) we learn more of the relationship between Agesilaus
and Megabates, son of Spithridates, while the Oxyrhynchus historian explicitly states
that the Spartan king took up Spithridates because of his son (*Hell. Oxy.* 16. 4 μάλιστα
μὲν ἕνεκα τοῦ μειρακίου).

to the mainstream of historical events,[80] and they are presented, with or without the use of direct speech, as one continuous unit rather than in a series of scattered episodes. What the novellas of the two works do have in common is the economy with which they are presented: Xenophon relates these stories briefly and without melodrama.

Ctesias is not the only author who seems to have left his mark upon the novellas of the *Cyropaedia*. Another writer who must be considered a likely influence upon—or inspiration for—the colourful tales in our work is Herodotus, 'the classic representative of the Greek novella'.[81] We have already noted that one of the novellas of the *Cyropaedia*, the story of Croesus, is clearly dependent upon Herodotus, and there is little doubt that Xenophon was well acquainted with Herodotus' work.[82] Herodotus' *History* contains a large number of novellas, which are presented in a wide variety of ways, unlike the *Cyropaedia*'s dramatic stories, which generally have a similar form. In Herodotus some novellas—the story of Polycrates' ring, Masistes' wife, Cyrus' childhood, etc.—are narrated as one continuous tale, while others, such as the tales of Periander, Pythius, Demaratus' birth, etc., are presented in more than one episode.[83] Several novellas are directly related to the main narrative thread of the *History*—e.g. the story of Syloson's flame-coloured cloak or Zopyrus at Babylon— while others are digressions, plain and simple, as with the tale of Rhampsinitus and the thief or Cleisthenes and the suitors.[84] Some characters appear in Herodotus' *History* both in and out of novellas (e.g. Croesus, Harpagus, Demaratus, Polycrates), reminding us of Gobryas and Gadatas of the *Cyropaedia*, while others (Gyges, Masistes' wife, Arion, Perdiccas, etc.) feature only in a single novella and then disappear. In other words, the novellas in Herodotus, unlike those of the *Cyropaedia*, are not necessarily episodic in structure, nor are they always woven into the main fabric of the story. Nor

---

[80] Gray 1989 argues that in the *Hell.* Xenophon is in fact more interested in the philosophical and moral qualities highlighted in these stories than in actual political events.

[81] Trenkner 1958: xiv. See also Aly 1936: 1173–4, who says that Herodotus is 'nicht der Schöpfer der Novelle . . . sondern ihr Entdecker'. Aly 1921 is the classic work on the novellas of Herodotus.

[82] See Keller 1911 and Riemann 1967: 20–7; Gray 1989 argues for the widespread influence of Herodotus on the *Hell.*

[83] Polycrates: Hdt. 3. 40–3; Masistes' wife: 9. 108–13; young Cyrus: 1. 107–22; Periander: 3. 50–3, 5. 92; Pythius: 7. 27–9, 38–9; Demaratus: 6. 61–3, 68–9.

[84] Cf. Hdt. 3. 139–40, 3. 150–60, 2. 121, 6. 126–30.

are Herodotus' tales presented chiefly by means of conversations: some novellas are composed almost entirely of dialogue (e.g. the story of Pythius), while others are narrated throughout in oratio obliqua (as with Arion or Rhampsinitus and the thief) or are presented within a speech (e.g. the chain of stories concerning Labda, Cypselus, Periander, Thrasybulus, and Melissa or the tale of Glaucus and the deposit).[85] Most stories—like those of Gyges and Candaules or Alexander and the partying Persians—are a blend of narrative and dialogue.[86] In short, Xenophon did not adopt the more formal characteristics of his novellas from Herodotus, since the tales in the *History* are much freer and varied in their form. Nevertheless, Xenophon may well have been influenced by the sheer quantity and diversity of tales in Herodotus and could have learnt from that work how such dramatic stories serve to enliven long narrative stretches. The brief and restrained presentation of the novellas of the *Cyropaedia*—interrupted, at times, by highly emotional moments—may also be due in part to Herodotus.

What of the content of Herodotus' *History*? If we look for traces or forerunners of Panthea in Herodotus, we find that the two types of women who feature in Ctesias—bold and intelligent warrior queens and cruel, strong-minded females who plot behind the scenes—are also present in the pages of the *History*.[87] Women of the first type include Semiramis, the Babylonian queen Nitocris, the Egyptian queen Nitocris, and the Amazons.[88] Tomyris, queen of the Massagetae, who defeats Cyrus on the battlefield and mutilates his body, and Artemisia, ruler of Halicarnassus and the only 'man' among Xerxes' advisers, are the two most outstanding examples of warrior queens.[89] Among the domestic but scheming figures we find Candaules' wife, Cassandane (mother of Cambyses), Eryxo (wife of Arcesilaus II), and Pheretime (mother of Arcesilaus III).[90] Atossa,

[85] Hdt. 7. 27–9, 38–9, 1. 23–4, 2. 121, 5. 92, 6. 86.

[86] Hdt. 1. 8–12, 5. 18–21. Heni 1976: 136–51 analyses the novella dialogues in Herodotus; he argues (138 n. 44, cf. p. 15) that Herodotus presents a novella entirely in oratio obliqua when the events narrated are more important than the story's characters. Other scholars think that Herodotus uses indirect speech as a means to distance himself from a tale and disclaim any responsibility for it—see Waters 1985: 69–70 and cf. Aly 1921: 241.

[87] Flory 1987: 42–6 notes the importance of the motif of the 'clever, vengeful queen' in Herodotus and discusses both types of women under this heading.

[88] Cf. Hdt. 1. 184, 1. 185–7, 2. 100, 4. 110–17.

[89] Tomyris: Hdt. 1. 205–14; Artemisia: 7. 99, 8. 68, 87–8, 93, 101–2.

[90] Candaules' wife: 1. 8–12; Cassandane: 3. 2–3; Eryxo: 4. 160; Pheretime: 4. 162, 165, 202, 205.

with her famous bedroom discussion with Darius, and Xerxes' cruel wife Amestris are the two most notable women in this group.[91] As in Ctesias (and Xenophon too, of course), there are several women who arouse strong passions in men: such are Ariston's third wife, Perkalos, and Cambyses' sister-wife.[92] At times these emotions lead to fatal consequences, as with Candaules' wife and the wife (and daughter) of Masistes.[93] Women in Herodotus are, then, objects of desire, but there is no romantic love story in the *History* along the lines of Panthea and Abradatas. The two most devoted couples described in Herodotus are Cyrus' adoptive parents—the herdsman Mithridates and his wife Cyno—and Amasis and Ladice. At first, we are told, Amasis has difficulties with his Greek wife but he grows to love her.[94] Such affection is not, however, equal to Panthea's passionate attachment to her husband.

Herodotus has a wide range of female characters, much wider than the two basic types of woman found in Ctesias.[95] There are several positive figures, good women, such as Gorgo, daughter of Cleomenes and wife of Leonidas, who is both virtuous and clever, and Polycrates' daughter, who prefers spinsterhood to losing her father.[96] Other women, while not quite as noble, serve as their husbands' companions (Harpagus' wife, Ladice, wife of Amasis) and advisers (Cyrus' foster mother, Sesostris' wife).[97] Yet others reprove (Cambyses' sister-wife), appease (Periander's daughter), assist (Otanes' daughter Phaidime), or save the very lives of (Intaphrenes' wife, Labda, mother of Cypselus) their menfolk.[98] While several women may have contributed to the fashioning of Panthea—the virtuous Gorgo, beautiful Rhodopis, coveted Perkalos (and wife of Ariston), distressed daughter of Hegetorides, militant Atossa, and widowed, suicidal Nitocris all come to mind—it is clear that the lady of Susa is a

---

[91] Atossa: 3. 133–4; cf. 7. 2–3. Amestris: 7. 114, 9. 110–12.

[92] Cf. Hdt. 6. 61–3, 6. 65, 3. 31–2.

[93] 1. 8–12, 9. 108–13.

[94] 2. 181 κάρτα μιν ἔστερξε; cf. the description of Mithridates and Cyno: ἦσαν δὲ ἐν φροντίδι ἀμφότεροι ἀλλήλων πέρι (1. 111). The childless Anaxandrides (5. 39–40) and Xerxes' brother, Masistes (9. 111), are also loyal and devoted husbands. Trenkner 1958: 24–5 sees the absence of love stories as the 'particular difference between Herodotus and romantic historiography'.

[95] For two good, brief surveys of women in Herodotus see Waters 1985: 128–30 and Gould 1989: 129–32; Dewald 1981 is a more detailed study.

[96] Hdt. 5. 51 and 7. 239, 3. 124.

[97] Hdt. 1. 109, 2. 181, 1. 111–12, 2. 107. (The advice given by Sesostris' wife is, of course, far from noble.)

[98] Hdt. 3. 32, 3. 53, 3. 68–9, 3. 119, 5. 92.

unique figure in her own right and is not simply a composite figure
borrowed from Herodotus' heroines.

We have seen that eunuchs feature in two of the novellas of the
Cyropaedia and that they are virtually omnipresent in Ctesias, but
such men are rarely found in Herodotus. Eunuchs are mentioned
several times in an offhand way, when they perform errands or act as
escorts or bodyguards; one steals his master's fortune.[99] The only
eunuch who is allotted any real role in Herodotus is Hermotimus,
Xerxes' chief eunuch, who, like Gadatas, has his revenge upon the
man who castrated him.[100] On the whole, eunuchs are at best minor
figures in Herodotus, and it seems unlikely that Gadatas or Panthea's
eunuchs are drawn from the *History*.

The bereaved Gobryas, on the other hand, whose son dies tragically at the hands of the young Assyrian king, does have several
counterparts in Herodotus. Astyages arranges a terrible end for
Harpagus' son, punishing father and son alike, while Prexaspes, a
leading Persian noble, watches his son being shot through the heart
by the mad Cambyses and is made to applaud the despot's marks-
manship. The Lydian Pythius, who infuriates Xerxes by his request
to have his eldest son released from the army, sees his child cut in
half, and Darius deals with a similar petition in equally cruel fashion,
killing all three of Oeobazus' sons. Psammenitus, king of Egypt, is
forced by Cambyses to witness the spectacle of his bridled and
trussed son being led to his death, for a reprieve comes too late to save
the boy. Herodotus' Croesus is another bereaved father whose son
dies tragically, even if not at the hands of a tyrant.[101] Herodotus also
tells of several bereaved wives, mothers, and sisters, and these female
figures—Tomyris, Nitocris the Egyptian queen, Eryxo, and Pheretime—are generally more vengeful than their male counterparts and
manage to punish the assassins.[102] In any event, Gobryas, who lost
his son because of the whims of a ruler, is reminiscent of several
figures in Herodotus.

Cruel, capricious despots along the lines of the young Assyrian
king of the *Cyropaedia* are not, of course, lacking in the pages of
Herodotus. Mad Cambyses—whose deeds include torturing the
embalmed body of Amasis, wounding the Apis calf, murdering his

---

[99] Hdt. 1. 117, 3. 4, 3. 77, 78, 4. 43; cf. 7. 187.
[100] Hdt. 8. 104–6; cf. below, sect. 3.
[101] Hdt. 1. 118–19, 3. 34–5, 7. 38–9, 4. 84, 3. 14–15, 1. 34–45.
[102] Cf. Hdt. 1. 213–14, 2. 100, 4. 160, 4. 162–7, 200, 202.

brother Smerdis, marrying two of his sisters and subsequently kill-ing one, shooting down Prexaspes' son in order to demonstrate his sobriety, attempting to kill Croesus, and burning up temple images—is the most oustanding example.[103] Cambyses is like the young Assyrian ruler in that he is unrelievedly bad (except for his final, penitent speech at 3. 65–6). Xerxes is a more complex charac-ter, but he too can be unaccountably harsh, as he is with Pythius, for example, and he rather arbitrarily cuts off a great many heads—including those of the dead Leonidas, the slandering Phoenicians, and the ship's captain who brings him safely to shore at the cost of others' lives.[104] The Persian ruler seems at his most unbridled in his passion, first for his brother's wife and then for her daughter, and in his subsequent arrogant behaviour towards Masistes (9. 108–13). Astyages is another ruler who can be cruel and vindictive, as can be seen from his original intention to kill his grandson Cyrus and his revenge upon the disobedient Harpagus.[105] There are several other harsh tyrants in the *History*, such as Periander and Polycrates, and Xenophon's young Assyrian king would not feel out of place among them. Such figures were not, of course, 'invented' by Hero-dotus, and Xenophon need not have turned to the Halicarnassian (or to Ctesias for that matter) for inspiration when drawing the portrait of his arrogant despot: the cruel king is a well-established type.

In summing up the possible influence of Herodotus on the novellas of the *Cyropaedia* we can single out one novella, the story of Croesus, which seems to have been written with Herodotus in mind. The other tales of the *Cyropaedia* include several favourite Herodotean themes and characters—e.g. cruel and capricious despots, bereaved fathers, and lively, influential women—but Xenophon's stories are more than variations on Herodotus' themes and include many original elements. The means used by Xenophon to present his novellas in the *Cyropaedia* do not stem from Herodotus, who narrates his stories in a wide variety of ways. Perhaps the chief influence of Herodotus on the tales of the *Cyropaedia* is their very inclusion in the work: Xenophon may have decided to introduce novellas into the *Cyropaedia* in the wake of Herodotus' novella-filled *History*.

Xanthus of Lydia is another predecessor of Xenophon who

---

[103] Hdt. 3. 16, 27–9, 30, 31–2, 34–5, 36, 37.
[104] Hdt. 7. 38–9, 7. 238, 8. 90, 8. 118.
[105] Hdt. 1. 108, 1. 117–19.

apparently included novellas in his semi-historical work.[106] In his
Lydiaca Xanthus seems to have included many sensational and
improbable stories, telling, for example, of a gluttonous king who ate
his own wife, of Amazons who blinded their male children, and of
female eunuchs.[107] He also includes tales of love and intrigue,[108] but
his two most romantic stories have survived only indirectly as fragments of Nicolaus of Damascus' universal history (*FGrH* 90 F 44, F
47). Scholars are divided in their views as to how faithfully Nicolaus
reproduces the original Xanthus, but it is generally agreed that the
core of these two stories comes from the *Lydiaca*.[109] While we do not
know if Xenophon in fact read or made use of Xanthus' original
work, it is none the less interesting to observe how much these two
(somewhat sensational)[110] Lydian tales have in common with the
novellas of the *Cyropaedia*. Thus Adyattes, the young Lydian prince,
kills Dascylus (the grandfather of Gyges) because he is jealous of his
father's high regard for him (*FGrH* 90 F 44. 11), reminding us both of
the Assyrian prince and of the Armenian king in the *Cyropaedia*.
Gyges of the *Lydiaca* is somewhat like the Mede Araspas, for he too
falls in love with the woman he is meant to be guarding for another;
in this case she is the king's bride (90 F 47. 6–7, 11). In these two
fragments (90 F 44 and F 47) Xanthus tells of several other romantic
involvements, including those of Damonno and Spermus, Kerses and
Ardy's daughter, and Gyges and the king's chambermaid;[111] all these
entanglements have political implications or consequences, as with
Araspas, Panthea, and Abradatas in the *Cyropaedia*. It is impossible to

---

[106] In discussions of the novella, particularly the early Ionian novella, the name of
Charon of Lampsacus is almost always coupled with that of Xanthus. See e.g.
Hausrath 1914: 443–4; Cataudella 1957: 46–7; Trenkner 1958: 24–5; Aly 1921: 215–
25. Charon is not discussed here because the novellas found in the fragments of his
work (*FGrH* 262 F 1, F 7, F 12, F 17) do not resemble the stories in Xenophon. In the
Cyr. we do not find such stratagems as that of having the enemy's horses dance to the
flute (F 1), or simply getting the other side intoxicated (F 17). Similarly, the women in
Charon—Lampsace (F 7) and the nymph (F 12)—are not at all like Panthea.

[107] *FGrH* 765 F 18 (cf. 90 F 22), 765 F 22, F 4a–b.

[108] See 765 F 8 and F 20, his version of Niobe's misfortunes.

[109] Jacoby on *FGrH* 90 F 1–102 (iic. 233–4) and Pearson 1939: 122–3 are strong
proponents of the view that these fragments of Nicolaus come directly from Xanthus'
work. Diller 1956 thinks that 90 F 44 and F 47 have undergone Hellenistic revision and
elaboration, but finds in the fragments many traces of the original *Lydiaca*, while von
Fritz 1967: 348–77, who argues that there was an intermediary Hellenistic influence at
work between Xanthus and Nicolaus, is willing to concede that Xanthus originally
included 'anekdotenhafte Erzählungen' in his work (376–7).

[110] See e.g. the plethora of amputated heads, wooden and real, in 90 F 44.

[111] Cf. 90 F 44. 2–3, F 44. 5, F 47. 8.

show that Xenophon was directly influenced by Xanthus, since we have no clear picture of what the *Lydiaca* was like. We do not even know, for example, if the passages of direct speech and dialogues found in the Nicolaus fragments—there is no direct speech in Xanthus' own *Lydiaca* fragments—were in the original work.[112] All we can say with any certainty is that Xanthus wrote colourful stories which were set against an Oriental background and linked to a historical narrative, before Xenophon wrote the *Cyropaedia*.[113]

This brief survey of novellas in historians who preceded Xenophon shows that the author of the *Cyropaedia* was following in the wake of others when he included in his allegedly historical narrative picturesque and dramatic tales, set in an Oriental milieu. Xenophon's dramatic stories and characters are similar to those found in Herodotus and Ctesias, but include many original elements which are more than variations upon extant novellas. Our author is, perhaps, even more original in the way he presents these tales: their episodic structure, numerous dialogues, and strong links with the main plot make them unique, even in relation to other works by Xenophon himself.

2. PANTHEA: THE FAIREST WOMAN IN ASIA

Panthea, the fairest woman in Asia, is the key figure in the longest and most famous story of the *Cyropaedia*. Her tale is the one episode in Xenophon's writings which, more than any other, led later Greek novelists to adopt the name 'Xenophon'.[114] We first hear of Panthea when we are told that the lady of Susa is included in the booty set aside for Cyrus after his first victory over the Assyrians (*Cyr.* 4. 6. 11). A fuller description of Panthea's background, circumstances, and appearance comes almost immediately afterwards, when Cyrus summons his childhood friend from Media, Araspas, and asks him to guard the fair prisoner for him (5. 1. 2 ff.). This is our first real

---

[112] See 90 F 44. 6, 9, F 47. 13, 14 vs. 765 F 1–F 30 and cf. n. 53 above. Here too Wacholder 1962: 68–9 argues that Nicolaus is responsible for the dialogues, while Biltcliffe 1969: 93 n. 32 plumps for Xanthus.

[113] The exact date of Xanthus' *Lydiaca* is debated by scholars (in relation to its supposed influence on Herodotus' work), but there is little doubt that Xanthus was a contemporary of Herodotus—see e.g. von Fritz 1967: 72 n. 49 and Drews 1973: 100.

[114] 'As though nineteenth-century English novelists had habitually signed their works "Richardson"': Heiserman 1977: 7; cf. Perry 1967: 167.

acquaintance with the Mede Araspas, and Xenophon identifies him[115] as the friend to whom young Cyrus presented his Median robe when he returned to Persia: this gift of the princely robe indicates that Araspas was Cyrus' best friend in Media (1. 4. 26).[116] Cyrus' grandfather, Astyages, later confiscates the robe and sends it (along with the other gifts that young Cyrus has presented) to his grandson in Persia. Cyrus reprimands his grandfather and insists that the presents be returned to their recipients. Thus the Persian ruler, even as a child, demonstrates that he is a zealous guardian of the property of others, but Araspas, as we shall see, has not taken to heart the lesson to be learnt from this childhood incident.

Xenophon tells us at the outset that Panthea's husband, Abradatas of Susa, was away on a diplomatic mission when the Assyrian camp was captured. His departure reminds us of Tigranes' absence during the military confrontation between Cyrus and the Armenians. Both Tigranes and Abradatas are noble, brave men who become allies of the Persian leader: since Xenophon cannot allow them at first to fight on behalf of their fellow countrymen against Cyrus, he simply removes them from the scene.

Araspas, summoned by Cyrus, is surprised to learn that the Persian ruler has not actually seen his beautiful captive, and the Mede now describes his first meeting with Panthea in an exceptionally vivid way. Panthea, we learn, is surrounded throughout this encounter by her maids. These loyal women first sit round her on the ground, and when she is ordered to stand they too rise. When Panthea wails, they immediately join in her cries. Perhaps Panthea tries to lose herself among her servants, for not only is she encircled by them, but she also dresses in clothing like theirs. None the less, the lady of Susa is conspicuous because of her stature, nobility, and

---

[115] See Tatum 1989: 164–5, 175–7 (and the nn. on 265–6) for the way Xenophon, as narrator, names his characters.

[116] This tale of a robe is one of several involving the presentation of clothing found in the *Cyr.*: see 1. 3. 3, 2. 4. 5–6, 8. 3. 3–4, 7–8; cf. 1. 3. 17. Robes were, of course, a favourite gift of Persian kings—cf. *Cyr.* 8. 2. 8, 8. 5. 18; *Anab.* 1. 2. 27; Hdt. 3. 22—and this may be why they feature so often in the pages of the *Cyr.* An additional explanation is that the Persians thought that a certain mystique or power was attached to clothing which came from the king, with the royal robes symbolizing the authority of the king himself: Herodotus' tales of Darius and Syloson's flame-coloured cloak (Hdt. 3. 139–40), Artabanus' donning of Xerxes' royal attire (7. 15–16), and Artaynte's disastrous request for Xerxes' robe (9. 109 ff.) all seem to support this view. See also Plut. *Artax.* 5. 2; Esther 6: 8, and cf. Sancisi-Weerdenburg 1980: 170–1, 1983: 28–9; Knauth 1975: 194.

elegance, and her appearance and every movement are carefully described by Araspas. The Mede tells Cyrus of her downcast expression while sitting on the ground, of the tears trickling down her dress and to her feet (poetically described as τὰ δάκρυα στάζοντα, 5. 1. 5), and of her cries and rending of her garments when she learns that she is intended for Cyrus. Panthea does not speak at all in this scene, but her actions are, in fact, more eloquent than any words would be. Araspas concludes his description by telling Cyrus that when Panthea tears her clothes in grief her lovely face, neck, and arms are suddenly revealed, and all those present are struck by her incomparable beauty: μήπω φῦναι μηδὲ γενέσθαι γυνὴ ἀπὸ θνητῶν τοιαύτη ἐν τῇ Ἀσίᾳ (5. 1. 7). This last comment by Araspas seems insensitive, for he notices Panthea's beauty rather than her distress, and one wonders if Xenophon means him to be so.[117]

In this introductory scene Panthea reminds us of a Homeric heroine, Penelope. Indeed, the very word δμωαί, used along with θεράπαιναι and δοῦλαι to describe Panthea's female attendants, seems to have Homeric overtones.[118] (We shall see that Panthea has a large retinue of servants, including eunuchs, male and female attendants, and a nurse, and in each episode of her novella Xenophon mentions those servants who best suit the occasion.) Penelope is another loyal wife who is separated from her husband and, like Panthea, she too is tall and beautiful (cf. e.g. *Od.* 18. 248–51).[119] Penelope also has no desire to beautify herself when her husband is away (*Od.* 18. 171–81) and she too can be found sitting low on the ground, in tears, and surrounded by loyal maids (*Od.* 4. 716–20).

In Herodotus we find another beautiful prisoner of war, the unnamed daughter of Hegetorides of Cos, who flees from the Persians at the battle of Plataea (Hdt. 9. 76), and it is interesting to contrast her behaviour with that of the modest Panthea. Hegetorides' daughter, who was but recently the mistress of a leading Persian noble, is also surrounded by a retinue of maids, but she dresses herself and her attendants with great care before approaching

---

[117] Philostratus, in his description of a painting of Panthea at her suicide (*Imag.* 2. 9. 5), has a similar touch: Panthea's pain, he says, does not cause her to become less beautiful and she lacerates her throat without disfiguring it.

[118] The poetic word δμωαί appears only here (5. 1. 6) in Xenophon; see Gautier 1911: 92 on 'le style . . . animé' and Homeric echoes of this passage.

[119] On the Greeks' equating stature with beauty see e.g. Hdt. 1. 60. 4 and the references collected by L. Breitenbach in his note on *Cyr.* 5. 1. 5; see also *Od.* 6. 107–8 and Stanford's note ad loc.

Pausanias.[120] The daughter of Hegetorides pleads her cause elo-
quently, while Panthea does not utter a word to her captors. Both
women receive the same encouragement from the men who now
hold their lives in the balance—γύναι, θάρσει (Hdt. 9. 76. 3), θάρρει,
ὦ γύναι (*Cyr.* 5. 1. 6)—but the daughter of Hegetorides is permitted
to go where she likes, while Panthea now belongs to Cyrus.[121]

Our first introduction to the fair lady of Susa resembles, even fore-
shadows, our last sight of her, at Abradatas' grave (7. 3. 2–16). In
both instances we find Panthea sitting in mourning on the ground
(5. 1. 4 χαμαὶ ... ἐκάθητο; 7. 3. 8 χαμαὶ καθημένην; cf. 7. 3. 5
κάθηται χαμαί). She is surrounded by faithful servants in both scenes
(5. 1. 4–6, 7. 3. 5, 14), but her husband is unavailable and she is in
great distress, crying and wailing (5. 1. 6 and 7. 3. 9 ἀνωδύρατο). In
our episode Panthea is at first veiled (5. 1. 4 κεκαλυμμένη) and in her
final appearance she is, in the end, covered once again—wrapped in
the same shroud as her husband (cf. 7. 3. 14 περικαλύψαι ... ἐνὶ
ἱματίῳ). One difference between the two scenes is that in the first
Panthea is silent, while in the second she addresses Cyrus, speaking
with much bitterness. So too in the final episode Panthea is the one to
encourage Cyrus, telling him, with great irony, ἀλλὰ θάρρει ... ὦ
Κῦρε (7. 3. 13), rather than being reassured (cf. 5. 1. 6 θάρρει, ὦ
γύναι) herself. None the less, in many ways Panthea's first appearance in the *Cyropaedia* anticipates—or mirrors—her final one.

Araspas urges Cyrus to go and see the fairest woman in Asia for
himself and is very surprised to discover that the Persian leader is not
interested in doing so. Cyrus explains that he is afraid that once he
sees Panthea he will be unable to resist returning again and again, and
thus will be led to neglect his duties. The Mede and Persian now
turn to a discussion of the workings of love; their ἐρωτικὸς λόγος—
which is continued at their next meeting—is unusual in being occa-
sioned by a woman. In the *Memorabilia* Socrates is also told by a
friend of a woman who is beautiful beyond words, Theodote. Unlike
Cyrus, he rushes off to see her at once, even though he too is aware of
the danger of being tempted to visit again and again (*Mem.* 3. 11. 1–
3). Socrates is, however, well able to withstand the charms of the
courtesan Theodote (cf. *Mem.* 3. 11. 15–18) and seems to take the

[120] Contrast Hdt. 9. 76. 1 with *Cyr.* 5. 1. 4–5.
[121] Panthea's combination of beauty and modesty also brings to mind another
'woman' found in Xenophon's writings—Arete, who meets Heracles at the crossroads
(*Mem.* 2. 1. 22).

dangers of passion seriously only when it comes to relations between men. Elsewhere in the *Memorabilia* Socrates warns Xenophon (no less!) of the pitfalls of love, after he learns that Critobulus has kissed Alcibiades' handsome son. He also reprimands Critias for his unseemly pursuit of Euthydemus and warns Critobulus that he must be discriminating in his advances towards young men.[122] In the *Symposium* Critobulus is aroused by Cleinias' beauty and speaks of the effects of love (*Symp.* 4. 10–22; cf. 23–8), and Socrates' long speech on love at the party (8. 1 ff.) is, in essence, meant to guide Callias in his relationship with young Autolycus. In other writers too talk of ἔρως usually concerns relationships between males: this is true of the speakers in Plato's *Symposium* and the speech by 'Lysias' in the *Phaedrus*.[123] In Aeschines' dialogue *Aspasia*, however, it is a discussion of Aspasia's talents which leads Socrates to reflect upon the whys and wherefores of love; we have already seen that Aeschines also included in this work the tales of two beautiful and influential Oriental women, Thargelia and Rhodogyne. Xenophon, in any event, changes the usual sex of the subject of these speeches when he has the lovely Panthea set off an ἐρωτικὸς λόγος.[124] This deviation seems deliberate: Artabazus, Cyrus' would-be wooer,[125] could easily have fulfilled the same function of introducing a discussion of the dangers of love, if his author so chose.

In the course of Araspas' debate with Cyrus on love, Xenophon repeatedly refers to the Mede as ὁ νεανίσκος (*Cyr.* 5. 1. 8, 9, 13, 18), even though he is Cyrus' childhood friend and presumably roughly the same age as the Persian leader. The word is meant to characterize Araspas and take the sting out of his future actions. Araspas is impetuous and inexperienced, Xenophon warns us, and it is only to be expected that he will later yield to temptation. The Mede, in any event, argues here that beauty is not an irresistible force since it does not affect everyone equally, the way that fire does. Araspas is, of

---

[122] *Mem.* 1. 3. 8–13, 1. 2. 29–30, 2. 6. 28 ff.

[123] See Lasserre 1944 for a survey of early ἐρωτικοὶ λόγοι. All we know of many of these early works is their title and author—e.g. a περὶ ἔρωτος by Simon the Cobbler (D.L. 2. 122) and by Simmias (D.L. 2. 124), a dialogue Ἐρωτικόν by Euclides (D.L. 2. 108), and a work entitled περὶ φύσεως ἔρωτος ἢ ἀρετῶν by Critias (DK 88 B 42). It is difficult to judge, but it seems that only Antisthenes' work περὶ παιδοποιίας ἢ περὶ γάμου ἐρωτικός (D.L. 6. 15; cf. frr. 114, 115 Caizzi) discussed women as well. Cf. Gigon 1953: 116–17.

[124] And even here Araspas and Cyrus use masculine (rather than feminine or mixed) terms when discussing erotic love—cf. Due 1989: 40.

[125] *Cyr.* 1. 4. 27–8; cf. 8. 4. 26–7, etc.

course, playing with fire, and later on Cyrus takes up the Mede's analogy, contending that gazing upon beautiful people is as fraught with danger as touching fire. The effects may not be felt immediately, but one is bound to be burnt in the end (5. 1. 16 αἴθεσθαι τῷ ἔρωτι). There are two similar comparisons between being in love and coming into contact with fire—upholding Cyrus', rather than Araspas', view of the matter—elsewhere in Xenophon. Socrates thinks that Critobulus, by kissing a handsome lad, is being more daring than if he were to jump into fire (*Mem.* 1. 3. 9), while Critobulus himself, whom Socrates describes as burning with passion,[126] is ready to walk through fire with his beloved Cleinias (*Symp.* 4. 16). In Plato, Socrates caught fire (*Charm.* 155 D ἐφλεγόμην) when he glanced inside Charmides' cloak, and he is reminded of a poet's warning to beware of beautiful boys.

Araspas goes on to argue that love is a matter of choice, as the avoidance of matches between brothers and sisters or fathers and daughters shows. One cannot pass a law against feeling hunger and thirst or heat and cold, but fear and law (5. 1. 10 φόβος καὶ νόμος) are sufficient to prevent incest. Here the young Mede Araspas is, of course, using very Greek arguments, not only bringing in the familiar *nomos–physis* antithesis,[127] but also using the outlawing of incest as an illustration of his point. While Greeks may have abhorred incest, Persians supposedly did not, and Xenophon seems to have forgotten for a moment that his interlocutors are not two Athenians, but a Mede and a Persian.[128]

Cyrus replies that if love were indeed a matter of volition, people should be able to stop loving at will. Instead, lovers are bound to those whom they love in chains stronger than iron, and are virtually enslaved. Although they often cry out in pain, they are unable to free themselves from the sickness, and in fact do not wish to escape (5. 1. 12). The Persian leader's analysis of the behaviour of lovers is very like discussions of ἔρως by both Xenophon and Socrates in the *Memorabilia* (1. 2. 22–3, 1. 3. 11), while his com-

[126] *Symp.* 4. 23 ἰσχυρῶς προσεκαύθη; cf. the description of a kiss as ὑπέκκαυμα at 4. 25.

[127] Cf. πέφυκε (5. 1. 10), πεφύκασι (5. 1. 11), and νόμος (5. 1. 10, 11).

[128] For the Greek attitude to incest see Eur. *And.* 173–6; Pl. *Laws* 838A–B; cf. *Mem.* 4. 4. 19–23. Persian attitude: Hdt. 3. 31 (vs. 1. 135); *FGrH* 765 F 31 (Xanthus); *FGrH* 688 F 44 (Ctesias); Δισσοὶ Λόγοι 2. 15; Antisthenes fr. 29 Caizzi. The Zoroastrian practice of next-of-kin marriage should also be noted in this context, although scholars disagree as to how widespread the custom was: see Boyce 1982: 75–7; Hornblower 1982: 360–1; Frye 1984: 97.

parison of love to an illness is an analogy regularly found in ἐρωτικοὶ λόγοι.[129]

Araspas counters Cyrus' arguments by roundly condemning
such lovers as wretched creatures. These lovers, he states, could
solve their difficulties by committing suicide, but turn instead to
stealing and do not respect the property of others. Cyrus, the Mede
adds, would be the first to condemn and punish such thieves. Good
people, while they may hanker after gold, horses, and beautiful
women, do not touch these things out of turn, and Araspas himself
is, he claims, living proof of this. Although he has seen Panthea and
certainly appreciates her beauty, he continues with his life as usual.
Araspas' vehement speech here is meant, of course, to underline his
subsequent downfall. The transition from besotted lovers to those
who take the belongings of others is most intelligible if it refers to
Araspas himself, for the Mede becomes obsessed by love for a
woman who belongs to another man—or actually to two other
men, Cyrus and Abradatas. Araspas, when faced with this moral
dilemma, does not choose to kill himself, and his statement that
Cyrus would be the first to chastise a thief is equally misguided, as
he himself later realizes.[130] The fact that young Araspas rashly
boasts here of his own invulnerability makes his later change of
heart all the more poignant.

Cyrus advises Araspas to avoid Panthea as he would a fire, and
he particularly warns him against gazing upon the lovely woman of
Susa for too long (5. 1. 16). In the *Memorabilia*, when Socrates warns
Xenophon of the dangers of love (*Mem.* 1. 3. 8 ff.) he compares
handsome people to scorpions, for both sting people and both are
capable of inducing madness. Scorpions must actually touch their
victims in order to do harm, adds Socrates, while good-looking
people can do damage from afar just by being looked upon (1. 3. 13
πάνυ πρόσωθεν; cf. *Cyr.* 5. 1. 16 τοὺς ἄπωθεν θεωμένους). The
Greeks seem to have believed that emanations—sometimes thought
of as shafts or missiles of love—were emitted from a (beautiful) person
and entered the observer's heart through his eyes, causing him to fall
in love.[131] This is probably why both Cyrus and Socrates

---

[129] Cf. Gorgias, *Helen* 19; Pl. *Phaedr.* 231 D; *Symp.* 207 A; Antisthenes fr. 109 Caizzi;
and see Lasserre 1944: 175–8 for further references to this topos.

[130] Contrast *Cyr.* 5. 1. 13 with 6. 1. 37.

[131] See e.g. Aes. *Ag.* 742; Eur. *Hipp.* 525–6; Gorgias, *Helen* 15–19; Pl. *Phaedr.*
251 B; cf. Hesychius s.v. ὀμμάτειος πόθος: διὰ τὸ ἐκ τοῦ ὁρᾶν ἁλίσκεσθαι ἔρωτι. See
too Thomson's note on Aes. *PV* 614–15 (= 590–1 in the usual numbering) and

advise so strongly against looking at beautiful people for long periods of time: ὄψις is bound to lead to love.

Araspas reassures Cyrus that he would not do anything wrong even if he should gaze at Panthea without pause, and the Persian compliments him, perhaps ironically, on his good intentions. He asks Araspas to take good care of the lady of Susa, for she may come in handy (ἐν καιρῷ) later on: Cyrus' ultimate interest in Panthea is the possible benefit or use that can be derived from her capture, and this is characteristic of the hero of the *Cyropaedia*.[132] His circumspect behaviour towards Panthea is not only the result of a Socrates-like moderation in sexual matters that is only to be expected from one of Xenophon's didactic figures,[133] but also stems from calculations of potential military or political advantage. Araspas has grouped beautiful women together with money and fine horses (with the women in third place): in other words, he has classified them as useful, as well as desirable, possessions. This is in fact Cyrus' view of Panthea: she is to be used, not sexually, but for other purposes. As we have already seen in relation both to Sambaulas and his ugly friend, and Cyrus and Artabazus, beauty and physical attraction take second place to utility in the *Cyropaedia*.[134]

Cyrus' request that Araspas guard Panthea carefully concludes their conversation, and immediately afterwards Xenophon tells us how the Mede, despite his protestations, falls in love.[135] Xenophon describes the process in one very long sentence, where the various factors at work (ἅμα μὲν . . . ἅμα δὲ . . . ἅμα δὲ . . . ἅμα δὲ . . .)[136] are shown to lead up to an unsurprising end result (5. 1. 18 ἐκ πάντων τούτων ἡλίσκετο ἔρωτι). Araspas becomes enamoured of Panthea not only because of her superior looks and character, but also because of her friendly, concerned attitude towards him: she

Pearson 1909: 256–7. This notion may be related to Empedocles' theory of effluences (ἀπορροαί) and sense-perception—see de Vries on Pl. *Phaedr.* 251 B; Bluck on *Meno* 76 C–D; Immisch 1927: 20 and 41.

[132] Cf. Tatum 1989: 163 ff.

[133] Cf. e.g. Xenophon's depiction of Agesilaus at *Ages.* 5. 4 ff.

[134] Cf. *Cyr.* 2. 2. 28–31, 4. 1. 22 ff., and above, ch. 3. 3.

[135] Araspas is, it seems, the first of a long series of figures who minimize the power of love only to succumb painfully later on; see Trenkner 1958: 26–7.

[136] This seems to be the only instance where Xenophon has ἅμα μὲν . . . followed by *three* repetitions of ἅμα δὲ . . . See *Cyr.* 2. 3. 19, 23, 6. 1. 24 (and cf. *Hell.* 5. 4. 62) for sentences of the form ἅμα μὲν . . . ἅμα δὲ . . . ἅμα δὲ . . . These sentences too are used to list several complementary factors which hold true at the same time. Xenophon also uses long, complex sentences when describing the downfall of several of his characters: see *Cyr.* 7. 2. 23–4; *Hell.* 6. 4. 31; and Tatum 1989: 48, 157–8, 170.

appreciates his kindness and has her servants attend to his needs, showing particular attention to him when he is ill. The lady of Susa seems to be following some of the advice Socrates has given the courtesan Theodote on the best way to attract suitors (*Mem.* 3. 11. 10–12). Socrates recommends to Theodote to welcome a dedicated admirer warmly, to attend to sick friends carefully, and to repay kindness: Theodote is to behave towards suitors just as Panthea treats Araspas. Socrates is, of course, an expert on matchmaking and love (cf. *Symp.* 3. 10), so that when Panthea acts, as it were, in accordance with his guidelines it is no wonder that the young Mede falls in love with her.

We hear no more of the love-stricken Araspas until Book 6, when Cyrus is looking round for a suitable spy (*Cyr.* 6. 1. 31 ff.). Cyrus is aware of the Mede's plight, for Araspas has threatened to use force against Panthea when he fails to win her over with words. The alarmed Panthea finds it necessary to inform Cyrus of these threats and sends her eunuch with a message to the Persian leader. The eunuch is mentioned here (6. 1. 33) for the first time, and he does seem a more suitable servant to tell tales of intrigue and lust than the maids we have encountered so far. The Persian leader's first reaction to the news is laughter, and we are reminded that earlier Araspas had laughed at Cyrus when he refused to see Panthea.[137] Cyrus does not address Araspas directly, but sends Artabazus to instruct the young Mede that Panthea is not to be forced to act against her own wishes. Artabazus takes Araspas to task severely, reprimanding him for his impiety, sinfulness, and lack of control. Cyrus' choice of representative here is puzzling, for Artabazus, who once pretended to be a relative of Cyrus in order to steal several kisses from him (1. 4. 27–8), is hardly a paragon of sexual rectitude himself. He may have been sent because he was a fellow Mede, or perhaps it is because Araspas' chief sin is not sexual indiscretion but failing to guard properly what was entrusted to him by Cyrus. Panthea is a deposit of a kind (cf. 6. 1. 35 παρακαταθήκην), and perhaps Artabazus spoke to Araspas in the way that Leutychides did when telling the Athenians of Glaucus and the deposit (Hdt. 6. 86). This exchange between the two Medes is one of the most interesting unrecorded conversations in the *Cyropaedia*. At its end Araspas is reduced to tears, ashamed and afraid of Cyrus' reaction. His grief (6. 1. 35 ὥστε ... πολλὰ μὲν δακρύειν ὑπὸ λύπης) shows how correct Cyrus' earlier observations on the behaviour of lovers were (cf. 5. 1. 12 κλαίοντας ὑπὸ λύπης).

[137] 6. 1. 34 ἀναγελάσας; cf. 5. 1. 9 καὶ ὁ νεανίσκος ἀναγελάσας εἶπεν.

Araspas' predicament leads Cyrus to think that the Mede would make an excellent candidate to spy upon the enemy. He invites Araspas to a private tête-à-tête, keeping their talk confidential, it seems, not only out of consideration for the shamefaced Mede but also because of his need to keep the plan secret. Their conversation is in fact a curious blend of two topics: reflections on love and a detailed plan of how Araspas is to spy on the enemy. Cyrus begins their talk by comforting Araspas, telling him that he has heard that the gods themselves have been worsted by love (6. 1. 36 ἔρωτος ἡττῆσθαι), to say nothing of prudent men. The argument (or excuse) that even the gods are unable to resist the power of love, and consequently men should not be blamed for their amorous involvements, is a familiar one.[138] Love is irresistible,[139] and that is why Cyrus himself has kept away from Panthea, following, so to speak, Socrates' advice in the *Memorabilia* that one should avoid passionate involvements if one wishes to behave prudently (*Mem.* 1. 3. 8 σωφρονεῖν). The Persian leader blames himself for exposing Araspas to temptation, and indeed their earlier discussion should have made it clear to Cyrus just how susceptible to Panthea's attractions his friend was. Araspas is most grateful to Cyrus for his forgiving attitude towards his all too human failings (cf. 6. 1. 37 σὺ μὲν ... εἰ ... πρᾷός τε καὶ συγγνώμων τῶν ἀνθρωπίνων ἁμαρτημάτων), and we are reminded of Cyrus' words when he urged Tigranes to forgive his father for having killed his teacher, the sophist: at first Cyrus addressed the Armenian king, saying ἀνθρώπινά μοι δοκεῖς ἁμαρτεῖν, and then turned to Tigranes with the request συγγίγνωσκε τῷ πατρί (3. 1. 40). The Persian leader benefits from the pardon he grants Araspas by being able to send him off as a spy; Tigranes does not derive any similar advantage from forgiving his father.

Araspas tells Cyrus how all the others have made him feel like sinking in shame: his enemies were pleased to learn of his misfortune and even his friends advised him to keep well out of Cyrus' way. It is interesting to note that Araspas has, along with his friends, a stock of

[138] Cf. Aristoph. *Clouds* 1079–82 (where the language is similar to our passage: Zeus is ἥττων ἔρωτος); Eur. *Tro.* 948ff.; Gorgias, *Helen* 19, etc. We have already noted several parallels between Gorgias' *Helen* and discussions of love in the *Cyr.*: these may be due to the fact that both writers make use of commonplaces or topoi on love, but perhaps Xenophon was directly influenced by the sophist here; see Nestle 1940–1: 42–3 (= 1948: 441–3) and cf. Classen 1984: 161–2. For further passages on the power of love see de Romilly 1976; cf. Heinimann 1945: 126–7, 131–2 on love as ἀνάγκη φύσεως.

[139] See *Cyr.* 6. 1. 36 τῷ ἀμάχῳ πράγματι and cf. Soph. *Ant.* 781ff.; Eur. fr. 430 N².

enemies within the Persian camp; normally only the Assyrians are referred to as enemies in the *Cyropaedia*.[140] Araspas' sorry reputation can be put to good use,[141] Cyrus explains, for if the Mede pretends to defect to the enemy, seemingly afraid of Cyrus' anger over Panthea, he will be readily accepted by the Assyrians and their allies. It is likely that Araspas will be made privy to their deliberations, adds the Persian leader, and he will then be able to report back in full detail on the enemy's plans. This ploy of sending a supposed defector—a man who seemingly has good cause to change sides—on an espionage mission is similar to Zopyrus' actions against the Babylonians on behalf of Darius (Hdt. 3. 153–60). In Herodotus Zopyrus, not Darius, is the one to conceive the plan, and he mutilates himself terribly in order to pretend that Darius has injured him, thus providing himself with an excuse for defecting to the Babylonians. None the less, there are several similarities between the two 'defectors': both Zopyrus and Araspas leave the Persian side under a (supposed) cloud in order to be accepted by—and spy upon—the 'Assyrians', both succeed in their espionage efforts while allegedly giving away their own side's secrets, and both are handsomely rewarded and honoured by their leaders.[142]

Araspas readily agrees to spy upon the enemy and Cyrus teasingly asks him if he will be able to leave the fair Panthea behind. The Mede in his reply theorizes once more on the character of love. Araspas explains that he has two souls, a good one and a bad one, rather than one soul which is capable of being both bad and good. He has learnt this from his recent encounter with that unjust sophist, love (6. 1. 41 νῦν τοῦτο πεφιλοσόφηκα μετὰ τοῦ ἀδίκου σοφιστοῦ τοῦ Ἔρωτος),[143] but with Cyrus as his ally Araspas is confident that his good soul will dominate. This passage of the *Cyropaedia* has certain Platonic overtones. In Plato's *Symposium* Socrates, quoting Diotime, describes Eros as φιλοσοφῶν διὰ παντὸς τοῦ βίου δεινὸς γόης καὶ φαρμακεὺς καὶ σοφιστής (203D), while the doctrine of two souls found here reminds commentators of several passages in Plato, even though

---

[140] See Dover 1974: 180ff. on the Greek tendency to take the existence of enemies for granted.

[141] *Cyr.* 6. 1. 38 ἐν καιρῷ; cf. 5. 1. 17.

[142] Hdt. 3. 156–60; *Cyr.* 6. 1. 42, 6. 3. 14–20.

[143] Later Greek novelists also take up this description of love as a σοφιστής; see e.g. Achilles Tatius 1. 10. 1 and cf. Anderson 1982. Araspas terms love an unjust or crooked (ἄδικος) sophist, but he is referring perhaps to the means by which he has been taught rather than the content of the teaching. The term σοφιστής is not in itself pejorative here; cf. Classen 1984: 156.

Plato often describes the soul as tripartite.[144] *Phaedrus* 237 D, a portion of Socrates' first ἐρωτικὸς λόγος, where he serves as a mouthpiece for a wily lover, is perhaps closest in tenor and context to our passage. Socrates, when trying to define love, contrasts the two guiding principles within people—the desire for pleasure and an acquired judgement which aims at what is best (ἐπίκτητος δόξα ἐφιεμένη τοῦ ἀρίστου)—and these two principles correspond, more or less, to Araspas' two souls, ἡ πονηρά and ἡ ἀγαθή (*Cyr.* 6. 1. 41). The doctrine presented here by the Mede, like that of the wily lover in Socrates' speech, is more popular than philosophical.[145]

Cyrus does not respond to Araspas' remarks with any philosophical musings of his own, but turns to some practical advice on how the Mede is to proceed as a spy. Araspas should supply the enemy with misleading information on Persian plans, advise them on military formations, and then return with up-to-date information on their battle strategy (6. 1. 42–3). The conversation between Cyrus and Araspas ends on this pragmatic note and the Mede sets out for the Assyrian camp according to plan, after leaving a false trail behind him: εἰπὼν πρός τινας ἃ ᾤετο συμφέρειν τῷ πράγματι (6. 1. 44) is Xenophon's gentle way of describing this deceit.

When Panthea hears that Araspas has gone,[146] she sends word to Cyrus offering to summon her husband, Abradatas, who will be, she promises, a far more loyal friend than Araspas was. Abradatas, who will bring with him as large a force as possible, will be glad to change sides, Panthea adds, for he has a score to settle with the young Assyrian king. Abradatas was on excellent terms with the old Assyrian ruler, but the new king once tried to separate Panthea and her husband by force. Panthea does not explain why the wanton (6. 1. 45 ὑβριστήν) young man tried to keep them apart, but presumably he had designs on the fair lady. While readers of the *Cyropaedia* may be disappointed not to be given all the details of a scandal which, like the story of Gadatas, deals with sexual jealousy, the fact that Panthea does not elaborate is in keeping with her delicate and circumspect

---

[144] See *Phaedr.* 237 D; *Rep.* 439 D; *Laws* 896 E; and cf. Arist. *Pol.* 1334^b17 ff.

[145] See Hackforth 1952: 41.

[146] Philostratus tells of a much later (2nd cent. AD) work describing Araspas' love for Panthea (*VS* 1. 22. 3). The tale seems to have been scandalous, for its author, Hadrian's secretary Celer, attributed it to an enemy of his, the rhetorician Dionysius of Miletus. Perry 1967: 169 suggests that Xenophon may have whitewashed the characters of Panthea and Araspas and suppressed an earlier, less ethical version of their relationship, but there is no real evidence for this theory.

behaviour. Abradatas, like Gobryas and Gadatas, the heroes of the two following novellas, will transfer his allegiance to Cyrus because he has been mistreated by the brash Assyrian despot; he too had been a loyal subject of the young king's father. Cyrus, apparently answering Panthea through a messenger (for the two do not seem to meet face to face until after Abradatas' death), asks her to send for her husband: his idea that the lady of Susa could prove useful has borne fruit.

Abradatas receives Panthea's summons and, recognizing his wife's σύμβολα, gladly[147] sets off with some thousand cavalrymen to join the Persian leader (6. 1. 46 ff.). This is the first we hear of any σύμβολα, which were, perhaps, tokens serving as proof of Panthea's identity, such as those used by Menelaus and Helen (Eur. *Hel.* 291) or the σήματα of Penelope and Odysseus (*Od.* 23. 108–10).[148] This is, at any rate, another bare allusion, like the brief reference to the provocative behaviour of the young Assyrian king towards Panthea, which Xenophon leaves to the imagination of his reader to fill in. Abradatas, when he reaches the Persian camp, sends word of his arrival to Cyrus, and the Persian leader has him brought at once to his wife. Panthea and Abradatas, reunited, naturally[149] embrace one another and then turn to talk of . . . Cyrus. Xenophon clearly intends the reunion between husband and wife to be a touching scene, describing how the two embrace after they scarcely hoped to meet again, but he is, it seems, even more anxious to extol his hero. No sooner does Panthea meet her husband again than she begins to list the Persian leader's virtues—his piety, self-restraint, and compassion towards her—and Abradatas' first thought too is one of gratitude towards Cyrus, rather than, for instance, concern for his wife. In our next (and final) glimpse of the pair (6. 4. 2–11) we learn a little more about their relationship; while Cyrus is again a topic of conversation between them, he is not the sole subject. Here, in any event, the single-minded concentration on the Persian leader jars: Xenophon has allowed didacticism to prevail over romanticism (or even realism) in this part of his tale.

[147] 6. 1. 46 ἄσμενος; cf. Panthea's prediction to Cyrus ἄσμενος ἂν . . . ἀπαλλαγείη (6. 1. 45).
[148] For σύμβολον as a prearranged token see Denniston on Eur. *El.* 577 and Page on Eur. *Med.* 613. Tuplin 1990: 17 thinks that Xenophon may be alluding here to the Eastern practice of using ciphers.
[149] 6. 1. 47 ὡς εἰκός; see 3. 1. 41 for a like remark by Xenophon on a similar occasion, the reunion of Tigranes and his wife, and cf. 2. 1. 2.

Abradatas leaves Panthea in order to present himself before Cyrus. Taking the Persian's right hand, he offers himself as friend, servant, and ally, and says that he will try to co-operate with Cyrus in any enterprise the latter undertakes. In this first meeting with the Persian leader Abradatas is dignified and displays a certain awareness of his own worth. When his compatriot Gobryas meets Cyrus for the first time in very similar circumstances—upon his defection—he is more humble, addressing the Persian leader as ὦ δέσποτα (4. 6. 2; cf. 5. 4. 42) rather than Abradatas' ὦ Κῦρε (6. 1. 48). Gobryas presents himself as a suppliant (ἱκέτης προσπίπτω), a vassal and ally (4. 6. 2 καὶ δίδωμί σοι ἐμαυτὸν δοῦλον καὶ σύμμαχον), rather than the man of Susa's more dignified friend, servant, and ally (6. 1. 48 φίλον σοι ἐμαυτὸν δίδωμι καὶ θεράποντα καὶ σύμμαχον). Gadatas, the third Assyrian who changes sides, bows down (5. 3. 18 προσκυνήσας) before the Persian leader the first time they meet and later addresses Cyrus as ὦ δέσποτα (5. 3. 28). Earlier Abradatas has been favourably compared to Cyrus in relation to his appearance, judgement, and power (5. 1. 6), so that his attitude towards Cyrus as a grateful, but equal, ally is probably a reflection of his nobility and high standing. The Persian leader accepts Abradatas' offer of an alliance and then sends him off to dine with Panthea. We next encounter the man of Susa fulfilling his promise to aid Cyrus and readying a hundred chariots for the forthcoming battle (6. 1. 50–1).

In the meantime Araspas' plan to infiltrate the enemy's command has, it seems, succeeded, for Cyrus learns from interrogating enemy prisoners that there are three men in charge of drilling the Assyrian forces—Croesus, a Greek,[150] and a Mede, said to be a deserter from the Persian side, i.e. Araspas. Cyrus, upon hearing of the Mede, exclaims 'may I get hold of him as I wish to' (6. 3. 11 ἀλλὰ . . . λαβεῖν μοι γένοιτο αὐτὸν ὡς ἐγὼ βούλομαι), a two-edged remark which Cyrus' men understand properly only shortly thereafter, when Araspas returns to the Persian camp. Cyrus greets Araspas warmly and explains to the others that the Mede did not depart in disgrace, but was sent to spy on the Assyrians. He then questions Araspas about the enemy's numbers and tactical procedures (6. 3. 14–21). The Egyptians, Araspas reports, appear to be the most dangerous opponents, and it is against them that Abradatas volunteers to fight

---

[150] The Greek encountered here is no doubt a fictional counterpart of Phalinus, the Greek military expert who fought at Artaxerxes' side in the *Anab.* (2. 1. 7). See Anderson 1970: 173 and cf. above, ch. 2. 2 at n. 130.

when Cyrus assigns the battle positions (6. 3. 35). Cyrus recommends casting lots for this hazardous post facing the enemy's phalanx and Abradatas wins the position by this method; he is fated, it seems, to undertake this dangerous task.

Cyrus' forces ready themselves for the contest with the Assyrians, and we find Abradatas putting on his armour for the forthcoming battle with Panthea at his side (6. 4. 2 ff.). She presents him with new golden armour which she has secretly fashioned for him, and her husband guesses that the gold has come from her own jewellery. Panthea explains that he is her most precious ornament, especially when he appears to others as he does to her. Panthea is anxious for Abradatas to impress others, and this desire for public recognition and honour, a typical attitude in the *Cyropaedia*, is something that she will return to immediately below. The lady of Susa, when helping her husband put on his new armour, tries to hide the tears falling down her cheeks: λανθάνειν μὲν ἐπειρᾶτο, ἐλείβετο δὲ αὐτῇ τὰ δάκρυα κατὰ τῶν παρειῶν (6. 4. 3) is Xenophon's poetic description.[151] With these two actions—supplying Abradatas with armour and crying at her husband's departure—Panthea brings to mind two different females in Homer: Thetis bringing Achilles the new armour she has had Hephaestus make for him (*Il.* 19. 10 ff.; cf. 18. 136 ff.) and Andromache bidding farewell to Hector (*Il.* 6. 394 ff.). The resemblances—and differences—between Panthea and Andromache are, as we shall see, particularly interesting.[152]

Abradatas, who is, Xenophon tells us, already attractive to begin with, looks handsome and noble in his golden armour (6. 4. 4). Such a lengthy and complimentary description of a character other than Cyrus is unusual in the *Cyropaedia*; Xenophon actually lingers less over Cyrus' own costume for the battle (7. 1. 2). So too in the course of the engagement itself Abradatas' actions—his exhortations to his companions, his swift assault upon the enemy, and his courageous death—are described in full (7. 1. 29–32; cf. 7. 3. 3) and come close to rivalling the amount of narrative devoted to the deeds of the hero of

---

[151] The words λείβω and παρειά are rarely found in prose: see Gautier 1911: 93 and cf. Higgins 1977: 6–7. Xenophon's language here is reminiscent of a passage in the *Odyssey* in which Odysseus is trying to hide his tears. Homer compares him to a widow mourning her fallen husband: δάκρυ δ' ἔδευεν ὑπὸ βλεφάροισι παρειάς ... πάντας ἐλάνθανε δάκρυα λείβων (*Od.* 8. 521–32).

[152] See e.g. Trenkner 1958: 26 and Delebecque's note *ad* 6. 4. 2 ff. in the Budé *Cyr.* for brief references to these Homeric echoes. Valla 1922: 120–1 has a more detailed comparison between Panthea and Andromache.

the *Cyropaedia* on the battlefield. Thus here, as in Homer,[153] a detailed arming scene serves as an indication that the hero will play an important role in the forthcoming fighting. We should remember that Abradatas, in addition to his role as Panthea's husband, is the only one of Cyrus' close friends or allies to be killed in battle, and that is why considerable attention is devoted to his *aristeia*.

When Abradatas is about to mount his chariot, Panthea asks those surrounding them to withdraw and then addresses her spouse (6. 4. 4 ff.). She begins by declaring that she loves Abradatas more than her own life (6. 4. 5 μεῖζον τῆς . . . ψυχῆς), reminding us of another devoted pair in the *Cyropaedia*, Tigranes and his wife: the Armenian prince had been prepared to give his life (3. 1. 36 κἂν τῆς ψυχῆς πριαίμην) to keep his wife from servitude. The lady of Susa tells her husband that she does not need to prove her loyalty to him: her actions are stronger testimony than any words could be. None the less, loving and faithful as Panthea is, her overwhelming concern is that Abradatas should distinguish himself in the coming battle. Panthea states that she would rather be buried with a brave Abradatas than live in shame with an ashamed man. Abradatas and Panthea must demonstrate their gratitude to Cyrus, who has treated the lady of Susa not as his slave or a mistress (ὡς ἐλευθέραν ἐν ἀτίμῳ ὀνόματι is the euphemism used by the delicate Panthea), but as if she were his brother's wife. In addition, Panthea reminds her husband, she has promised the Persian leader that Abradatas will prove a far better and more loyal man than Araspas was (6. 4. 8; cf. 6. 1. 45).

In this farewell scene with her husband Panthea exhorts Abradatas to be courageous and fight bravely. She has asked the others present to depart, not so as to exchange a few last intimacies with her husband—compare Andromache's regrets at *Il.* 24. 744–5—but in order to rouse Abradatas to valiant action on the battlefield. If Panthea's situation—that of a tearful wife parting from her husband, who is going to die in the fighting—is similar to that of Andromache in book 6 of the *Iliad*, her words and outlook are not at all like that of the Homeric heroine. Andromache tries to dissuade Hector from returning to the fighting and thinks only of the disastrous personal consequences for herself and their son Astyanax if he should be killed (*Il.* 6. 405 ff.). It is Hector who, like Panthea, is concerned with the opinion of others. He is anxious to avoid seeming a coward (*Il.* 6. 443 κακός), just as Panthea fears living in shame (*Cyr.* 6. 4. 6 ζῆν μετ'

[153] Cf. Griffin 1980: 19, 36–7.

αἰσχυνομένου αἰσχυνομένη), while Andromache concentrates on her own personal situation. Her wish that she may die too if Hector is killed[154] stems from sorrow and despair, and is not at all like Panthea's vision of sharing Abradatas' heroic end as the greatest good (6. 4. 6 τῶν καλλίστων).[155] Panthea's words here foreshadow, of course, her own death at Abradatas' side, but at the time of her suicide she sees her husband's death in an entirely different light. The lady of Susa may shed tears in this farewell scene, just as Andromache does,[156] but in spirit she is closer to Herodotus' Atossa, who in the seclusion of their bedroom urges Darius to enter into a war in order to demonstrate to the Persians that their ruler is a man (Hdt. 3. 134).[157] Perhaps it is not a coincidence that both Atossa and Panthea, when urging their husbands to fight, are influenced by their feeling of obligation to another man, Democedes and Cyrus respectively. In this scene and in her previous appearance, where she suggested to Cyrus that her husband join the Persian's forces, Panthea seems closest to the scheming Oriental women who appear so often in the pages of Herodotus and Ctesias.

Abradatas is not offended in the least that Panthea finds it necessary to remind him to fight valiantly, even after he has volunteered for—and been allotted—one of the most dangerous battle positions; in fact, he is pleased by her words (6. 4. 9). Placing his hand on Panthea's head and looking upward to heaven, he prays to Zeus to prove a worthy husband to his wife and a worthy friend to Cyrus. Returning for a moment to the parting between Hector and Andromache, we find that Hector too offers a prayer to Zeus (and the other gods), but this concerns his son Astyanax (*Il.* 6. 475–81). The child Astyanax, a (nearly) silent presence at his parents' farewell, is ever uppermost in their thoughts,[158] and in a certain sense Cyrus plays the same role as Astyanax at the final meeting between Abradatas and Panthea. The pair from Susa have Cyrus in mind during much of their conversation and he is almost a silent, third presence at their discussion.

---

[154] *Il.* 6. 410–11; compare Hector's similar petition at 464–5.

[155] Panthea's attitude here may have been influenced by the Spartan tradition of women exhorting their menfolk to valorous deeds.

[156] *Cyr.* 6. 4. 3; *Il.* 6. 405, 484, 496.

[157] See Schaps 1982: 198 for several further instances of Greek women encouraging men to be more warlike. Such stories, states Schaps, are more common than tales of women urging their menfolk not to fight.

[158] Cf. *Il.* 6. 407–8, 432, 466 ff.

Abradatas mounts his chariot and closes the door, and Panthea, with her husband out of reach, embraces the chariot-box and secretly follows as he drives away. Abradatas, turning round, bids Panthea farewell once again and asks her somewhat brusquely to leave: θάρρει, Πάνθεια, καὶ χαῖρε καὶ ἄπιθι ἤδη (6. 4. 10). Panthea's eunuchs and maidservants lead her to her carriage, have her lie down, and hide her from view. The lady of Susa is, presumably, overcome by grief, and one imagines that the eunuchs take care of her carriage's departure while the female servants comfort her. In her reluctance to be parted from her husband Panthea reminds us once again of Andromache, who also has to be dismissed by her husband (Il. 6. 490 ἀλλ' εἰς οἶκον ἰοῦσα τὰ σ' αὐτῆς ἔργα κόμιζε), and is then surrounded by maidservants who share in her grief. Abradatas, who is understandably reluctant to have his wife follow him to the battle-field, speaks more impatiently than Hector does: in the Iliad it is Hector who lingers and delays the final parting.[159] In any event, the ruler of Susa is far more gentle in dismissing Panthea than Sophocles' Ajax is towards Tecmessa, in yet another reminiscence of the Hector–Andromache scene (Soph. Aj. 578 ff.).

Only after the beautiful lady of Susa is out of sight, Xenophon tells us, do onlookers turn to gaze at Abradatas, decked out in his armour (6. 4. 11); this is a final narrative touch in a dialogue full of vivid movement, props, and gestures. The setting of this conversation moves from indoors (probably inside a tent), where Panthea tearfully helps Abradatas don his armour, to outdoors, where the ruler of Susa departs in his chariot. The audience present at this exchange also changes: at first the couple are surrounded by attendants whom Panthea dismisses in order to converse with Abradatas privately, and later, at their final parting outside, eunuchs, maids, and bystanders are again to be found. Only rarely are the settings and actions accompanying conversations in the Cyropaedia more prominent than in the Panthea novella, and this is true of the final scene of the tale as well.

Once Abradatas takes up his allotted spot in the battle line-up, he converses briefly with Cyrus, who encourages him and advises him to go and exhort his men (7. 1. 15–18). Abradatas' actual role in the battle—his valiant attack upon the Egyptian phalanx, the mutilation of his body, and his death together with the loyal few who have fought at his side—is narrated in its proper chronological place, as part of

[159] Il. 6. 515–16; cf. 6. 496, where Andromache is said to turn around frequently (ἐντροπαλιζομένη).

Xenophon's running description of the battle of Thymbrara. We later return to Abradatas' demise, for after the capture of Sardis Cyrus enquires after him and learns from one of his servants that the ruler of Susa has been killed (7. 3. 2 ff.). The servant informs the Persian ruler that Panthea has taken Abradatas' body for burial near the River Pactolus, where a grave is being dug. Panthea, having decked out her husband for burial, is sitting on the ground, clutching her husband's head to her knees (7. 3. 4–6). The information relayed by the servant to Cyrus, in an address somewhat like a messenger speech in tragedy, could have been presented to the reader directly by Xenophon, as part of his narrative.[160] By having a servant tell Cyrus of Abradatas' death, Xenophon makes his reader concentrate on the Persian's reaction, thus building up tension and interest in the forthcoming encounter between Cyrus and Panthea.

Cyrus reacts by hitting his thigh—a gesture indicating vexation and grief[161]—and rushing to the scene of the burial, after leaving instructions for ornaments and sacrificial animals to be brought to the graveside (7. 3. 6–7). The burial accorded to Abradatas seems more Greek than Persian, perhaps because he is an Assyrian. The corpse was, it seems, bathed in the River Pactolus, a pollution which is not in accordance with Persian custom, at least according to Herodotus (1. 138). Abradatas is to be inhumed without being embalmed in wax (cf. Hdt. 1. 140) or exposed to the elements according to the Zoroastrian practice.[162] The sacrifice of animals at the burial site in Abradatas' honour is, apparently, in line with Persian customs, but Xenophon may also have been influenced by the slaughter of sheep and cattle to be found at the funeral rites of Homeric heroes, such as Patroclus and Achilles.[163]

Cyrus finds Panthea sitting on the ground, holding Abradatas' head on her lap (7. 3. 8). This is the customary gesture of the chief mourner at a funeral: Andromache mourns Hector in just this way.[164] Although Xenophon does not mention the fact, this is, it seems, the first time that Cyrus actually sets eyes on Panthea. It is

---

[160] Both the beginning and the end of the servant's speech—the description of Abradatas' death and of Panthea sitting on the ground with her husband's corpse—are in fact narrated again separately (cf. 7. 1. 30, 7. 3. 8).

[161] Cf. e.g. *Il.* 15. 113.

[162] See above, ch. 2. 7 at n. 336.

[163] See Arr. *Anab.* 6. 29. 7; cf. *Il.* 23. 166–7; *Od.* 24. 65–6.

[164] *Il.* 24. 724. For this gesture of holding or touching a dead person's head see Macleod on *Il.* 24. 712.

certainly the first direct exchange between the two recorded in the *Cyropaedia*; perhaps Cyrus does not permit himself to see the fair lady of Susa until she no longer belongs to another man. The Persian leader first sheds tears for the dead Abradatas and then addresses his spirit, ὦ ἀγαθὴ καὶ πιστὴ ψυχή (*Cyr.* 7. 3. 8). Cyrus' choice of adjectives may be meant to echo Panthea's original promise to him that her husband will prove a better and more loyal man (6. 4. 8 ἄνδρα καὶ πιστότερον καὶ ἀμείνονα; cf. 6. 1. 45) than Araspas. Cyrus then clasps Abradatas' hand in a gesture of farewell[165] only to have the hand come away with his own, for Abradatas has been badly mangled by the Egyptians. Panthea, weeping, takes the hand from Cyrus and fits it back into place.

This gruesome incident of Abradatas' severed hand is compared by commentators to the tale of the clever thief in Herodotus, whose detachable arm is seized by Rhampsinitus' daughter (Hdt. 2. 121).[166] A more relevant parallel is the mutilation of Cyrus the Younger at Cunaxa, for he had his head and right arm cut off by Artaxerxes' men.[167] In fact the circumstances of Abradatas' death resemble Cyrus' end in many ways.[168] Both men launch an attack on the enemy's closely formed ranks (*Anab.* 1. 8. 26 τὸ στῖφος; *Cyr.* 7. 1. 30 πολλῷ στίφει, cf. 7. 3. 3), with the aid of only a few close friends (*Anab.* 1. 8. 25 οἱ ὁμοτράπεζοι, 1. 9. 31 οἱ . . . φίλοι καὶ συντράπεζοι; *Cyr.* 7. 1. 30 οἱ . . . ἑταῖροί τε . . . καὶ ὁμοτράπεζοι), for the rest of their forces have rushed off to pursue the enemy (*Anab.* 1. 8. 25; *Cyr.* 7. 1. 30, 7. 3. 3). Both Abradatas and Cyrus the Younger fight valiantly but are killed together with their close companions, and their corpses are, as we have seen, mutilated. Thus the mangling of Abradatas' body, while an unsavoury occurrence, is not in fact far removed from the experience of Xenophon himself. Ctesias, in his full-scale depiction of the death of Cyrus the Younger, also includes a scene in which Parysatis gathers Cyrus' scattered limbs for burial and mourns her son, and this may have influenced

---

[165] Again, this is a customary gesture; cf. *Cyr.* 3. 2. 14 and 8. 7. 28.

[166] Several scholars consider this incident inappropriate and incongruous; see Keller 1911: 257 and Breitenbach 1966: 1718, who thinks that this 'makabre Szene' indicates that Xenophon has adapted the entire Panthea novella from another source.

[167] *Anab.* 1. 10. 1; compare Ctesias' more detailed version, *FGrH* 688 F 16. 64, 66, F 20.

[168] Cf. Tatum 1989: 181–2 with n. 22. Anderson 1970: 165–91 finds that many details in the fictional battle of Thymbrara (*Cyr.* 7. 1) were written in reaction to the actual happenings at Cunaxa.

the way the weeping Panthea tends Abradatas' pitiful remains in our episode.[169]

We now learn that the widowed Panthea has done a complete turn-about in her attitude towards war. She blames herself—and Cyrus too (7. 3. 10 ἴσως δὲ καὶ διὰ σέ, ὦ Κῦρε)—for her husband's death, because she has foolishly exhorted him to prove himself a loyal friend to Cyrus on the battlefield, with no thought of the consequences for himself. The lady of Susa, who had told her husband that she much preferred a glorious, shared death to a life together in disgrace, is now bitter and repentant: she will indeed shortly join Abradatas in death, but Panthea clearly derives little comfort from her husband's heroic end. One wonders if, given another opportunity to address her husband, her choice of glory over life would be repeated. This sad and reproachful Panthea is perhaps a more convincing and human figure than the earlier exhorting one, but she is a surprising creation of the author of the *Cyropaedia*. It is Cyrus' viewpoint—that Abradatas, who has died victorious, has been granted the fairest end of all—which, as we have seen, is the usual attitude in the work.[170] The Persian leader continues to demonstrate his appreciation of the glories attached to victory by pressing on Panthea all the outer trappings—fine burial-clothing and decorations, animals for sacrifice at the graveside, and an impressive monument—used to honour a fallen hero.

Cyrus is concerned about Panthea's future and promises to arrange an escort for her to the place of her choice; he does this out of respect for her self-restraint and virtue. All Panthea need do, says the Persian, is reveal to him to whom she wishes to be conveyed. The lady of Susa replies in terrible irony that Cyrus need have no fear about her concealing the identity of the person whom she wishes to join: ἀλλὰ θάρρει . . . ὦ Κῦρε, οὐ μή σε κρύψω πρὸς ὅντινα βούλομαι ἀφικέσθαι (7. 3. 13). Cyrus does not understand the ambiguity of her remark, although the style is akin to his own two-edged wish, earlier, to get hold of Araspas (6. 3. 11).[171]

The Persian leader takes his leave of Panthea, pitying her, we are told, for having lost such a husband and pitying Abradatas for never being able to see his wife again. This reference to *seeing* Panthea is

---

[169] See Photius' brief summary of Ctesias: ὡς Παρύσατις . . . πενθοῦσα Κῦρον καὶ μόλις ἐκομίσατο τὴν κεφαλὴν αὐτοῦ καὶ τὴν χεῖρα (*FGrH* 688 F 16. 66); cf. F 24, F 25, F 41.

[170] See above, ch. 2. 6, on the usual attitude towards war and victory in the *Cyr.*

[171] Compare too Ajax's ambiguous monologue before his suicide (Soph. *Aj.* 646ff.).

perhaps an allusion to the lady's great beauty—a more open remark would be inappropriate at this scene of mourning. So too the Persian's reassurance that Panthea will not be left friendless and his delicate probing as to where she would like to go may be more than a 'feed' to her final ironic statement: perhaps Cyrus is ready to arrange a match for the lady of Susa with the man of her choice. It is not altogether unlikely that the Persian considers himself a suitable candidate for the role of protector and future spouse. Cyrus' offer, in any event, makes it clear that Panthea's suicide stems solely from love of her husband; unlike Andromache, for example, she need not worry how she will fare without her husband's protection, and her grief is perhaps less selfish than that of the Homeric heroine. Had Panthea not killed herself, it seems likely that she would have eventually married one of Cyrus' chief lieutenants (if not the Persian leader himself), just as the daughter of Gobryas does. The only way to preserve the lady of Susa's image as a faithful wife untarnished is the way that Xenophon has chosen, to have Panthea join her husband in death.

After Cyrus' departure Panthea bids her eunuchs withdraw so that she can mourn Abradatas as she wishes—ὡς βούλομαι (7. 3. 14), another ambiguous phrase that is not understood correctly by those who surround her. Eunuchs are often involved in the burial of their masters in Ctesias,[172] and their attendance here at Abradatas' grave is not surprising. More unexpected is the presence of Panthea's nurse, to whom the lady of Susa now turns with the request that she be covered with the same shroud as Abradatas, after she dies. This is the first we hear of any τροφός; she is presumably Panthea's childhood nurse, who now serves as her mistress' confidante. Xenophon introduces her here, only minutes before Panthea's death, in a role very like that of the nurses in tragedy, for she now tries to dissuade her mistress from suicide, in the manner of, for example, Hermione's nurse in the *Andromache* (811 ff.) and Deianira's in the *Trachiniae* (874 ff.).[173] Panthea is deaf to her servant's entreaties and the nurse

[172] Cf. *FGrH* 688 F 13. 9, F 13. 23, F 15. 47.

[173] Other nurses who serve as confidantes are found in Euripides' *Medea*, *Hippolytus*, and *Stheneboea*; for the latter see Page 1942: No. 16, lines 10–12. See Steven's note on *And.* 802 ff. and Herzog-Hauser 1937: 1498. Trenkner 1958: 66 thinks that this stock character in Euripides was 'undoubtedly a contemporary type'; the gravestone *IG* ii² 7873 (dated to the second half of the 4th cent.) provides real-life evidence for such a relationship between a nurse and her ward. In Ctesias Parysatis has a trusted maid and confidante, called Γίγγη or Γίγις, who is privy to her plot to poison her daughter-in-law Stateira, but she is not described as a τροφός in the extant fragments (*FGrH* 688 F 27. 70, F 29).

withdraws, allowing the lady of Susa to unsheath a dagger long held in readiness (7. 3. 14 πάλαι παρεσκευασμένον) and stab herself to death. Panthea dies with her head on her husband's breast and the nurse, fulfilling her last wish, wraps the pair in a joint shroud.

Xenophon allots Panthea a dignified, restrained, and economical end: he does not show us the over-wrought nurse pleading with her mistress, nor does he have the lady of Susa indulge in a long emotional speech before her death, in the manner of such tragic heroines as Phaedra, Alcestis, Deianira, and Evadne in Euripides' *Supplices*. Panthea has planned her suicide in advance, as her hidden dagger shows, and she puts an end to herself quickly and quietly because she has no desire to live without her husband. Grief-stricken widows who voluntarily join their husbands in death are found in two plays of Euripides, and Xenophon may have been acquainted with these tragic heroines.[174] In Plato Socrates speaks of the many people who voluntarily descend to Hades in the hope of being united with their loved ones (*Phaedo* 68 A), and Xenophon probably knew of several instances of people who willingly died together with (συνθανεῖν) or in the wake of (ἐπαποθανεῖν) another, both in fiction and in fact.[175] Indeed, we have just seen that the close friends and companions of both Abradatas and Cyrus the Younger[176] chose to die with their leaders. Turning to the East, we hear from Herodotus how Thracian wives customarily joined their husbands in death. Each male Thracian had several wives, and when a husband died there was a contest among them as to who was his favourite and should be granted the honour of being killed and buried alongside her husband (Hdt. 5. 5). Ctesias tells us that Sardanapallus' wife joins her husband (and his mistresses) on the huge funeral pyre that the king erected after his defeat by the Medes (*FGrH* 688 F 1q), but it is not clear whether she did so on her own initiative. Diodorus Siculus (19. 33–4) describes the Indian custom of suttee, which, according to his account, arose not from the passionate devotion of wives to their husbands, but in order to prevent women from poisoning unsatisfactory

---

[174] Laodameia in the *Protesilaus* (frr. 647–57; cf. esp. fr. 656) and Evadne in the *Supplices* (980 ff.).

[175] See e.g. Jocaste in Eur. *Phoen.* 1455 ff. and the παιδικά who fights to the very end at the side of his lover, the Spartan Anaxibius, described in the *Hell.* (4. 8. 39); for further instances see Hirzel 1908: 78–9 and compare his discussion of suicide in tragedy, 93–100. For pre-Euripidean tales of a bereaved wife committing suicide see Trenkner 1958: 71 n. 2 and Collard on Eur. *Supp.* 980–1113.

[176] Cf. *Oec.* 4. 19.

spouses. None the less, Diodorus includes the story of a man's two
wives who vie for the privilege of being buried with him, and this tale
probably comes from the much earlier Alexander historian, Onesicritus;[177] Xenophon may have been acquainted with the Indian
practice. In sum, Panthea's suicide, her wish to die because her husband is dead, has precedents both in Greek life and literature and in
Oriental practice.

When Panthea's three eunuchs see what their mistress has done,
they quickly follow suit, pulling out their daggers and stabbing
themselves to death on the spot (*Cyr.* 7. 3. 15). The closest parallel to
their act of self-sacrifice is again to be found on the battlefield of
Cunaxa, where, according to one of the two versions Xenophon
gives, the eunuch Artapates, Cyrus' most loyal sceptre-bearer,[178]
draws out his dagger and kills himself when he sees that his master
has died.[179] In Ctesias the eunuchs of Sardanapallus also die with
their master on the funeral pyre (*FGrH* 688 F 1b 27. 2), but again we
do not know if they volunteered to do so. Herodotus (7. 107) tells of
Borges' great funeral pyre, which included his wife, children,
mistresses, and servants.

Cyrus is stunned by the news of Panthea's suicide and rushes back
to the scene to see if he can assist in any way. He mourns Panthea's
death but also admires her action, and this feeling of esteem mingled
with sadness (rather than horror) is probably the reaction Xenophon
wishes to induce in his readers as well. All that remains for the
Persian leader to do is arrange a fitting funeral for the pair and erect a
huge monument over their grave (7. 3. 16). The brief description of
the tomb of Panthea and Abradatas is the only mention of such
monuments in the *Cyropaedia*: we hear nothing of the tombs of
Astyages, Cambyses, or Mandane, although Cyrus himself does
describe the kind of burial he would like (cf. 8. 7. 25, 27). In Ctesias,
on the other hand, a description of the burial and tombstone of
leading figures seems to have been a regular feature of the *Persica*: the
monuments of Ninus, Zarinaea, Astyages, and Darius are all
described.[180]

---

[177] Cf. Strabo 15. 1. 30 and Hornblower 1981: 94 n. 71.

[178] For the evidence that sceptre-bearers were eunuchs see Guyot 1980: 82 and 87
n. 118; on Artapates as a eunuch see Lewis 1977: 16 n. 81.

[179] φασι . . . ἑαυτὸν ἐπισφάξασθαι σπασάμενον τὸν ἀκινάκην (*Anab.* 1. 8. 29); compare our passage: σπασάμενοι . . . τοὺς ἀκινάκας ἀποσφάττονται (*Cyr.* 7. 3. 15).

[180] Cf. *FGrH* 688 F 1b 7. 1, F 5. 34. 5, F 9. 6, F 13. 19. At *Cyr.* 7. 3. 15 there is also a
description of the monument erected for Panthea's dead eunuchs. These lines are

The colourful romantic tale of the lady of Susa ends with her death and neither Panthea, nor Abradatas, nor Araspas is mentioned again in the *Cyropaedia*. One last question remains: what is the source of this dramatic story? The fact that the novella serves Xenophon's literary aims so well—since it enlivens what would otherwise be a long, rather tedious section devoted to military doings and yet is firmly linked to the main plot of the work—is perhaps the strongest argument for Xenophon's authorship of the tale, or at least for considerable revision of an existing account by him. It is hard to imagine that a story developed in its entirety by another would fit into the *Cyropaedia* so neatly and successfully. The novella seems neither wholly Greek (despite the heroine's very Greek name)[181] nor wholly Oriental, and the three kinds of attendants found in the tale—maidservants, eunuchs, and a nurse—point respectively to the three most recognizable influences at work: Homer, Ctesias and other stories of the Persian court, and Greek tragedy. It seems reasonable to conclude that it is Xenophon who has blended and combined these various elements; it is much less likely that the author of the *Cyropaedia* simply copied the story, in its entirety, from an unknown source, either Greek or Persian.

3. GOBRYAS AND GADATAS: TWO ASSYRIAN DEFECTORS

The Assyrian noble Gobryas is the leading figure in our next novella. Xenophon introduces him simply by telling us that after Cyrus' first victory over the Assyrians Gobryas, an elderly Assyrian, arrived at the Persian camp accompanied by a cavalry guard (4. 6. 1 ff.). We learn of Gobryas' background and reasons for approaching the Persian leader only when Cyrus does: his story is unfolded in the course of their first conversation. Gobryas, addressing Cyrus most humbly, introduces himself, explaining that he is an Assyrian noble with a stronghold, a considerable estate, and one thousand cavalrymen at his disposal. He was a loyal friend and ally of the old Assyrian king, who has just been killed in the battle with the Persians, but Gobryas

deleted by Dindorf, who is followed by most editors. Dindorf terms the passage 'absurdum recentioris Graeculi additamentum' and notes that neither Zonaras (*Epit. Hist. 3. 23*) nor Tzetzes (*Hist. Var. Chil. 3. 799*) includes any reference to this section in their close summaries of this part of the *Cyr.* One argument in favour of the received text is that it is precisely the kind of detail that Ctesias would have included.

[181] Cf. Tatum 1989: 175–6.

now wishes to transfer his allegiance to Cyrus because of his hatred for the old king's son and successor.

While neither Herodotus nor Ctesias makes any mention of an Assyrian (i.e. Babylonian) named Gobryas who defects to Cyrus, we know from Babylonian sources that there was indeed such a historical personage. The cuneiform Nabonidus Chronicle, when relating the events of the monarch's seventeenth year, 539 BC, the year of Cyrus' conquest of Babylon, tells us that 'Ugbaru [= Gobryas], governor of the Guti, and the army of Cyrus entered Babylon.'[182] According to the Chronicle, Cyrus himself entered Babylon only later, and Gobryas died shortly thereafter. In broad outline, then, Xenophon's account corresponds to the cuneiform source: both tell of an important Babylonian who is on Cyrus' side, facilitates the capture of Babylon, and enters that city ahead of the Persian ruler.[183] The 'Assyrian' Gobryas of the *Cyropaedia* should be distinguished from the Persian of the same name who appears in Herodotus as one of Darius' fellow conspirators: this latter Gobryas is the father of Mardonius and served, it seems, as the satrap of Babylonia under both Cyrus and Cambyses.[184] In any event, it seems that our Gobryas is not a figure invented by Xenophon: he is based on an authentic Babylonian ally of Cyrus. We do not know, however, which elements of the Assyrian's tale in the *Cyropaedia* come from Xenophon's (unknown) source and which are the product of his own imagination. It would be especially interesting to know whether the reason given for Gobryas' defection, the senseless killing of his son, was an element added by Xenophon.

[182] Nabonidus Chronicle 3. 15–16; the translation is that of Grayson 1975a: 109–10. Pritchard 1969: 305–7 has another convenient English translation. Two different forms of the name Gobryas—Ugbaru and Gubaru—appear in this section of the Chronicle (3. 12–22) and two different people *may* be meant: cf. Grayson's note on 3. 15; Oppenheim 1985: 544 with n. 4; and cf. below, n. 184.

[183] See Scheil 1914, who notes the correspondences between Xenophon's Gobryas and the individual described in the Nabonidus Chronicle. He thinks that Gobryas should be identified with a commanding officer of Nebuchadrezzar by that name, who had been active some 20 years earlier; see, however, the objections of Clay 1921 and cf. Schwenzner 1923. Cf. also Dandamaev 1989: 42–3 with n. 2; Beaulieu 1989: 226–30.

[184] Cf. Hdt. 3. 70ff., 6. 43, etc. This seems to be the consensus of the majority of scholars—cf. e.g. Kuhrt 1988: 122: '*If* Ugbaru and Gubaru in the Chronicle are identical, then this personage (presumably the figure from which the Gobryas of Xenophon . . . is ultimately derived) is definitely *not* the same person as the later governor'—but untangling the various Persian and Babylonian Gobryases is no simple task. See the variety of views found in a single volume of the *Cambridge History of Iran*: Mallowan 1985: 411 vs. Diakonoff 1985: 144 vs. Oppenheim 1985: 544; and cf. Cook 1983: 30–1, 46, 168, and Frye 1984: 94–5 with n. 25.

Gobryas now relates to Cyrus the circumstances of his son's death (4. 6. 2–7). He is deeply agitated by the tragedy, and Xenophon indicates this not by describing Gobryas' gestures or expressions or emotional state, but by the language he has the Assyrian use to tell his tale. Gobryas' speech contains what seems to be the highest concentration of tragic or poetic words in the *Cyropaedia*, and the vocabulary of tragedy is well suited to convey his misery.[185] In addition, the Assyrian uses long, convoluted sentences, with various clauses left dangling—cf. in particular *Cyr.* 4. 6. 3—since he is, as we are meant to see, too overcome by grief to present the story in an orderly and coherent fashion.

Gobryas had only one son, a loving and devoted child, who was invited by the old Assyrian king to court in order to marry the king's daughter. The crown prince invited Gobryas' son to go hunting with him and they rode together as friends, with the Assyrian prince allowing his companion a free hand since he considered himself a far better horseman. Gobryas' son killed a bear and a lion in quick succession, but only after the prince had aimed at each in turn and missed them. When Gobryas' son exclaimed in delight at his own skill, the prince could contain his jealousy no longer: he snatched a spear and stabbed his companion to death (*Cyr.* 4. 6. 3–4).

We have seen that Ctesias tells a similar story of the monarch Artaxerxes I's fury at Megabyxus' prowess in hunting, and Curtius Rufus reports a parallel incident concerning Alexander and a young man from his royal guard.[186] The Assyrian prince, it seems, is unused to hunting and competing freely with others in a friendly manner. In this respect he presents a strong contrast to Cyrus, who as a youth in Media resisted Astyages' suggestion that he take advantage of royal prerogative and have his fill of hunting ahead of his companions. Cyrus enjoyed the friendly rivalry and praised his successful friends without the least bit of jealousy.[187] During young Cyrus' stay in Media he came close to meeting the Assyrian prince, when the latter set out on another ill-fated hunting expedition. In this episode the Assyrian, about to be married, travels to the Assyrian–Median border to hunt for game for his wedding. He is accompanied by a

---

[185] Cf. γαμέτην (*Cyr.* 4. 6. 3), αἰχμήν (4. 6. 4), τάλας (4. 6. 5), γοωμένη (4. 6. 9), and the further list in Gautier 1911: 107 n. 1 (cf. 91–2). See also Holden's note on *Cyr.* 4. 6. 5.

[186] *FGrH* 688 F 14. 43 (and cf. Plut. *Mor.* 173 D); *Exp. Alex.* 8. 6. 7.

[187] *Cyr.* 1. 4. 15 οὐδ᾽ ὁπωστιοῦν φθονερῶς; compare the Assyrian prince, who tries to hide his jealousy: κατέσχεν ὑπὸ σκότου τὸν φθόνον (4. 6. 4).

large military force and consequently decides to make a foray into Media itself, so that his expedition will prove all the more productive and impressive. Astyages and Cyaxares, hearing of the invasion, rush to the frontier with their cavalry and the teenaged Cyrus joins them. The Medes attack, following a plan proposed by Cyrus, and the Assyrians are forced to retreat (1. 4. 16–24). Thus early on in the *Cyropaedia* there is a near confrontation between the Persian and the Assyrian in which both behave in characteristic fashion: Cyrus is bold and ingenious and the Assyrian prince is proud and over-ambitious. The failure of the small Assyrian force at Media fore-shadows their later large-scale defeat at the hands of Cyrus.

Gobryas mourns his son deeply, stressing the fact that the youth was a beloved, only son and that he no longer has a male child. The Assyrian noble contrasts his present grief-stricken old age with his former cheerful existence, and touchingly describes the sorrow of an old man burying a beloved young son. This theme of bereaved fathers and missing sons, which appears, as we have seen, fairly frequently in the pages of Herodotus, is also found in our two remaining novellas. Gadatas refers to his childless state, to the sons he will never have, while Croesus briefly mentions his son who perished in the prime of life.[188] The circumstances surrounding the killing of Gobryas' son—his death by means of a spear during a hunting party, at the hands of a supposed friend—are reminiscent, in fact, of the fatal end of Croesus' son Atys in Herodotus' version of the story (Hdt. 1. 34–45). Xenophon presents the bereaved Gobryas with great sympathy and delicacy, and this has led one scholar to suggest that our passage was written after Xenophon's own son, Gryllus, was killed at Mantinea.[189]

Gobryas goes on to say that the Assyrian prince never displayed any remorse over his evil deed, although his father, the king, did express his sorrow and sympathy. Gobryas, who would never have turned against his friend, the old king, cannot possibly live under the rule of his son's murderer; the latter is, in any event, aware of the bereaved father's animosity towards him. The hope of revenge, concludes the elderly Assyrian noble, is his sole source of comfort (*Cyr.* 4. 6. 6–7). Perhaps Gobryas insists upon his devotion to his former master, the old Assyrian king, because the loyalty of a defector is normally open to suspicion. All three of Cyrus' Assyrian allies join

[188] Gadatas: *Cyr.* 5. 4. 12, 30; cf. 5. 3. 19. Croesus: 7. 2. 20.
[189] Cf. Delebecque 1957: 391–2.

him because they are innocent victims of their cruel ruler: in the black-and-white world of the *Cyropaedia* all those identified with the Persian cause must be of unblemished character and cannot simply betray their own country.

In both the Herodotean and Ctesian versions of Cyrus' rise to power the Persian has a close ally and adviser who helps him in the early stages of his conquests—Harpagus and Oebares respectively. Gobryas comes closest to filling this role in the *Cyropaedia*, even if Xenophon's Cyrus only rarely follows his advice. Gobryas, in fact, bears more than a superficial resemblance to Harpagus in Herodotus, for each joins forces with Cyrus because his own ruler has wantonly murdered his only son. Herodotus' Harpagus plays a much more active part in establishing Cyrus' rule than Xenophon's Assyrian does, for he encourages or actually incites the Persian to rebel, while Gobryas (along with almost everyone else in the *Cyropaedia*) is more of a tool in Cyrus' hands. Gobryas turns against the Assyrian ruler partly because he realizes that the young king is aware of his hostility towards him, and this is much more realistic than the situation in Herodotus, where Astyages simply forgets that he has wronged Harpagus and appoints him commander of the Median forces. Finally, both Gobryas and Harpagus ultimately achieve their aim and avenge their sons' deaths.[190]

Cyrus goes to visit Gobryas soon after this first meeting in order to become better acquainted with his new ally; we have already looked at the symposium the two hold at Gobryas' estate.[191] At his estate the Assyrian presents to Cyrus his marriageable daughter, a sad, beautiful maiden who, as we have seen, is reminiscent of Panthea. The next scene in our novella is a conversation between Gobryas and the cruel Assyrian ruler, conducted through messengers (*Cyr.* 5. 3. 5–7). Gobryas approaches the king on Cyrus' behalf, for while the Persians are ready to do battle, the Assyrians do not march out to meet them. The Assyrian noble tells his former ruler that if he will come out to defend his country, Gobryas himself will join him; if not, Gobryas will be compelled to submit to the Persian victors. The despot responds with a sharp and pointed blast, reminding Gobryas that he is still his king. The Assyrian ruler states that while he does not regret killing Gobryas' son, he is now sorry that he has not killed the father as well. He is not ready to begin fighting and recommends that

---

[190] Cf. Hdt. 1. 117–19, 123–4, 127, 129.
[191] *Cyr.* 5. 2. 1 ff.; see above, ch. 3. 4.

Gobryas return with his men in thirty days. Gobryas replies that he hopes to continue to vex the young king and then departs.

This exchange between Gobryas and the young king is the one passage in the *Cyropaedia* where we come closest to meeting the arrogant Assyrian ruler in the flesh. Elsewhere his actions are always reported indirectly—either by Xenophon, as narrator, or by one of the characters of the *Cyropaedia*. Similarly his father, the old Assyrian king, is shown only once, exhorting his soldiers to bravery before their battle with the Persian forces.[192] In his brief 'live' appearance the young Assyrian lives up to his reputation and behaves in cruel and arrogant fashion. His opening words δεσπότης ὁ σὸς λέγει (5. 3. 6) are meant to put Gobryas in his place as a rebellious upstart and establish the young king's authority: his father would never have spoken to the elderly Assyrian in that way. Oriental rulers are often addressed as ὦ δέσποτα, and in the *Cyropaedia* Gobryas, Gadatas, and Croesus all use the appellation at times when speaking to Cyrus,[193] but here it is the king who finds it necessary to use the term δεσπότης of himself. In Herodotus there are three kings who refer to themselves as δεσπότης—Darius addressing the Scythian ruler, Cambyses speaking to Psammenitus, and Xerxes lashing the Hellespont[194]—and in all three instances it is because their authority over the person (or object) they address is recent or not fully acknowledged, as is the case with the Assyrian king here. The king's unwillingness to fight is somewhat like the Scythians' rejection of Darius' efforts to engage them in battle in Herodotus (4. 125 ff.), although here the Assyrian ruler does eventually take up the challenge, only to be defeated. There is one positive aspect to Gobryas' parley with the enemy: their exchange is short and straightforward and the two sides are openly hostile, so that there is none of the deceit, double-dealing, or mutual suspicion which often characterizes negotiations elsewhere in Xenophon.[195]

An exchange of messages between enemies before they clash, such as we have here, is found fairly regularly both in Ctesias and in

---

[192] *Cyr.* 3. 3. 43–5; cf. above, ch. 2. 6.
[193] See e.g. Hdt. 1. 90, 7. 38, 8. 102, etc., and cf. *Cyr.* 4. 6. 2, 5. 4. 42, 5. 3. 28, 7. 2. 9; cf. 7. 3. 3 and 4. 5. 11.
[194] Hdt. 4. 126–7, 3. 14, 7. 35.
[195] See e.g. *Anab.* 2. 3. 17–29, 2. 5. 2–27; *Hell.* 3. 1. 20–8, 3. 4. 5–6; contrast *Hell.* 4. 1. 29–39. Wencis 1977 and Hirsch 1985: 14–38 discuss the constantly recurring themes of deceit and suspicion in the (negotiations of the) *Anab.* On negotiations in the *Hell.* see Gray 1981: 324–6, 328–30.

Herodotus. In the *Persica* the Indian king sends Semiramis a threatening letter before she launches her attack upon him, but she dismisses his words contemptuously. Ctesias' Astyages threatens an unperturbed Cyrus before their clash, and his Darius and Scythian king exchange nasty letters before they go to war.[196] In Herodotus too Astyages and Cyrus communicate briefly before they meet in battle, and Tomyris, queen of the Massagetae, sends messages to Cyrus before each of their two confrontations. Darius and the Scythian king exchange messages and the Persian king later receives symbolic gifts meant as a warning, before a battle that never actually takes place. Alexander, sent as an ambassador by Mardonius, attempts to negotiate with the Athenians before the battle of Plataea.[197] Our exchange betwen Gobryas and the young Assyrian belongs to this tradition of pre-battle exchanges in which the two enemies vilify one another, although generally it is the leaders of the two opposing sides who address one another. Xenophon avoids a direct confrontation between Cyrus and the young Assyrian king throughout the *Cyropaedia*: the two do not meet face to face on the battlefield, either as young men in Media or at the critical Persian–Assyrian conflict at Thymbrara, and they do not even address one another indirectly through messengers before the battle. Gobryas, in his dealings here with the Assyrian despot, is Cyrus' emissary, as he is, in a sense, later on when he actually kills the enemy king.

When Gobryas returns to the Persian camp with the Assyrian's reply, Cyrus recalls that Gobryas had told him of another potential Assyrian defector, the eunuch Gadatas.[198] Gadatas, another so-called friend of the Assyrian prince, attracted the attention of the prince's mistress at a drinking-party. When this woman complimented Gadatas upon his beauty, congratulating the woman who would become his wife, the Assyrian prince had his friend seized and castrated. The prince then circulated a different version of the incident, claiming that Gadatas had attempted to seduce his mistress (*Cyr.* 5. 2. 27–8).

The prince's behaviour, reprehensible as it is, is not altogether without parallel in Eastern harems and courts. There are at least two other Oriental stories where the sexual jealousy of a royal figure

---

[196] *FGrH* 688 F 1b 18. 1–2, 90 F 66. 33, 688 F 13. 20.

[197] Hdt. 1. 127, 1. 206, 208, 212, 4. 126ff., 8. 140ff.

[198] It has been argued that our Gadatas should be identified with the satrap of Ionia of that name whom Darius reprimands in a letter—cf. Meiggs and Lewis 1969, No. 12—but this identification is not generally accepted; see Mallowan 1985: 414–15.

comes to a head at a drinking-party: Ahasuerus has Haman executed
for coming too close to Queen Esther when pleading for his life at a
party she has arranged (Esther 7: 7–10), and Amestris insists, at the
king's birthday dinner, that Xerxes hand over Masistes' wife to her
because of the monarch's relations with mother and daughter (Hdt.
9. 110–12). More generally, Ctesias has several tales of royal figures
behaving cruelly towards others because of their sexual involvements. Ninus threatens to blind Onnes if he does not relinquish
Semiramis, Amestris tortures the Greek doctor Apollonides because
of his affair with her daughter Amytis, and Parysatis takes her
revenge upon the entire family of Terituchmes, her disloyal son-in-
law who is in love with another woman. Amytis, Megabyxus' wife
and the daughter of Xerxes, is let off lightly and simply scolded by
her father for her sexual misdemeanours, while Parysatis' lover is
killed by her son Artaxerxes.[199] In Herodotus we find further strong
reactions by royal Orientals to sexual offences: Candaules' wife
insists that Gyges assassinate her husband because he has exposed
her to view, while Xerxes has Sataspes impaled after he fails to
circumnavigate Libya, because he has raped Zopyrus' daughter.[200]
We have already seen how frightened Araspas was to face Cyrus even
after an unsuccessful attempt to seduce Panthea, and all these stories
point to the fact that Eastern rulers took sexual matters very much to
heart.[201] While the Assyrian prince's sexual jealousy is not without
precedent, the punishment he inflicts, castration, is cruel and
unusual, and perhaps that is why the prince found it necessary to
present his own account of Gadatas' supposed misdeed. Gadatas is, it
should be recalled, the son of an Assyrian noble even more powerful
than Gobryas. The incident involves a mistress of the Assyrian prince
and not his wife,[202] perhaps because the Eastern (or at least Persian)
custom was to have mistresses and concubines, but not wives, present
at such drinking-parties.[203] In any event, the prince's jealousy is
much less understandable when a mere mistress is involved.

[199] *FGrH* 688 F 1b 6. 9–10; F 14. 44; F 15. 56, F 16. 61; F 13. 32 (and 14. 34); F 16. 60.
[200] Hdt. 1. 8–12, 4. 43. For an interesting discussion of the parallels between Herodotus' two 'Harem-Liebesgeschichten'—Gyges and Candaules, and Xerxes and
Masistes' wife—see Wolff 1964.
[201] Cf. Plut. *Artax*. 27. 1.
[202] Or one of his wives. We have seen that the prince was about to be married long
ago when he set out on his hunting escapade in Media (1. 4. 16 ff.). This would mean
that Gobryas' daughter was intended to be an additional wife (4. 6. 9); there may have
been several others.
[203] See Plut. *Mor*. 613 A; *Artax*. 26. 4–5; and cf. Hdt. 5. 18, 9. 110; Athen. 145 D.

Gobryas tells Cyrus that he is confident that Gadatas will join their side, for he and the eunuch have often spoken to each other freely— obviously against the Assyrian prince—in the past. The Persian leader asks Gobryas to approach the eunuch at an opportune time (thereby glossing over the difficulties involved in slipping through enemy lines to Gadatas, who lives at the very gates of Babylon)[204] and to sound him out. If Gadatas wishes to join them, Gobryas should keep the matter secret, suggests Cyrus, for there is no greater advantage in war than having a friend pose as an enemy (*Cyr.* 5. 3. 9).[205]

The Persian and the Assyrian now consider how they can best make use of the eunuch. They work out a plan, with Cyrus putting forward a series of suggestions and Gobryas approving, or sometimes adding to, the Persian's proposals (5. 3. 11–14). Even though Babylon is the Assyrian's home territory and it is he who is acquainted with Gadatas, Cyrus, as usual, takes the initiative and plots their next moves. The plan is for the Persians to pretend to attack Gadatas' territory and to allow him to capture some of their forces. These captives will reveal that they intend to assault the Assyrian fortress which is used to direct operations against the Hyrcanians and the Sacians, and Gadatas will use this 'information' as a pretext to enter the fortress without arousing suspicion. Cyrus will then attack the stronghold, and with the eunuch's assistance from within the fortress should fall into Persian hands. Gobryas contacts Gadatas, who readily agrees to co-operate. Xenophon does not actually show us the reunion of the two Assyrians but simply summarizes the secret meeting between them in one sentence (5. 3. 15). We can assume that the two commiserated over their sufferings at the hands of the cruel young king and that Gobryas praised Cyrus in glowing terms, encouraging the eunuch to become his ally. Their situation is somewhat like the reunion of Panthea and Abradatas (6. 1. 47), without, of course, the romantic element. After their meeting all goes as planned and the fortress is captured.

The story of Zopyrus' self-mutilation and infiltration of Babylon on behalf of Darius, found in Herodotus, has already been mentioned in

---

[204] Cf. *Cyr.* 5. 2. 29 ff.

[205] Cyrus has learnt about the desirability of deceiving one's foes from his father Cambyses before setting out on his long campaign (1. 6. 27–37). Gadatas is the first spy whom the Persian recruits and Araspas is the second; later Cyrus sends members of an Indian delegation and several of his own men disguised as slaves to spy upon the Assyrians—cf. 6. 2. 2–3, 9–11.

relation to Araspas' espionage mission.[206] Gadatas' entry into the Assyrian fortress also seems closely related to Zopyrus' exploit, particularly in the deliberate dispatch of Persian military forces to be captured by a supposed ally of the enemy in order to enhance his credibility. In the case of Zopyrus several thousand of Darius' men are actually killed as part of his plan, while with Gadatas Cyrus' men are only cross-examined (and presumably tortured) in public; later these men help the eunuch secure the inside of the fortress.[207] Gadatas is also somewhat like another figure in Herodotus whom we have already encountered, Cyrus' ally Harpagus, for he too is considered above suspicion by his compatriots and allowed to command forces opposed to Cyrus, even though he has been treated so cruelly by his own king.

It is not without significance that the eunuch Gadatas' chief exploit takes place inside the fortress, rather than together with Cyrus out on the battlefield. A eunuch's place is generally within an establishment or at its gates, and this is true of the noble Gadatas later on as well, when as a member of Cyrus' court in Babylon he is both chief sceptre-bearer and in charge of running the Persian's entire household from within.[208] Eunuchs were customarily the keepers of the keys, and in the *Persica* we find several eunuchs who are called upon to admit, in secret, people who conspire against the head of their household and thus play a role similar to that of Gadatas here.[209]

After the fortress is captured, Gadatas hurries out to meet Cyrus for the first time (5. 3. 18 ff.). The eunuch bows down to the Persian, in accordance with the custom, adds Xenophon—probably referring to Assyrian practice, although neither Abradatas nor Gobryas, for example, has greeted Cyrus in this fashion. Thus far in the *Cyropaedia* only Assyrian captives have bowed down to Cyrus, and it is only much later, at the royal procession in Babylon, that the Persians do obeisance for the first time.[210] While Gadatas' bow may be no more than the physical equivalent of Gobryas' first greeting to Cyrus, ὦ δέσποτα (4. 6. 2), the eunuch, despite his noble lineage, seems very submissive and meek in all his dealings with the Persian leader. Gadatas greets Cyrus with the words χαῖρε Κῦρε (5. 3. 18) and the

---

[206] Hdt. 3. 153 ff.; cf. above, sect. 2.

[207] Hdt. 3. 155, 157; *Cyr.* 5. 3. 16–17.

[208] 8. 4. 2 ἡ πᾶσα ἔνδον δίαιτα; cf. 5. 3. 14, 18 (where the word ἔνδον is again used in conjunction with Gadatas).

[209] Cf. *FGrH* 688 F 1p and F 1b 24. 4, F 13. 16, F 15. 48.

[210] 4. 4. 13, 8. 3. 14.

Persian, playing upon the meaning of the word, tells the eunuch that he is obliged to feel joyous, for Gadatas has enabled him to turn the fortress over to his allies. The Persian leader, referring at once to the eunuch's plight, says that while the Assyrian king has deprived him of the ability to have children, he has not taken away Gadatas' capacity to acquire friends, and his new allies will try to be no less helpful than any offspring would have been. Gadatas has no opportunity to reply to this rather tactless pronouncement, for the Hyrcanian leader rushes in to express his gratitude to Cyrus for the capture of the stronghold; Cyrus points out that Gadatas should be thanked as well (5. 3. 18–21).

The next conversation betwen Gadatas and Cyrus is a brisk, businesslike affair, since the eunuch must return home quickly in order to ward off an attack on his own land by the Assyrian king. Cyrus arranges to follow him with an army as quickly as possible (5. 3. 26–9). The Assyrian king, aided by a treacherous member of Gadatas' cavalry, comes close to defeating the eunuch and Gadatas himself is wounded by the traitor. Cyrus and his men then arrive opportunely on the scene and drive the Assyrians away (5. 4. 1–9). The subsequent encounter between Gadatas and Cyrus is a happy one. Gadatas is delighted to greet his rescuer and expresses himself effusively and emotionally; this is true of his later appearances in the *Cyropaedia* as well.[211] Gadatas is extremely grateful to Cyrus for his intervention, saying that he has done little to deserve such help and pointing out, in surprisingly Gorgianic style, that all would have been lost for him without the Persian's assistance (5. 4. 11 ὡς νῦν τὸ μὲν ἐπ' ἐμοὶ οἴχομαι, τὸ δ' ἐπὶ σοὶ σέσωμαι). Referring back to Cyrus' promise that the eunuch's new friends will prove as devoted as any children might have been (5. 3. 19), Gadatas states that even if he had been able to father children, he is uncertain that his own sons would have been as loyal to him as Cyrus is. Fathers are often pained by their children, Gadatas continues, as the case of the Assyrian king and the crown prince shows: once again we encounter the motif of fathers and sons.

Gadatas is a fairly young man, a contemporary of Gobryas' son and the young Assyrian ruler, so that the comparison of his relationship with Cyrus to that between a father and his son is inappropriate; brothers would be a more fitting designation. Panthea states that the Persian leader has treated her as he would a brother's wife, while the

[211] See e.g. 5. 4. 30–1, 6. 1. 1–5.

elderly Gobryas looks upon Cyrus as a substitute son, but those foster relationships are chronologically tenable.[212] It is clear that the question of children arises in relation to Gadatas because he is a eunuch, but his comparison of Cyrus to a son[213] may also have been influenced by the story of the eunuch Artembares, as recorded in Nicolaus of Damascus' reworking of Ctesias.[214] Artembares serves as Astyages' chief wine-pourer and trains young Cyrus to serve wine at the king's table. The eunuch becomes very fond of the Persian lad, treating him as affectionately as a son,[215] and receives permission from Astyages to adopt Cyrus and have him inherit his own position as cupbearer. Just as Xenophon has his young Cyrus pour wine once only, in what seems to be a sideways glance at Ctesias,[216] Gadatas' paternal attitude towards the Persian may also be another fleeting reference to the story of Cyrus' youth, as it appears in the *Persica*.

Cyrus points out to the eunuch that he did not come to Gadatas' rescue by himself, but together with an entire army of Persians, Medes, Hyrcanians, Armenians, Sacians, and Cadusians, just as he has earlier reminded the grateful Hyrcanian leader that Gadatas played an important part in gaining control of the frontier fortress. At this stage, before the conquest of Babylon,[217] the Persian leader does his utmost to unite all his various friends and allies into one cohesive unit, and he is willing to forgo the adulation of others in order to foster such unity. Gadatas responds to Cyrus' hints and provides gifts and food for the entire army (5. 4. 13–14).

The Persian and Assyrian next converse when Cyrus' army is about to depart from the eunuch's territory: this is the most emotional of their dialogues (5. 4. 29 ff.). Gadatas presents Cyrus with many gifts, saying that all of his property is at the Persian's disposal, for he will never have a child of his own to inherit the estate. When he dies, continues the eunuch emotionally, his name and race will be extinguished. Gadatas swears by the gods who see and hear all things[218] that he has said and done nothing to deserve the injury that he has suffered. His denial is emphatic, with five of the twelve words he

---

[212] Cf. 6. 4. 7, 4. 6. 2.
[213] See also below, 5. 4. 30.
[214] *FGrH* 90 F 66. 5–7; cf. above, n. 24.
[215] 90 F 66. 6 φιλοφρονησάμενος ὡς ἂν υἱῷ.
[216] *Cyr.* 1. 3. 8 ff.; see above, ch. 3. 2.
[217] But not afterwards—cf. 8. 2. 26–8.
[218] 5. 4. 31 οἳ καὶ ὁρῶσι πάντα καὶ ἀκούουσι πάντα; see *Cyr.* 8. 7. 22 and *Mem.* 1. 4. 18 for similar descriptions of the gods by Cyrus and Socrates respectively.

uses in his oath meaning 'no': καὶ ταῦτα . . . οὔτε ἄδικον οὔτε αἰσχρὸν οὐδὲν οὔτε εἰπὼν οὔτε ποιήσας ἔπαθον (5. 4. 31). The eunuch, overcome by his sad plight, then bursts into tears and is unable to continue speaking. While all four of the main characters of the novellas of the *Cyropaedia*—Panthea, Gobryas, Gadatas, and Croesus—find themselves in tragic situations, only two, Panthea and Gadatas, are reduced to tears by their fate, and Panthea is, of course, a woman.

Cyrus pities Gadatas, Xenophon tells us, but he offers no words of comfort and turns to the practical matter at hand—the gifts proffered by the Assyrian. The Persian leader, anxious to build up his cavalry, is glad to accept the horses brought by Gadatas, but he refuses the other presents because he is unable to reciprocate the eunuch's generosity. He asks Gadatas to safeguard the gifts for him, but the Assyrian replies that he is hardly in a position to do so. As long as he was on good terms with the Assyrian ruler, explains Gadatas, he considered his father's estate ideal, since it is near enough to Babylon to allow him all the advantages of urban living and yet is removed from the bustle of a big city. Now, however, he is situated dangerously close to powerful enemies (5. 4. 32–4). This description of Gadatas' estate in days of old is unexpected: the Assyrian sounds a bit like Ischomachus, weighing the advantages of urban as against rural living.[219] It should be recalled, perhaps, that Xenophon himself spent many years on a rural estate at Scillus, close to Olympia.[220]

The eunuch realizes that he should have thought of the consequences of having an angry enemy at his doorstep before he transferred his allegiance to Cyrus. None the less, he acted as he did because his soul, injured and outraged, was indifferent to questions of safety and was filled—or pregnant (5. 4. 35 κυοῦσα), a peculiar word for the eunuch to use—with thoughts of revenge. The new Assyrian ruler is hated by the gods and men alike, continues Gadatas, and he despises people, not if they do him some harm but if he suspects that they are superior to him. When Gadatas roundly condemns the Assyrian king and stresses his desire for revenge upon the man who had him castrated, we are reminded of another vengeful eunuch, Hermotimus, the chief eunuch of Xerxes, who appears in Herodotus (8. 105–6). Hermotimus was taken as a prisoner of war to Sardis and sold to Panionius of Chios, who made a profession of castrating good-looking youths. Years later, when Hermotimus, who had risen to become Xerxes' favourite eunuch,

[219] Cf. e.g. *Oec.* 11. 14–18.   [220] See *Anab.* 5. 3. 7 ff.

met Panionius, he managed to get the Chian and his family into his power by pretending to be a grateful friend. Hermotimus then had his revenge, forcing Panionius to castrate his four sons, and the sons their father. Before this terrible act is performed, the furious eunuch addresses Panionius in a speech which is similar in many ways to Gadatas' words to Cyrus here. Hermotimus, like Gadatas, bemoans his fate as a eunuch, also asserting that he has done nothing to deserve such treatment and similarly condemning the man who has acted so vilely. Both Gadatas and Hermotimus succeed in their quest for vengeance, but in Herodotus Hermotimus confronts the man who has injured him and condemns him face to face. In the *Cyropaedia* there is no direct exchange between Gadatas and the young Assyrian king, not even when the eunuch enters the royal palace and assassinates him.

Gadatas claims that the Assyrian ruler injures those who seem superior to him; this was the case both with Gobryas' son, who was a better marksman, and Gadatas himself, who presumably is more handsome than the prince. The Assyrian despot's jealousy leads him to surround himself with scoundrels as allies, adds the eunuch sarcastically, so that Cyrus need not worry about fighting any brave Assyrians, for their ruler will dispose of them by himself. Xenophon's Hiero has similar views about the way a tyrant acts towards outstanding compatriots. Hiero complains to Simonides that a tyrant must fear brave, wise, and just men since they may object to his regime, and hence he must resort to unworthy men as allies.[221] Similarly, in the Persians' constitutional debate in Herodotus Otanes contends that a tyrant is jealous of the best of his subjects and takes pleasure in the worst.[222] The Assyrian despot of the *Cyropaedia* behaves, then, in typically tyrannical fashion.

Gadatas concludes by saying that although the allies of the Assyrian king are unworthy, they are still capable of harassing him. Cyrus takes his new ally's worries to heart and suggests that Gadatas fortify his estate and then join the Persians on their campaign. The eunuch breathes a sigh of relief at Cyrus' invitation and adds that he would like to take his mother along. The mention of Gadatas' mother, who is presumably an elderly widow dependent on her none too powerful son, is another touch added by Xenophon in order to make the eunuch seem a weak and somewhat pathetic figure. We hear nothing, for instance, of any elderly dependants of Gobryas,

---

[221] *Hiero* 5. 1–4; cf. 2. 17–18.   [222] Hdt. 3. 80. 4; cf. Pl. *Rep.* 567 B–C.

Panthea, or Abradatas. Gadatas readies his household for the departure, leaving behind garrisons to guard his forts and taking both
friends and untrustworthy associates along with him on the campaign. The Persian leader's invitation to the eunuch is not altogether
altruistic, since Cyrus thinks that Gadatas will prove a useful companion, and indeed the eunuch does supply information on roads,
water supplies, and provisions in the area: the best interests of both
Gadatas and Cyrus conveniently coincide.

Before turning to the final episode in the stories of Gobryas and
Gadatas, their entry into Babylon and the assassination of the king, it
is worth looking at one further episode in which Gadatas features,
Cyr. 6. 1. 1–5. Cyrus and his allies have gathered in front of Cyaxares'
tent, waiting for the Mede leader to join them in a council of war on
whether or not to continue their campaign against the Assyrians.
Cyrus' men bring forward many of their new allies, who beg the
Persian leader to remain. Among these is Gadatas, who is accompanied by Hystaspas. Cyrus, Xenophon tells us, knows that the
eunuch is consumed by fear that the allied forces will disband and he
teases him, saying that Gadatas does not really want him to stay but
is simply parroting Hystaspas' words. The eunuch, who does not
seem to realize that Cyrus is joking, raises his hands to heaven and
swears that he has approached the Persian leader on his own
initiative, since without the Persian army all will be lost for him.
Cyrus then turns to banter with Hystaspas, who is able to reply to the
Persian leader in kind and teases Cyrus in this semi-serious
exchange.[223] Gadatas, who cannot forget his vulnerable position for
even a moment, cuts a sorry and pathetic figure, and again one
suspects that he is presented in this way because he is a eunuch.
Gobryas and the Hyrcanian leader are two other allies of Cyrus who
have a great deal to lose if the Persian army withdraws, but we do not
see them being teased in front of Cyaxares' tent: instead they are
found inside, at the council of war itself, presenting their case with
great dignity. If Gadatas is often portrayed as a weak and emotional
character, he is also allotted various notable military feats: at times
we are allowed to remember that he is a noble, and not just a eunuch.
Such exploits include his original 'battle' with Cyrus and infiltration

---

[223] The combination of play and earnest found here—cf. οἱ μὲν δὴ τοιαῦτ᾽ ἔπαιζον
σπουδῇ πρὸς ἀλλήλους (6. 1. 6)—is rather unexpected at a gathering of military leaders
about to discuss war plans; normally this semi-serious tone is found only in the symposia of the *Cyr.*

of the frontier fortress, his winning over of an Assyrian garrison by persuasion, and his victory over the other Assyrian defectors in the horse-races. In addition, Gadatas contributes military equipment to the allied forces and is in command of 10,000 horsemen at the royal procession held after the conquest of Babylon.[224] His most outstanding deed is, of course, his part in the conquest of Babylon.

In his attempt to take Babylon (*Cyr.* 7. 5. 1 ff.) Cyrus first surveys the city's massive high walls and concludes that an assault on them is virtually impossible; he then seems to plan to organize a siege and starve the Babylonians into submission instead.[225] After Chrysantas suggests fording the Euphrates, the Persian leader arranges for ditches to be dug, thus making the city accessible by draining the river. Cyrus decides to attack on the night of a Babylonian festival, when the enemy will be occupied in drinking and carousing. He calls his forces together, exhorts and advises them, and then has Gobryas and Gadatas lead the way into the city and the royal palace. Some of the enemy are killed, others flee while shouting aloud, and Gobryas and his men join in the shouting, pretending to be fellow revellers. The Assyrian defectors head straight for the palace gates and fall upon the sentries there, who are drinking by a fire. The clamour reaches the palace and the king sends out messengers to see what is wrong. Gobryas and Gadatas then rush through the open gates to the king himself, who awaits them, dagger in hand. Gadatas, Gobryas, and their men kill the king and his attendants: Babylon has been captured. The two Assyrian defectors bow down and thank the gods for allowing them their vengeance upon the wicked king and then kiss Cyrus' hands and feet, crying for joy (7. 5. 26–32).

Xenophon's description of the conquest of Babylon by Cyrus resembles in many ways the account found in Herodotus (1. 189–91). Both writers agree that the city was hostile to the Persian leader and

---

[224] See 5. 3. 15–18, 5. 4. 51, 8. 3. 25, 6. 1. 19, 21, 8. 3. 17, 7. 5. 24 ff. At the same time that Gadatas takes over one Assyrian fort by using persuasion (5. 4. 51) Cyrus, typically, captures two other strongholds by means of harsher tactics—assault and intimidation.

[225] Xenophon's account of the capture of Babylon by Cyrus is not very lucid. Cyrus, apparently, has no real intention of besieging the city and simply wishes to confuse the Babylonians, but the Persian leader does not make this clear at the start to his own followers—cf. *Cyr.* 7. 5. 7 and the troublesome phrase ὅπως ὅτι μάλιστα ἐοίκοι πολιορκήσειν παρασκευαζομένῳ (7. 5. 12) with Holden's note ad loc.; see also Keller 1911: 257–8. Cyrus also comes up rather abruptly with a plan to divert the Euphrates (7. 5. 9), and the exact method he uses to drain the river is unclear; see Breitenbach 1966: 1711–12.

had to be captured by force. In both versions Cyrus originally intends to besiege the city, but is daunted by the fact that the Babylonians have a huge store of provisions. The Persian leader, in both accounts, then diverts the Euphrates in order to gain entrance into the city and his attack takes place at the time of a festival, when many of the Babylonians are drinking and making merry.[226] The Book of Daniel (5: 1 ff.) also tells of Babylon being captured by 'Darius the Mede' at the time of a great feast, when the king and his court have drunk a great deal. This stratagem of taking advantage of an intoxicated enemy is found elsewhere as well: in Herodotus Cyrus kills and captures many of the Massagetae after they wine and dine on Persian fare, and the clever thief puts Rhampsinitus' guards to sleep by sharing with them the wine he has 'accidentally' spilt, thus recovering his brother's body. Charon of Lampsacus has another such tale of making the enemy drunk.[227]

Unlike Xenophon, Herodotus does not refer to the fate of the king of Babylon (whom he calls Labynetus, son of Labynetus and Nitocris, 1. 188), and he makes no mention, of course, of the part played by the Assyrian defectors Gobryas and Gadatas. In any event, neither Herodotus' version nor that of Xenophon matches the account of Babylon's capture found in the cuneiform evidence, the most authentic historical record.[228] According to the Nabonidus Chronicle (3. 15 ff.), 'Ugbaru [= Gobryas] . . . and the army of Cyrus entered Babylon without battle' and Nabonidus himself was arrested. Some ten days later Cyrus entered the city and he was greeted ceremoniously, as a victor and liberator.[229] There is no mention of the fact that Persian rule began in Babylon during a festival, although according to some translations of the Chronicle reference is made to the drinking of wine at the beginning of the

[226] Hostile city: Hdt. 1. 190; *Cyr.* 7. 5. 2, 13, 14, cf. 58. Capture by force: Hdt. 1. 190–1; *Cyr.* 7. 5. 20–31. Intention to besiege: Hdt. 1. 190; *Cyr.* 7. 5. 7. Babylonian stores: Hdt. 1. 190. 2; *Cyr.* 7. 5. 13. Euphrates diverted: Hdt. 1. 191. 1–5; *Cyr.* 7. 5. 15–16. Festival and merry Babylonians: Hdt. 1. 191. 6; *Cyr.* 7. 5. 15, cf. 21, 25, 26, 27. For a further comparison of the two accounts see Keller 1911: 257–8; Breitenbach 1966: 1711–12.

[227] Hdt. 1. 211, 2. 121 δ; *FGrH* 262 F 17.

[228] For a recent survey of the available sources on the Babylonia of Cyrus' time and an account of the conquest of Babylon see Kuhrt 1988: 112–28. Dougherty 1929: 167–200 is an attempt to reconcile the various Greek and cuneiform sources: see too Ravn 1942: 90–1; Smith 1944: 30–48; Burn 1984: 54–5.

[229] The Chronicle, whose language is obscure here, states that green twigs or palm-branches were strewn along the path which Cyrus used. See Oppenheim 1985: 539, 543; Kuhrt 1988: 121 n. 68.

description of the fall of Babylon.[230] The Cyrus Cylinder, which is less historical and more propagandist than the Chronicle,[231] tells of how Marduk had Cyrus enter Babylon without any battle and delivered Nabonidus into the Persian's hands: the people of Babylon were jubilant. In actual fact, then, Cyrus did not have to take the city of Babylon by force.[232] He captured Nabonidus, the ruler of Babylon, but apparently did not execute him.[233]

This brings us to the question of the identity of the nameless Assyrian rulers—father and son—found in the *Cyropaedia*. Which historical figures, if any, lie behind Xenophon's kindly, elderly Assyrian king and his son, the wicked young ruler? One possibility is that the father in Xenophon, the original Assyrian king, is Nabonidus and the crown prince is his son, Belshazzar. The historical Nabonidus spent ten years in self-imposed exile in Teima, an oasis in the Arabian desert, returning to the capital only a few years before the city's capture, and during his absence his son Belshazzar reigned in his stead, as co-regent, in Babylon.[234] Thus Xenophon (or his source) may have assumed that Belshazzar was the actual ruler of

[230] Dougherty 1929: 169 (and cf. 195) translates 3. 7 of the Nabonidus Chronicle as 'the abundance of wine was ample among the [troops]', while the version of Grayson 1975*a*: 109 is 'He [i.e. Nabonidus] made a libation of wine.' Oppenheim, the translator in Pritchard 1969, considers the passage unintelligible and does not give a translation—see 306 n. 8. Kuhrt 1988: 121 notes that the Chronicle (3. 16–18) stresses that no rites or cultic acts were interrupted at the temples even after Gobryas' troops entered Babylon and suggests that this fact led to Herodotus' story of a festival taking place at the time of the city's capture; Beaulieu 1989: 226 thinks that the tradition of festivities might reflect historical fact.

[231] An English translation of the Cylinder is in Pritchard 1969: 315–16; for an analysis of the inscription see Oppenheim 1985: 545–51; Dougherty 1929: 175–9; and the further references in Kuhrt 1987: 49 n. 80.

[232] Kuhrt 1990*b*: 123–4 points out that Cyrus' entry into Babylon was 'carefully orchestrated' and followed a hard-won battle, including much slaughter and looting, at Opis; cf. Kuhrt 1990*a*: 181.

[233] Scholarly opinion varies as to whether or not Nabonidus was executed: the second volume of the *Cambridge History of Iran* again—cf. above, n. 184—contains a variety of views. Diakonoff 1985: 147 thinks that Nabonidus was spared, as (apparently) does Oppenheim 1985: 542, while Mallowan 1985: 414 argues, partly on the basis of *Cyr.* 7. 5. 29–30, that the Babylonian ruler was killed. Dandamaev 1989: 47–50, Beaulieu 1989: 231, and Kuhrt 1990*a*: 185 all refer to the Dynastic Prophecy, a recently discovered Babylonian text—cf. Grayson 1975*b*: 24–37—which is a brief history of the kings of Babylon cast in the form of a pseudo-prophecy. In this text (2. 19–21) it is 'predicted' that the king of Elam (i.e. Cyrus) will settle the deposed Nabonidus in another land. This statement is confirmed by the Babylonian historian Berossus (*FGrH* 680 F 9), who says that Cyrus took pity on Nabonidus and exiled him to a remote province.

[234] See Tadmor 1965 for a chronology of Nabonidus' movements (and inscriptions), and cf. Beaulieu 1989: 149–71. Oates 1986: 131–5 is a briefer account.

Assyria (i.e. Babylonia) at the time of Nabonidus' stay in Teima and that Nabonidus was dead rather than in exile.[235] In the *Cyropaedia*, however, the elderly Assyrian king is a fairly positive figure: his former subjects all speak highly of him and his only crime is his desire to add Media to his empire. His son, on the other hand, is unabashedly evil, known above all for his impiety and hubris.[236] This picture of a wicked, impious king fits in well with the very black portrait of Nabonidus found in the (Persian-inspired) Babylonian sources—especially in the Cyrus Cylinder and the 'Verse Account of Nabonidus'.[237] In these cuneiform sources Nabonidus is a wicked man and a heretic, who prefers the cult of the moon-god Sin over the traditional worship of Marduk. He moves the images of the gods about, neglects various temples, and fails to celebrate the new year festival. In addition, he mistreats his subjects ('Verse Account', col. 1). In the Cyrus Cylinder Nabonidus is unfavourably contrasted with Cyrus, who is depicted as a saviour chosen by Marduk. While opposition to Nabonidus' rule may not have been solely, or even chiefly, on religious grounds,[238] it is clear that he was quite unpopular in Babylon and that he was attacked by Persian propagandists for his unrighteous behaviour. Thus word of Nabonidus' bad reputation may have reached Xenophon through Persian sources, and Nabonidus, although close to 70 at the time of Babylon's capture,[239] seems a much more likely candidate for the role of the villainous young Assyrian king of the *Cyropaedia*. If Nabonidus is the younger Assyrian of the *Cyropaedia* we are left with the problem of identifying his father, the elderly king. Nabonidus was not the son of Labashi-Marduk, the previous ruler, but ascended to the throne after conspiring against his king. Herodotus seems to think that Nabonidus was the son of Nebuchadrezzar,[240] and Xenophon may have thought so as well.

[235] This same argument is used to explain why in the Book of Daniel (5: 1–6: 1), Belshazzar is king of Babylon at the time of its fall; see Dougherty 1929: 196–7; Lehmann-Haupt 1902; Beaulieu 1989: 231.

[236] Elderly Assyrian king: 4. 6. 2, 5, 6, 5. 4. 12, 6. 1. 45; cf. 1. 5. 2–3. Young Assyrian ruler: *Cyr.* 4. 6. 4, 5. 2. 27, 28, 6. 1. 45, 7. 5. 32. Beaulieu 1989: 90–8 argues that Belshazzar was in fact the evil son of a kindly, aged father.

[237] For an English translation of the 'Verse Account of Nabonidus' see Pritchard 1969: 312–15.

[238] Cf. Oppenheim 1985: 540–2, 546–7, 550–1; Oates 1986: 133–4. Kuhrt 1990c argues that there is no real evidence for religious opposition to Nabonidus.

[239] Oates 1986: 134.

[240] Hdt. 1. 74–7 and 1. 188. 1; he calls both kings Labynetus. See MacGinnis 1986: 79 for the various identifications of the two Labynetuses by scholars. In the Book of Daniel Belshazzar is thought to be the son of Nebuchadrezzar.

Another possibility is that Nebuchadrezzar is the model for the elderly king, while his son and short-lived heir, the unpopular Amel-Marduk (Evil-Merodach), is the young Assyrian king, but both father and son ruled Babylon before it fell to Cyrus and the Persians. In short, there is no simple way to identify the two Assyrian rulers of the *Cyropaedia* with any pair of historical Babylonian kings.[241]

The assassination of the young Assyrian king, the final scene in the Gobryas–Gadatas novella, contains no dialogue; it is the only important episode in the novella that does not include conversation. Gadatas, Gobryas, and their forces are simply shown making their way into the palace and killing the king, who awaits them with dagger held in hand. It is surprising that Xenophon does not dramatize the actual assassination: he could have included, for example, speeches by the two Assyrian defectors, vilifying the king one last time before executing him, or a plea by the king to be spared. In both Herodotus and Ctesias there are similar stories involving the murder of a reigning king within the palace walls, and their accounts are much livelier. Herodotus, when telling of the assassination of the Magi pretenders to the throne by the seven Persian conspirators (3. 77–9), has a full description of the event. He tells of the conspirators' entry into the palace, the Magi taking up their weapons, and the actual struggle between the Magi and the seven. Herodotus even includes an exchange between Gobryas and Darius in the midst of the fight, in which the former urges the latter to kill the Magus at all costs. Ctesias' parallel account of the same event (*FGrH* 688 F 13. 16) is, as is to be expected, even more colourful. The seven Persians, who have the eunuchs Artasuras and Bagpates, keeper of the keys, join their plot, come upon the Magus ruler in bed with a Babylonian concubine. The Magus, having no other weapon at hand, fights them off with a couch-leg but is eventually overpowered. In another assassination scene (F 15. 48) Secundianus, aided by the eunuch Pharnacyas, kills his half-brother Xerxes only a short time after the latter ascends to the throne. The killing takes place during a festival, when Xerxes is asleep in the palace after drinking his fill. This story, in the abridged version given us by Photius, clearly resembles our scene, for both killings take place during a festival when the victims are fairly drunk, and both involve two conspirators—a noble and a eunuch. Eunuchs also participate in the assassination of the Magus

---

[241] See too Miller's discussion in appendix II of the Loeb *Cyr.*, 456–7.

in Ctesias' version, and Xenophon may have been influenced by the *Persica* when fashioning Gadatas' role in the *Cyropaedia*.

Why does Xenophon describe the assassination of the Assyrian king so briefly? One reason may be that, as with Abradatas' death in the course of the battle of Thymbrara, he does not wish to interrupt the swift narrative of events—the conquest of Babylon—in order to linger over a diverting, dramatic episode: such a pause would break up the continuity of his tale. Another possibility is that Xenophon did not consider a drawn-out death scene especially edifying or entertaining. In any event, with the death of the wicked Assyrian king the novellas of the two Assyrian defectors come to an end. Both Gobryas and Gadatas can be encountered later in the *Cyropaedia*,[242] but no further reference is made to their tribulations at the hands of the young Assyrian ruler.

4. CROESUS: A WISE MONARCH?

Croesus is the leading figure in the last of our four novellas. We have already seen that the king of Lydia first appears in person in the *Cyropaedia* only after he comes under Cyrus' control, following his capture at Sardis. The first exchange between Cyrus and the Lydian monarch in our work (7. 2. 9ff.) was undoubtedly written by Xenophon with Herodotus' account of Croesus in mind. Herodotus' story of the meeting between Croesus and Solon, the tale of the Lydian's two sons, Croesus' frequent consultations of the oracle at Delphi, his first encounter with Cyrus after the capture of Sardis—all have left their mark on our dialogue. This influence expresses itself in different ways: at times Xenophon seems to assume his readers' acquaintance with Herodotus' *History*, alluding only briefly to stories found there and taking it for granted, as it were, that his readers can fill in the gaps by themselves. Elsewhere in this first conversation between the two rulers Xenophon deliberately strays from his predecessor's account.[243]

Cyrus enters Sardis the morning after the capture of the city, and the Lydian monarch, who has shut himself up in his palace,

[242] See e.g. *Cyr.* 8. 4. 1 ff.

[243] For a detailed, thoughtful comparison between *Cyr.* 7. 2. 9–29 and Herodotus' account of Croesus see Lefèvre 1971. Keller 1911 and Riemann 1967: 20–7 also compare the two authors, and the following discussion draws upon all three scholars. For other Greek versions of the life of Croesus see Weissbach 1931: 456–7.

immediately calls for him, presumably in order to ask for protection for himself and his men. The Persian leader arranges for a force to guard Croesus, but has no time for the defeated king himself. Cyrus has discovered that the Chaldean contingent of his army, who have entered and captured the city together with the Persians the night before, have left their posts in order to loot the rich capital. An enraged Cyrus summons the Chaldean leaders and dismisses them from his army, warning them that they will now be exposed to danger. The penitent Chaldeans offer to return the booty at once and Cyrus has them turn it over to the obedient Persians who have stayed at their posts, for he thinks that the discipline of the Persians should be rewarded (7. 2. 1–8). Only after dealing with this reckless plundering of Sardis is the Persian leader able to devote himself to Croesus: Xenophon uses this incident with the Chaldeans in order to set the stage for the discussion of treasure which takes place between the two leaders at their first meeting.[244] This concern with the preservation or guarding of wealth—which also arises at the first encounter between Croesus and Cyrus in Herodotus (1. 88–90)—recurs in the two other conversations that the Lydian and the Persian rulers hold in the *Cyropaedia*.

Croesus is brought before Cyrus and greets him meekly—χαῖρε ὦ δέσποτα (7. 2. 9)[245]—saying that fate has decreed that Cyrus will be called his master henceforth. The Persian, rather unexpectedly, wishes Croesus well in return, reminding him that they are both human, after all (7. 2. 10 ἐπείπερ ἄνθρωποί γέ ἐσμεν ἀμφότεροι). Cyrus seems unusually benevolent here, particularly if we bear in mind that Croesus was the leader of the enemy forces allied against him, and as such has caused him a great deal of trouble. In a similar situation—a first meeting with a defeated enemy immediately after his capture—Cyrus behaves much more sternly towards the Armenian king. The key to the Persian's humane attitude here seems to lie in Herodotus and his version of the first meeting, at the funeral pyre, between Croesus and Cyrus. There the Persian leader, after hearing of Croesus' discussion with Solon, comes to realize that he and the Lydian are equally mortal: καὶ τὸν Κῦρον ... μεταγνόντα τε καὶ ἐννώσαντα ὅτι καὶ αὐτὸς ἄνθρωπος ἐὼν ἄλλον ἄνθρωπον ... ζῶντα πυρὶ διδοίη (Hdt. 1. 86. 6). In the *Cyropaedia* Cyrus comes to

---

[244] See Tatum 1989: 153 for a different interpretation of the Chaldean incident.

[245] For the use of δεσπότης by various characters in the *Cyr.* see above, sects. 2 and 3 at n. 193; Tatum 1989: 153 overlooks these usages.

this first meeting equipped with an awareness of his own—and Croesus'—mortality, and he brings it up at the very start of the conversation without having been enlightened by Croesus. The Lydian, in turn, makes no mention of Solon. Thus Cyrus, in Xenophon's version, fills to a certain extent the role given to Solon in Herodotus: at the least, he possesses a portion of Solon's wisdom.[246]

Cyrus' next words to Croesus are again somewhat unexpected: the Persian leader would like to ask the Lydian's advice. Cyrus only rarely asks the advice of others in the *Cyropaedia*, and Croesus, an enemy and rival who has just been subdued, is an unlikely counsellor: here too it seems that the influence of Herodotus is at work. The Lydian king is eager to oblige Cyrus, reminding us of Herodotus' Croesus, who in fact volunteers his counsel without being asked.[247] The same problem is discussed in both Xenophon and Herodotus: the looting of Sardis. We have seen that in the *Cyropaedia* this question troubles Cyrus even before his meeting with Croesus; although the Persian has resolved the Chaldean affair by himself, he is concerned with the ramifications of the incident. Cyrus would like to reward his deserving soldiers but is afraid that if he allows them to loot Sardis indiscriminately the city will be destroyed and the worst men will end up with the largest share of the booty (7. 2. 11). In Herodotus, it should be recalled, Croesus points out to the Persian leader that the victorious Persian soldiers are pillaging what is now Cyrus'—and not his own—city. Herodotus' Lydian warns Cyrus that the Persians, who are both undisciplined and unused to money, will be spoilt by their new wealth, and that the one who takes the most will be bound to rebel against Cyrus. Croesus then suggests a way to confiscate the spoils without angering the Persian soldiers (Hdt. 1. 88–9). Thus one of Cyrus' two worries in the *Cyropaedia*—that his worst soldiers will be the most acquisitive—is already discussed by the Herodotean Croesus, while his other concern, that the city of Sardis will be ruined, is not. In Herodotus Croesus thinks of how to keep Cyrus' newly acquired wealth and inexperienced Persian soldiers safe from harm, while in Xenophon the Lydian worries more directly about his own city and subjects.[248] Croesus' plan for having

---

[246] Cf. Lefèvre 1971: 283–5. Lefèvre is less convincing when he argues that Cyrus, in Xenophon's version, is meant to replace Apollo as well (292–3).

[247] *Cyr.* 7. 2. 10; Hdt. 1. 88. 2, cf. 1. 207. 1.

[248] Croesus of the *Cyr.* does not have any suggestions on how the Persian leader is to distribute booty among his soldiers or restrain the more avaricious of his men, and later Cyrus will successfully handle this problem by himself: cf. *Cyr.* 8. 4. 29–36.

the Lydians turn over their wealth and preserving the city intact is simple: he will approach his fellow Lydians, telling them that he has won a guarantee from Cyrus that there will be no sacking of the city or removal of women and children. In return, promises Croesus, the Lydians will willingly hand over all the wealth of Sardis to the Persians and the unravaged city will be filled afresh, the following year, with many good things. Cyrus can always reconsider the question of spoils later, concludes the Lydian monarch, but in the meantime the Persian can begin his take-over of the riches of Sardis by emptying out Croesus' own treasuries (7. 2. 12–14).

The Persian leader, Xenophon tells us, adopts all of Croesus' recommendations; such an immediate, wholesale acceptance of the proposal of another by Cyrus is very rare indeed in the *Cyropaedia*. After Cyrus' long conversation with his father in Book 1 of the *Cyropaedia*, in which the Persian king instructs his son on how to behave in the forthcoming military expedition (1. 6), it is very unusual to find Cyrus following the advice of others. None the less, here the Persian leader consults with Croesus, listens to his advice, and implements all of the Lydian's proposals.[249] Croesus not only offers immediate, specific advice, but explains his reasoning, speaking in more general fashion of the economic foundations of a city. His comment that a city's handicrafts are the source of its affluence is especially noteworthy.[250] Here, then, Croesus is a repository of general knowledge and a wise counsellor, while Cyrus seeks, and follows, his advice. Croesus continues in this role of adviser to the Persian leader in his two later appearances in the *Cyropaedia*, just as the Herodotean Croesus counsels Cyrus (and Cambyses) several times. On these later occasions in the *Cyropaedia*, however, the Lydian volunteers his suggestions unasked and Cyrus does not accept them quite so wholeheartedly: Croesus is no longer very wise.

In his second encounter with Croesus in the *Cyropaedia* (7. 4. 12–13) Cyrus is about to depart from Sardis, taking many wagon-loads of booty with him. Croesus presents the Persian with an exact written inventory of the contents of each wagon and explains that the lists will enable Cyrus to check on his men and see whether or not they have delivered all the goods entrusted to them. Cyrus thanks Croesus for

---

[249] 7. 2. 14 ταῦτα μὲν δὴ πάντα οὕτω συνήνεσε ποιεῖν ὁ Κῦρος ὥσπερ ἔλεξεν ὁ Κροῖσος.

[250] 7. 2. 13 αἱ τέχναι . . . ἃς πηγάς φασι τῶν καλῶν εἶναι; for this meaning of τέχναι cf. 5. 3. 47 and 6. 2. 37.

the inventory, but reminds him that the men are conveying booty to which they themselves are entitled, so that stealing would, in effect, mean stealing from themselves. None the less, Cyrus makes use of the Lydian's lists, having his lieutenants check up on the men responsible for delivering the wagon-loads. Croesus offers at this second meeting unsolicited advice—advice again related to the preservation of treasure—which Cyrus seems to reject but actually makes use of. The Persian, while proclaiming his faith in his men, does arrange to keep them under surveillance: Cyrus manages to have his cake and eat it too. The argument which Cyrus uses here— that his men would only be robbing themselves—seems a variation on Croesus' words to Cyrus in Herodotus, when the Lydian points out that the Persians are looting what is now Cyrus' city and not his own: οὔτε πόλιν τὴν ἐμὴν οὔτε χρήματα τὰ ἐμὰ διαρπάζει . . . ἀλλὰ φέρουσί τε καὶ ἄγουσι τὰ σά (Hdt. 1. 88).[251] Here too Xenophon seems to be writing with Herodotus' *History* in mind.

It should be noted that even in Herodotus Croesus is not always the wise adviser, nor is Cyrus simply one who consistently receives advice. In the *History* the Lydian monarch is at first in need of sage advice himself, and he is counselled by Bias/Pittacus, Sandanis, and, of course, Solon.[252] After his defeat Croesus is transformed into an adviser, guiding both Cyrus and Cambyses, and he retains that role to the very end of his days.[253] His suggestions do not, however, always prove valuable, as Cambyses points out.[254] Herodotus' Cyrus, although generally the recipient of advice (from Harpagus, Croesus, etc.), is capable of devising his own schemes when the need arises, and at the very end of the *History* the Persian ruler himself appears as a wise adviser, warning of the dangerous effects of a soft climate.[255] Thus Herodotus allows a certain fluidity or flexibility in the roles of adviser and recipient of advice,[256] but it is true that when Croesus and Cyrus converse in the *History* the Lydian is always the teacher and the Persian his pupil. In the *Cyropaedia* Xenophon has the two rulers virtually exchange parts, proceeding by stages. At their first meeting Cyrus requests Croesus' advice and does as the Lydian suggests

---

[251] Cf. Delebecque's note ad loc. in the Budé *Cyr.* Hdt. 7. 147 is another instance of a monarch's wise distinction between 'theirs' and 'ours'.

[252] Hdt. 1. 27, 1. 71, 1. 29–33.

[253] Hdt. 1. 155–6, 207, 3. 34, 36.

[254] Hdt. 3. 36; cf. Stahl 1975.

[255] Hdt. 9. 122; cf. 1. 125–6.

[256] Cf. Lattimore 1939.

(7. 2. 10–14), but is asked by Croesus in turn, as we shall see, for his opinion on a different matter (7. 2. 25). When the two next converse, about the need for an inventory of the wagon-loads of booty, Cyrus again accepts the Lydian's advice, which is unsolicited this time, but does so reluctantly, contributing his own words of wisdom (7. 4. 12–13). Finally, at their third and last discussion the Persian leader rejects Croesus' unsolicited counsel outright, and Cyrus is clearly meant to be the wiser of the two.

At this third encounter between Croesus and Cyrus in the *Cyropaedia* (8. 2. 15–23) the Persian leader demonstrates that friends, rather than treasuries, are the best place to deposit one's riches. Croesus warns Cyrus that he is squandering his wealth by distributing so much to his friends and suggests that the Persian ruler store his riches in a treasury instead. Cyrus responds by proving that friends make the best and safest treasure-houses. He sends Hystaspas round to his friends with a request for funds and the sum total promised by Cyrus' well-wishers proves much larger than the amount that Croesus thought the Persian leader could amass on his own. Cyrus then points out at length that those who acquire money justly and use it well are happier than those who store up vast amounts of wealth.[257] Here, then, Cyrus rejects Croesus' advice on money matters. This conversation between Croesus and the Persian leader is introduced by Xenophon in a chapter of the *Cyropaedia* devoted to praise of Cyrus and the efforts he makes to win the affection of his subjects. Xenophon lauds his hero and describes Cyrus' actions and sayings very much in the manner he uses for Socrates in the *Memorabilia*.[258] The conversation between Cyrus and Croesus falls into two parts—the discussion before and after Hystaspas' appeal to Cyrus' friends—reminding us of the two-part dialogues of advice in the *Memorabilia*. Here, as in the *Memorabilia*, a third person is introduced to carry out a plan, and there is a pause while instructions are carried out.[259] Cyrus' fairly lengthy exhortation at the end of the dialogue is another *Memorabilia*-like feature of the conversation. Thus, in his third conversation with Croesus in the *Cyropaedia* Cyrus is so much

---

[257] Cf. above, ch. 3. 5 at n. 131.

[258] Note in particular καὶ λόγος δὲ αὐτοῦ ἀπομνημονεύεται (*Cyr.* 8. 2. 14) and the introduction to the third Croesus–Cyrus encounter: καλὸν δ' ἐπίδειγμα ... λέγεται Κῦρος ἐπιδεῖξαι Κροίσῳ (8. 2. 15).

[259] Third person introduced: *Mem.* 2. 9. 4 ff. Pause while instructions are executed: *Mem.* 2. 7. 12, 2. 9. 4, 3. 1. 4. For two-part advice dialogues in the *Mem.* see above, ch. 2. 1 at n. 64.

the teacher that he is made to resemble Xenophon's favourite didactic figure of all, Socrates, while Croesus, who has little to say after his initial suggestion, clearly plays the role of disciple to the Persian leader: Herodotus has been left far behind. In sum, Xenophon, when portraying the relationship between Cyrus and Croesus, plays with the roles of adviser and recipient of advice, moving from the characterization of Croesus as counsellor and Cyrus as pupil found in Herodotus to his own idealized portrait of the Persian as a wise leader who rarely needs to consult others.

Returning to the initial meeting between Croesus and Cyrus in the *Cyropaedia*, we find that Cyrus now questions Croesus about his past, allowing us a further, more colourful glimpse into the Lydian's background. Cyrus begins by asking Croesus about his relationship with Apollo and the Delphic oracle (7. 2. 15). In Herodotus' version of the first meeting between the two rulers a puzzled and angry Croesus requests permission from Cyrus to send messengers to Delphi, in order to discover why he has been so dangerously misled by the oracle. It is only after he receives an explanation from the Pythian priestess that Croesus is willing to acknowledge his own share in his downfall (Hdt. 1. 90–1). Here, Cyrus already knows of the Lydian's connection with the oracle and he wonders about the responses from Delphi—that is, he wonders how Croesus, an obedient and generous follower of Apollo, has ended up in his present unfortunate situation. Croesus, in Xenophon, is not surprised at his defeat at the hands of the Persians, and realizes at once, immediately after his capture, that he is entirely to blame.[260] The lessons which both Cyrus and Croesus learn slowly and at some cost in Herodotus—on mortal limitations, on personal culpability—are quickly absorbed, almost taken for granted, in the *Cyropaedia*.

The Lydian king has, he tells Cyrus, behaved badly towards Apollo from the very start, testing the oracle's credibility rather than approaching it with a specific request. Even gentlemen, to say nothing of gods, do not like being mistrusted, continues Croesus. None the less, the oracle responded to the Lydian's test and knew what strange things Croesus was doing far away from Delphi. Croesus' account here of his dealings with the oracle is brief to the point of obscurity, and is best understood with Herodotus at hand: Xenophon seems to assume that his readers are familiar with the *History* and he quickly summarizes this section of the Lydian's tale.

[260] Cf. Riemann 1967: 24–5.

According to Herodotus (1. 46–8), exactly a hundred days after he sent messengers off to various oracles Croesus boiled a tortoise and a lamb together in a bronze cauldron; the oracle at Delphi described his doings accurately. In Herodotus it is not actually stated that the Lydian ruler was wrong to put the oracle to the test and Croesus is not reprimanded for his impiety, not even in the final response he receives from Delphi, in which the Pythian priestess explains how he has consistently misconstrued the oracle's words (Hdt. 1. 91). None the less, this action of his is surely meant to contribute to the Herodotean picture of Croesus as an arrogant and hubristic man who is bound to fall. Elsewhere in the *History* such attempts to tamper with the divine, or test it, often end in disaster. Amasis' warning to Polycrates and Artabanus' attempts to conjure up Xerxes' dream by sleeping in the king's bed are two such examples, while the case of Aristodicus, who successfully tests the truth of an oracle, is perhaps a counter-example.[261]

In the *Cyropaedia* Croesus now tells Cyrus of the second time he consulted the Delphic oracle: he asked what he should do in order to have children. This question does not have any parallel in Herodotus, and we are meant to understand that Xenophon's Croesus did not have any children[262] for many years. The Lydian king does not receive any reply at first, presumably because Apollo was angered by his initial approach, but he appeases the god with rich offerings and sacrifices and is finally told that he will have children. Here Croesus uses the treasures he sends to Delphi as a kind of bribe or incentive to prompt a reply, rather than as a thank-you offering after the oracle has granted a reply, as in Herodotus. Croesus tells Cyrus that he subsequently had two sons but that they were of no avail, for one is permanently mute while the other was killed in the prime of life. Once again Xenophon is apparently looking back to the *History*, for Croesus' description of his two sons in our dialogue closely parallels Herodotus' initial description of the two.[263] Herodotus gives full details of the tragic death of Atys at the hands of Adrastus and also tells of how Croesus' second son miraculously regained his power of speech and saved his father's life when Sardis was captured.[264]

---

[261] Hdt. 3. 40–3, 7. 15–18, 1. 157–9.

[262] Or perhaps sons—cf. *Cyr.* 7. 2. 26.

[263] Compare ὁ μὲν γὰρ κωφὸς ὢν διετέλει, ὁ δὲ ἄριστος γενόμενος ἐν ἀκμῇ τοῦ βίου ἀπώλετο (*Cyr.* 7. 2. 20) with ἦσαν δὲ τῷ Κροίσῳ δύο παῖδες, τῶν οὕτερος μὲν διέφθαρτο, ἦν γὰρ δὴ κωφός, ὁ δὲ ἕτερος τῶν ἡλίκων μακρῷ τὰ πάντα πρῶτος (Hdt. 1. 34).

[264] Hdt. 1. 34–45, 1. 85.

Xenophon's brief mention of Croesus' dead son seems to allude to the Atys–Adrastus tale in Herodotus, but he apparently rejects the second story, stating that Croesus' other son remained (7. 2. 20 διετέλει) mute.

The Lydian monarch's next approach to the oracle comes, he tells Cyrus, because he is overcome by the misfortunes concerning his children. He asks Apollo what he should do in order to pass the remainder of his life most happily: τί ἂν ποιῶν τὸν λοιπὸν βίον εὐδαι-μονέστατα διατελέσαιμι;(7. 2. 20). This question is perhaps best understood against the background of Solon's conversation with Croesus in Herodotus, since there too Croesus is concerned with the question of happiness.[265] When he is asked by the Lydian king to name men who are happy, Solon repeatedly stresses that men can be judged fortunate only after their lives are over—that is, only if their good fortune continues to the very end of their days.[266] Our Croesus seems to take this warning of Solon into account when he frames his question to the oracle, since he asks, in the wake of his family's misfortunes, how he is to be happy for the rest of his days, rather than asking, for instance, what he should do to change his luck or how he can become happy.

The oracle's response to Croesus—quoted verbatim, so to speak, in verse form—is σαυτὸν γιγνώσκων εὐδαίμων, Κροῖσε, περάσεις (*Cyr.* 7. 2. 20). This is, of course, the famous Delphic maxim γνῶθι σαυτόν: Croesus must know himself, and in this way will go through life happy. The oracle quoted here (and the question which prompts it) does not appear in other extant accounts of Croesus and was probably invented by Xenophon himself.[267] Croesus' earlier consultation of the Delphic oracle, on having children, also appears only in the *Cyropaedia*, and again seems to have been fabricated by Xenophon, but there he simply summarizes Apollo's reply—ἔσοιντο (*Cyr.* 7. 2. 19)—rather than producing a full-fledged oracle. The second oracle conforms to the general pattern of oracular responses: it is in dactylic hexameter, Croesus, the petitioner, is addressed in the second person, and his name appears in the vocative. Only the type

---

[265] Hdt. 1. 29–33; cf. Lefèvre 1971: 288.

[266] Hdt. 1. 32. 7 πρὶν δ᾽ ἂν τελευτήσῃ ἐπισχεῖν μηδὲ καλέειν κω ὄλβιον; cf. 1. 30. 4, 1. 31. 3, 1. 32. 5, 9, 1. 33.

[267] Cf. Parke and Wormell 1956: i. 139, who call the oracle in Xenophon 'crudely impossible'. Fontenrose 1978: 304 agrees, saying that both oracles in the *Cyr.*—on the children and 'Know thyself' (= Q 104 and Q 105 in his numbering)—were invented by Xenophon.

of dactylic hexameter used—spondees in each of the first four feet—is rather rare.[268] The lesson which Xenophon has Apollo teach Croesus here, 'Know thyself', is a traditionally pious one, but it is none the less disconcerting to find Xenophon, a petitioner of the Delphic oracle on his own behalf,[269] concocting or 'forging' an oracle for literary purposes.

Upon receiving this reply from Delphi Croesus was, he tells Cyrus, pleased, thinking that the oracle had prescribed a very easy task, since everyone knows who he himself is. Initially, then, Croesus takes the famous injunction γνῶθι σαυτόν—an injunction which was inscribed over the entrance to Apollo's sanctuary at Delphi and ascribed to various wise men such as Thales, Chilon, etc.[270]—at its face value. The Lydian monarch thinks that he already knows who he is, i.e. knows that he is (named) Croesus. In his superficial approach to the maxim Croesus reminds us of another figure in Xenophon, Euthydemus of the *Memorabilia* (4. 2. 24 ff.). Young Euthydemus, who has been to Delphi twice, has to be taught by Socrates that 'Know thyself' does not simply mean knowing one's name, but knowing one's capabilities. This—the recognition of his own abilities or capacities—is precisely the lesson Croesus learns through his encounters with Cyrus. When the Lydian king stays peaceably at home all goes well for him, but after joining the Assyrian's campaign against Cyrus his troubles begin afresh, since the Assyrians and their allies, including Croesus, are defeated in their first clash with the Persians. Only when the Lydian recognizes his inferiority to the Persians and withdraws from the battle are his safety and well-being guaranteed. Through their first engagement in battle Cyrus unwittingly teaches Croesus to know himself—as an inferior rival.[271]

---

[268] For a brief characterization of oracular responses see Parke and Wormell 1956: ii, p. xxv. According to Parke and Wormell, p. xxx, the metrical pattern found in our hexameter occurs in only two other oracular responses. Of the six components of oracular poetry noted by Fontenrose 1978: 177–9, our one-line oracle contains three: (A) salutation, (B) restatement of the question, and (E) message.

[269] *Anab.* 3. 1. 5–8; cf. 5. 3. 5, 6. 1. 22.

[270] See Pl. *Prot.* 343A–B; *Charm.* 164D; and the further references collected by O'Brien 1967: 80–2. Interestingly, Chilon is supposed to have been enjoined by the Delphic oracle γνῶθι σαυτόν in reply to his question 'What is best?', but the sources for this story are all later than the *Cyr.*—see Parke and Wormell 1956: ii, No. 423, and Fontenrose 1978: Q 77. On γνῶθι σαυτόν in general see Wilamowitz 1926.

[271] When Socrates explains to Euthydemus the true meaning of the maxim 'Know thyself', he uses just such an example: those cities which do not know their own capabilities and fight against stronger ones lose either their territory or their freedom (*Mem.* 4. 2. 29).

Croesus' newly acquired knowledge of himself, his recognition of his own limitations in the military sphere, is short-lived, and soon afterwards he allows himself to be chosen commander-in-chief of the Assyrians and their allies. The life of luxury he leads, the gifts he receives, the flattery and entreaties of others, and the prospect of becoming the greatest of men—all these factors puff Croesus up, he explains to Cyrus, and lead him to accept the leadership of the army (*Cyr.* 7. 2. 23). It is interesting to note that the means used to persuade Croesus here—gifts and soft words—are precisely those he himself uses to coax an answer from the Delphic oracle. Thus once again Croesus does not know himself, that is, he does not acknowledge his own limitations. The Lydian adds that he was particularly wrong in thinking that he could defeat the Persian leader. Cyrus, notes Croesus, is descended from the gods, comes from a royal line of kings, and has practised virtue from childhood onwards, whereas he himself is descended from a man who gained both his kingdom and his freedom on the same day. This description of Cyrus as a scion of gods and kings—πρῶτον μὲν ἐκ θεῶν γεγονότι, ἔπειτα δὲ διὰ βασιλέων πεφυκότι, ἔπειτα δ' ἐκ παιδὸς ἀρετὴν ἀσκοῦντι (*Cyr.* 7. 2. 24)—is, of course, extravagant. In his introduction to the *Cyropaedia* Xenophon announces his intention to tell the reader what he has learnt of Cyrus the Great, concentrating in particular, as Croesus does here, on the Persian's ancestry, appearance and character, and education.[272] When Xenophon discusses Cyrus' origins he simply notes that his clan, the Persidae, take their name from the hero Perseus,[273] and unlike the Lydian king here, he does not hint at any divine descent. The only other figure in the *Cyropaedia* who refers to the Persian leader's supposed descent from the gods is Artabazus, Cyrus' loyal Mede suitor (4. 1. 24). Artabazus is an ardent admirer of Cyrus, eager to recruit his fellow countrymen to the Persian cause, so that his enthusiasm is understandable, but the reason for Croesus' fulsome praise of Cyrus here is less clear. Perhaps, once again, Xenophon wishes to counter, indirectly, the less happy accounts of Cyrus' origins and upbringing found in both

---

[272] 1. 1. 6 ἐσκεψάμεθα τίς ποτ' ὢν γενεὰν καὶ ποίαν τινὰ φύσιν ἔχων καὶ ποίᾳ τινὶ παιδευθεὶς παιδείᾳ. Immediately afterwards (1. 2. 1 ff.) Xenophon does in fact describe these three features—γενεά, φύσις, παιδεία—of Cyrus' background. In our passage, incidentally, Croesus appears to use the word φύσις differently, as a synonym of γενεά rather than 'nature' or 'character'.

[273] 1. 2. 1 οἱ δὲ Περσεῖδαι ἀπὸ Περσέως κλήζονται; cf. Hdt. 7. 61.

Herodotus and Ctesias; perhaps the captive Croesus is indulging in simple flattery.[274]

Croesus not only praises Cyrus, the descendant of gods and kings, but also mentions, in contrast, his own ignoble ancestry.[275] The founder of Croesus' royal house who was a servant before he became king is, of course, Gyges, who was, according to Herodotus, one of Candaules' bodyguards.[276] Here Croesus alludes to his famous ancestor very briefly, so that once again Xenophon seems to be referring his readers to Herodotus' *History* and the full account of Gyges' rise to power found there.[277] According to Herodotus, the oracle at Delphi had given notice that in the fifth generation after Gyges, i.e. in Croesus' time, Gyges' crime would have to be paid for, but Croesus ignored the prediction (Hdt. 1. 13, 91). Perhaps, then, by this oblique allusion to Gyges in our dialogue Croesus hints at something else that he should have known about himself: he is the descendant of Gyges and is fated to be punished for his forefather's impious acts.

Croesus readily admits his culpability for his present unfortunate situation, but he now feels that he does know himself: defeat has been a swift teacher. The Lydian ends his speech with a question: does Cyrus think that his new self-knowledge will in fact guarantee his happiness, as Apollo has promised? The Persian leader, explains Croesus, is in the best position to know since he now controls the Lydian's welfare. Croesus' doubts about Apollo's veracity—cf. ἔτι δοκεῖς ἀληθεύειν τὸν Ἀπόλλω . . . ; (7. 2. 25)—would seem to indicate that he has not entirely changed his old ways. His question is, in essence, a plea for Cyrus to treat him kindly, and the Persian so understands it. Cyrus replies only indirectly, by offering to restore to Croesus his wife, daughters, friends, attendants, and customary pleasures of the table, but not his weapons: Croesus will not be

---

[274] Cf. Tatum 1989: 264–5 n. 18.

[275] Cyaxares is another figure who contrasts his origins with those of the Persian leader, and the scene—the sole confrontation between the · Mede despot and his nephew in the *Cyr.*—is, in a sense, the reverse of the present one, for Cyaxares stresses his own royal lineage and hints at Cyrus' lowly origins (5. 5. 8; cf. above, ch. 2. 5).

[276] Hdt. 1. 8. 1 τῶν αἰχμοφόρων; cf. 1. 91. 1 δορυφόρος. Gyges is called a shepherd at Pl. *Rep.* 359 D.

[277] Hdt. 1. 8–13. Other non-Herodotean tales of Gyges were also in circulation in Xenophon's time, as can be seen from Pl. *Rep.* 359 C–360 B and a fragment of Nicolaus of Damascus (*FGrH* 90 F 47), which is largely drawn from Xanthus of Lydia; cf. above, n. 109. Smith 1902 has a valuable discussion and analysis of the various sources on Gyges. Since Xenophon repeatedly alludes to Herodotus in this section of the *Cyr.*, it seems likely that his Gyges, like his Croesus, is drawn from the Halicarnassian.

allowed to wage wars. Cyrus makes these concessions to the Lydian, he says, because he pities him his former happiness. We are reminded of Cyrus' humane, compassionate attitude displayed at the very opening of this dialogue, and of the merciful stance of Herodotus' Cyrus which underlies it.

It is interesting to compare again Cyrus' attitude towards Croesus here with his earlier position concerning another vanquished opponent, the Armenian king. The Persian leader was unwilling at first to pardon the Armenian because he was suspicious of the ruler's instant contrition and change of heart following his defeat (3. 1. 17). Often, Cyrus tells Tigranes, a proud man can be humbled by defeat, only to recover and behave arrogantly once again (3. 1. 26), and this is precisely the pattern that Croesus has followed—attacking Cyrus, withdrawing after he recognizes his inferiority, only to be puffed up with pride and attack once more. Cyrus forgives the Armenian king because such a course of action best suits his own interests, but we hear nothing of any humanitarian fellow-feeling towards his foe of the kind we find here. Even after pardoning the Armenian Cyrus negotiates with him over the release of his family. Here the Persian leader is magnanimous from the start, restoring Croesus' family and luxurious lifestyle to him at once, but he does forbid the Lydian all military initiative and keeps a close eye on him henceforth. The Persian's words to Croesus may be gentler than those he addressed to the Armenian king, but his actions are similarly pragmatic.

Croesus is delighted by the terms Cyrus offers him, saying that he now knows that his life will indeed be a most happy one. Cyrus will be treating the Lydian as Croesus himself treats the person he loves the best—his wife—allowing him all the riches and luxuries of life with no part in the military actions undertaken to acquire them. The luxurious life of ease which Cyrus now allows the Lydian king is the very way of life which Croesus recommends for the rebellious Lydians, as a means to tame them, in Herodotus (1. 155). By stripping the Lydians of their arms, dressing them in flowing garments, and teaching them to engage in music and trade, states the Herodotean Croesus, Cyrus will turn Lydian men into women. In the *Cyropaedia* Cyrus deprives Croesus of his arms while allowing him luxuries, but it is the Lydian who gladly foresees that he will now lead a woman's life, so that here too the roles of teacher and pupil, or adviser and recipient of advice, are not as clearly demarcated as in Herodotus. Croesus embraces his effeminate new lifestyle wholeheartedly, reminding us of several effete rulers in Ctesias, such as Ninyas, Sardanapallus, and Nanarus the Babylonian.[278] Our Croesus does not, however, go to the extremes that these rulers do, for we do not hear of him wearing women's clothing or carding wool together with his mistresses. We have seen that these effete rulers are countered or complemented by various bold Oriental women who take upon themselves the tasks of men, so that male and female roles are, at times, shifted about. In Herodotus Xerxes exclaims that his men have turned into women and his women into men, in the wake of Artemisia's seemingly courageous actions in battle,[279] and this blurring of masculine and feminine functions is best exemplified, even symbolized, by Semiramis' cloak, which is especially designed to disguise whether its wearer is male or female.[280] Semiramis wears this garment on her way to assisting her husband and Ninus in the very masculine mission of conquering Bactria. The theme of effete men and vigorous women is a popular one in novellas, but it should be remembered that the effeminate rulers of these tales can suddenly demonstrate their virile qualities if the need arises. The pair Nanarus and Parsondes, the pampered Babylonian satrap and his captive enemy who is forced to become a music-girl, is probably the best illustration of such transformations. The womanish satrap Nanarus is quite ruthless when it comes to dealing with his foe, while the manly Parsondes turns from courageous hunter and fighter to effeminate flute-player and then back again to dangerous enemy in the course of the tale.[281] Similarly, the effete Sardanapallus leaves the harem behind and fights boldly for the control of his empire when put to the test; his courageous suicide is admired by many.[282] Perhaps Cyrus, who wonders at Croesus' good-humoured acceptance of his new status, suspects that the Lydian too may undergo another change of heart, for he now takes Croesus along as a companion wherever he goes, either—Xenophon is careful to explain—because he thinks that he will prove useful or because he considers that to be the safest course. Croesus, as we have seen, does attempt to demonstrate his usefulness in his two later appearances in the *Cyropaedia*, but by the time of their third encounter Cyrus has

[278] Cf. above, sect. 1 with n. 44.
[279] Hdt. 8. 88 οἱ μὲν ἄνδρες γεγόνασί μοι γυναῖκες, αἱ δὲ γυναῖκες ἄνδρες.
[280] *FGrH* 688 F 1b 6. 6 οὐκ ἦν διαγνῶναι τὸν περιβεβλημένον πότερον ἀνήρ ἐστιν ἢ γυνή.
[281] *FGrH* 90 F 4.
[282] *FGrH* 688 F 1b 25–7, F 1q.

resumed his usual role of wise leader. After this third meeting the Lydian monarch no longer serves as a counsellor and, in a sense, outlives his usefulness; we hear no more of Croesus and the last of the four novellas of the *Cyropaedia* comes to a close.

Before concluding this chapter it is worth looking once again at the question of Xenophon's sources for the novellas of the *Cyropaedia*. We have seen the many similarities between the dramatic tales of the work and other stories, set against a Persian or Oriental background, written by contemporary or earlier Greek writers. The resemblance is most obvious in the case of the Croesus novella, which was clearly written by Xenophon with Herodotus close at hand, but many features of the other novellas of the *Cyropaedia* have fairly close parallels in Herodotus, Ctesias, etc. The stories that Xenophon tells, while more than pallid variations on, or imitations of, tales in other Greek writers, are sufficiently like them to eliminate the necessity of assuming that the *Cyropaedia*'s novellas stem from more remote Persian material. On the other hand, the inclusion of an apparently historical figure such as Gobryas, who does not appear in other extant Greek sources, would seem to indicate that Xenophon had access to Persian-based material of some kind.

Even after examining all the available relevant sources, we cannot determine where the stories of the *Cyropaedia* come from. One can either credit Xenophon with enough imagination to have invented most of the details of these lively tales on his own or else attribute the more colourful scenes of his novellas to unknown sources. In either case, Xenophon is manifestly well in control of this material. He tells the stories in a vivid and dramatic way, skilfully using narrated dialogues as the chief means of presenting them. These tales enliven his narrative, but Xenophon ensures that they are firmly linked to the main plot and action of the *Cyropaedia*. Whatever their source, the novellas of the *Cyropaedia* are, on the whole, Xenophon's own creation.

5

Xenophon and his Hero

Throughout most of the *Cyropaedia* there is little doubt that Cyrus is meant to be an ideal figure, a successful ruler whose model conduct is well worth emulating. So Xenophon introduces him at the very opening of the *Cyropaedia* and so the Persian leader appears for most of the work: Cyrus is wise, virtuous, and ever successful in achieving his ambitions. We have seen that Xenophon believes in teaching by example, with an outstanding hero to serve as paradigm—e.g. Agesilaus of the *Agesilaus*, Socrates of the *Memorabilia*, Xenophon himself in the *Anabasis*[1]—and it is no surprise to find that the Cyrus of the *Cyropaedia* is, on the whole, another such paragon of virtue. None the less, at times Xenophon has Cyrus behave in surprising or inconsistent fashion and it is this question—the relationship between Xenophon and his hero in the *Cyropaedia*—which is the subject of this chapter.

One outstanding fact about Cyrus is that he is virtually omnipresent in the *Cyropaedia*—he is nearly always 'on stage' and closely involved with every aspect of the work. There are very few occasions when we are allowed to ignore his existence, and if others are allowed to share the limelight it is only for a brief period and because Xenophon has a specific purpose in mind, a purpose which someone other than his hero is better qualified to serve. Thus Cambyses, Cyrus' father, is shown teaching his son because Cambyses is meant to be a model father and teacher, while the hero of the *Cyropaedia* (who was not, it seems, an ideal parent) is—just this once—an eager and enthusiastic pupil. Abradatas is a focus of attention at Thymbrara because he is the only important character in the *Cyropaedia* who is going to die bravely on the battlefield. Panthea, of course, introduces romance into the work; Cyrus himself is perhaps too intent upon his conquests to be swept away by passion. So too

[1] Cf. above, chs. 1. 1, 2. 1 at n. 3.

Pheraulas muses at length on the value of wealth because he, unlike Cyrus, can relinquish control over his property.[2]

Other characters in the *Cyropaedia* are allowed to appear centre stage only because they serve as foils, less successful rivals to the Persian leader. This is, for example, the role allotted to Cyaxares and, to a lesser extent, Tigranes. Perhaps the most interesting—because the most inexplicable—character in the *Cyropaedia* is Adusius, a wise and experienced soldier who serves as Cyrus' deputy. Adusius appears in only one section of the work (7. 4. 1 ff.), where he uses guile and clever negotiation to bring two warring Carian factions together. This diplomatic Persian officer seems to have been invented by Xenophon especially for the Carian episode; in Herodotus, for example, the Carians are subdued by Cyrus' lieutenant, Harpagus.[3] It is not clear why Cyrus himself could not have played the peacemaker in this episode, and such positive, independent characters are very rare in the *Cyropaedia*.[4]

Since Cyrus is found in nearly every episode of the *Cyropaedia*, he participates in the vast majority of the dialogues of the work. The Persian leader is absent only when there are intimate conversations between husband and wife (e.g. Tigranes and his wife, Panthea and Abradatas), exchanges between other rulers and their subjects (the young Assyrian king and Gobryas, Cyaxares and a Mede officer), or a rare conversation between two new acquaintances (Pheraulas and the Sacian).[5] It is usually Cyrus who acts as a spokesman for Xenophon's didactic ideas in the *Cyropaedia*, but occasionally another figure—e.g. Gobryas, an unnamed Persian, and, most notably, Cyrus' father, Cambyses—is permitted to reflect upon favourite moralistic themes of Xenophon.[6] We have seen that Cyrus need not be the teaching figure, the 'Socrates' of didactic conversations, but that he often plays a role similar to that of the philosopher in the *Memorabilia*.[7]

[2] See above, chs. 1. 2, 4. 2, 3. 5.

[3] Hdt. 1. 174. See Breitenbach 1966: 1711, who calls the Adusius–Carian episode 'eine typisch xenophontische Erfindung'; cf. 1714. Schwartz 1889: 190 n. 2 (= 1956: 170 n. 2) also thinks that Xenophon invented Adusius, calling him an idealized Spartan harmost; he compares our passage to *Hell.* 5. 4. 55.

[4] We have encountered other characters who appear just once in the *Cyr.*, but these figures—e.g. Aglaitadas, Sambaulas (2. 2. 11–17, 28–31; cf. above, ch. 3. 3), and the insolent Daiphernes (8. 3. 21–3)—have a specific, stereotyped role to play; unlike Adusius, their part cannot be taken over by the Persian leader.

[5] *Cyr.* 3. 1. 41, 6. 1. 47, 6. 4. 2–11 (and cf. above, ch. 4. 2), 5. 3. 5–7, 4. 5. 9–12, 8. 3. 30–2, 35–48 (and cf. above, ch. 3. 5); see also 8. 3. 7–8, 8. 4. 31.

[6] Cf. 5. 2. 14 ff. (and see above, ch. 3. 4), 5. 3. 2–4, 1. 6. 1 ff. (and see above, ch. 2. 2).

[7] Cf. above, ch. 2. 7.

Xenophon's rather single-minded concentration upon his hero is particularly noticeable whenever any plans are proposed or decisions are made in the *Cyropaedia*. Cyrus does have advisers at times—he consults with Gadatas and Gobryas and holds discussions with his loyal lieutenants, Hystaspas, Pheraulas, and in particular Chrysantas—but on the whole the Persian leader is the chief initiator of strategies and programmes in the work. Generally Cyrus comes up with a plan or proposal on his own, and his companions either supply some necessary information or simply go along with his ideas; at the very most the Persian leader's partners assist him in devising a course of action. Often Cyrus rejects the counsel—both solicited and unsolicited—of his followers, friends, and allies.[8] In virtually all of the conversations in the *Cyropaedia* in which plans are formulated there is only one 'correct' view, that expressed by Cyrus.[9] Even if others do make proposals or suggestions of their own, very little space is allotted to the presentation of their ideas, which are then turned down by the Persian leader.

Often in the *Cyropaedia* proposals are not made during discussions between two or three individuals—that is, in planning dialogues—but are outlined in speeches addressed to a large group of allies, officers, etc. in an assembly or council. Here too Cyrus almost invariably suggests the plan and there is never any opposition to his proposals. The assemblies of the *Cyropaedia* in which decisions are reached all follow the same pattern: Cyrus announces or suggests a plan and his motion is then generally seconded by one of his close followers. All those present then express their support for the idea and the Persian leader closes the assembly with specific instructions on the way the new plan is to be implemented.[10] There are also two councils in the *Cyropaedia* (5. 1. 19–29, 6. 1. 6–22) where Cyrus meets his allies in order to decide whether to continue their war against the Assyrians. Each of the allied leaders expresses his view in turn, but all speak in one voice, unanimously supporting the decision that suits

---

[8] Cyrus initiates a course of action: *Cyr.* 1. 4. 18–19, 2. 4. 9–17, 3. 3. 13–20, 4. 2. 13–14, 4. 5. 36–55, 6. 1. 31–44, 6. 2. 1–3, 7. 1. 6–9, 15–18. Others assist him: 4. 1. 10–12, 5. 3. 8–14, 7. 1. 19–20; cf. 1. 4. 11–12. Cyrus rejects advice of others: 2. 1. 8, 3. 3. 29–33, 46–7, 48–56, 4. 1. 10–11, 5. 2. 29–37, 5. 4. 41–50, etc.

[9] The exception is *Cyr.* 4. 1. 13–23, Cyaxares' attempts to dissuade Cyrus from continuing their campaign against the Assyrians, where Xenophon allows us to see that there are two sides to the question; cf. above, ch. 2. 5.

[10] See *Cyr.* 2. 1. 10–13, 4. 2. 38–47, 4. 3. 3–23, 7. 5. 71–8. 1. 6. At 5. 3. 29–45 and 6. 2. 23–41 there is no loyal seconder, while at 2. 3. 1–16 there are two; cf. 7. 5. 41–57, where Chrysantas acts as Cyrus' agent.

Cyrus, to continue with the war. The assemblies and councils of the *Cyropaedia* are even less controversial or free-ranging than the planning dialogues; only one position, the orthodox one, is ever presented.

Elsewhere—in other writers and in other works by Xenophon himself—councils and assemblies are often used to illustrate the conflicting considerations involved in formulating a plan or reaching a decision. Herodotus, for example, has a series of war councils in which Xerxes must choose between very different courses of action recommended to him by his advisers.[11] We are also shown the lively debate between Darius, Otanes, and Gobryas on the best way to be rid of the Magus and the deliberations of Otanes, Megabyxus, and Darius on the form of government to be established after he is gone.[12] Thucydides too uses antithetical speeches to present two conflicting proposals and to illuminate the various factors that have influenced a decision.[13] Xenophon himself uses the same method of presentation in the *Hellenica* at times,[14] but it is particularly interesting to compare the assemblies, councils, and conversations in which plans are formed in the *Anabasis* with those of the *Cyropaedia*. In some of the many assemblies convened by the Ten Thousand there is general agreement from the very start on the plan to be adopted, and at times a single speech is sufficient to win the consent of all concerned;[15] this is similar to the situation in the *Cyropaedia*. None the less, in the *Anabasis* there are also a great many conferences in which a variety of views are put forward before a decision is reached.[16] Even more noteworthy are a series of exchanges between Xenophon and Chirisophus in which they disagree about a course of action to be undertaken or a plan to be adopted.[17] These dialogues in the *Anabasis* both point to opposing tactical considerations and hint at the friction between the Athenian and the Spartan.[18]

[11] Hdt. 7. 8–11, 7. 234–7, 8. 67–9.

[12] Hdt. 3. 71–3, 80–2.

[13] Thuc. 1. 67–86, 3. 36–49, 6. 9–23, 6. 32–41, etc.

[14] See e.g. *Hell.* 7. 1. 1–14 (and cf. 6. 3. 4–17), 6. 5. 33–49.

[15] General agreement: *Anab.* 3. 1. 33–47, 3. 2. 1–39, 6. 4. 10–13. Single speech (by Xenophon): 4. 8. 9–14, 7. 3. 2–6.

[16] *Anab.* 2. 1. 7–23, 3. 1. 15–32, 4. 6. 6–19, 5. 1. 2–14, 5. 6. 1–14, 5. 6. 22–34; cf. Clearchus' manipulations at 1. 3. 9–20.

[17] *Anab.* 3. 4. 38–42, 3. 5. 4–6, 4. 1. 19–22, 4. 7. 3–7; cf. 3. 3. 11–19.

[18] See 4. 6. 14–16 and cf. 4. 6. 3; Cawkwell 1972: 18–21 discusses the relationship between Chirisophus and Xenophon. *Anab.* 2. 4. 2–7, 7. 2. 12–13, 7. 7. 1–12 are other instances of dialogues where plans are discussed and clashes between opposing points of view are dramatized.

In the *Cyropaedia*, when Xenophon invariably has plans evolve along the lines suggested by the Persian leader, he demonstrates that his hero is a brilliant and original military thinker, quick to take advantage of every opportunity afforded him, but he pays a certain price as well. In the end these councils and discussions are not interesting precisely because Cyrus never has any need to alter his decisions or take account of the opinions of others. This situation is not dissimilar to the effect Xenophon's portrayal of Cyrus as consistently and conscientiously pious has upon us. We have seen that the Persian leader is careful to fulfil all his obligations to the gods and that his sacrifices are always well received, but that this uniformly positive picture, in the long run, makes the religion of the *Cyropaedia* seem routine and unthinking.[19]

While readers of the *Cyropaedia* may find that Cyrus is at times too (boringly) good to be true, it seems safe to say that this is not Xenophon's intention: he is just being excessively didactic. Very occasionally we find that Xenophon's didacticism so gets the better of him that he presents Cyrus in an inconsistent way: the author makes use of his model hero to press home a point at the cost of having him behave in an uncharacteristic manner. Thus Cyrus, who likes nothing better than addressing his friends and allies at great length, expresses on one occasion great disdain for rhetoric because his author wants to stress that deeds are more important than words.[20]

This desire to instruct his readers on the ideal way to behave seems to be the main factor which influenced Xenophon when he fashioned the episodes and speeches of the *Cyropaedia*. At times, however, he forgets his didacticism and places his hero in situations which are not necessarily paradigmatic because he wishes to correct or balance in some way the various stories related to Cyrus the Great found in other writers. Thus, Astyages, the kindly grandfather of the *Cyropaedia*, arranges a feast shortly after he becomes acquainted with young Cyrus, just as his Herodotean counterpart does, but his dinner-party, unlike the one in Herodotus, is a cheerful affair. At the party Cyrus plays at being cupbearer, and in this oblique way Xenophon also refers to Ctesias' account of the rise of young Cyrus.[21] Sometimes this glance at other writers' accounts leads to incon-

---

[19] See above, ch. 2. 2 at n. 122.
[20] *Cyr.* 3. 3. 48–56; cf. above, ch. 2. 6.
[21] *Cyr.* 1. 3. 4 ff.; cf. above, ch. 3. 2.

sistencies. The eunuch Gadatas displays a paternal attitude towards Cyrus, despite the fact that they are near contemporaries, and this is probably because a eunuch is responsible for Cyrus' early promotions in Ctesias–Nicolaus.[22] So too Cyrus of the *Cyropaedia* behaves much more humanely and compassionately towards Croesus than he does towards another vanquished ruler, the Armenian king, and it is most likely that this behaviour owes much to Herodotus' account of the first meeting between the two rulers. Herodotus, in a sense, is the real author of the compassionate Cyrus who first encounters Croesus in the *Cyropaedia* and readily—but most uncharacteristically—accepts all of the advice that the Lydian king has to offer. Later, as we have noted, Xenophon has his hero revert to type and reject the suggestions of the Lydian king.[23] Occasionally we are even allowed a glimpse at the darker side of the historical conquests of Cyrus the Great, for Xenophon has the Persian leader override the king of the Medes, Cyaxares, and usurp his power. Similarly, on his deathbed the hero of the *Cyropaedia* emphasizes to his sons too vehemently the importance of brotherly love, because Xenophon and his readers are aware of the actual strife that will arise between the pair.[24] In sum, Xenophon occasionally introduces a jarring note or has his hero do the unexpected, either for pedagogical purposes or because he wishes to counteract, explain away, or simply refer to other versions of the life of Cyrus the Great current in his time. None the less, for most of the *Cyropaedia* Xenophon seems to identify with Cyrus, and portray him quite simply as a model figure to be emulated: there are very few hints of any distance between the author and his hero.

2. CYRUS IN BABYLON

The question of Xenophon's intentions and attitude towards his protagonist becomes more complex when we come to the final sections of the *Cyropaedia*, those following the conquest of Babylon (7. 5 ff.). It is true that in the very last scene of the work, Cyrus' departure from this world (8. 7), Xenophon portrays the Persian ruler as a heroic figure, whose death reminds us of Socrates' end. The

---

[22] Cf. above, ch. 4. 3.
[23] See above, ch. 4. 4.
[24] Above, ch. 2. 5, 7.

Cyropaedia does not, however, end on this elevated note. Instead there is a bitter, sarcastic epilogue (*Cyr.* 8. 8) in which the well-run and admirable government created by Cyrus is contrasted with the decadent Persian empire of Xenophon's day. According to this final chapter, Cyrus' empire began to crumble and decay immediately after his death (8. 8. 2 εὐθὺς . . . πάντα δ᾿ ἐπὶ τὸ χεῖρον ἐτρέποντο). By telling his readers that Cyrus' life's work began to disintegrate as soon as he was gone, Xenophon seems to undermine the value of many of the customs and institutions he has painstakingly outlined throughout the eight books of the *Cyropaedia*, and this angry final chapter seems so inconsistent and out of place that it has, as we have seen, often been condemned as inauthentic.[25] However, if we look carefully at the entire last part of the work (7. 5–8. 7), we shall see that Xenophon indicates to his readers, well before the final chapter, that Cyrus is not always an ideal ruler and that the government he has created is, of necessity, less than perfect. After the conquest of Babylon, when Cyrus goes about establishing his empire and its administration, it is difficult to view the Persian ruler as consistently heroic and admirable: there is a gap between his original ideas of good conduct and the notions and actions he adopts as ruler of Babylon.

The difficulties begin immediately after the conquest of Babylon, with Cyrus' desire to establish himself (κατασκευάσασθαι)[26] there in a manner befitting a king (7. 5. 37). Cyrus wishes to appear in public only rarely and in majestic fashion, but is anxious to avoid arousing jealousy. Consequently he contrives a way to win his friends' approval for this new way of life. His stratagem was a simple one. He stood in a public place one morning and allowed all who wished to do so to approach him with requests; naturally, great crowds soon gathered. The Persian leader's close friends were forced to fight their way through the throng to reach Cyrus, only to be kept waiting at his side all day long. Cyrus dismissed his friends at night with the request that they return early the next morning in order to talk with him. They hurried off gladly, Xenophon tells us, having been forced

---

[25] See above, ch. 1. 3.

[26] Holden (in his commentary ad loc.) states that κατασκευάσασθαι refers to a physical establishment, a palace for Cyrus; he may be influenced by the fact that Cyrus has just allocated houses to his allies (7. 5. 35). But the continuation of the sentence—where we learn that the Persian leader would like to appear as infrequently and as impressively as possible—indicates that Sturz's 'se gerere' (found in his lexicon s.v. κατασκευάζω) is the correct translation; cf. Luccioni 1947: 237 n. 224.

to neglect nature's calls throughout the day.[27] The following day the crowds surrounding Cyrus were even larger and the Persian leader stationed men around himself to fend off all but his friends and allies, so that they could hold their discussion. Cyrus' companions quickly realize, as they are meant to do, that the Persian ruler must be protected and secluded from the masses if they are to have any opportunity to see him themselves. The end result of their talk is that Cyrus, following the suggestion of his friends,[28] moves into the Babylonian royal palace. Almost immediately afterwards he selects a personal and palace bodyguard to serve him (7. 5. 37–58).[29]

It is only natural that Cyrus should wish to reap the fruits of victory—i.e. take over the Babylonian king's palace and be respected from afar—but the way he goes about doing so is slightly disturbing.[30] The Persian leader devises a stratagem which he uses against his *friends*, and he manipulates them into offering him what he considers his due. Long ago (1. 6. 38) Cyrus has been taught by his father Cambyses that a good commander must know how to invent and make use of new stratagems—against the enemy. Here, for the first time, we find Cyrus tricking his friends for reasons other than military security.[31] Xenophon could easily have shown Cyrus as first being disturbed by masses of petitioners and only then deciding, along with his friends, that he must become a less accessible figure. Instead, the crowds are arranged by Cyrus himself and the effect on the reader is disquieting.

We are left even more uneasy by Cyrus' next move, his forming a bodyguard composed of eunuchs. It is not clear from Xenophon's wording here—πάντας τοὺς περὶ τὸ ἑαυτοῦ σῶμα θεραπευτῆρας ἐποιήσατο εὐνούχους (7. 5. 65)—whether we are meant to understand that Cyrus actually had those who served under him castrated or merely chose his bodyguard from a pool of available eunuchs,[32]

[27] This sort of homely, vulgar detail is rarely found in the *Cyr.*; compare Artabazus' ironic remark that he spent the day envied, but unfed, at Cyrus' side (7. 5. 53).

[28] Cf. above, ch. 3. 6, on the role played here by Chrysantas.

[29] Guyot 1980: 78–9 notes that both Hellanicus (*FGrH* 4 F 178) and Ctesias (*FGrH* 688 F 1b 21. 2, 7) associate a ruler's isolation from his subjects with his use of court eunuchs. Cyrus, whose new bodyguards are eunuchs, fits this pattern.

[30] We are reminded, perhaps, of the more drastic ruse used by Herodotus' Pisistratus, who wounds himself and his mules in order to be supplied with a bodyguard (Hdt. 1. 59).   [31] Cf. *Cyr.* 2. 4. 15, 6. 3. 11.

[32] Zonaras, in his epitome of the *Cyr.*, paraphrases as τοὺς . . . περὶ τὸ ἑαυτοῦ σῶμα θεραπευτῆρας ἐξέτεμε καὶ εὐνούχους πεποίηκε (*Epit. Hist.* 3. 25), but most scholars reject this interpretation and think that Cyrus selected eunuchs to serve as bodyguards. Cf. Delebecque's note ad loc. in the Budé *Cyr.*

but it seems unlikely that the first interpretation is correct. Herodotus terms castration an abominable act (8. 105–6), and this attitude appears to be the general Greek view.[33] In the *Cyropaedia* itself we have seen that one of the worst deeds performed by the young Assyrian king is the emasculation of Gadatas; Cyrus is hardly likely to repeat his enemy's crime on a much greater scale. In any event, the very use of eunuchs as servants was a strange and barbaric custom in Greek eyes, as Xenophon seems well aware, for he carefully lists all of his hero's reasons or rationalizations for making use of eunuchs as bodyguards, taking pains to indicate throughout that he is presenting Cyrus'—rather than his own—reflections.[34] The Persian leader, we are told, thinks that eunuchs are free to love their masters above all others because they are without family ties. They are particularly vulnerable to ill treatment by others and are consequently grateful to a master who affords them protection. Eunuchs, like gelded horses and castrated bulls or dogs, become less aggressive and self-assertive, but are still capable of performing their duties well. They are extremely loyal to their masters, even in times of misfortune, and although physically weaker than other men, eunuchs too can ply a sword in battle (7. 5. 59–65).

All of Cyrus' arguments may well be valid, but the Persian's utilitarian and selfish outlook, his 'zynische Beschönigung'[35] of the issue, is hardly calculated to lay Greek scruples to rest. The views attributed to Cyrus may simply be a less than successful attempt by Xenophon to explain away a sticky fact of Persian life, but it is also possible that Cyrus is deliberately portrayed here in somewhat negative fashion. Xenophon often omits or transmutes unsavoury features of the historical Cyrus' life in the *Cyropaedia*, and he could well have ignored the entire eunuch question. Alternatively, by changing his story only slightly—for example, a group of the defeated Assyrian king's former eunuchs approach Cyrus with the request that he take them on as servants and, using the above arguments, convince him—Xenophon could have dealt with the issue while presenting Cyrus in a more favourable light. As the *Cyropaedia* stands, Cyrus, on his own initiative, forms a bodyguard composed of

[33] For the Greek attitude towards eunuchs see Hug 1918: 449–55.

[34] Cf. [Κῦρος] ἐνόμισε . . . ἔγνω . . . ὁρῶν . . . ἡγήσατο . . . ἡγεῖτο . . . ἐφαίνετο αὐτῷ . . . ἐτεκμαίρετο . . . ταῦτα γιγνώσκων . . . ἐποιήσατο εὐνούχους (7. 5. 59–65), and see Montgomery 1965: 137–8.

[35] Thus Hug 1918: 451. Breitenbach 1966: 1738, Lewis 1977: 20, and Guyot 1980: 81–3 all point out how unusual our passage is.

eunuchs and also organizes a palace guard of ten thousand Persian spearmen (7. 5. 65–8).

Next (7. 5. 71–86) comes a speech by Cyrus to the Persian and allied leaders on the need for continued discipline, moderation, and the practice of virtue on their part—old, familiar themes[36]—if they are to keep and administer the empire properly. The Persian leader suggests that the leaders spend their time at the royal court just as the ὁμότιμοι back in Persia do, and that their children be educated at court as well. Cyrus seems to be proposing that the old practices of the Persian court be transferred to Babylon, and, spurred on by Chrysantas, many men agree to stay and put themselves at their ruler's disposal (8. 1. 1–6). Cyrus quickly establishes a bureaucracy along military lines for administering the fiscal side of the empire (8. 1. 9–15), and then turns to the training of his associates (8. 1. 16 κοινῶνας).[37] He employs, we learn, various means to compel the nobles to attend his court, and those absent are automatically suspected of wrongdoing. One method used to guarantee attendance was to have an absentee noble's possessions seized by a close friend of Cyrus. When the noble came forward to complain, Cyrus would at first postpone giving him a hearing, and even after allowing him his say would delay giving his verdict. Another, more drastic measure used by the Persian leader was to confiscate all of a missing noble's property and hand it over to another, more loyal friend (8. 1. 16–20). These measures, it should be recalled, were directed against the Persians and Cyrus' allies, not against the vanquished Babylonians. Plainly, then, Cyrus' court in Babylon is *not* run in the same way as the Persian court described by Xenophon at the beginning of the *Cyropaedia* (1. 2. 2–15). In Persia only the need to work for a living keeps men away from their civic duties. Persian elders, rather than their king Cambyses, serve as judges of both public and private affairs, even dealing with capital cases. These elders also choose all the other magistrates and handle requests for military aid and troops. So too the Persian authorities, rather than their king, fix the amount of war booty that must be contributed to the state treasury.[38]

---

[36] See Due 1989: 96–100 for an analysis of *Cyr.* 7. 5. 70–8. 1. 8 and its many parallels with 1. 6, Cambyses' long conversation with his son.

[37] There is an interesting change in terminology in the *Cyr.* after the conquest of Babylon (7. 5 ff.). The ὁμότιμοι have all but disappeared (cf., however, 7. 5. 85; 8. 5. 21 only confirms this point), to be replaced by κοινῶνες or κοινωνοί (7. 5. 35, 36, 8. 1. 16, 25, 36, 40, etc.; the manuscripts often confuse the two). Does this mean that Cyrus no longer has equals or peers, only partners? [38] Cf. *Cyr.* 1. 5. 4–5, 4. 5. 16–17.

Cambyses, as we have seen, is described as a kind of 'constitutional monarch', who accepts the city's decrees and is ruled by the law: property rights are respected in Persia and are not subject to the whims of the ruler.[39] Cyrus of Babylon is not limited by all these checks, rules, and constraints: he is the standard of justice, a living, seeing law (cf. 8. 1. 22 βλέποντα νόμον) who supersedes—albeit only to improve upon—any written statutes.

This implicit contrast between Cambyses' government in Persia and his son's rule in Babylon is made explicit by Xenophon during Cyrus' first visit home after his great conquests (8. 5. 21–7). Cyrus, bearing gifts and animals for sacrifice, enters his native country accompanied only by his friends, having left his army outside the Persian borders. We are not told, as might be expected, of any warm, tumultuous welcome for the conquering hero.[40] Instead, we find that Cambyses convenes a meeting between Persian nobles and his son: he is afraid that the delicate balance of power in Persia will be disrupted by Cyrus. Cambyses negotiates a compact between Cyrus and the Persian nobles whereby each party is to respect the other's rights and come to its aid in time of need.[41] Cyrus, declares Cambyses, will be king of Persia after his death, but he seems to expect that his son will visit Persia only rarely, leaving the actual duties of kingship—mainly religious ones—to another member of the royal family. Cambyses warns Cyrus that he is not to rule Persia as he does the rest of his empire, with a view to his own advantage (8. 5. 24 ἐπὶ πλεονεξίᾳ). This characterization of Cyrus' rule over his empire is significant: during his stay in Media the young Cyrus had been warned by his mother that πλεονεξία is a quality of tyrants, as opposed to kings (1. 3. 18). While we cannot conclude from Cambyses' statement that Cyrus is to be considered a tyrant,[42] it is clear that Xenophon is distinguishing here between two distinct regimes—the traditional Persian 'constitutional monarchy' described in Book 1 and Cyrus' more despotic rule over his empire, as outlined in Books 7 and 8 of the *Cyropaedia*. If one of Xenophon's aims in the work is to describe an ideal form of government, at best only one of these two very different regimes can be said to represent such an ideal.[43]

---

[39] Cf. *Cyr.* 1. 3. 17–18 and above, ch. 2. 3.   [40] Cf. *Cyr.* 3. 3. 2.

[41] Commentators compare the compact arranged here between Cyrus and the Persian people to the covenant between the Spartan kings and their state described in the *Lac. Pol.* (15. 1–7); see e.g. Tatum 1989: 78–9 and cf. Hirsch 1985: 99, who considers the compact of the *Cyr.* an Iranian feature.   [42] Cf. Tatum 1989: 77–8.

[43] For an excellent discussion of this point see Carlier 1978: 138–43.

Returning to Cyrus' court at Babylon, we find that the Persian ruler has decided that he and his companions should adopt the Median form of dress—their rich robes, high shoes, and elaborate make-up—in place of the simple and austere Persian style.[44] This decision is surprising, to say the least.[45] Not only does Cyrus' proposal here present a strong contrast to the rejection of cosmetics and other artificial aids to the appearance expressed by another hero in Xenophon, Ischomachus of the *Oeconomicus* (10. 2–9),[46] but it is also inconsistent with earlier episodes in the *Cyropaedia* itself. We are told, for example, that the young Cyrus is fascinated by his rouged and richly attired grandfather and delighted to receive an elaborate Median costume of his own—because he is a child (1. 3. 2–3). Persian dress is traditionally much plainer, and when an older Cyrus leaves Media to return home he is careful to leave his Median robe behind (1. 4. 26). Later, Cyrus clashes with his Mede uncle over the question of clothes. Cyaxares thinks that Cyrus will impress an Indian delegation favourably if he is attired in decorative Median robes, while Cyrus contends that he will make a better impression by arriving on the scene as quickly as possible, adorned with sweat and haste.[47] Cyaxares concedes that his nephew's attitude is the correct one, but he has not really taken the lesson to heart, for he later keeps a large group of his allies, who are about to hold a war council, waiting while he dresses (6. 1. 1). It is perhaps not insignificant that when he finally does arrive on the scene, elaborately costumed, his contribution to the ensuing discussion is minimal. In short, throughout most of the *Cyropaedia* elaborate make-up and dress are shown to be an indulgence, an affectation of the idle (cf. 8. 8. 15–17). Even after Cyrus institutes Median dress he slips back into his old moralizing attitude one last time. After distributing Median robes to his men, to be worn during the grand inaugural procession at Babylon, the Persian leader is asked what he himself will wear. Cyrus replies that *his* costume does not matter—for him the best possible adornment is

---

[44] *Cyr.* 8. 1. 40–2; cf. 8. 3. 1–4, 13–14.

[45] So surprising that most editors delete *Cyr.* 8. 1. 40–2 (but not, apparently, the passages in 8. 3); see Holden and Delebecque in their commentaries ad loc.

[46] Many scholars note this contrast between Cyrus and Ischomachus: see e.g. Anderson 1974: 178–9; Breitenbach 1966: 1739; Holden on *Cyr.* 8. 1. 40–2.

[47] *Cyr.* 2. 4. 1, 5–6. In Xenophon's writings the working up of a sweat is often considered a virtue: cf. *Cyr.* 1. 2. 16, 1. 6. 17, and the further references in Due 1989: 108. See also *Mem.* 2. 1. 28; *Oec.* 11. 12; *Symp.* 2. 18; and in particular *Oec.* 4. 20–5, where the bedecked and bejewelled younger Cyrus surprises Lysander by his willingness to engage in sweat-filled exercise.

having adorned his friends.[48] In actual fact the Persian ruler arrives at the procession decked out in majestic purple, and he is made to appear larger than life so that all those present are overwhelmed by the splendour of his costume (8. 3. 13–14). Why does Cyrus change his views, rejecting Persian simplicity and adopting Mede artifice?

It seems that the Persian ruler thinks that it is not enough for rulers to be better than their subjects: they must bewitch them as well, and making use of the pomp and trappings of royal power is one way to ensure that a government will be properly respected.[49] Here too we see Cyrus adding to or, to be more exact, straying from his father's teachings. Cambyses has advised his son that the best way to guarantee the willing obedience of one's subjects is, simply, to be better than they are and thus convince them that it is to their own advantage to obey (1. 6. 21–2). He has nothing to say about a ruler having to enchant or dazzle his subjects; Cambyses himself and his nobles dress simply.[50] Cyrus' new techniques certainly seem effective: when he makes his grand entrance in the procession all prostrate themselves before him (8. 3. 14). None the less, Xenophon rather cynically adds that perhaps all those present bow down to the Persian leader, not because they are impressed by his appearance but because they have been commanded to do so. The author of the *Cyropaedia* also notes that this is the first time that the Persians prostrate themselves before their leader. Given the Greeks' feelings about προσκύνησις,[51] one wonders whether Xenophon's readers are meant to think that this new Persian attitude is a good one.

Cyrus, as ruler, undergoes a similar change in his attitude towards rich and elaborate food. He has stated, time and again, that one should eat only simple food in moderate quantities, stressing that 'hunger is the best relish'.[52] Often, too, this traditional Persian approach is opposed to the practices of the Medes.[53] If in his youth

---

[48] *Cyr.* 8. 3. 3–4; cf. 6. 4. 3; *Anab.* 1. 9. 23. Cyrus' attitude here is not all that different from Cyaxares' when he tried to persuade Cyrus to wear an elaborate Median robe for the meeting with the Indian delegation. Cyaxares had said that if his nephew were to be impressively attired it would also reflect well on him (2. 4. 5). When Cyrus prefers speed, sweat, and discipline as decorations, we are made to feel that his uncle is ignoring the essentials and concentrating upon outer trappings, but here the Persian leader's adornment of his men is meant to be taken as thoughtful and generous.

[49] *Cyr.* 8. 1. 40, 8. 3. 1; cf. 7. 5. 37. See Wood 1964: 64–5 and cf. Breebaart 1983: 123–4.

[50] 1. 3. 2; cf. 4. 5. 54.

[51] Cf. Arrian, *Anab.* 4. 11. 9, and see Tuplin 1990: 23–4.

[52] *Cyr.* 1. 5. 12 and 4. 5. 4; cf. 4. 2. 38, 5. 2. 16–17, etc.; see above, ch. 3. 2.

[53] 1. 3. 4, 1. 6. 8, 4. 5. 7, etc.; cf. 8. 8. 16, 20.

Cyrus did not enjoy or appreciate his grandfather's rich table (1. 3. 4–6), as ruler of Babylon he is served expensive and elaborate meals which could well rival those of Astyages (8. 2. 4 ff.). It is interesting to note, in fact, how closely Cyrus has come to resemble his grandfather. They are now alike in their dress, eating habits, aloofness from their subjects, and their attitude towards the law, self-aggrandizement, and the property of others.[54] This state of affairs is all the more striking if we remember that at the beginning of the *Cyropaedia* Astyages is deliberately and unfavourably contrasted with Cyrus' father, Cambyses.[55]

Cyrus, as head of an empire, also reminds us of a different tyrant who appears in Xenophon's writings, Hiero. The Persian ruler, like Hiero, would like to have good men help him rule his empire, but is afraid of competition from potential rivals. Both Cyrus and Hiero need to surround themselves with a loyal bodyguard, and both find that their lofty position has deprived them of the opportunity to enjoy society and companionship. The two rulers also enjoy some of the same advantages: Hiero and Cyrus hear only praise, enjoy rich foods, and are well equipped to reward their friends and harm their enemies. In the *Hiero* Simonides suggests to the tyrant two methods of making himself more popular—enriching himself by enriching his friends and delegating the task of punishing to others, while awarding prizes by himself—and these two methods are already employed by Cyrus.[56]

Hiero is forced to rid himself of able men and make use of less worthy ones (*Hiero* 5. 2), but in Babylon Cyrus overcomes the problem by using a combination of carrot and stick to keep his men loyal to himself but at odds with one another. Thus he sympathizes with his men in good fortune and bad, honours worthy men with food specially sent from his table, gives them lavish gifts, and uses them as 'treasurers' for his wealth. He also sends doctors and medicines to them when they are ill.[57] On the other hand, the Persian ruler makes

---

[54] Dress: 8. 1. 40–2 and 8. 3. 13–14, 1. 3. 2. Food: 8. 2. 4 ff., 1. 3. 4 ff. Aloofness: 8. 3. 19–23, 1. 3. 8. Law: 8. 1. 22, 1. 3. 18. Self-aggrandizement: 8. 5. 24, 1. 3. 18. Property: 8. 1. 20, 1. 4. 26. Cyrus does not, however, acquire Astyages' fondness for drink (1. 3. 10).

[55] 1. 3. 2 ff., esp. 2, 11, 18; cf. above, ch. 2. 3, ch. 3. 2.

[56] Dangerous rivals: *Cyr.* 8. 1. 46–8; *Hiero* 5. 1, 6. 15–16. Bodyguard: *Cyr.* 7. 5. 58 ff.; *Hiero* 2. 8 ff., 6. 10–11, etc. No society: *Cyr.* 7. 5. 39 ff.; *Hiero* 6. 1–3. Praise: *Cyr.* 8. 2. 12; *Hiero* 1. 14–15. Food: *Cyr.* 8. 2. 4; *Hiero* 1. 16–25. Help friends, harm enemies: *Cyr.* 8. 2. 7, 13, etc.; *Hiero* 2. 2. Enriching friends: *Cyr.* 8. 2. 15 ff.; *Hiero* 11. 13. Rewards, not punishments: *Cyr.* 8. 1. 17, 39, 8. 2. 27; *Hiero* 9. 3.

[57] Cf. *Cyr.* 8. 2. 1–2, 3–4, 7–9, 15–23, 24–5.

use of great numbers of spies, the 'eyes and ears of the king',[58] so that men everywhere are afraid to speak out against him. Cyrus organizes contests, we are told, not only in order to encourage the pursuit of excellence but also to stir up contention and rivalry among his nobles (8. 2. 26). He also has litigants and competitors of all kinds choose their own judges, realizing that the contestants will hate those who give judgements against them, but will not feel particularly grateful towards those who decide in their favour. In this way, Xenophon tells us, Cyrus contrives that all the most powerful men at his court should like him more than they do each other.[59]

This policy of 'divide and conquer' again leaves us uneasy.[60] In the past Cyrus, though well aware of the merits of contests and competitions, had been bothered by the jealousy and rivalry they engendered and was anxious to channel his men's negative feelings against the Assyrian enemy. The Persian ruler also did his utmost to foster unity and friendship among his various friends and allies.[61] Once, we are told, men praised Cyrus spontaneously and willingly because they were impressed by him, but now, with spies everywhere, they have no choice but to speak well of him.[62] Even the Persian leader's more benign actions, such as his distribution of lavish presents, do not necessarily lead to desirable results. Thus we are told that Cyrus' generous gifts caused men to prefer him to their brothers, fathers, and children (8. 2. 9). In view of the Persian ruler's own strictures to his sons on the naturalness and importance of fraternal devotion (8. 7. 14–16; cf. 8. 8. 4), such loyalty on the part of his subjects, though convenient for Cyrus, could hardly have been considered virtuous even by him.

In this part of the *Cyropaedia* all of the Persian ruler's seemingly kind and thoughtful policies are consistently shown to be motivated by utilitarian, if not selfish, considerations.[63] From the very start Cyrus has been both kindly and selfish, but in the past the Persian's own best interests and the interests of others have always conveniently coincided: there was no conflict between the good of Cyrus

---

[58] For a detailed discussion of the various sources on, and interpretations of, the Persian king's eye(s) and ears see Hirsch 1985: 101–34.

[59] *Cyr.* 8. 2. 26–8; cf. 8. 1. 48.

[60] See Breebaart 1983: 126–7 for an interesting attempt to explain Cyrus' promotion of envy and distrust among the nobles as intended 'to keep the engine of all-embracing unselfish monarchical virtue going'.

[61] Cf. e.g. *Cyr.* 3. 3. 10, 5. 4. 13.   [62] See *Cyr.* 1. 4. 25, 3. 1. 41, 3. 3. 4, etc. vs. 8. 2. 12.

[63] See Farber 1979: 501 on the pragmatism behind Cyrus' φιλανθρωπία, and cf. Due 1989: 163–70.

and the good of others. For every gift Cyrus bestows, every kindly action he performs, he receives some benefaction in return, and his generosity towards others is well rewarded. So, for example, when Cyrus behaves circumspectly towards Panthea he gains her husband as an ally. He invites the frightened Gadatas to join the Persians on their campaign, and in return receives much useful information on local conditions. He is open-minded about having able, non-Persian soldiers join his army, and consequently gains a better army for himself; there are many further examples of this kind.[64] After the conquest of Babylon, we are increasingly aware of only one party—the Persian leader himself—benefiting from these seemingly generous acts. A king, says Cyrus, like a shepherd, must keep his charges happy while making use of or deriving benefit from them (8. 2. 14): one cannot but suspect that they are kept happy only because it causes them to produce better and more abundant fleece. It is instructive to compare this statement by Cyrus with a similar one attributed to Socrates in the *Memorabilia* (3. 2. 1). Agamemnon, Socrates says, is called ποιμένα λαῶν because, like a shepherd with a flock, a general must see to it that his troops are safe and supplied with their needs, and that they fulfil their function. Socrates makes no mention of the military leader using or benefiting from his men, only of the soldiers improving their lot. The Persian ruler's attitude here seems much closer to that of Thrasymachus in the *Republic* (343 A–B).[65]

A good case in point is Cyrus' behaviour towards his slaves. The Persian leader, we are told, takes pains never to let his slaves go hungry or thirsty, and feeds them with titbits from his table, hoping to engender their good will as one does with dogs (8. 2. 4). During hunting expeditions free men are not provided with food, but Cyrus carefully leads the slaves to drink, as with beasts of burden, and pauses to allow them to have a meal so that they will not be too hungry. Cyrus' solicitude for his slaves earns him the title 'father', for his care has reconciled them to a state of lifelong servitude: ἐπεμέλετο αὐτῶν ὅπως ἀναμφιλόγως ἀεὶ ἀνδράποδα διατελοῖεν (8. 1. 44). Are we meant only to admire such a 'father'?[66]

[64] See above, ch. 4. 2, 3, ch. 3. 3, and esp. ch. 3. 5 at n. 133.

[65] See Adam on *Rep.* 343 A 7 and cf. Skemp 1952: 52–66 on the shepherd metaphor and its Persian origin; cf. also Pl. *Laws* 694 E–695 B and Tatum 1989: 232–3.

[66] Some editors find this attitude too difficult to digest and delete the last five words of 8. 1. 44; see Holden ad loc. Schneider's remark (quoted by Dindorf ad loc.) that these words should be taken as Xenophon's judgement and not that of the slaves is probably right, and the text need not be altered. See also Luccioni 1947: 241.

An interesting example of this new, ambivalent attitude of Xeno-phon towards his hero is a brief tale involving Cyrus and his soldiers. When the Persian leader distributes among his forces a great deal of booty taken from Sardis, some of the men think that if he has given so much away he must have kept an even greater amount of money for himself. Others are quick to deny the charge and defend their leader, saying that he prefers giving away money to possessing it. Cyrus, hear-ing of these rumours, assembles his men, displays to them all the treasure that can be seen, and lectures them on the true value of wealth (8. 4. 29–36). The situation described here—Cyrus confronting a group of detractors—is virtually unique in the *Cyropaedia*.[67] This brief sketch of soldiers debating the merits of their leader is, of course, not unrealistic and reminds us of the *Anabasis*,[68] but up to this point we have never seen soldiers criticizing Cyrus: all have admired him fervently. The soldiers may suspect the Persian leader of wrongdoing, but Cyrus lectures his men didactically on the proper attitude towards riches, and it seems clear that his author agrees with these sentiments. Thus, in this brief incident Xenophon both indicates that his hero is not universally popular and has Cyrus express moral platitudes.

Each of the less than ideal features of Cyrus' behaviour as ruler of an empire, taken by itself, is perhaps no more than slightly disquieting; viewed cumulatively, they are disturbing and require some sort of explanation. The discrepancies and difficulties are too numerous and obtrusive not to have been deliberately included by Xenophon. On the other hand, Cyrus and his rule continue to be praised as exemplary, and there are scenes in Book 8—such as the third, *Memorabilia*-like encounter between Croesus and Cyrus,[69] the cheerful symposium at Babylon,[70] and Cyrus' peaceful departure from this world—where the Persian ruler seems more of a model figure than ever.[71]

Why does Xenophon introduce these inconsistencies? The answer appears to be that Cyrus, after the conquest of his empire, has become a benevolent despot, and Xenophon wishes to show us that

[67] The closest parallel is at 6. 2. 12, where the unhappy Persian soldiers are afraid, but not angry or jealous.

[68] See e.g. *Anab.* 5. 6. 19, 5. 7. 2.

[69] 8. 2. 15 ff.; cf. above, ch. 4. 4.

[70] 8. 4. 1 ff. We have seen, however, that at this symposium both Hystaspas and Gobryas hesitate before speaking their minds freely to Cyrus, thus hinting at the changed relationship between the Persian ruler and his closest companions; cf. above, ch. 3. 6 at n. 139.

[71] 8. 7; cf. above, ch. 2. 7. See also Hirsch 1985: 98 for an enumeration of Cyrus' positive features as ruler after he conquers Babylon.

both—benevolence and despotism—are needed to run a large empire successfully.[72] At times Xenophon emphasizes the autocratic, even tyrannical nature of his hero's rule and at times he describes Cyrus' kind and outstanding character, which has been in evidence throughout the *Cyropaedia*, but it is the two taken together which make his regime so uniquely successful. This is one of the important lessons of the *Cyropaedia*, and it has several corollaries.

The first is that absolute rule or despotism is the kind of regime needed to govern a large and varied empire well. Once master of an empire, Cyrus begins to act as a despot both because he wishes to be treated as a king and because such measures are necessary if he is to remain in control. We have seen that Xenophon consistently shows his hero as deliberately initiating or adopting some of the least attractive features of his new regime, and we are given his well-thought-out and highly practical reasons for doing so. This lends an air of necessity, even inevitability, to Cyrus' actions. If the sovereign of a large and varied empire is to succeed in its government, he must, it seems, become an absolute and remote figure. Cyrus, once in Babylon, changes or ignores many of the teachings of his father Cambyses, and he rejects, in essence, the Persian 'constitutional monarchy'. The ideal and idyllic society of Cyrus' youth had left him dissatisfied even before he set out on his great conquest. It does not actively encourage the pursuit of great gain and glory, and one can grow old there, practising virtue, with nothing to show for it (1. 5. 8 ff.). The simple rustic Persian monarchy, with its careful system of checks and balances, is excellent as a training-ground for Cyrus but does not leave him enough scope for his ambitions and capabilities. It is not, as Xenophon himself realizes, a realistic model of government for a large and far-flung empire. One must choose, apparently, between the careful and virtuous rule of a small-scale polity and the more extensive, but despotic, rule of an empire.

The second consequence of Cyrus' enlightened absolutism is that it must in fact be enlightened. The rule established by the Persian leader in his empire depends to a large extent on the character of the man in charge: ὅταν μὲν ὁ ἐπιστάτης βελτίων γένηται, καθαρώτερον τὰ νόμιμα πράττεται· ὅταν δὲ χείρων, φαυλότερον (8. 1. 8; cf. 8. 8. 5).

---

[72] Flory 1987: 121–7 has a very interesting analysis of the tyrannical means used by Herodotus' Deioces the Mede—secret police, spies, remoteness—to preserve his rule (Hdt. 1. 96–100). These methods are essential, argues Flory, to an ideal monarchy, and Herodotus means to portray Deioces as a wise, if manipulative, philosopher king.

Cyrus uses methods which are very effective in his own hands but are, in themselves, far from perfect. His achievement as a ruler was unique (1. 1. 4), but this is, in part at least, because he failed to create institutions or inaugurate ways of life which would guarantee its continuation. In Books 7 and 8 Xenophon often describes practices Cyrus initiated in Babylon and then adds that they are still found ἔτι καὶ νῦν, i.e. in fourth-century Persia.[73] Some of these passages can be taken simply as an attempt to glorify Cyrus—many of the Persian practices known in Xenophon's time are shown by him actually to have been devised long ago by his clever hero—but there may be more to some of the ἔτι καὶ νῦν passages than that. If the present-day Persian government is less than perfect, Xenophon seems to imply, it is not because the practices instituted by Cyrus have been abolished or neglected: they still exist, but are not a sufficient safeguard of success.[74]

Xenophon, in the very opening of the *Cyropaedia* (1. 1. 1 ff.), has mentioned Cyrus' career as an exception to the general observation that it is difficult, if not impossible, to rule men. Before ending his book he must explain why Cyrus is an exception, demonstrating not only the positive side of his achievements—how he acquired a large empire of obedient subjects—but also the negative one: why Cyrus was unique and did not manage to arrange for his good works to last beyond his lifetime.[75] When Xenophon portrays Cyrus as a benevolent despot, he does answer both these points, well before the epilogue. Cyrus' good character and virtue guarantee the well-being of his empire, but these are his own special characteristics. The despotism he inaugurates is what is left to the following generation of Persians—along with the conquered empire—and it is a poor legacy. The epilogue only serves to confirm this point, if in an extreme and outspoken way.[76]

Xenophon does not criticize the hero of the *Cyropaedia*—his hero—

---

[73] Cf. 7. 5. 70, 8. 1. 6–7, 20, 24, 36, 8. 2. 4, 7–9, 8. 3. 9, 10, 13, 34, 8. 4. 5, 8. 5. 21, 27, 8. 6. 5, 9, 14, 16, etc.

[74] There are, of course, other ways of understanding the ἔτι καὶ νῦν passages, which are not restricted solely to Books 7 and 8 of the *Cyr.*; see below. Sometimes these passages are simply used by Xenophon to stress a particular point and are patently false (e.g. 8. 5. 27). Elsewhere such references to the present are meant to display Xenophon's intimate knowledge of Persia: see Lewis 1977: 23 n. 130, 53 n. 21, 74 n. 158, etc. Delebecque 1957: 395–404 has a fairly comprehensive collection and discussion of the ἔτι καὶ νῦν passages; cf. Due 1989: 33–8.

[75] Cf. Higgins 1977: 158 n. 70, who sees a 'clear necessity for a balancing falling action to complement the first chapter' of the *Cyr.*, and cf. Tatum 1989: 220–1.

[76] See Luccioni 1947: 251–3 and Carlier 1978: 160–3.

overtly, nor does he explicitly state that the inheritance which the Persian leader has bequeathed is wanting in any way. None the less, in the final portions of the *Cyropaedia* Xenophon has Cyrus institute practices which cannot be considered, either by the author himself or by his readers, ideal. Thus there is a certain distance or tension in this final section of the work between Xenophon and his hero: in order to become an efficient ruler of an empire, Cyrus has had to change, and changing means departing from some of his old, exemplary ways. Xenophon lets us see—but never explicitly says—that the developments initiated by Cyrus after the conquest of Babylon will eventually lead to the moral downfall of his regime, and indeed in the epilogue he states that Cyrus' empire begins to disintegrate immediately after he dies (8. 8. 2).

3. THE ENDING OF THE *CYROPAEDIA*

This brings us to the problematic epilogue. If Xenophon is uncharacteristically reticent and only hints in the final sections of the work (7. 5–8. 7) that the seeds of destruction have been sown by Cyrus himself, the sharp, sarcastic tone of the epilogue (8. 8) leaves little to the reader's imagination. The blunt, outspoken criticisms of contemporary Persian mores and the unfavourable comparisons with the noble habits and customs of Cyrus' time found in this final chapter make it plain to every reader how much the Persians have deteriorated. The belligerent tone and sudden change of attitude towards the Persians are just one of the difficulties raised by the final chapter: there are also several contradictions between descriptions of Persian customs found in the main body of the *Cyropaedia* and those in the epilogue. Such discrepancies occur even in relation to various practices instituted by Cyrus or common in his day which Xenophon has specifically mentioned as still existing in his own time, ἔτι καὶ νῦν.[77] These contradictions should not, perhaps, be taken too seriously: they do not relate to important matters and stem, in all likelihood, from a combination of carelessness and inconsistency on

---

[77] See *Cyr.* 8. 8. 8 vs. 1. 2. 16 (on exercise); 8. 8. 12 vs. 8. 1. 34–6 (on hunting); 8. 8. 13, 19 vs. 4. 3. 23 (on horsemanship); 8. 8. 9 vs. 1. 2. 11 (on number of daily meals); 8. 8. 10, 12 vs. 5. 2. 17 (on temperance); etc. In the first three instances Xenophon mentions that these customs are still upheld in his own day (ἔτι καὶ νῦν). See Holden ad loc., Delebecque 1957: 405–9, Hirsch 1985: 92–4, and Due 1989: 36–8 for various attempts to deal with this difficulty.

Xenophon's part. We have seen that one way to idealize Cyrus is to claim that his influence on Persian habits is felt to this very day; a second method is to show how much better he was than present-day Persians. For most of the *Cyropaedia* Xenophon uses the first means, while in the epilogue he uses the second.

Scholars are agreed that the final chapter of the work cannot be faulted on linguistic grounds and is written in Xenophon's style.[78] Another argument used to establish the authenticity of *Cyr.* 8. 8 is the parallel instance of the *Lacedaemonion Politeia*, where we again find an epilogue (chapter 14) which seems at odds with the rest of the work, for Xenophon criticizes contemporary Spartans after praising the Spartans of long ago.[79] It is worth remembering that the opening of the *Lacedaemonion Politeia* is also very like that of the *Cyropaedia*,[80] and perhaps such beginnings and endings were a feature of *politeia* literature.[81] While many modern readers would perhaps prefer another ending to the *Cyropaedia*, none of the ancients ever objected to the epilogue. On balance, there is no compelling reason to reject the authenticity of *Cyr.* 8. 8, particularly if Xenophon has in fact paved the way for the disappointing successors to Cyrus in the very measures he outlines in the Babylonian section of the work.

Just as Xenophon's opening does not hint at the rich variety of subjects and scenes that will follow in the *Cyropaedia*, so too the epilogue is not in any sense a summary of the work. We have seen that the penultimate chapter of the *Cyropaedia*, Cyrus' farewell scene (8. 7), with its complex blend of sources and aims, is a kind of microcosm of the entire composition:[82] as such, it would have served very well as an ending to the work.[83] It is a measure of Xenophon's increasing detachment from his hero in the final sections of the *Cyropaedia* that he did not choose to have Cyrus' tranquil, idealized death conclude his work.

---

[78] The only unusual linguistic feature of the epilogue is the frequent use of the particle μήν; see Holden on *Cyr.* 8. 8; Gautier 1911: 130 n. 1; Luccioni 1947: 247–8 n. 281. Tatum 1989: 224 (with n. 10) notes how the final sentence of the *Cyr.* (8. 8. 27) is similar to the endings of other works by Xenophon.

[79] See Hirsch 1985: 95 and the further references there; cf. Due 1989: 21.

[80] Compare *Lac. Pol.* 1. 1–2 with *Cyr.* 1. 1. 1–3, and see above, ch. 1. 1 at n. 42.

[81] Chapter 14 is the penultimate, not the final, chapter of the *Lac. Pol.* in the manuscript tradition, but several scholars transpose the two final chapters; cf. the discussions in Breitenbach 1966: 1751–2; Higgins 1977: 66–7; Hirsch 1985: 95.

[82] Above, ch. 2. 7.

[83] Cf. Tatum 1989: 216.

Bibliography

The following is a list of all the modern references cited in the notes, with the exception of standard commentaries (e.g. How and Wells on Herodotus).

Aalders, G. J. D., 1953: 'Date and Intention of Xenophon's *Hiero*', *Mnemosyne*, 6: 208–15.

Albertus, J., 1908: *Die παρακλητικοί in der griechischen und römischen Literatur* (diss. Strasburg).

Aly, W., 1921: *Volksmärchen, Sage und Novelle bei Herodot und seinen Zeitgenossen* (Göttingen; repr. 1969).

—— 1936: 'Novelle', *RE* xvii/1. 1171–9.

Anderson, G., 1982: *Eros Sophistes: Ancient Novelists at Play* (Chico, Calif.).

Anderson, J. K., 1970: *Military Theory and Practice in the Age of Xenophon* (Berkeley).

—— 1974: *Xenophon* (London).

Andrieu, J., 1954: *Le Dialogue antique* (Paris).

Arnim, H. von, 1923: *Xenophons Memorabilien und Apologie des Sokrates* (Copenhagen).

Asheri, D., 1983: *Fra ellenismo e iranismo* (Bologna).

Atkinson, K. M. T., 1956: 'The Legitimacy of Cambyses and Darius as Kings of Egypt', *JAOS* 76: 167–77.

Avery, H. C., 1972: 'Herodotus' Picture of Cyrus', *AJP* 93: 529–46.

Barigazzi, A., 1957: review of Cataudella, *La novella greca*, in *Athenaeum*, 35: 371–5.

Barker, E., 1960: *Greek Political Theory* [5] (London).

Barkowski, O., 1923: 'Sieben Weise', *RE* iiA/2. 2242–64.

Bassett, S. E., 1917: 'Wit and Humor in Xenophon', *CJ* 12: 565–74.

Beaulieu, P. A., 1989: *The Reign of Nabonidus, King of Babylon (556–539 B.C.)* (New Haven).

Bell, J. M., 1978: 'κίμβιξ καὶ σοφός: Simonides in the Anecdotal Tradition', *QUCC* 28: 29–86.

Bernays, J., 1885: 'Philons Hypothetika', in id., *Gesammelte Abhandlungen*, 262–82 (Berlin).

Bigwood, J. M., 1976: 'Ctesias' Account of the Revolt of Inarus', *Phoenix*, 30: 1–25.

—— 1983: 'The Ancient Accounts of the Battle of Cunaxa', *AJP* 104: 340–57.

—— 1986: '*POXY* 2330 and Ctesias', *Phoenix*, 40: 393–406.

Biltcliffe, D. A. W., 1969: 'P. Ox. No. 2330 and its Importance for the Study of Nicolaus of Damascus', *RM* 112: 85–93.

Bischoff, H., 1932: *Der Warner bei Herodot* (diss. Marburg) = Marg 1965: 302–19, 681–7 (excerpted).

Blundell, M. W., 1989: *Helping Friends and Harming Enemies: A Study in Sophocles and Greek Ethics* (Cambridge).

Bonner, R. J., and Smith, G., 1930–8: *The Administration of Justice from Homer to Aristotle*, 2 vols. (Chicago).

Bowie, E. L., 1986: 'Early Greek Elegy, Symposium and Public Festival', *JHS* 106: 13–35.

—— 1990: '*Miles Ludens*? The Problem of Martial Exhortation in Early Greek Elegy', in Murray 1990: 221–9.

Bowra, C. M., 1953: *Problems in Greek Poetry* (Oxford).

Boyce, M., 1955: 'Zariadres and Zarēr', *BSOAS* 17: 463–77.

—— 1957: 'The Parthian *Gōsān* and Iranian Minstrel Tradition', *JRAS* 10–45.

—— 1968: 'Middle Persian Literature', in *Iranistik: Literatur* (Handbuch der Orientalistik, 4. 2. 1), 31–66 (Leiden and Cologne).

—— 1982: *A History of Zoroastrianism*, ii (Leiden).

—— 1988: 'The Religion of Cyrus the Great', in A. Kuhrt and H. Sancisi-Weerdenburg (eds.), *Achaemenid History*, iii. *Method and Theory*, 15–31 (Leiden).

Breebaart, A. B., 1983: 'From Victory to Peace: Some Aspects of Cyrus' State in Xenophon's *Cyrupaedia*', *Mnemosyne*, 36: 117–34.

Breitenbach, H. R., 1950: *Historiographische Anschauungsformen Xenophons* (diss. Basel).

—— 1966: 'Xenophon von Athen', *RE* ixA/2. 1569–2051 (repr. separately Stuttgart, 1966).

Bremmer, J., 1983: 'The Importance of the Maternal Uncle and Grandfather in Archaic and Classical Greece and Early Byzantium', *ZPE* 50: 173–86.

—— 1990: 'Adolescents, *Symposion*, and Pederasty', in Murray 1990: 135–48.

Briant, P., 1982: *Rois, tributs et paysans* (Paris).

Brown, T. S., 1978: 'Suggestions for a Vita of Ctesias of Cnidus', *Historia*, 27: 1–19.

Browne, E. G., 1902: *A Literary History of Persia*, i (London).

Bruns, I., 1896: *Das literarische Porträt der Griechen im fünften und vierten Jahrhundert* (Berlin).

Burn, A. R., 1960: *The Lyric Age of Greece* (London).

—— 1984: *Persia and the Greeks*² (repr. of 1962 edn. with postscript by D. M. Lewis) (London).

Burnyeat, M. F., 1977: 'Socratic Midwifery, Platonic Inspiration', *BICS* 24: 7–16.

Burrow, T., 1973: 'The Proto-Indoaryans', *JRAS* 123–40.

Caizzi, F. D., 1966: *Antisthenis Fragmenta* (Milan).

Calder, W. M., 1983: 'The Oath "By Hera" in Plato', in *Mélanges Delebecque*, 35–42 (Aix-en-Provence).

Calhoun, G. M., 1919: 'Oral and Written Pleading in Athenian Courts', *TAPA* 50: 177–93.

Calogero, G., 1957: 'Gorgias and the Socratic Principle *Nemo sua sponte peccat*', *JHS* 77: 12–17.

Carawan, E. M., 1983: '*Erotesis*: Interrogation in the Courts of Fourth-century Athens', *GRBS* 24: 209–26.

Carlier, P., 1978: 'L'idée de monarchie impériale dans la *Cyropédie* de Xénophon', *Ktema*, 3: 133–63.

Cataudella, Q., 1957: *La novella greca* (Naples).

Cawkwell, G., 1972: 'Introduction', in *Xenophon*: The Persian Expedition, 9–48 (Harmondsworth).

Chaumont, M. L., 1973: 'Chiliarque et curopalate à la cour des Sassanides', *Iranica Antiqua*, 10: 139–65.

Christensen, A., 1936: *Les Gestes des rois dans les traditions de l'Iran antique* (Paris).

Chroust, A. H., 1957: *Socrates, Man and Myth* (London).

Cizek, A., 1975: 'From the Historical Truth to the Literary Convention: The Life of Cyrus the Great Viewed by Herodotus, Ctesias and Xenophon', *AC* 44: 531–52.

Classen, C. J., 1984: 'Xenophons Darstellung der Sophistik und der Sophisten', *Hermes*, 112: 154–67.

Clay, A. T., 1921: 'Gobryas, Governor of Babylonia', *JAOS* 41: 466–7.

Connor, W. R., 1989: 'Historical Writing in the Fourth Century B.C. and the Hellenistic Period', in P. E. Easterling and B. M. W. Knox (eds.), *Cambridge History of Classical Literature*, i/3. *Philosophy, History and Oratory*, 46–59 (Cambridge).

Cook, J. M., 1983: *The Persian Empire* (London).

Dadachanjee, R. K., 1904: 'On the *Cyropaedia*', *Journal of the Bombay Branch of the Royal Asiatic Society*, 21: 552–61.

Dandamaev, M. A., 1989: *A Political History of the Achaemenid Empire* (trans. W. J. Vogelsang) (Leiden).

Davies, J. K., 1971: *Athenian Propertied Families* (Oxford).

Delatte, A., 1933: *Le Troisième Livre des souvenirs Socratiques de Xénophon* (Liège).

Delebecque, É., 1957: *Essai sur la vie de Xénophon* (Paris).

Denniston, J. D., 1954: *The Greek Particles*² (Oxford).

Devereux, G., 1973: 'The Self-blinding of Oidipous in Sophokles: *Oidipous Tyrannos*', *JHS* 93: 36–49.

Dewald, C., 1981: 'Women and Culture in Herodotus' *Histories*', in H. Foley (ed.), *Reflections of Women in Antiquity*, 91–125 (New York).

Diakonoff, I. M., 1985: 'Media', in Gershevitch 1985: 36–148.

Dickermann, S. O., 1909: *De argumentis quibusdam apud Xenophontem Platonem Aristotelem obviis e structura hominis et animalium petitis* (diss. Halle).

Dihle, A., 1956: *Studien zur griechischen Biographie* (Göttingen).

Diller, H., 1956: 'Zwei Erzählungen des Lyders Xanthos', in *Navicula Chiloniensis (Studia . . . Jacoby)*, 67–78 (Leiden).

Dittmar, H., 1912: *Aischines von Sphettos* (Philologische Untersuchungen, 21) (Berlin).

Dodds, E. R., 1951: *The Greeks and the Irrational* (Berkeley and Los Angeles).

Dörrie, H., 1956: *Leid und Erfahrung: Die Wort- und Sinn-Verbindung παθεῖν-μαθεῖν im griechischen Denken* (Akad. Mainz, Abh. d. Geist. u. Soz. Klasse, 5) (Wiesbaden).

Dougherty, R. P., 1929: *Nabonidus and Belshazzar* (New Haven).

Dover, K. J., 1965: 'The Date of Plato's *Symposium*', *Phronesis*, 10: 2–10 = 1988: 86–101.

—— 1974: *Greek Popular Morality in the Time of Plato and Aristotle* (Oxford).

—— 1986: 'Ion of Chios: His Place in the History of Greek Literature', in J. Boardman and C. E. Vaphopoulu-Richardson (eds.), *Chios: A Conference at the Homereion in Chios 1984*, 27–37 (Oxford) = 1988: 1–12.

—— 1988: *The Greeks and their Legacy: Collected Papers*, ii (Oxford).

Drews, R., 1973: *The Greek Accounts of Eastern History* (Cambridge, Mass.).

Ducrey, P., 1968: 'Aspects juridiques de la victoire et du traitement des vaincus', in J. P. Vernant (ed.), *Problèmes de la guerre en Grèce ancienne*, 231–43 (Paris).

Due, B., 1989: *The* Cyropaedia: *Xenophon's Aims and Methods* (Aarhus).

Ehlers, B., 1966: *Eine vorplatonische Deutung des sokratischen Eros* (Zetemata, 41) (Munich).

Erasmus, S., 1954: 'Der Gedanke der Entwicklung eines Menschen in Xenophons *Kyrupädie*', in *Festschrift für Fr. Zucker*, 111–25 (Berlin).

Erbse, H., 1960: 'Textkritische Bemerkungen zu Xenophon', *RM* 103: 144–68.

—— 1961: 'Die Architektonik im Aufbau von Xenophons *Memorabilien*', *Hermes*, 89: 257–87.

Farber, J. J., 1979: 'The *Cyropaedia* and Hellenistic Kingship', *AJP* 100: 497–514.

Fehling, D., 1985: *Die sieben Weisen und die frühgriechische Chronologie* (Berne).

—— 1989: *Herodotus and his 'Sources': Citation, Invention and Narrative Art* (revised Eng. trans. J. G. Howie) (Leeds).

Fehr, B., 1990: 'Entertainers at the *Symposion*: The *Akletoi* in the Archaic Period', in Murray 1990: 185–95.

Field, G. C., 1967: *Plato and his Contemporaries*[3] (London).

Finley, J. H., 1967: *Three Essays on Thucydides* (Cambridge, Mass.).

Finley, M. I., 1972: *The World of Odysseus*[2] (Harmondsworth).

Flacelière, R., 1961: 'A propos du *Banquet* de Xénophon', *RÉG* 74: 93–118.

Flory, S., 1987: *The Archaic Smile of Herodotus* (Detroit).

Fontenrose, J., 1978: *The Delphic Oracle* (Berkeley and Los Angeles).

Forster, E. S., 1912: *Isocrates:* Cyprian Orations (Oxford).

Friedländer, P., 1913: 'ΥΠΟΘΗΚΑΙ', *Hermes*, 48: 558–616.

Fritz, K. von, 1935: 'Antisthenes und Sokrates in Xenophons Symposion', *RM* 84: 19–45.

—— 1967: *Die griechische Geschichtsschreibung*, i/2 (Berlin).

Frost, F. J., 1980: *Plutarch's* Themistocles*: A Historical Commentary* (Princeton).

Frye, R. N., 1976: *The Heritage of Persia*[2] (London).

—— 1984: *The History of Ancient Iran* (Handbuch der Altertumswissenschaft, iii. 7) (Munich).

Gaiser, K., 1959: *Protreptik und Paränese bei Platon* (Tübinger Beiträge zur Altertumswissenschaft, 40) (Stuttgart).

—— 1977: 'Griechisches und christliches Verzeihen: Xenophon, *Kyrupädie* 3. 1. 38–40 und Lukas 23, 34a', *Wiener Studien*, Beiheft 8 (= *Latinität und alte Kirche: Festschrift für R. Hanslik*), 78–100.

Galinsky, G. K., 1972: *The Herakles Theme* (Oxford).

Gärtner, H., 1984: (ed.) *Beiträge zum griechischen Liebesroman* (Hildesheim, Zurich, and New York).

Gautier, L., 1911: *La Langue de Xénophon* (Geneva).

Gershevitch, I., 1968: 'Old Iranian Literature', in *Iranistik: Literatur* (Handbuch der Orientalistik, 4. 2. 1), 1–30 (Leiden and Cologne).

—— 1985: (ed.) *Cambridge History of Iran*, ii. *Median and Achaemenian Periods* (Cambridge).

Gharib, B., 1968: 'A Newly Found Old Persian Inscription', *Iranica Antiqua*, 8: 54–69.

Giangrande, G., 1976: 'On an Alleged Fragment of Ctesias', *QUCC* 23: 31–46.

Giannantoni, G., 1983–5: *Socraticorum Reliquiae*, ii–iii (Naples).

Gigon, O., 1946: 'Xenophontea', *Eranos*, 44: 133–40.

—— 1947: *Sokrates: Sein Bild in Dichtung und Geschichte* (Berne).

—— 1953: *Kommentar zum ersten Buch von Xenophons Memorabilien* (Basle).

—— 1956: *Kommentar zum zweiten Buch von Xenophons Memorabilien* (Basle).

Gill, C., 1973: 'The Death of Socrates', *CQ* 23: 25–8.

Gilmore, J., 1888: *The Fragments of the* Persika *of Ktesias* (London).

Gomperz, H., 1912: *Sophistik und Rhetorik* (Berlin).

Gould, J., 1989: *Herodotus* (London).

Gray, V. J., 1981: 'Dialogue in Xenophon's *Hellenica*', *CQ* 31: 321–34.

—— 1985: 'Xenophon's "Cynegeticus"', *Hermes*, 113: 156–72.

—— 1986: 'Xenophon's *Hiero* and the Meeting of the Wise Man and Tyrant in Greek Literature', *CQ* 36: 115–23.

—— 1989: *The Character of Xenophon's* Hellenica (London).

Grayson, A. K., 1975*a*: *Assyrian and Babylonian Chronicles* (Locust Valley, NY).

—— 1975*b*: *Babylonian Historical-Literary Texts* (Toronto).

Grayson, C. H., 1975: 'Did Xenophon Intend to Write History?', in B. Levick (ed.), *The Ancient Historian and his Materials: Essays in Honour of C. E. Stevens*, 31–43 (Farnborough).

Greiffenhagen, G., 1966: 'Der Prozeß des Ödipus', *Hermes*, 94: 147–76.

Griffin, A., 1982: *Sikyon* (Oxford).

Griffin, J., 1980: *Homer on Life and Death* (Oxford).

Griffith, M., 1977: *The Authenticity of 'Prometheus Bound'* (Cambridge).

Gulley, N., 1968: *The Philosophy of Socrates* (London).

Gutglueck, J., 1988: 'From *ΠΛΕΟΝΕΞΙΑ* to *ΠΟΛΥΠΡΑΓΜΟΣΥΝΗ*: A Conflation of Possession and Action in Plato's *Republic*', *AJP* 109: 20–39.

Guthrie, W. K. C., 1969–75: *A History of Greek Philosophy*, iii–iv (Cambridge).

Gutschmid, A. von, 1892: *Kleine Schriften*, iii (Leipzig).

Guyot, P., 1980: *Eunuchen als Sklaven und Freigelassene in der griechisch-römischen Antike* (Stuttgart).

Hackforth, R., 1952: *Plato's* Phaedrus (Cambridge).

Harrison, A. R. W., 1971: *The Law of Athens*, ii (Oxford).

Hartmann, I. I., 1889: *Analecta Xenophontea Nova* (Leipzig).

Harvey, F. D., 1984: 'The Wicked Wife of Ischomachos', *EMC* 28: 68–70.

Hausrath, A., 1914: 'Die ionische Novellistik', *Neue Jahrb. für Kl. Alt.* 17: 441–61.

Hawtrey, R. S. W., 1981: *Commentary on Plato's* Euthydemus (Philadelphia).

Heinimann, F., 1945: *Nomos und Physis* (Basle; repr. 1965).

Heiserman, A., 1977: *The Novel before the Novel* (Chicago).

Heni, R., 1976: *Die Gespräche bei Herodot* (diss. Heidelberg).

Herzog-Hauser, G., 1937: 'Nutrix', *RE* xvii/2. 1491–500.

Higgins, W. E., 1977: *Xenophon the Athenian: The Problem of the Individual and the Society of the Polis* (Albany).

Hinz, W., 1976: *Darius und die Perser*, i (Baden-Baden).

Hirsch, S. W., 1985: *The Friendship of the Barbarians: Xenophon and the Persian Empire* (Hanover and London).

Hirzel, R., 1895: *Der Dialog: Ein literarhistorischer Versuch*, i (Leipzig).

—— 1908: 'Der Selbstmord', *Archiv für Religionswissenschaft*, 11: 75 ff., 243 ff., 417 ff. (repr. separately Darmstadt, 1967).

Höistad, R., 1948: *Cynic Hero and Cynic King* (Uppsala).

Homeyer, H., 1962: 'Zu den Anfängen der griechischen Biographie', *Philologus*, 106: 75–85.

Hornblower, J., 1981: *Hieronymus of Cardia* (Oxford).

Hornblower, S., 1982: *Mausolus* (Oxford).

—— 1987: *Thucydides* (London).

Hoschander, J., 1923: *The Book of Esther in the Light of History* (Philadelphia).

Hudson-Williams, H. L., 1950: 'Conventional Forms of Debate and the Melian Dialogue', *AJP* 71: 156–69.

Hudson-Williams, T., 1910: *The Elegies of Theognis* (London).

Hug, A., 1918: 'Eunuchen', *RE* suppl. iii. 449–55.

Immisch, O., 1927: *Gorgiae Helena* (Berlin and Leipzig).

Irwin, T., 1974: review of L. Strauss, *Xenophon's Socrates*, in *Philosophical Review*, 83: 409–13.

Jacoby, F., 1912: 'Herodorus', *RE* viii/1. 980–7 = 1956*b*: 241–5.

—— 1922: 'Ktesias', *RE* xi/2. 2032–73 = 1956*b*: 311–32.

—— 1947: 'Some Remarks on Ion of Chios', *CQ* 41: 1–17 = 1956*a*: 144–68.

—— 1956*a*: *Abhandlungen zur griechischen Geschichtschreibung* (Leiden).

—— 1956*b*: *Griechische Historiker* (Stuttgart).

Jebb, R. C., 1893: *The Attic Orators*², i (London).

Joël, K., 1901: *Der echte und der Xenophontische Sokrates*, ii/1–2 (Berlin).

Jones, J. W., 1956: *The Law and Legal Theory of the Greeks* (Oxford).

Keller, W. J., 1911: 'Xenophon's Acquaintance with the History of Herodotus', *CJ* 6: 252–9, 347.

Kent, R. G., 1953: *Old Persian: Grammar, Texts, Lexicon*² (New Haven).

Kerferd, G. B., 1981: *The Sophistic Movement* (Cambridge).

Keulen, H., 1971: *Untersuchungen zu Platons 'Euthydem'* (Wiesbaden).

Klima, O., 1968: 'Avesta. Ancient Persian Inscriptions. Middle Persian Literature', in J. Rypka (ed.), *History of Iranian Literature* (trans., ed. K. Jahn), 1–67 (Dordrecht).

Knauth, W., 1975: *Das altiranische Fürstenideal von Xenophon bis Ferdousi* (in collaboration with S. Nadjmabadi) (Wiesbaden).

Knox, B. M. W., 1957: *Oedipus at Thebes* (New Haven).

Körte, A., 1927: 'Aufbau und Ziel von Xenophons Symposion', *Verh. Sächs. Akad. Wiss., Leipzig, Phil.-hist. Kl.* 79: 3–48.

Krömer, D., 1977: 'Kyros' Unsterblichkeitsbeweis bei Xenophon und Cicero', *Würzburger Jahrbücher*, 3: 93–104.

Kuhrt, A., 1987: 'Usurpation, Conquest and Ceremonial: From Babylon to Persia', in D. Cannadine and S. Price (eds.), *Rituals of Royalty: Power and Ceremonial in Traditional Societies*, 20–55 (Cambridge).

—— 1988: 'Babylonia from Cyrus to Xerxes', in J. Boardman, N. G. L. Hammond, D. M. Lewis, and M. Ostwald (eds.), *Cambridge Ancient History*, iv². 112–38 (Cambridge).

—— 1990*a*: 'Achaemenid Babylonia: Sources and Problems', in H. Sancisi-Weerdenburg and A. Kuhrt (eds.), *Achaemenid History*, iv. *Centre and Periphery*, 177–94 (Leiden).

—— 1990*b*: 'Alexander and Babylon', in J. W. Drijvers and H. Sancisi-Weerdenburg (eds.), *Achaemenid History*, v. *The Roots of the European Tradition*, 121–30 (Leiden).

—— 1990*c*: 'Nabonidus and the "Babylonian priesthood"', in M. Beard and J. North (eds.), *Pagan Priests*, 119–58 (London).

Kurke, L., 1990: 'Pindar's Sixth *Pythian* and the Tradition of Advice Poetry', *TAPA* 120: 85–107.

Lacey, A. R., 1971: 'Our Knowledge of Socrates', in G. Vlastos (ed.), *The Philosophy of Socrates*, 22–49 (Garden City, NY).

Larsen, J. A. O., 1962: 'Freedom and its Obstacles in Ancient Greece', *CP* 57: 230–4.

Lasserre, F., 1944: "Ἐρωτικοὶ Λόγοι", *MH* 1: 169–78.

Lateiner, D., 1989: *The Historical Method of Herodotus* (*Phoenix* suppl. 23) (Toronto).

Latham, K. J., 1981: 'Hysteria in History: Some Topoi in War Debates of Homer, Herodotus and Thucydides', *Museum Philologum Londiniense* 5: 54–67.

Latte, K., 1920: *Heiliges Recht* (Tübingen).

Lattimore, R., 1939: 'The Wise Adviser in Herodotus', *CP* 34: 24–35.

Lavagnini, B., 1922: 'Le origini del romanzo greco', *Annali della Scuola Normale Superiore di Pisa*, 28: 9–104 = Gärtner 1984: 68–101 (excerpted).

Lefèvre, E., 1971: 'Die Frage nach dem βίος εὐδαίμων: Die Begegnung zwischen Kyros und Kroisos bei Xenophon', *Hermes*, 99: 283–96.

Lehmann-Haupt, C. F., 1902: 'Gobryas und Belsazar bei Xenophon', *Klio*, 2: 341–5.

Lévy, E., 1976: *Athènes devant la défaite de 404* (Paris).

Levy, R. (trans.), 1967: *The Epic of the Kings: Shah-Nama, the National Epic of Persia by Ferdowsi* (London).

Lewis, D. M., 1977: *Sparta and Persia* (Leiden).

—— 1984: 'Postscript', in Burn 1984: 587–609.

Lloyd, G. E. R., 1966: *Polarity and Analogy* (Cambridge).

—— 1979: *Magic, Reason and Experience* (Cambridge).

Luccioni, J., 1947: *Les Idées politiques et sociales de Xénophon* (Paris).

—— 1953: *Xénophon et le socratisme* (Paris).

Luschnat, O., 1942: *Die Feldherrnreden im Geschichtswerk des Thukydides* (*Philologus* suppl. 34) (Leipzig).

MacDowell, D. M., 1978: *The Law in Classical Athens* (London).

—— 1990: 'The Meaning of ἀλαζών', in E. M. Craik (ed.), *'Owls to Athens': Essays on Classical Subjects Presented to Sir Kenneth Dover*, 287–92 (Oxford).

MacGinnis, J. , 1986: 'Herodotus' Description of Babylon', *BICS* 33: 67–86.

Macleod, C. W., 1974: 'Form and Meaning in the Melian Dialogue', *Historia*, 23: 385–400 = 1983: 52–67.

—— 1983: *Collected Essays* (Oxford).

Mallowan, M., 1985: 'Cyrus the Great (558–529 B.C.)', in Gershevitch 1985: 392–419.

Marg, W. (ed.), 1965: *Herodot: Eine Auswahl aus der neueren Forschung*² (Wege der Forschung, 26) (Darmstadt).

Martin, J., 1931: *Symposion: Die Geschichte einer literarischen Form* (Studien zur Geschichte und Kultur des Altertums, 17. 1 and 2) (Paderborn).

Mattingly, H. B., 1977: 'Poets and Politicians in Fifth-century Greece', in K. H. Kinzl (ed.), *Greece and the Eastern Mediterranean in Ancient History and Prehistory (Studies . . . Schachermeyr)*, 231–45 (Berlin and New York).

Maxwell-Stuart, P. G., 1976: 'Pain, Mutilation and Death in Herodotus VII', *La parola del passato*, 31: 356–62.

Mayrhofer, M., 1978: *Supplement zur Sammlung der altpersischen Inschriften* (Vienna).

Meiggs, R., and Lewis, D. M., 1969: *A Selection of Greek Historical Inscriptions* (Oxford).

Meister, K., 1978: 'Stesimbrotos' Schrift über die athenischen Staatsmänner und ihre historische Bedeutung (*FGrHist* 107 F1–11)', *Historia*, 27: 274–94.

Momigliano, A., 1971: *The Development of Greek Biography* (Cambridge, Mass.).

—— 1977: 'Eastern Elements in Post-Exilic Jewish and Greek Historiography', in id., *Essays in Ancient and Modern Historiography*, 25–35 (Oxford).

Montgomery, H., 1965: *Gedanke und Tat: Zur Erzählungstechnik bei Herodot, Thukydides, Xenophon und Arrian* (Lund).

Morrison, D. R., 1988: *Bibliography of Editions, Translations, and Commentary on Xenophon's Socratic Writings (1600–Present)* (Pittsburgh).

Morrow, G. R., 1962: *Plato's Epistles* (Indianapolis).

Müller, C. W., 1975: *Die Kurzdialoge der Appendix Platonica* (Studia et Testimonia Antiqua, 17) (Munich).

Murray, O., 1980: *Early Greece* (London).

—— 1983: 'The Symposion as Social Organisation', in R. Hägg (ed.), *The Greek Renaissance of the Eighth Century B.C.: Tradition and Innovation*, 195–9 (Stockholm).

—— 1990: (ed.) *Sympotica: A Symposium on the* Symposion (Oxford).

Nestle, W., 1940–1: 'Xenophon und die Sophistik', *Philologus*, 94: 31–50 = 1948: 430–50.

—— 1948: *Griechische Studien* (Stuttgart).

Neuhaus, O., 1901: 'Die Überlieferung über Aspasia von Phokaia', *RM* 56: 272–83.

Nickel, R., 1979: *Xenophon* (Erträge der Forschung, 111) (Darmstadt).

Nöldeke, T., 1930: *The Iranian National Epic* (trans. L. T. Bogdanov) (Bombay; repr. Philadelphia, 1979).

North, H., 1966: *Sophrosyne: Self-knowledge and Self-restraint in Greek Literature* (Ithaca, NY).

Nussbaum, G. B., 1967: *The Ten Thousand: A Study in Social Organization and Action in Xenophon's* Anabasis (Leiden).

Oates, J., 1986: *Babylon* [2] (London).

Ober, W. B., 1982: 'Did Socrates Die of Hemlock Poisoning?', *Ancient Philosophy*, 2: 115–21.

O'Brien, M. J., 1967: *The Socratic Paradoxes and the Greek Mind* (Chapel Hill).

Olmstead, A. T., 1948: *History of the Persian Empire* (Chicago).

Oppenheim, A. L., 1985: 'The Babylonian Evidence of Achaemenian Rule in Mesopotamia', in Gershevitch 1985: 529–87.

Paap, A. H. R. E., 1970: *The Xenophon Papyri* (Papyrologica Lugduno-Batava, 18) (Leiden).

Page, D. L., 1942: *Greek Literary Papyri*, i (London).

Parke, H. W., and Wormell, D. E. W., 1956: *The Delphic Oracle*, 2 vols. (Oxford).

Patzer, A., 1970: *Antisthenes der Sokratiker* (diss. Heidelberg).

Pearson, A. C., 1909: 'Phrixus and Demodice', *CR* 23: 255–7.

Pearson, L., 1939: *Early Ionian Historians* (Oxford).

Pease, S. J., 1934: 'Xenophon's *Cyropaedia*, "the compleat general"', *CJ* 29: 436–40.

Pelling, C., 1990: 'Childhood and Personality in Greek Biography', in id. (ed.), *Characterization and Individuality in Greek Literature*, 213–44 (Oxford).

Pellizer, E., 1990: 'Outlines of a Morphology of Sympotic Entertainment', in Murray 1990: 177–84.

Perry, B. E., 1967: *The Ancient Romances* (Berkeley and Los Angeles).

Pizzagalli, A., 1942: 'L'epica iranica e gli scrittori greci', *Atene e Roma*, 10: 33–43.

Posner, E., 1972: *Archives in the Ancient World* (Cambridge, Mass.).

Powell, J. G. F., 1988: *Cicero, Cato Maior De Senectute* (Cambridge).

Pritchard, J. B. (ed.), 1969: *Ancient Near Eastern Texts Relating to the Old Testament* [3] (Princeton).

Pritchett, W. K., 1971: *The Greek State at War*, i (Berkeley).

—— 1979: *The Greek State at War*, iii. *Religion* (Berkeley and Los Angeles).

Radermacher, L., 1967: *Aristophanes' 'Frösche'* [3] (Vienna).

Ramage, E. S., 1961: 'An Early Trace of Socratic Dialogue', *AJP* 82: 418–24.

Ravn, O. E., 1942: *Herodotus' Description of Babylon* (trans. M. Tovborg-Jensen) (Copenhagen).

Rawson, E., 1969: *The Spartan Tradition in European Thought* (Oxford).

Reinhardt, K., 1960: 'Herodots Persergeschichten', in id., *Vermächtnis der Antike: Gesammelte Essays zur Philosophie und Geschichtsschreibung*, ed. C. Becker, 133–74 (Göttingen) = Marg 1965: 320–69.

Reitzenstein, R., 1893: *Epigramm und Skolion* (Gießen).

Reverdin, O., 1962: 'Crise spirituelle et évasion', in id. (ed.), *Grecs et barbares* (Entretiens Hardt, 8), 83–120 (Geneva).

Richter, E., 1893: 'Xenophon-Studien', *Jahrb. f. Klass. Phil.*, suppl. 19: 57–155.

Riemann, K. A., 1967: *Das herodoteische Geschichtswerk in der Antike* (diss. Munich).

Robert, L., 1938: 'Inscriptions du dème d'Acharnai: Le serment des éphèbes athéniens', in id., *Études épigraphiques et philologiques*, 296–307 (Paris).

Roberts, C. H., 1954: '*P. Oxy.* 2330: Ctesias, *Persica*', *Oxyrhynchus Papyri*, 22: 81–4.

Robinson, R., 1953: *Plato's Earlier Dialectic* [2] (Oxford).

Robinson, T. M., 1979: *Contrasting Arguments: An Edition of the* Dissoi Logoi (New York).

Rohde, E., 1914: *Der griechische Roman und seine Vorläufer* [3] (Leipzig).

Romilly, J. de, 1956: *Histoire et raison chez Thucydide* (Paris).

—— 1976: 'L'excuse de l'invincible amour dans la tragédie grecque', in J. M.

Bremer, S. L. Radt, and C. J. Ruijgh (eds.), *Miscellanea Tragica in Honorem J. C. Kamerbeek*, 309–21 (Amsterdam).

Rösler, W., 1990: '*Mnemosyne* in the *Symposion*', in Murray 1990: 230–7.

Sancisi-Weerdenburg, H., 1980: *Yauna en Persai* (diss. Leiden).

—— 1983: 'Exit Atossa: Images of Women in Greek Historiography on Persia', in A. Cameron and A. Kuhrt (eds.), *Images of Women in Antiquity*, 20–33 (London).

—— 1985: 'The Death of Cyrus: Xenophon's *Cyropaedia* as a Source for Iranian History', *Acta Iranica*, 25: 459–71.

Schachermeyr, F., 1965: 'Stesimbrotos und seine Schrift über die Staatsmänner', *SB Wien. Akad.* 247/5: 3–23.

Schaerer, R., 1969: *La Question platonicienne*² (Neuchâtel).

Schaps, D., 1982: 'The Women of Greece in Wartime', *CP* 77: 193–213.

Scharr, E., 1919: *Xenophons Staats- und Gesellschaftsideal und seine Zeit* (Halle; repr. Tübingen 1974).

Scheil, V., 1914: 'Le Gobryas de la Cyropédie et les textes cunéiformes', *Revue d'Assyriologie*, 11: 165–74.

Schwartz, E., 1889: 'Quellenuntersuchungen zur griechischen Geschichte', *RM* 44: 161–93 = 1956: 136–74.

—— 1943: *Fünf Vorträge über den griechischen Roman*² (Berlin).

—— 1956: *Gesammelte Schriften*, ii (Berlin).

Schwartz, M., 1985: 'The Old Eastern Iranian World View According to the Avesta' and 'The Religion of Achaemenian Iran', in Gershevitch 1985: 640–63, 664–97.

Schwenzner, W., 1923: 'Gobryas', *Klio*, 18: 41–58, 226–52.

Shahbazi, A., 1977: 'The "Traditional Date of Zoroaster" Explained', *BSOAS* 40: 25–35.

Shaked, S., 1982: 'Two Judeo-Iranian Contributions: Iranian Functions in the Book of Esther', in id. (ed.), *Irano-Judaica*, 292–303 (Jerusalem).

Siewert, P., 1977: 'The Ephebic Oath in Fifth-century Athens', *JHS* 97: 102–11.

Sinclair, T. A., 1967: *A History of Greek Political Thought*² (London).

Skemp, J. B., 1952: *Plato's* Statesman (New Haven).

Slater, W. J., 1990: 'Sympotic Ethics in the *Odyssey*', in Murray 1990: 213–20.

Slings, S. R., 1981: *A Commentary on the Platonic* Clitophon (Amsterdam).

Smith, K. F., 1902: 'The Tale of Gyges and the King of Lydia', *AJP* 23: 261–82, 361–87.

Smith, S., 1944: *Isaiah, Chapters XL–LV* (London).

Snell, B., 1966: 'Zur Geschichte vom Gastmahl der Sieben Weisen', in id., *Gesammelte Schriften*, 115–18 (Göttingen).

Stahl, H.-P., 1975: 'Learning through Suffering? Croesus' Conversations in the History of Herodotus', *YCS* 24: 1–36.

Starr, C. G., 1975: 'Greeks and Persians in the Fourth Century B.C., Part I', *Iranica Antiqua*, 11: 39–99.

Stephens, S. A., 1985: 'The Ancient Title of the *Ad Demonicum*', *YCS* 28: 5–8.

Stokes, M. C., 1986: *Plato's Socratic Conversations* (Baltimore).

Strauss, L., 1948: *On Tyranny: An Interpretation of Xenophon's* Hiero (New York).

—— 1970: *Xenophon's Socratic Discourse: An Interpretation of the* Oeconomicus (Ithaca, NY).

Stroheker, K. F., 1953: 'Zu den Anfängen der monarchischen Theorie in der Sophistik', *Historia*, 2: 381–412.

Stronach, D., 1985: 'Pasargadae', in Gershevitch 1985: 838–55.

Strycker, E. de, 1962: review of Gaiser, *Protreptik und Paränese bei Platon*, in *Gnomon*, 34: 13–21.

Susemihl, F., 1887: 'Der Idealstaat des Antisthenes und die Dialoge Archelaos, Kyros und Herakles', *Jahrb. f. klass. Phil.* 135: 207–14.

Sutton, D., 1989: 'The Satyr Play', in P. E. Easterling and B. M. W. Knox (eds.), *Cambridge History of Classical Literature*, i/2. *Greek Drama*, 94–102 (Cambridge).

Tadmor, H., 1965: 'The Inscriptions of Nabunaid: Historical Arrangement', *Assyriological Studies*, 16: 351–63.

Tarrant, D., 1955: 'Plato as Dramatist', *JHS* 75: 82–9.

Tatum, J., 1989: *Xenophon's Imperial Fiction: On* The Education of Cyrus (Princeton).

Tecuşan, M., 1990: '*Logos Sympotikos*: Patterns of the Irrational in Philosophical Drinking. Plato outside the *Symposium*', in Murray 1990: 238–60.

Thesleff, H., 1967: *Studies in the Styles of Plato* (Helsinki).

—— 1978: 'The Interrelation and Date of the *Symposia* of Plato and Xenophon', *BICS* 25: 157–70.

Thompson, H. A., and Wycherley, R. E., 1972: *The Athenian Agora*, xiv. *The Agora of Athens* (Princeton).

Thompson, S., 1955–8: *Motif-index of Folk-literature*, 6 vols. (Copenhagen).

Tigerstedt, E. N., 1965: *The Legend of Sparta in Classical Antiquity*, i (Lund).

Tod, M. N., 1948: *A Selection of Greek Historical Inscriptions*, ii (Oxford).

Toher, M., 1989: 'On the Use of Nicolaus' Historical Fragments', *CA* 8: 159–72.

Tomin, J., 1987: 'Socratic Midwifery', *CQ* 37: 97–102.

Trenkner, S., 1958: *The Greek Novella in the Classical Period* (Cambridge).

Treu, M., 1966: 'Ps.-Xenophon: Πολιτεία Ἀθηναίων', *RE* ixA/2. 1928–82.

Tuplin, C., 1990: 'Persian Decor in *Cyropaedia*: Some Observations', in J. W. Drijvers and H. Sancisi-Weerdenburg (eds.), *Achaemenid History*, v. *The Roots of the European Tradition*, 17–29.

Ullrich, F., 1908: *Entstehung und Entwickelung der Literaturgattung des Symposion*, i (Würzburg).

Valla, D., 1922: 'Il Mito di Pantea', *Atene e Roma*, 3: 119–24.

Vlastos, G., 1981: '*ΙΣΟΝΟΜΙΑ ΠΟΛΙΤΙΚΗ*', in id., *Platonic Studies*², 164–203 (Princeton).

Vlastos, G., 1983: 'The Socratic Elenchus', *OSAP* 1: 27–58.

Vorrenhagen, E., 1926: *De orationibus quae sunt in Xenophontis Hellenicis* (diss. Elberfeld).

Vries, G. J. de, 1963: 'Novellistic Traits in Socratic Literature', *Mnemosyne*, 16: 35–42.

Wacholder, B. Z., 1962: *Nicolaus of Damascus* (Berkeley and Los Angeles).

Wade-Gery, H. T., 1932: 'Thucydides, the Son of Melesias', *JHS* 52: 205–27 = 1958: 239–70.

—— 1958: *Essays in Greek History* (Oxford).

Waters, K. H., 1985: *Herodotos the Historian* (London and Sydney).

Weiskopf, M., 1989: *The So-called 'Great Satraps' Revolt', 366–360 B.C.* (*Historia* Einzelschriften, 63) (Stuttgart).

Weissbach, F. H., 1924: 'Kyros', *RE* suppl. iv. 1129–66.

—— 1931: 'Kroisos', *RE* suppl. v. 455–72.

Wellman, R. R., 1976: 'Socratic Method in Xenophon', *JHI* 37: 307–18.

Wencis, L., 1977: '*Hypopsia* and the Structure of Xenophon's *Anabasis*', *CJ* 73: 44–9.

West, M. L., 1971–2: *Iambi et Elegi Graeci*, 2 vols. (Oxford).

—— 1974: *Studies in Greek Elegy and Iambus* (Berlin and New York).

—— 1978: *Hesiod,* Works and Days (Oxford).

—— 1985: 'Ion of Chios', *BICS* 32: 71–8.

Whitehead, D., 1990: *Aineias the Tactician* (Oxford).

Widengren, G., 1959: 'The Sacral Kingship of Iran', in *La regalità sacra* (*Numen* suppl. 4), 242–57 (Leiden).

Wilamowitz, U. von, 1926: 'Erkenne dich selbst', in id., *Reden und Vorträge*[4], ii. 171–89 (Berlin).

Woldinga, G. J., 1938–9: *Xenophons Symposium, Prolegomena en Commentaar* (diss. Amsterdam).

Wolff, E., 1964: 'Das Weib des Masistes', *Hermes*, 92: 51–8 = Marg 1965: 668–78.

Wood, N., 1964: 'Xenophon's Theory of Leadership', *C&M* 25: 33–66.

Woodruff, P., 1982: *Plato,* Hippias Major (Oxford).

Yarshater, E., 1983: 'Iranian National History', in id. (ed.), *Cambridge History of Iran*, iii/1. *The Seleucid, Parthian and Sasanian Periods*, 359–477 (Cambridge).

—— 1988: 'The Development of Iranian Literatures', in id. (ed.), *Persian Literature*, 3–37 (Albany, NY).

Young, T. C., 1988: 'The Consolidation of the Empire and its Limits of Growth under Darius and Xerxes: Imperial Organization and Cultural Achievement', in J. Boardman, N. G. L. Hammond, D. M. Lewis, and M. Ostwald (eds.), *Cambridge Ancient History*, iv[2]. 79–111 (Cambridge).

Zaehner, R. C., 1961: *The Dawn and Twilight of Zoroastrianism* (London).

Ziegler, K., 1964: *Plutarchos von Chaironeia* (Stuttgart) (rev. repr. of *RE* xxi. 636–962).

Index Locorum

Bold numbers indicate a main entry. Passages appearing twice on the same page are not cited twice in the index.

8. 2. 13: 293 n.
8. 2. 14: 295
8. 2. 15–23: 115 n., 179–81, 197, 270–1, 293 n., 296 n.
8. 2. 24–5: 293 n.
8. 2. 26–8: 256 n., 294 n.
8. 2. 26: 65 n., 294
8. 2. 27: 293 n.
8. 3: 56 n.
8. 3. 1–4: 291 n.
8. 3. 1: 292 n., 293 n.
8. 3. 3–4: 26 n., 174 n., 222 n., 292 n.
8. 3. 3: 189 n.
8. 3. 5 ff.: 173
8. 3. 5: 182
8. 3. 7–8: 177, 182, 222 n., 281 n.
8. 3. 9: 298 n.
8. 3. 10: 298 n.
8. 3. 11: 56
8. 3. 13–14: 291 n., 292
8. 3. 13: 298 n.
8. 3. 14: 254 n.
8. 3. 17: 260 n.
8. 3. 19–23: 293 n.
8. 3. 21–3: 281 n.
8. 3. 24: 56 n.
8. 3. 25 ff.: 65 n., 174
8. 3. 25: 97 n., 173, 260 n.
8. 3. 26: 175 n.
8. 3. 28: 127 n.
8. 3. 30–2: 281 n.
8. 3. 32: 174 n., 175
8. 3. 33: 176 n.
8. 3. 34: 183, 298 n.
8. 3. 35–50: 132, **173–83**
8. 3. 35–48: 281 n.
8. 4. 1 ff.: 97 n.
8. 4. 1–27: **132–5,** 151, **183–90**, 265 n., 296 n.
8. 4. 2: 254 n.
8. 4. 5: 298 n.
8. 4. 9–10: 83 n.
8. 4. 9: 150
8. 4. 12: 150
8. 4. 13–16: 169
8. 4. 14: 95
8. 4. 24–6: 169
8. 4. 24: 198
8. 4. 26–7: 167, 225 n.
8. 4. 29–36: 267 n., 296
8. 4. 31: 281 n.
8. 4. 32–6: 26 n.
8. 5. 17–20: 103 n.

8. 5. 17: 99 n.
8. 5. 18–20: 169
8. 5. 18: 222 n.
8. 5. 20: 99 n.
8. 5. 21–7: 290
8. 5. 21: 289 n., 298 n.
8. 5. 22 ff.: 55
8. 5. 22–7: 72 n.
8. 5. 24: 293 n.
8. 5. 27: 298 n.
8. 5. 28: 16 n., 169 n.
8. 6. 5: 298 n.
8. 6. 9: 298 n.
8. 6. 10–13: 110 n.
8. 6. 14: 298 n.
8. 6. 16: 298 n.
8. 7: **115–31**, 285, 296 n., 300
8. 7. 2: 58
8. 7. 3: 57, 59 n.
8. 7. 14–16: 294
8. 7. 22: 256 n.
8. 7. 25: 244
8. 7. 27: 244
8. 7. 28: 240 n.
8. 8: 23, 286, 299–300
8. 8. 2–3: 81
8. 8. 2: 127 n., 299
8. 8. 4: 23 n., 294
8. 8. 5: 297
8. 8. 8: 299 n.
8. 8. 9: 299 n.
8. 8. 10: 150, 158, 299 n.
8. 8. 12: 299 n.
8. 8. 13: 299 n.
8. 8. 15–17: 291
8. 8. 16: 170, 292 n.
8. 8. 19: 299 n.
8. 8. 20: 292 n.
8. 8. 27: 300 n.

Hellenica
1. 5. 4–7: 189
1. 6. 8–11: 111 n.
1. 7. 16 ff.: 85
2. 3. 24–34: 85
2. 3. 35–49: 85
2. 3. 56: 130
2. 4. 13–17: 111 n.
2. 4. 16: 175
2. 4. 17: 112 n.
3. 1. 10–28: 214
3. 1. 20–8: 250 n.
3. 1. 22: 85
3. 1. 24–8: 85

General Index

Abradatas 2, 193–4, 232–8, 259
  absence 222
  arming scene 235–6
  and Cyrus the Younger 240–1
  death 238–9, 240–1, 243, 280
  dignified 234
  parting from Panthea 235–8
  reunion with Panthea 233, 253
  see also Panthea
Achaemenid rulers:
  appoint successors 123
  fraternal strife 124–5
  tombs of 128–9
  virtues of 73
  and Zoroastrianism 19–20, 128
Adusius 281
Aeneas Tacticus 71
Aeschines Socraticus 33 n., 38, 45 n.,
  46 n., 141 n.
  Alcibiades 148
  Aspasia 25, 150 n., 166, 187 n., 202–3,
  225
  Callias 161 n.
Agariste's suitors 146–7, 186 n.
Agesilaus:
  death 122
  didactic 26
  idealized 8
  and Lysander 106 n.
  matchmaker 188, 213
  in old age 120
  and Pharnabazus 99, 184 n., 213
  temperate and hardy 26, 67, 156 n.,
  171, 228 n., 280
Agesilaus 7, 120
Aglaitadas 162–3, 167–8, 190, 281 n.
alienation of affections 92, 106–7, 220
Amorges 117
Anabasis:
  biographical elements 6–7
  critical soldiers in 296
  date of 11 n.
  deceit in 250 n.
  decision-making in 283
  novellas 212–13
  and *Persica* 211–13

symposia 151–2, 173, 174
trials 83–4
ἀνάκρισις 81, 86–7
analogies:
  applied to interlocutor himself 28–9,
  40–1, 82–3, 106–7
  in *Cyr.* 295
  in Herodotus 29 n.
  in *Hiero* 45
  in *Oec.* 46–7
  used by Socrates 39–41
  in Xen., *Symp.* 49
Andromache 22 n., 235–9, 242
anthologies of learned writings 186
Antisthenes 3 n., 12, 141 n., 148, 171 n.
  Cyrus 8–10
  in Xenophon 36, 37, 48–9, 93, 135,
  137, 138, 171, 179–80, 188, 190
ἀπορία 44, 60, 69, 82–3, 90
Araspas 192–4, 220, 221–32, 236, 240,
  252, 254
Ardashir I 17–18, 20, 21
Armenian king:
  and Croesus 266, 277, 285
  and sophist 24, 91–2, 106 n., 132 n.,
  182 n., 220, 230
  trial of 40 n., 78–85, 94–7, 102 n., 130,
  198 n., 213 n.
Armenian sophist 24, 91–4, 107, 109,
  131, 132 n., 198 n., 230
Artabazus 56 n., 132–4, 173, 287 n.
  and Araspas 193–4, 228–9
  and Cyrus 166–7, 189–91, 197, 214,
  225, 275
Aspasia 187 n., 225
  'Ionian' 212–13
Assyrian crown prince:
  assassination of 265–6
  cruel 205, 218–19
  and Gadatas 195–6, 204, 220, 255–60,
  288
  and Gobryas 168, 250–1, 281
  and Gobryas' son 21, 168–9, 194, 246–9
  identity of 262–4
  not pampered 60
  and Panthea 232–3